SOCIAL CLASS

SOCIAL CLASS

How Does It Work?

Annette Lareau and Dalton Conley
EDITORS

Russell Sage Foundation • New York

The Russell Sage Foundation

Library of Congress Cataloging-in-Publication Data

Social class : how does it work? / edited by Annette Lareau and Dalton Conley.
    p. cm.
  Includes bibliographical references.
  ISBN 978-0-87154-506-0
  1. Social classes—United States. 2. Class consciousness—United States. I. Lareau, Annette. II. Conley, Dalton, 1969–
    HN90.S6S545 2008
    305.50973—dc22

                                                    2007049696

Contents

About the Authors

Annette Lareau is professor of sociology at the University of Maryland.

Dalton Conley is University Professor at New York University, adjunct professor of community medicine at the Mount Sinai School of Medicine, and a research associate at the National Bureau of Economic Research (NBER).

Clem Brooks is Rudy Professor of Sociology at Indiana University at Bloomington.

Richard M. Carpiano is assistant professor of sociology and Michael Smith Foundation for Health Research Scholar at the University of British Columbia, where he is also a faculty affiliate of the Human Early Learning Partnership (HELP).

John Goldthorpe is an emeritus fellow of Nuffield College, Oxford, and the British Academy, and a member of the Academia Europaea and the Royal Swedish Academy of Sciences.

David B. Grusky is professor of sociology at Stanford University, director of the Center for the Study of Poverty and Inequality at Stanford, and coeditor of the Stanford University Press Social Inequality Series.

Angel L. Harris is assistant professor of sociology and African American studies at Princeton University.

Roger D. Hodge is the editor of *Harper's Magazine.*

Michael Hout is professor of sociology and demography at the University of California at Berkeley.

Michelle Jackson is a research fellow in the Centre for Research Methods in the Social Sciences (Department of Politics and International Relations) at Nuffield College, Oxford.

Karyn Lacy is assistant professor of sociology and African American studies at the University of Michigan.

Bruce G. Link is a research scientist at New York State Psychiatric Institute and professor of epidemiology and sociomedical sciences (in psychiatry) at the Mailman School of Public Health at Columbia University.

Jeff Manza is professor of sociology at New York University.

Leslie McCall is associate professor of sociology and a faculty fellow at the Institute for Policy Research at Northwestern University.

Mary Pattillo is associate professor of sociology and African American studies at Northwestern University.

Jo C. Phelan is associate professor of sociomedical sciences and codirector of the Center for the Study of Social Inequalities and Health at the Mailman School of Public Health at Columbia University.

Janny Scott has been a reporter for *The New York Times* since 1994.

Ray Suarez joined *The NewsHour* in October 1999 as a Washington-based senior correspondent and also serves as a backup anchor.

Kim A. Weeden is associate professor and chair of sociology at Cornell University.

Elliot B. Weininger is assistant professor of sociology at the State University of New York at Brockport.

Erik Olin Wright is Vilas Distinguished Professor of Sociology at the University of Wisconsin.

Acknowledgments

THE PAPERS in this book first were presented at a conference at New York University. This conference was co-organized by the editors along with David Grusky and Mike Hout; we thank them for their role in making this project a reality. We are particularly grateful to the president of the Russell Sage Foundation, Eric Wanner, and the Russell Sage Foundation for generously supporting the conference. We are also indebted to David Grusky and the Stanford Center for the Study of Poverty and Inequality for financial assistance, as well as to the University of Maryland Department of Sociology, the Consortium for the Study of Race and Ethnicity at the University of Maryland, and the Maryland Population Research Center for their contributions. At New York University, Carse Ramos at the Center for Advanced Social Science Research provided priceless administrative support for the project. The Center for Advanced Social Science Research at New York University also made a generous financial contribution.

Intellectually, a number of people provided critical feedback to the authors, including the anonymous reviewers and, especially, Michèle Lamont, who offered comments at the conference itself. At the Foundation, Suzanne Nichols has been particularly helpful in overseeing the production of the book. At the University of Maryland, Aleia Clark provided important research assistance; Silviu Romaniuc and Stephan Heuer assisted in production. The University of Maryland and the Center for the Advanced Study of the Behavioral Sciences generously provided a fellowship year at CASBS during which Annette Lareau worked on this volume. Finally, Annette Lareau gratefully acknowledges the emotional support of her husband, Samuel Freeman, during the editorial process. Although he personally objects to "meddling editors" and was constantly encouraging authors to ignore his wife's editorial advice ("Just nod, agree, and do what you want," he suggested), he nonetheless provided her with invaluable emotional sustenance, comfort, and good humor.

PART I

CONCEPTIONS OF SOCIAL CLASS

Introduction:
Taking Stock of Class

Annette Lareau

Social class has an odd place in sociology. On the one hand, class is prominently featured in many core aspects of the discipline. Its centrality has a long lineage: the theoretical foundations for studying social class were established by many of the leading figures of sociology, including Marx and Weber (Wright 2005). Comparing and contrasting these theoretical perspectives is a time-honored tradition in graduate education. Similarly, some sociology professors report that their favorite moments in the classroom involve contesting young people's presumption of the viability of the American Dream. From dramatic charts showing that the "wealthiest 1 percent of all Americans accounted for 38 percent of the nation's total net worth" to pictures taken with hidden cameras showing how elites gather for summer leisure in exclusive enclaves such as the Bohemian Grove, sociology professors routinely suggest in lectures that classes exist in the United States (Giddens, Duneier, and Appelbaum 2007; Domhoff 2006).[1] They also demonstrate that, ideological support to the contrary, there is a limited amount of mobility in American society (McNamee and Miller 2004; see also Alvarez and Kolker 2001).

On the other hand, few contemporary empirical studies that use the concept of class find their way into academic journals. This is inconsistent with the "pride of place" that class occupies in sociology's theoretical traditions. Rather than measure and analyze "class," studies often use the terms "inequality," "stratification," "family background," or specific indicators (such as education, wealth, income, or occupation)—sometimes interchangeably. As a result, considerable murkiness swirls around the empirical study of social class. As shown in this chapter, reasonable people disagree about the best way to define the concept of social class, and many, leery of conceptual ambiguity and confusion, avoid the term altogether.

There are other troubles. For example, the debate about whether the concept of class is even worth retaining in empirical research remains unresolved. Fifty years ago, Robert Nisbet (1959) proclaimed that "the term social class . . . is nearly valueless for the clarification of the data of wealth, power, and social status" (11). Somewhat later, Terry Nichols Clark and Seymour Martin Lipset (1991) asserted that social classes were "dying." In their 1996 book *The Death of Class,* Jan Pakulski and Malcolm Waters continued to challenge the viability of the concept of social class in the study of politics:

> Class has collapsed and is decomposing, leaving only the merest traces of its effects. If it ever was real and salient, and we are certainly prepared to admit that class was a sturdy historical reality, it is no longer. . . . Classes are dissolving . . . the most advanced societies are no longer class societies. (Pakulski and Waters 1996, 7)[2]

Building on these studies, Paul Kingston, in *The Classless Society* (2001), launches a full-scale assault on the value of the concept of class in the American context. He argues that "groups of people sharing common economic positions—what are commonly designated as 'classes'—do not share distinct similar, life-defining experiences." He suggests that "class theories misrepresent the structure of inequality in contemporary American society." Kingston is particularly concerned with the lack of empirical evidence: "Class theory has not only been developed with little empirical validation, but has been advanced in the face of much disconfirming research" (Kingston 2001, 1, 3). These resounding critiques suggest that the empirical evidence does not support the continued salience of the concept of social class.

Are these critiques of the concept of social class correct? One way to address this issue is to examine the significance of class across different spheres of social life. Indeed, as the field has become increasingly specialized, many researchers are knowledgeable about a relatively specific topic. Within sociology, subfields (for example, the sociology of education) are divided into further subfields. In this climate, it is hard to perceive common themes in the research spanning the discipline. It is particularly difficult to discern whether "class" is a viable concept that has empirical meaning across a variety of subfields. Thus, to take stock of the viability of the concept of social class, an assessment would surely benefit by a broader perspective—one that looks not simply at a single dimension of social life but "horizontally" across many.

In addition, the studies that do exist often appear to be orthogonal to one other. Exchanges among scholars taking stock of the state of empirical research on class are rare.[3] The field could fruitfully be moved forward by more conversation about the various definitions of class, an assessment of critical decision-points in empirical research, and the strengths and weaknesses of the different approaches. Such a conversation would advance our understanding of the various conceptions of social class in sociology, the ways in which social class is presented and discussed in the media and public life, and the range of definitions that are being used today in empirical research.

This book addresses these issues. It seeks to determine whether there is evidence to support the viability of the concept of social class across a number of spheres: identity, education, politics, health, family life, and urban communities. In addition, the volume seeks to assess the varying definitions of social class that are used in empirical work and to elucidate important challenges facing the researchers doing empirical work. In fact, the project was conceived as an effort to bring together scholars who share an interest in analyzing social class but who also offer differing approaches to the topic. It grew out of a conference on the topic that took place at New York University in April 2006. The conference was a lively gathering with a vibrancy of intellectual exchange.[4] This was partly due to the fact that the conference brought together a relatively small group of faculty and graduate students—eighty persons—who shared common interests but were not used to such a gathering of qualitative and quantitative scholars as well as scholars working in a diversity of subfields. The conference, like this volume, also sought to cast a broad net. The conference organizers stressed the importance of being inclusive in the conception of class, pushing the boundaries of efforts to examine class empirically, and facilitating a critical conversation on the limits as well as the strengths of various approaches to class. Hence, the editors also asked journalists from leading national publications (the *New York Times*, television's *NewsHour with Jim Lehrer*, and *Harper's* magazine) to share their thoughts on the meaning and use of the concept of class in the public sphere. Their thoughtful essays, which are included here as an epilogue to the chapters by sociologists, clearly convey the confusion surrounding the concept of class in American society.

For example, Janny Scott, a reporter who took a leadership role in the *New York Times* series on social class, reflects on the difficulty in getting others to understand what they were doing (*New York Times* 2005). She recounts an early meeting with a senior editor concerning the project:

> I said I had been thinking, was there [a way] to make a beat out of writing about class. It seemed to me that class difference was out in the open in New York City in a way that was maybe less so in other places. Once you got tuned into it for whatever reason, class assumptions and dynamics seemed to permeate

nearly every encounter. Class was the subtext in our daily lives, I suggested. But we rarely looked at it squarely. Maybe I could write about that.

He looked at me across the table. He was really smart. He cocked his head. "I think that you are saying something important but I don't know what."

Unlike the comparable series carried out by *New York Times* reporters on "How Race Is Lived in America" (*New York Times* 2002), other reporters and editors did not quite understand what they were studying. Scott had to keep explaining it and trying to convince others that there was a story to be written. In the six-part series, one headline used the term "shadowy divides" to highlight the place that class holds in the lives of ordinary Americans.

This ambiguity was not simply in the eyes of the public. Janny Scott and other *New York Times* reporters spoke to dozens of sociologists and other social scientists doing research on inequality. They were struck by the lack of consensus about the appropriate definition of social class, as Scott relays in her chapter: "Some of the people we were interviewing told us class was defined by income. Some said it was more about education or about wealth. Some said occupation was the key. We were ruthless; we had a deadline; we decided, almost for the sake of argument, that class was the product of a combination of all four."

In her chapter, she calls for social scientists to make progress on this issue: "It would be helpful if there were more agreement about what we mean when we use the word 'class.' "

The Chapters: What Do They Show?

The chapters tour many important realms of social life: identity, health, politics, education, family, and urban life. Of course, this list is not complete. It is striking, however, that there are similar results across all of the spheres in that birth into a specific class, even broadly conceived, does shape life chances. Those raised in the middle class and upper middle class (to use terminology that is, admittedly, contested) have strikingly more favorable life chances than those raised in the working class (Beller and Hout 2006; Conley 1999). For example, there is universal agreement that good health and a longer life expectancy are highly desirable. Richard Carpiano, Bruce Link, and Jo Phelan show in chapter 8 that there is a clear consensus on the importance of social position in achieving good health and a long life (see also Conley, Strully, and Bennett 2003; House et al. 1994). Jeff Manza and Clem Brooks's look in chapter 7 at active citizenship, in the form of political participation, also leaves little doubt about the class patterns there. In chapter 3, John Goldthorpe and Michelle Jackson show that, as a result of their class origins, some British youth who do not perform well on a crucial educational exam have more favorable outcomes than their performance would lead one to expect. In the United States, enrollment in and graduation from college play a pivotal role in shaping future class destinations. In chapter 4, Elliot Weininger and I show that working class youth depend heavily on educational institutions in this transition, while middle class youth get the benefit of additional "concerted cultivation" and "customization" in the transition to college. Parents' informal knowledge of how colleges work and their deployment of class-based resources can make a crucial difference.

Still, the power of class can vary. As Michael Hout shows in chapter 1, class-based patterns are clearest at the ends of the distribution. There is more "churning" in the middle, he asserts. Nevertheless, he demonstrates, when prompted, only 3 percent of Americans fail to self-identify with a social class. In most cases, their self-identifications reflect objective circumstances. But circumstances do not necessarily coalesce to send a clear class signal. The Ivy League professional with a six-figure income and the high school dropout with a succession of low-wage jobs have no trouble naming their class position. In contrast, underpaid social workers with a master's degree and the affluent shopkeeper with the high school diploma have a harder time choosing between middle and working class. Overall, however, Hout's evidence challenges the "death of class" argument.

As the chapters in this book make clear, some authors believe it is a mistake to study class without taking into account other powerful social forces, including race. From this perspective, Mary Pattillo suggests in chapter 9 that race "inflects" class and that the dynamics of social exclusion cannot be fully understood without attention to race. In chapter 5, Karyn Lacy and Angel Harris argue that there is considerable variation within the black middle class; they also find that income and education have a differential impact on the identity of adolescents.[5]

The relationship between gender and class is another complex topic. Early studies tended to focus exclusively on men, ignoring the issue of gender altogether (Acker 1973). With the dramatic increase in women's labor force participation in recent decades, and particularly the participation of married women with young children, this approach has become much more problematic (Crompton 1993, 93–97; Leiulfsrud and Woodward 1987). Efforts to resolve it have faced many challenges (for a review of the issues, see Zipp and Plutzer 1996, 2000). The chapter in this volume by Leslie McCall weighs in on part of this issue. She finds that between 1970 and 2000, "evidence . . . support[s] the claim that inequalities among men and women are qualitatively different if quantitatively similar, suggesting that we do need to examine gender and class inequalities simultaneously."[6] McCall and many others believe that class studies would be improved by a fuller reckoning with gender dynamics in empirical research.

The significance of contingency also surfaces in other areas. As Dalton Conley makes clear in chapter 6, there are important variations among siblings raised in the same family. But this variability among siblings, Conley suggests, is not an indication that social structure is unimportant. Rather, it suggests the need for a more sophisticated understanding of the impact of the social structural forces shaping each individual's life course. Rather than having a global impact on children's destinations, family background and familial class position may have a *contingent* impact.

In the remaining portion of this introduction, I discuss three cross-cutting themes in the volume: the degree to which empirical research is directly linked to a conceptual model, the degree of specificity in the definition of class, and the kinds of questions that the research intends to illuminate. The chapters do not agree on the proper approach to class research on these key issues.

Conceptual and Theoretical Linkages in Class Research

Of course, theoretical models of social class have provided more or less clearly definable approaches: for example Marx, Weber, and Bourdieu all offer an analysis of how class works (Weininger 2002; Wright 2005). According to sociological theory and methodology books, these conceptual models should provide a pathway for guiding our empirical analyses of social class. In this textbook model, any effort to understand the mechanisms through which social class position has an impact on daily life would begin by focusing on translating the broader conceptual model into a researchable question. The conceptual issues would be the driving force.

This model is rarely followed. Rather than being nurtured by theoretical questions, empirical research is often heavily influenced by methodological issues. For example, the accessibility of secondary data sets, available methodological approaches to analyzing data, and pressures to develop one's career by publishing frequently and rapidly (among other factors) frequently play a defining role in shaping the research process. Many critical questions cannot be answered with existing data. Nationally representative data sets are expensive to collect—to say nothing of data that would facilitate cross-national comparisons. Few data include key variables that correspond to our conceptual models. For example, we seldom have access to detailed measures of authority relations in the workplace, the amount of job-specific expertise required by particular jobs, the informal cultural knowledge used in the workplace, or current conditions in the regional labor market. Nor do data sets typically provide details about the small group of people who are extremely privileged in their wealth or in their very high-level managerial authority.[7] Yet detailed information would be very helpful in differentiating empirical support for, say, the approaches developed by Marx, Weber, and Bourdieu (Breen 2005; Weininger 2005; Wright 2005). Absent such data, scholars with very different theoretical beliefs must sometimes make use of similar, if not identical, measures. In the realm of qualitative research, the labor-intensive character of research restricts the analysis to a small number of cases. As a result, it is most common for researchers to study one social class; studies comparing different social class and racial groups are rare. All research is incomplete. But the gap between the richness of the theoretical concepts of social class and the available empirical studies in both quantitative and qualitative research is striking indeed.

Given the emphasis in graduate training on the role of theory in driving empirical work, most researchers discuss in a perfunctory fashion the critical role that theory should play in the formulation of studies. It is striking, then, how the authors of a chapter in this book, David Grusky and Kim Weeden, discuss this approach. "We . . . reject the standard presumption . . . that measurement choices may be justified by simply proffering a definition that appears to motivate such choices." They believe that definitions of class should be subject to an empirical test:

> Our goal is . . . to develop methods that make it possible to subject class models of all kinds to convincing empirical test. . . . The conventional definition-based legitimation of measurement decisions should be replaced, we will argue, with an empirical legitimation that requires analysts to demonstrate that their preferred measure in fact adequately captures the structure of inequality.

Instead of stating a definition and then defending a choice by referring to a conceptual argument, Grusky and Weeden prefer "empirical legitimation" of a measure. This drive for an empirically based definition of class presumes, of course, that current data provide accurate, detailed, and comprehensive measures of critical factors. This seems unlikely.

In addition, there are reasons to believe that whole swaths of social life that are probably associated with social class are missing from nationally representative data sets. Indeed, some topics are well worn, while others are virtually absent from discussion.[8] To mention just one example, our understanding of the feelings of pain and exclusion that can be connected to upward mobility is not particularly deep. Although Bourdieu clearly writes about the importance of self-exclusion and the withdrawal from interaction, it is hard for surveys to be sufficiently nuanced on this point. Some journalists, such as Alfred Lubrano in his book *Limbo* (2003), have shown that upwardly mobile individuals—"straddlers" of two different worlds—report uneasiness in negotiating the cultural aspects of middle class life, even after spending years in middle class jobs. Yet few studies capture these feelings of unease in a sophisticated fashion. At the conference, after a long discussion on the relative merits of the gradational and relational approaches to class (discussed later in the chapter), Michèle Lamont called for researchers "to broaden the agenda" to ensure the "long-term health" of the field:

> The field of class analysis [is] always coming back [to] these questions that have, I think, to some extent paralyzed the field for a long time: "Is it A or B?" . . . Why do we go back to these questions as opposed to asking ourselves to look at the very wide range of questions that have not been asked yet? The field would be more vital, I think, if we moved toward thinking about new questions as opposed to working toward digging a deeper and deeper hole around issues that are belabored.[9]

How Specific a Definition of Class Do We Need?

In the literature, there is significant variability in the degree of generality or precision in definitions of class. This can be due to the particular conception of class that researchers make use of in their work. For example, scholars influenced by the work of Pierre Bourdieu deploy an encompassing concept that includes economic capital and cultural capital (see Bourdieu 1984). In other cases, however, differences in specificity grow out of methodological commitments. Researchers using ethnographic methods, for example, do not examine one variable while controlling for others; rather, they study people who come into their purview bearing an intersecting web of class "variables." Hence, most work using ethnographic methods also assumes a more general conception of class rather than a specific one.

Some approach the topic of social class with a desire for greater precision. As David Grusky reflected after the conference:

> I [was] struck that some of the participants quite cavalierly used "class" to refer to variables I would never label as such (for example, education, income)—a revelation of sorts because some of us obsess endlessly about how class might be defined in contradistinction to measures of education, income, and the like. It was striking that a field that has been so built around the concept of class has evidently made so little headway and that so much dissensus could still prevail. Is the concept of income equally poorly specified in economics? I suspect not. Why, by contrast, is the concept of class still so ambiguously defined in our field? Does that speak to the peculiar social organization of sociology? Or to inherent problems with the class concept itself?

One debate concerns the use of a synthetic definition of class (such as the socioeconomic index) compared to a strategy of using individual variables (such as education or occupation). Over the years there have been many debates in the literature about the proper methodological approach to the measurement of socioeconomic status (Haug 1977; Haug and Sussman 1971; Hollingshead 1971; Mueller and Parcel 1981). Recently, in a series of papers, Robert Hauser, John Robert Warren, and their colleagues have taken stock of socioeconomic indices (Hauser and Logan 1992; Hauser and Warren 1997; Warren and Hauser 1997; Warren, Sheridan, and Hauser 1998). In a long paper in *Sociological Methodology*, Warren and Hauser (1997, 177) emphatically state their position: "We conclude that composite indexes of occupational socioeconomic status [SES] are scientifically obsolete." While some scholars may consider this matter to be long settled, the use of SES measures continues in the field. In addition, others continue to see value in a combined measure of class position (Marsh et al. 2007).

At the conference, there was a discussion of the value of a synthetic index of social class. As the transcript of his comments makes clear, John Goldthorpe of Nuffield College, Oxford, vehemently objected to a global concept of class:

> [Some see] class as some kind of *umbrella concept* that aims to capture all the various aspects of social inequality that we know exist in contemporary societies. It may perhaps exclude racial and ethnic inequalities or gender inequalities, but it still covers a pretty broad swath of other inequalities. That's the umbrella concept of class, and it's not one for which I have very much sympathy: it just leads to muddled and confused thinking. What I would favor in place of that—and I think others here share this view, including Erik Olin Wright [2005; see also chapter 11]—is that it is better to have a *fairly specific, narrowly defined concept of class* [Goldthorpe 2007], which one can then use along with other concepts that try to capture other aspects of structured social inequality.

The fact that many of those present at the conference shared Goldthorpe's view became clear as participants discussed the Blau and Duncan (1978) socioeconomic index. Bart Landry of the University of Maryland also vigorously objected to the SES approach:

> I think that SES is just an abomination. . . . I encouraged one of my students to look at different measures of class, and he went through the literature on SES and tried to find out how people use it. Well, lo and behold, most people who use SES don't tell you how they combine those variables. And so you are left completely in the dark about what they have there. . . . I think that it would be nice if some of us would try to get beyond that.

Perhaps because of the power of the American ideology of individualism, American sociological researchers have been more likely to rely on SES than have their European counterparts. John Goldthorpe expressed puzzlement about the ubiquitous use of SES here:

> I share the dislike of SES. I've never really understood its popularity in American sociology. But it's not the gradational aspect of it that worries me. Maybe there is something in . . . this gradational approach. It is the more synthetic aspect—putting together, as if [it] usually happens, income and education—[that troubles me].

Goldthorpe also pointed out that the index was developed before the advent of multivariate analysis. In addition, the original intent of the index was quite different from the use to which it is put today:

> I think it's worth remembering that the most important SES measure that is used in American sociology, the Duncan SEI index, began as an attempt [to achieve] a proxy measure for occupational prestige. That was the original idea, to get an occupational prestige scale for all occupations. So it didn't really begin as a synthetic measure. It began as a measure of occupational prestige. But then it kind of took [on a life of] its own.

He saw it as unnecessary: "What I find very odd about synthetic measures, in this age when we can do multivariate analysis . . . with great ease, [is that] if you think that income and education are important, then just put them in the analysis separately. Why put them in on some rather arbitrary combination?"

But others disagree with the drive for as specific a measure of social class as possible. Dalton Conley also sees debate over definitions of social class as ultimately fruitless. He emphasizes that research on class fails to offer powerful equations that predict behavior (that is, equations that explain a great deal of the variance in behavior). In chapter 16, he offers a reflection on what is missing in our current studies of social class. Given his concern that available measures cannot capture the subtle nature of class, he openly embraces an umbrella or "kitchen sink" approach:

> Rather than spend more time and effort in trying to refine lofty conceptual apparatuses, I would argue for a "kitchen sink" approach: even when we include every form of social hierarchy we can measure, our empirical models do rather poorly in explaining meaningful outcomes. . . . What's more . . . when we measure any social hierarchy—class included—we tend to point to, but never name precisely, exactly what we mean. As a result, I argue that we should embrace a folk-concept of class and include in our models all forms of social hierarchy that appear to hold empirical weight, ascriptive or achieved. These may range from social networks to income flows and wealth stocks to physical appearance. Especially in an age when cultural, social, human, bodily, and financial capital are fluid and exchangeable, this would appear to be the most robust strategy.[10]

Other researchers concur.[11] Thus, there is a real disagreement among scholars in the field on the level of precision that is needed for high-quality research.

In addition to the disagreements about the degree of precision necessary in studies of class and the best kinds of indicators to rely on, there is also confusion and a lack of clarity around the very word "class" and the more frequently used term "inequality." At present, the strengths and weaknesses attached to these two terms remain unclear in the sociological literature. In my view, however, the term "class" has significant advantages over the term "inequality." Specifically, "class" does evoke a notion of *groups* or collectivities; this means that implicit in the term "class" is a notion of a form of social structure.[12] By contrast, the term "inequality" typically does not evoke a notion of groups or social structure in a similar way. Indeed, the term "inequality," with the emphasis on the ranking of the amount of a resource that is held, is easily compatible with a focus on individuals and, in some cases, individualism. This is an important distinction, since sociology is the study of groups and social institutions. Indeed, there is a risk that, in focusing on individuals, attention to social structure can be downplayed or lost, as Erik Olin Wright worries about in his chapter.[13]

Why Do Researchers Study Class?

In this final section, we turn to an issue other than the degree to which researchers have conceptually infused definitions of class or the level of precision they expect. Instead, we look at the overall purpose of the research. Erik Olin Wright delineates six distinct approaches to the study of class.[14] He suggests that most of the chapters in the volume fall into one of them: "Nearly all of the chapters in this volume revolve around the third of the six class analysis questions: how can we explain variations in life chances in contemporary American society?" He terms this approach a *gradational* one, according to which researchers examine variations in individuals' objective circumstances. His image here is one of studying individuals on the "rungs on the ladder":

> How are people *objectively located* in distributions of material inequality? In this case, class is defined in terms of material standards of living, usually indexed by income or, possibly, wealth. Class, in this agenda, is a *gradational* concept; the standard image is of rungs on a ladder, and the names for locations are accordingly such things as upper class, upper middle class, middle class, lower middle class, lower class, under class.

Wright objects to the disproportionate attention to how people obtain "the cultural, motivational, and educational resources they use to acquire their position in the system of stratification, mainly through the way these resources affect their entry into jobs." This line of research, which he believes continues to dominate quantitative inequality research, says "little . . . about the determinants of the inequalities in the positions themselves that people occupied." Wright prefers what he terms a *relational approach*. Rather than focus on individual life chances, this approach, for example, focuses on "the nature of . . . the positions themselves." He sees the relational approach as a "more complex and demanding" approach to the study of class. In this approach, he asks:

> What *explains* inequalities in life chances and material standards of living? This question [focuses on] identifying causal mechanisms that help determine salient features of that system. When class is used to explain inequality, [class is defined] by *the relationship of people to income-generating resources* or assets of various sorts.

Wright includes opportunity hoarding as one example of this approach (Tilly 1998). This concept is meant to draw the eye of the investigator beyond the individual to look at collective patterns of exclusion and inclusion. The chapter by Mary Pattillo, for example, takes up opportunity hoarding in neighborhood politics. Her examination of a Chicago neighborhood clearly illustrates a concerted effort by middle- and upper-income residents to exclude poor potential neighbors. Even as the racial demographics of the neighborhood changed from all-white to all-black, the rhetoric of "protecting and preserving" the neighborhood as a middle class place continued. As part of their effort to keep the neighborhood "up to their standard," some residents fought to exclude residents they defined as undesirable.[15]

In the discussion at the conference, others suggested that opportunity hoarding is not the only structural dynamic that needs to be incorporated into class analysis. Hannah Bruckner of Yale University, for example, argued that we must also consider the consequences of cumulative advantage:

> The [papers are], in my point of view, somewhat truncated in terms of relational concepts of class that are a little bit broader than just opportunity hoarding. What I am referring to is the concentration of advantage and disadvantage in communities and schools and workplaces that have cumulative effects. It is not just individuals that have a certain class, it's being an individual of a certain class and an *environment* where class members are concentrated or not concentrated. I think Mary Pattillo's paper was an exception, and you could read the health paper [by Richard Carpiano, Bruce Link, and Jo Phelan] [in this way] as well, but this kind of contextualization of social class, I think, would give us a robust handle on class effects.[16]

Efforts to surpass the preoccupation with the allocation of individuals would also need, however, to differentiate between opportunity hoarding and other approaches. Indeed, Wright takes the view that the analysis of opportunity hoarding is also flawed. To be sure, he approvingly points out that opportunity hoarding captures one of the central mechanisms of social exclusion: there is "causal interdependence between the advantages of one group and the disadvantages of another, and thus improvements in the latter are a threat to the former." However, he considers this approach to be incomplete, for it ignores an "additional causal process that generates inequality"—exploitation.[17] As he writes: "This is a stronger form of relational interdependency than in a relation of simple exclusion, for here there is an ongoing relationship between the *activities* of the advantaged and disadvantaged persons, not just a relationship between their *conditions*. Exploitation and domination are forms of structured inequality that simultaneously require the continual active cooperation between exploiters and exploited, dominators and dominated, and generates systematic antagonisms of their interests."[18] In chapter 11, Wright draws a contrast between opportunity hoarding and studies of domination and exploitation. According to Wright, employers' goal of producing cost-effective products is dependent on the availability of a low-cost labor supply. He calls for research that engages more directly with the relations of production, particularly exploitation.

There are many ways in which we could describe the state of empirical research on social class, but "conceptually coherent" would not be one of them. The field is turbulent, chaotic, conflicted, and broken into a number of sub-areas where researchers have very different methodological approaches. As a result, many researchers never engage one another or talk to one another. It can also be hard to see the overlap in studies that use different methodological approaches; studies sometimes seem orthogonal to one another.

In gathering these chapters together, we have sought to take stock of where things stand on empirical research on class. As this introduction suggests, the chapters in this volume do provide evidence of the importance of social class, particularly at key points in the class structure. The authors also offer, however, differing, and conflicting, assessments of how to define social class. Thus, the book reflects some of the turbulence and liveliness of the field. The field may never reach a complete consensus around a single, "standard" definition of class. In addition, the impact of social class may be contingent, and a sophisticated analysis of class may need to be interwoven with an analysis of other factors, including gender and race. But if we could improve the detail and empirical richness of the data as well as the conceptual coherence, then the field might be able to move forward. This is an important goal.

The author gratefully acknowledges the helpful comments of the anonymous reviewers and of David Grusky, Michael Hout, Paul Dean, Steve Martin, Pamela Barnhouse Walters, Elliot B. Weininger, and Julia Wrigley. All errors, of course, are the responsibility of the author.

Notes

1. Most of the grids, tables, and portraits of the American class structure are in books designed for teaching; see, for example, Gilbert (2002), Kerbo (2005), and Thompson and Hickey (2007). Also, we would like to note that although this book does include one chapter on Britain, all of the others deal with American society; to make the discussion less cumbersome we simply use the term "American society."

2. There have been numerous pieces of writing in this academic battle. Michael Hout (2007, personal communication) succinctly summarized the various skirmishes: "Clark and Lipset (1991) argued that social classes were 'dying' as a widespread anti-authority/anti-hierarchy strand in Western civilization undercut the privileges of achievement. Goldthorpe and Marshall (1992) and Hout, Brooks, and Manza (1993) shot back noting the growth of inequality, the persistence of social origins as a factor in mobility, the prevalence and, it seemed, significant increase in health disparities, the rising role of money in electoral politics, and rising residential segregation. Clark and Lipset retorted that they meant politics—class was less of a factor than it used to be. That prompted the Hout, Brooks, and Manza piece (1995) that showed its persistence in American elections and the Evans (1999) volume that showed persistence in countries like the United States, United Kingdom, and Germany, where class was one factor among many, but decline in Scandinavia, where class used to be the only factor in voting. Then came Pakulski and Waters on class identity waning. Wright's book, *Class Counts* (1997a), was, among many things, Wright's counter to Clark and Lipset (2001) and Pakulski and Waters (1996). Kingston [weighed in and] brought [in] American Exceptionalism. All the while Grusky and Weeden were asking how many classes are there and are they rooted in broad and deep distinctions or functional ones?" See also Manza and Brooks (1996), Evans (1999), Clark (2003), Wright (1996), and Goldthorpe and Marshall (1992), among others.

3. There have been some important collections on the topic, but some are older, including Hall (1997) and McNall, Levine, and Fantasia (1991). Erik Olin Wright has published extensively on the topic (1989, 1997a, 1997b, 2005). See also Crompton (1993), Perrucci and Wysong (1999), and Wysong and Perrucci (2007). For edited collections on inequality, see, among others, Duncan and Brooks-Gunn (1997), Neckerman (2004), and Grusky and Szelényi (2007). See also the *New York Times* series, "Class Matters" (*New York Times* 2005).

4. The conference was taped. The discussion in the last session was transcribed. Portions of the transcription are included in this volume (with the permission of the speakers). This transcription is the basis of the Goldthorpe epilogue as well as for some of the points made later in this introduction.

5. The intersection of class and race remains challenging. Some have called for the development of intersectionality (that is, "an analysis claiming that systems of race, economic class, gender, sexuality, ethnicity nation and age form mutually constructing features of social organization"; Collins 1998, 278; see also Collins and Anderson 1995). Others have focused more on comparing the experience of different racial and ethnic groups on class issues. For example, there is a voluminous literature comparing the experience of African Americans and whites on key elements of class—for example, studies of race and wealth (Conley 1999; Oliver and Shapiro 2006; Shapiro 2004), education (Bowen and Bok 1998; Jencks and Phillips 1998; Weis 2007; Wells and Crain 1997); and occupational experiences (Moss and Tilly 1995; Pager 2007; Royster 2003; Smith 2005; Young 2006), to name only a few. The black middle class has clearly grown in recent decades, and racial segregation in housing has profoundly shaped key aspects of the

experiences of black middle class families (Massey and Denton 1996; Pattillo-McCoy 1999). In addition, there is increasing attention to variations within the black middle class (Lacy 2007).

6. McCall reports that this gender difference was stronger in the earlier period than the later one. There is evidence that marriage patterns are becoming more homogenous (Buchmann and DiPrete 2006; Schwartz and Mare 2005), which would mean that husbands and wives would be more like one another in their class positions than less alike. But women continue to make less money than men; gender segregation remains powerful in many occupations (Charles and Grusky 2004).

7. In a nationally representative sample, the number of individuals in this category will be extremely small. Data requirements call for a minimum number of cases per cell. The rarity of this group precludes the production of data sets with sufficient cases for analysis. Although it is theoretically possible that survey researchers could oversample this population, the high expense, combined with the difficulties of gaining access effectively, precludes this option. There have been a few studies based on interviews with or observations of upper class families. The classic ones were by Digby Baltzell (1958/1971), but there have been a few more recent studies of upper class women (Ostrander 1984) and boarding schools for the upper class (Cookson and Persell 1985). Journalistic studies are much more common (Chernov 1998; Lundberg 1969). The most common studies of the upper class are the studies of the composition of boards of directors of major corporations and the interlocking web of social connections in this group (Allen 1987; Allen and Broyles 1989, 1991; Burris 2000, 2007; Domhoff 2006; see also Mills 1956).

8. Ethnographic studies often raise important questions that are either not taken up by survey research or addressed with measures that lack nuance and sophistication. The range of topics is enormous and includes class and family life (Hansen 2005; Lareau 2003; Rubin 1976), downward mobility (Newman 1988, 1993), the insecurity of the labor market (Newman 2006; Rubin 1976; Weis 2004), the black middle class (Lacy 2007; Pattillo-McCoy 1999; Shapiro 2004), the labor process and family life (Halle 1984), moral boundaries by class and race (Lamont 1992, 2000), class and art taste (Halle 1993), class and kinship (Bott 1971; Fischer 1982; Hansen 2005), and class and education (Bernstein 1971; Heath 1983; Lareau 2003; Weis 2007). See also the classic studies of class and community, including Lynd and Lynd (1934, 1982), Warner (1960), Hoggart (1957), and Hollingshead (1949, 1953), as well as classic studies by C. Wright Mills (1956, 1956/1999). See also the PBS documentary *People Like Us: Social Class in America* (Alvarez and Kolker 2001) and the documentary *Born Rich* (Johnson 2003).

9. When asked the kinds of examples she had in mind, Lamont wrote: "How people think of themselves as advantaged or penalized; the relationship they have with this self-concept—shame, pride, guilt, etc.; how class differences are negotiated at the micro level, including the work we do to help people of other groups save face and feel comfortable across the class divide."

10. In Conley's view, the gross inadequacy of current measures should not, however, stop researchers from doing empirical work. In his chapter, he uses

maternal education as a "proxy" for his measure of social class, to examine sibling differences in key life outcomes. The varying outcomes for brothers and sisters in the same family, however, are not a basis for rejecting the value of the ideas of social class. But it does raise important ambiguities.

11. As noted earlier, particularly for those using comparative historical methods or ethnographic methods, the analytic process is also not very conducive to the kind of specificity that Goldthorpe champions. If one works closely with only six or twelve cases (such as families), it is much more reasonable to take a broader ("umbrella") approach to defining social class than a specific one (Lareau 2003).

12. This difference can be seen in the origins of the terms cited in the *Oxford English Dictionary* (OED 1971) (see also Williams 1985). The term "class" first appeared in the 1600s in English but originated in ancient Rome: "Class: *Roman History.* Each of the six divisions or orders of the Roman people in the constitution assembly ascribed to Servius Tullius. 1. A division or order of society according to status; a rank or grade of society." By contrast, "inequality"—the "state or condition of being unequal" ("want of equality")—highlights the notion of a ranking, of having more or less than someone of something. "1. Want of equality between persons or things; disparity
    a. In respect to magnitude, quantity, number, intensity, or other physical quality
    b. In respect of dignity, rank, or circumstances; Social disparity; the fact of occupying a more or less advantageous position
    c. In respect of excellence, power, or adequacy."

13. One conference participant, Julia Wrigley of CUNY Graduate Center, commented on the lack of attention to the role of the state in the chapters in the book: "There is remarkably little discussion of the state, yet surely there is some kind of power structure, which is maintaining [and] supporting different classes, promoting other classes, the interests of them all in various ways. . . . And that wasn't part of the analysis here. It seems as if that has moved into comparative historical sociology in a very major way, where it's easier to see the actions of workings of states when you are looking over long time spans, different kinds of societies, different entities. . . . [But] it is so absolutely fundamental to . . . class analysis."

14. Wright's questions are: "(1) How are people objectively located in distributions of material inequality? (2) What explains how people, individually and collectively, subjectively locate themselves and others within a structure of inequality? (3) What explains inequalities in life changes and material standards of living? (4) What social cleavages systematically shape overt conflicts? (5) How should we characterize and explain the variations across history in the social organization of inequalities? (6) What sorts of transformations are needed to eliminate oppression and exploitation within capitalist societies?"

15. This study of opportunity hoarding, with its emphasis on the stockpiling of scarce resources by some individuals, is a theme developed by others. Pamela Barnhouse Walters, for example, stresses the "zero-sum" nature of American education. She notes that there are limited numbers of openings at elite univer-

sities, which provide access to high-level "good jobs," and that privileged parents' attempts to secure a seat at one of those elite universities for their own children constitute, at the same time, an effort to exclude others (Walters 2007).

16.   Bruckner's point about the importance of studying the environment was echoed by others. For example, Bruce Link, co-author of chapter 8 (on health), noted: "In the health field one of the angles is to sort of blame people for their bad behavior. And at the contextual level . . . I get benefits because of the neighborhood that I live in, there are parks where I can exercise . . . [there is] my occupation where they [provide] health benefits, or my marriage where my wife bugs me. . . . Hannah Bruckner's point about contextual effects as opposed to individual effects [is] really critical."

17.   Goldthorpe sees the issue of exploitation as the crucial difference between his work and Wright's: "I think over the years, in the way in which Erik's thinking and mine have developed, we've come a lot closer together than we once were. And I have never actually liked the label put on my approaches—neo-Weberian. I have always said that [my work] certainly takes something from Weber; it also takes something from Marx, perhaps even more from the Austrian Marxists of the early twentieth century, such as Karl Renner, who introduces this idea of the service relationship. So I think it is pretty eclectic. But I think ideas should be judged by their consequences, not by their providence. I think the remaining area of disagreement between Erik and myself turns, as he said, on the concept of exploitation. I can see that [that] is a useful concept [in] political rhetoric, but it does not do much for me as an analytical concept in sociology."

18.   Goldthorpe, among others, faulted Wright for the normative and moral dimension of his sixth question. Wright rejected the complaint: "I don't consider the sixth question as a normative question. . . . The sixth one said: What sorts of transformations are necessary in capitalist society in order to eliminate oppression and exploitation? Now, the question is motivated by a commitment, a particular set of value commitments. But the question asks a causal question: what sort of changes would have these effects? It is refutable. . . . When we ask questions—What sorts of chances would reduce the inequalities of opportunity of young black men and white men?—that is not a normatively driven question. . . . So I am not evoking the notion of exploitation primarily as a moral concern when I do so analytically. It's a particular claim about the character of interconnections of interests of actors, which is stronger than just the exclusionary interest-conflicts. There is a form of interdependence between advantaged and disadvantaged, privileged and underprivileged—you can use various terms—in which the privileged need the underprivileged. That's why the immigration debate is so interesting in these terms. It is incorrect that elites just want them to disappear. It would not be in the interests of elites for the illegal immigrants to disappear, because they provide all of these cheap services. That is a different kind of relationship from one which is just opportunity hoarding. And you need a language for talking about that. I use a charged language for reasons which you might object to, but the concept itself I don't think is one that there should be any objections to."

References

Acker, Joan. 1973. "Women and Social Stratification: A Case of Intellectual Sexism." *American Journal of Sociology* 78(4): 936–45.

Allen, Michael P. 1987. *Founding Fortunes: A New Anatomy of the Super-Rich in America.* New York: Dutton.

Allen, Michael P., and Philip Broyles. 1989. "Class Hegemony and Political Finance: Presidential Campaigning Contributions of Wealthy Capitalist Families." *American Sociological Review* 54(2): 275–87.

———. 1991. "Campaign Finance Reforms and the Presidential Campaign Contributions of Wealthy Capitalist Families." *Social Science Quarterly* 72(4): 738–50.

Alvarez, Louis, and Andrew Kolker, producers and directors. 2001. *People Like Us: Social Class in America.* PBS documentary film first broadcast September 23, 2001. Information available at http://www.pbs.org/peoplelikeus.

Baltzell, E. Digby. 1958/1971. *Philadelphia Gentlemen: The Making of a National Upper Class.* Chicago, Ill.: Quadrangle Books.

Beller, Emily, and Michael Hout. 2006. "Intergenerational Social Mobility: The United States in Comparative Perspective." *The Future of Children* 16(2): 19–36.

Bernstein, Basil. 1971. *Class, Codes, and Control: Theoretical Studies Towards a Sociology of Language.* New York: Schocken Books.

Blau, Peter M., and Otis Dudley Duncan. 1978. *The American Occupational Structure.* New York: Free Press.

Bott, Elizabeth. 1971. *Family and Social Network.* New York: Free Press.

Bourdieu, Pierre. 1984. *Distinction: A Social Critique of the Judgment of Taste.* Cambridge, Mass.: Harvard University Press.

Bowen, William G., and Derek Bok. 1998. *The Shape of the River: Long-Term Consequences of Considering Race in College and University Admissions.* Princeton, N.J.: Princeton University Press.

Breen, Richard. 2005. "Foundations of Class Analysis in the Weberian Tradition." In *Approaches to Class Analysis,* edited by Erik Olin Wright. Cambridge: Cambridge University Press.

Buchmann, Claudia, and Thomas DiPrete. 2006. "The Growing Female Advantage in College Completion: The Role of Parental Education, Family Structure, and Academic Achievement." *American Sociological Review* 71(4): 515–41.

Burris, Val. 2000. "The Myth of Old Money Liberalism: The Politics of the Forbes 400 Richest Americans." *Social Problems* 47(3): 360–78.

———. 2007. "Who Rules? An Internet Guide to Power Structure Research." Accessed at http://www.uoregon.edu/~vburris/whorules.

Charles, Maria, and David B. Grusky. 2004. *Occupational Ghettos: The Worldwide Segregation of Women and Men.* Stanford, Calif.: Stanford University Press.

Chernov, Ron. 1998. *Titan: The Life of John D. Rockefeller Sr.* New York: Random House.

Clark, Terry Nichols. 2003. "The Breakdown of Class Politics." *The American Sociologist* 34(1–2): 17–32.

Clark, Terry Nichols, and Seymour Martin Lipset. 1991. "Are Social Classes Dying?" *International Sociology* 6(4): 397–410.

———. 2001. *The Breakdown of Class Politics: A Debate on Post-Industrial Stratification.* Washington and Baltimore, Md.: Woodrow Wilson Center Press and Johns Hopkins University Press.

Collins, Patricia Hill. 1998. *Fighting Words: Black Women and the Search for Justice.* Minneapolis, Minn.: University of Minnesota Press.

Collins, Patricia Hill, and Margaret L. Anderson, editors. 1995. *Race, Class, and Gender.* Belmont, Calif.: Wadsworth.

Conley, Dalton. 1999. *Being Black, Living in the Red: Race, Wealth, and Social Policy in America.* Berkeley, Calif.: University of California Press.

Conley, Dalton, Kate W. Strully, and Neil G. Bennett. 2003. *The Starting Gate: Birth Weight and Life Chances.* Berkeley, Calif.: University of California Press.

Cookson, Peter W., Jr., and Caroline Hodges Persell. 1985. *Preparing for Power: America's Elite Boarding Schools.* New York: Basic Books.

Crompton, Rosemary. 1993. *Class and Stratification: An Introduction to Current Debates.* Cambridge: Polity Press.

Domhoff, G. William. 2006. *Who Rules America? Power, Politics, and Social Change,* 5th ed. Boston, Mass.: McGraw Hill. For "Links and Further Reading," see http://sociology.ucsc.edu/whorulesamerica/links.html.

Duncan, Greg J., and Jeanne Brooks-Gunn, editors. 1997. *Consequences of Growing Up Poor.* New York: Russell Sage Foundation.

Evans, Geoffrey, editor. 1999. *The End of Class Politics? Class Voting in Comparative Context.* Oxford: Oxford University Press.

Fischer, Claude S. 1982. *To Dwell Among Friends: Personal Networks in Town and City.* Chicago, Ill.: University of Chicago Press.

Giddens, Anthony, Mitchell Duneier, and Richard Appelbaum. 2007. *Introduction to Sociology,* 6th ed. New York: W. W. Norton.

Gilbert, Dennis. 2002. *American Class Structure in an Age of Growing Inequality,* 6th ed. Belmont, Calif.: Wadsworth.

Goldthorpe, John. 2007. *On Sociology,* vols. 1 and 2. Stanford, Calif.: Stanford University Press.

Goldthorpe, John, and Gordon Marshall. 1992. "The Promising Future of Class Analysis." *Sociology* 26(3): 381–400.

Grusky, David B., and Szonja Szelényi. 2007. "Introduction." In *The Inequality Reader: Contemporary and Foundational Readings in Race, Class, and Gender,* edited by David B. Grusky and Szonja Szelényi. Boulder, Colo.: Westview Press.

Hall, John R. 1997. "The Reworking of Class Analysis." In *Reworking Class,* edited by John R. Hall. Ithaca, N.Y.: Cornell University Press.

Halle, David. 1984. *America's Working Man: Work, Home, and Politics Among Blue-Collar Property Owners.* Chicago, Ill.: University of Chicago Press.

———. 1993. *Inside Culture: Art and Class in the American Home.* Chicago, Ill.: University of Chicago Press.

Hansen, Karen V. 2005. *Not-So-Nuclear Families: Class, Gender, and Networks of Care.* New Brunswick, N.J.: Rutgers University Press.

Haug, Marie R. 1977. "Measurement in Social Stratification." *Annual Review of Sociology* 3: 51–77.

Haug, Marie R., and Marvin B. Sussman. 1971. "The Indiscriminate State of Social Class Measurement." *Social Forces* 49(4): 549–63.

Hauser, Robert M., and John Allen Logan. 1992. "How Not to Measure Intergenerational Occupational Persistence." *American Journal of Sociology* 97(6): 1689–711.

Hauser, Robert M., and John Robert Warren. 1997. "Socioeconomic Indexes for Occupations: A Review, Update, and Critique." *Sociological Methodology* 27: 177–298.

Heath, Shirley Brice. 1983. *Ways with Words: Language, Life, and Work in Communities and Classrooms.* Cambridge: Cambridge University Press.

Hoggart, Richard. 1957. *The Uses of Literacy: Changing Patterns in English Mass Culture.* Boston, Mass.: Beacon Press.

Hollingshead, August B. 1949. *Elmtown's Youth: The Impact of Social Classes on Adolescents.* New York: Wiley & Sons.

———. 1953. "Social Stratification and Psychiatric Disorder." *American Sociological Review* 18(2): 163–69.

———. 1971. "Commentary on 'The Indiscriminate State of Social Class Measurement.' " *Social Forces* 49(4): 563–67.

House, James S., James M. Lepkowski, Ann M. Kinney, Richard P. Mero, Ronald C. Kessler, and A. Regula Herzog. 1994. "The Stratification of Aging and Health." *Journal of Health and Social Behavior* 35(3): 213–34.

Hout, Michael, Clem Brooks, and Jeff Manza. 1993. "The Persistence of Classes in Postindustrial Societies." *International Sociology* 8(3): 259–77.

———. 1995. "The Democratic Class Struggle in the U.S. Presidential Elections, 1952–1992." *American Sociological Review* 60: 805–28.

Jencks, Christopher, and Meredith Phillips, editors. 1998. *The Black-White Test Score Gap.* Washington: Brookings Institution Press.

Johnson, Jamie, producer and director. 2003. *Born Rich.* HBO documentary film. Information available at http://www.hbo.com/docs/programs/born_rich/synopsis.html.

Kerbo, Harold R. 2005. *Social Stratification and Inequality.* Boston, Mass.: McGraw Hill.

Kingston, Paul. 2001. *The Classless Society.* Stanford, Calif.: Stanford University Press.

Lacy, Karyn. 2007. *Blue-Chip Black: Race, Class, and Status in the New Black Middle Class.*

Lamont, Michèle. 1992. *Money, Morals, and Manners.* Chicago, Ill.: University of Chicago Press.

———. 2000. *The Dignity of Working Men: Morality and the Boundaries of Race, Class, and Immigration.* Cambridge, Mass.: Harvard University Press.

Lareau, Annette. 2003. *Unequal Childhoods: Class, Race, and Family Life.* Berkeley, Calif.: University of California Press.

Leiulfsrud, Hakon, and Alison Woodward. 1987. "Women at Class Crossroads: Repudiating Conventional Theories of Family Class." *Sociology* 21(3): 393–412.

Lubrano, Alfred. 2003. *Limbo: Blue-Collar Roots, White-Collar Dreams.* New York: Wiley & Sons.

Lundberg, Ferdinand. 1969. *The Rich and the Super-Rich.* New York: Bantam Books.

Lynd, Robert S., and Helen Merrell Lynd. 1934. *Middletown: A Study in American Culture.* New York: Harcourt Brace Jovanovich.

———. 1982. *Middletown in Transition: A Study of Cultural Conflicts.* New York: Harcourt Brace Jovanovich.

Manza, Jeff, and Clem Brooks. 1996. "Does Class Analysis Still Have Anything to Contribute to the Study of Politics? Comments." *Theory and Society* 25(5): 717–24.

Marsh, Kris, William A. Darity, Jr., Philip N. Cohen, Lynne M. Casper, and Danielle Salters. 2007. "The Emerging Black Middle Class: Single and Living Alone." *Social Forces* 86(2): 735–62.

Massey, Douglas, and Nancy Denton. 1996. *American Apartheid.* Cambridge, Mass.: Harvard University Press.

McNall, Scott G., Rhonda F. Levine, and Rick Fantasia, editors. 1991. "Introduction." In *Bringing Class Back In*, edited by Scott G. McNall, Rhonda F. Levine, and Rick Fantasia. Boulder, Colo.: Westview Press.

McNamee, Stephen J., and Robert K. Miller Jr. 2004. *The Meritocracy Myth*. Lanham, Md.: Rowman & Littlefield.

Mills, C. Wright. 1956. *White Collar: The American Middle Classes*. New York: Oxford University Press.

———. 1956/1999. *The Power Elite*. New York: Oxford University Press.

Moss, Philip, and Chris Tilly. 1995. " 'Soft' Skills and Race: An Investigation of Black Men's Employment Problems." Working paper, Russell Sage Foundation. Accessed at http://epn.org/sage/rstill.html.

Mueller, Charles W., and Toby L. Parcel. 1981. "Measures of Socioeconomic Status: Alternatives and Recommendations." *Child Development* 52(1): 13–30.

Neckerman, Kathryn M., editor. 2004. *Social Inequality*. New York: Russell Sage Foundation.

New York Times. 2002. *How Race Is Lived in America: Pulling Together, Pulling Apart*. New York: Times Books.

———. 2005. *Class Matters*. New York: Times Books. Accessed at http://www.nytimes.com/pages/national/class.

Newman, Katherine S. 1988. *Falling from Grace: The Experience of Downward Mobility in the American Middle Class*. New York: Vintage Books.

———. 1993. *Declining Fortunes: The Withering of the American Dream*. New York: Basic Books.

———. 2006. *Chutes and Ladders: Navigating the Low-Wage Labor Market*. New York: Russell Sage Foundation.

Nisbet, Robert A. 1959. "The Decline and Fall of Social Class." *Pacific Sociological Review* 2(1): 11–17.

Oliver, Melvin, and Thomas Shapiro. 2006. *Black Wealth/White Wealth: A New Perspective on Racial Inequality*. London: Routledge.

Ostrander, Susan A. 1984. *Women of the Upper Class*. Philadelphia, Pa.: Temple University Press.

Oxford English Dictionary. 1971. Oxford: Oxford University Press.

Pager, Devah. 2007. *Marked: Race, Crime, and Finding Work in an Era of Mass Incarceration*. Chicago, Ill.: University of Chicago Press.

Pakulski, Jan, and Malcolm Waters. 1996. *The Death of Class*. London: Sage Publications.

Pattillo-McCoy, Mary. 1999. *Black Picket Fences: Privilege and Peril Among the Black Middle Class*. Chicago, Ill.: University of Chicago Press.

Perrucci, Robert, and Earl Wysong. 1999. *The New Class Society*. Lanham, Md.: Rowman & Littlefield.

Royster, Deidre. 2003. *Race and the Invisible Hand: How White Networks Exclude Black Men from Blue-Collar Jobs*. Berkeley, Calif.: University of California Press.

Rubin, Lillian B. 1976. *Worlds of Pain: Life in the Working-Class Family*. New York: Basic Books.

Schwartz, Christine R., and Robert D. Mare. 2005. "Trends in Educational Assortative Marriage from 1940 to 2003." *Demography* 42(4): 621–46.

Shapiro, Thomas. 2004. *The Hidden Cost of Being African American: How Wealth Perpetuates Inequality*. Oxford: Oxford University Press.

Smith, Sandra. 2005. " 'Don't Put My Name on It': Social Capital Activation and Job-Finding Assistance Among the Black Urban Poor." *American Journal of Sociology* 111(July): 1–57.

Thompson, William E., and Joseph V. Hickey. 2007. *Society in Focus: An Introduction to Sociology*, 6th ed. Boston, Mass.: Allyn & Bacon.

Tilly, Charles. 1998. *Durable Inequality*. Berkeley, Calif.: University of California Press.

Walters, Pamela Barnhouse. 2007. "Sustaining Privilege: Opportunity Hoarding in American Education." Unpublished paper, Indiana University.

Warner, W. Lloyd. 1960. *Social Class in America*. New York: Harper & Row.

Warren, John Robert, and Robert M. Hauser. 1997. "Social Stratification Across Three Generations: New Evidence from the Wisconsin Longitudinal Study." *American Sociological Review* 62(August): 561–72.

Warren, John Robert, Jennifer T. Sheridan, and Robert M. Hauser. 1998. "Choosing a Measure of Occupational Standing." *Sociological Methods and Research* 27(1): 3–76.

Weininger, Elliot B. 2002. "Class and Causation in Bourdieu." In *Current Perspectives in Social Theory*, vol. 21, edited by Jennifer M. Lehmann. Greenwich, Conn.: JAI Press.

———. 2005. "Foundations of Pierre Bourdieu's Class Analysis." In *Approaches to Class Analysis*, edited by Erik Olin Wright. Cambridge: Cambridge University Press.

Weis, Lois. 2004. *Class Reunion: The Remaking of the American White Working Class*. London: Routledge.

———, editor. 2007. *The Way Class Works: Readings on Family, School, and the Economy*. London: Routledge.

Wells, Amy Stuart, and Robert L. Crain. 1997. *Stepping Over the Color Line: African-American Students in White Suburban Schools*. New Haven, Conn.: Yale University Press.

Williams, Raymond. 1985. *Keywords: A Vocabulary of Culture and Society*. Oxford: Oxford University Press.

Wright, Erik Olin. 1989. *The Debate on Classes*. London: Verso.

———. 1996. "The Continuing Relevance of Class Analysis." *Theory and Society* 25(5): 697–716.

———. 1997a. *Class Counts: Comparative Studies in Class Analysis*. Cambridge: Cambridge University Press.

———. 1997b. "Rethinking, Once Again, the Concept of Class Structure." In *Reworking Class*, edited by John R. Hall. Ithaca, N.Y.: Cornell University Press.

———. 2005. *Approaches to Class Analysis*. Cambridge: Cambridge University Press.

Wysong, Earl, and Robert Perrucci. 2007. "Organizations, Resources, and Class Analysis: The Distributional Model and the U.S. Class Structure." *Critical Sociology* 33(1–2): 211–46.

Young, Alford A., Jr. 2006. *The Minds of Marginalized Black Men: Making Sense of Mobility, Opportunity, and Future Life Chances*. Princeton, N.J.: Princeton University Press.

Zipp, John F., and Eric Plutzer. 1996. "Wives and Husbands." *Sociology* 30(2): 235–52.

———. 2000. "From Housework to Paid Work." *Social Science Quarterly* 81(2): 538–54.

Chapter 1

How Class Works: Objective and Subjective Aspects of Class Since the 1970s

MICHAEL HOUT

MARX AND Engels founded class analysis with their famous claim, in *The Communist Manifesto,* that "the history of all hitherto existing societies is the history of class struggle." Class analysts have struggled ever since to live down the founders' boldness. Past and present societies turn out to be more complex than class struggle admits. But it is a serious error of both logic and fact to conclude that just because class falls short of explaining "all hitherto existing society," it is somehow insignificant. As Erik Olin Wright notes in *Class Counts* (1997, 1), "Class is a pervasive social cause and thus it is worth exploring its ramifications for many social phenomena." For birthweight and cause of death, when to marry and who to marry, where to live and where to eat, what to say and how to say it, class matters.[1] Scholars debate which aspect of class makes a difference and precisely how the several components of class combine to affect a specific outcome of interest, but the question "Are social classes dying?" has been answered with a loud no.[2] This chapter elaborates on how class remains salient by focusing on what everyday people tell us about their class location and how it relates to what we know about their education, occupation, and income.

Wright's (2005a) challenge—"If 'class' is the answer, what is the question?"—orients many chapters in this volume, including mine. He poses six questions that "class" might be answering. I go after the second of them: "What explains how people, individually and collectively, subjectively locate themselves and others in a structure of inequality?" To subjectively locate themselves and others, people have to correctly perceive the extent of social inequality, correctly identify where inequality comes from, and then correctly find their place in the unequal scheme of things. Little wonder, then, that the revolutionaries of one hundred years ago called out for a vanguard class to lead people through the complexities, and more's the wonder that Americans today find coherent answers to questions about their class position.

What Do We Mean by "Class"?

To start the discussion, we can think of class as how people earn their money, how much money they have, or what they do with their money.[3]

For statistical analysis and descriptive work, any or all three can be useful. Sociologists tend to favor the first concept—that how people make their money defines their class. The original idea was that the so-called social relations of production set in motion historical forces that shaped consciousness and action. These days the concept addresses interests more directly—the idea being that people who earn their money the same way share interests in preserving or advancing their collective welfare. This approach can preserve the important idea that classes exist in relation to one another. A sociologist could think of class as rooted in where the money comes from without thinking it matters because some classes depend on the existence of other classes to get their money, but it is nearly impossible to maintain that one class exploits another without simultaneously embracing the idea that class is about where the money comes from. As examples, Kim Weeden and David Grusky (2005; chapter 2, this volume) frame classes as ways of earning a living in a given division of labor, but they do not interrogate the relation of any one class to another; Wright (1997, 2005b), on the other hand, makes the relation between exploiter and exploited paramount.

Class in this sense also resolves the conundrum of people on predictable trajectories. Young medical students, White House interns, and others who see their low income as a short spell of "paying dues" are in most ways class equals with the people who currently occupy the positions to which they aspire. Less certainly, we might also hypothesize that people in their late fifties who have a decent income but no pension to speak of might be already identifying with the struggles that lie not too far ahead of them.

Others, mostly economists, put money, no matter its origin, at the center of their models. People make choices under time and budget constraints. Having money relieves the budget constraint on action. Trade-offs still exist because nobody has an infinite amount of money. But the more money a person accumulates, the less constrained that person's actions become. Not everyone does the same thing with their money. Some buy more things; others save. The point is that more income means more choices. People with looser budget constraints make different choices than people with tight budgets. And in that circumscribed way, class matters. In less circumscribed ways, too, money itself matters. In politics, the classic derivation is that people with money resist taxes in general and progressive taxation in particular (Downs 1957). In the United States today, high-income people care about different government services than the ones that matter to low-income people. High-income people support spending on public universities and roads, for example, but do not think the government should give poor people money. Meanwhile, low-income people favor spending more on social welfare programs and drug treatment as well as raising the minimum wage.[4]

Lifestyle—what people do with the money they have—is an important consideration in Pierre Bourdieu's approach to class (see Lamont 1992, 2000; Lareau and Weininger, this volume; Weininger 2005). Bound up with privilege and interests is "habitus," the specific orientation to social life that predisposes some classes to one mode of being and other classes to other modes. These are serious aspects of class analysis, but I do not consider them here both because habitus is as much a dependent variable as an independent variable and because the data at my disposal were not designed to address this issue.

Popular conceptions of class also bring up lifestyle issues as typified by Roger Hodge's list of class terms (this volume). Many items on his class list—rich, poor, professional, blue collar, white collar, Wall Street, suit, service worker, Ivy League, state school, preppy, public, college boy—invoke where the money comes from. But his other terms blend location, consumption, and reputation in terms such as ghetto, skank, trailer trash, redneck, and fabulous. These informal appellations blend privilege, taste, and geography in ways that indicate Americans' fascination with class, distinction, and respect. As Hodge says, they expose the myth of classless America as, itself, a myth. The blending makes them useless as explanatory tools, even if we could reduce them to measurement, but they might make interesting research subjects in their own right if somebody could establish their relative currency and had an analysis strategy for parsing the relative contributions of privilege, taste, and so on.

If we are interested in describing social patterns, then virtually any notion that captures how people differentiate themselves into "haves" and "have-lesses" will serve that purpose—some better, some worse. And so, for descriptive work, researchers use a wide array of measures and observations to capture class differences. Since my aims are primarily descriptive, I show in the rest of the chapter that people's answers to simple questions make common sense and correlate with the most straightforward battery of objective conditions—education, occupation, and income.[5] I also present evidence of variation in how education, occupation, and income relate to subjective-class placement to test others' theories of how class works (or does not).

To move from description to a causal explanation, though, much more is required. My descriptive data show that what people say goes with what they do for a living and what they have. An explanation would tell *why* they say what they do. Done right, a causal statement inexorably links being in one class rather than another with having one idea rather than another. Optimally, a powerful theory would imply a specific classification scheme, which, in turn, would embed in the necessary distinction of one category from another the explanation of why they differ. This complete package of theory, classification scheme, and explanation is class analysis as Marx and Engels understood it, and class analysis as some of their successors still see it. But for the most part the more comprehensive schemes have a weaker empirical record than the demographic approaches like mine that show associations too strong to ignore but do not link theory, classification, and explanation.

Class Awareness and Identification

What Americans say about social class depends on what question they are asked and what answers are suggested to them. Perhaps a skeptic could make the case that this regularity implies that Americans are unsure about what they think. But to me it looks like survey respondents pay attention to what we ask them. The American National Election Study (ANES) and the General Social Survey (GSS) are two large projects that assess Americans' opinions on a variety of subjects and have done so for a long time.[6] The ANES frequently asked at least part of its sample this question about social class: "There's been some talk these days about different social classes. Most people say they belong either to the middle class or the working class. Do you ever think of yourself as belonging in one of these classes?" At various times from 1956 to 2000, about two-thirds of American adults said they did think of themselves as belonging to one of those two classes (68 percent over all the years), and there was no consistent trend.[7]

The follow-up to the question "Do you belong to a class?" is, obviously enough, "Which one do you belong to?" In 2000, 59 percent of Americans eligible to vote said "middle class" and 41 percent said "working class." In the 1950s, people split the other way around: 40 percent said "middle class," and 60 percent said "working class." Equal numbers chose "middle class" and "working class" from the 1960s through 1992. The one-third of people who initially said they did not belong to either the middle or working class were asked, "Well, if you had to make a choice, would you call yourself middle class or working class?" Throughout the years, the people who initially denied class membership said they were working class by a 56 percent to 37 percent majority. (About 1 percent volunteered "lower" or "poor," 1 percent volunteered "upper" or "rich," 3 percent said there are no classes, and 1 or 2 percent gave uncoded responses.)[8]

Table 1.1   Subjective Social Class: All Persons and Employed Respondents Twenty-Five Years and Older

Class	All Respondents	Employed Respondents
Upper class	4%	3%
Middle class	47	46
Working class	44	48
Lower class	5	3
Number of cases	7,518	4,806

Source: General Social Survey (GSS), 2000 to 2004.
Note: Cases weighted to adjust for sample design.

The GSS asks just one direct question of all its respondents: "If you were asked to use one of four names for your social class, which would you say you belong in: the lower class, the working class, the middle class, or the upper class?" This question gets an answer from 99.4 percent of the people who hear it. Americans in the present decade split more or less equally between responding "middle class" and "working class" (as in the ANES data of the 1960s through the 1990s). This wording yields more "upper" and "lower" answers, however, than the ANES question. (Three to 5 percent choose "lower," and 3 to 5 percent choose "upper.") Table 1.1 illustrates this general finding with data from the 2000 to 2004 GSS. The "middle class" answer edged out "working class" by four percentage points here. Restricting attention to people who have jobs, the slight advantage swings to "working class." When Richard Centers (1949) first asked this exact question in 1945, 49 percent identified as working class and 45 percent as middle class. Americans' answers changed remarkably little in sixty years. Considering the increases in education, professional employment, income, homeownership, and other economic indicators since 1945, it would be reasonable to expect the middle class to have grown more than just two points and the working class to have declined by more than five points. For subjective changes to lag so far behind objective changes hints that many Americans answer based on their relative education, occupation, and income, perhaps discounting improvements that all share. The multivariate analysis I present later in this chapter is consistent with this idea, as is much research on subjective well being (Hout 2003).

Retired people and homemakers identify as middle class significantly more than people in the labor force do. Retirees' earning days are behind them, so their annual family incomes understate their standard of living. Presumably they have lower expenses, especially if they have paid off their mortgage; they may also have some savings, and it could be that they simply continue to think of their class position as that of their lifestyle before retirement. In any event, their identities are somewhat marginal to the class awareness debates, though they should perhaps get more attention.

Homemakers are marginal in a different way. Most of them are engaged in a division of labor that puts the need to earn money on their spouse. Their class identity reflects their family income pretty much as employed people's identity does (Baxter 1994). Because they have no current position in the occupational division of labor, however, their answers make no reference to any specific position in the occupational structure, unlike the answers of employed or retired people. Their spouse's occupation dominates their class placement.

Employed people express a working class identity slightly more often than they say they are middle class—48 percent compared to 46 percent (3 percent said lower class and 3 percent said upper class). Detailed breakdowns by employment status (not shown) show that extreme answers are slightly less common among the employed than among the retired and students; homemakers resemble the employed.

The ANES and GSS coach respondents with references to the middle and working classes in their questions. Open-ended questions that do not prompt respondents with any answer categories get far more mentions of the middle class and far fewer mentions of the working class. In 1964 a mere 6 percent of American adults volunteered "working class" in response to the question "What social class do you consider yourself a member of?" (Hodge and Treiman 1968). Our 1991 survey of American adults (Hout, Wright, and Jankowski 1992) returned more mentions—16 percent—but it is nonetheless a rare American who thinks "working class" without a prompt.[9] The modal reply in the 1991 survey was to mention the upper, middle, and lower classes (or equivalents like rich, middle, and poor, or high, middle, and low).[10] Richard Coleman and Lee Rainwater (1978) got similar responses in a regional study. They noted the similarity between this characterization of the American class structure and the conclusions reached by the "community studies" tradition (Lockwood 1966; Warner, Meeker, and Eells 1960).

Some scholars (most recently, Kingston 2000) have looked to this kind of evidence that Americans rarely use the term "working class" to question the salience of the working class identity in particular and, occasionally, class identities altogether. That goes too far, I think. Over 90 percent of Americans offer an answer to open-ended class questions, 99.4 percent answer the closed-ended question, and two-thirds of the electorate say they are a "member" of a social class. Americans are "class-aware," as Mary Jackman and David Jackman (1983) put it. Most need prompting before they use the working class label; perhaps "working class" reflects some vestige of the cold war. But there is definitely class awareness in the United States in this decade.

As David Halle (1984) famously pointed out, references to "working man" are far more prevalent than references to "working class," even in factory settings. I would add that the references to "working families" in the 2006 congressional election race raised class issues far more than they brought up issues about labor force participation.

Having demonstrated that Americans will answer class questions, I now turn to whether their answers make substantive sense; the alternative is that they represent random acquiescence to the survey situation—that is, that their answers indicate little more than their politeness and tell us nothing about their class awareness. The first way to tell whether the answers are substantive or merely polite is to see whether the answers correlate with the education, occupation, and income of the respondents. The second way is to see whether the answers correlate with things that class is supposed to predict.

Of course, others have taken this approach before. From their research it is clearly more reasonable to say that Americans have flexible—and maybe multiple—class identities than to say they have none. The social science literature on class identification in the 1960s emphasized "status inconsistencies" attributable to the modest correlations between income, occupation, and education (Hodge and Treiman 1968). People understand what goes into being middle class or working class in the abstract, but many find themselves in complicated positions that imply different class identities. "A merchant marine seaman, who was buying an apartment house for investment purposes . . . thought he was 'about middle class as an apartment house owner, and working class as a merchant marine'" (Yoshino 1959, 114; quoted in Hodge and Treiman 1968, 535). Factory foremen with no high school diploma but substantially above-average incomes and suburban tract homes have similar split identities. Small-town schoolteachers with advanced degrees but incomes below the national average may be less conflicted about their middle class status, yet some identify with the working class, especially the ones who are married to factory workers. And we will see later that entrepreneurs, regardless of education, answer according to the incomes of their clientele: if they sell car parts or farm supplies, they are less likely to identify as middle class than if they sell suits to businessmen.

Complexity exists in the loose connections between objective characteristics and in the ways in which workplaces and home settings mobilize different aspects of people's identities. Halle (1984, 205) elaborated the "complexity" argument based on his participant-observations in a New Jersey refinery (known by the pseudonym "Imperium"):

> The concept of the working man expresses both class and gender consciousness for Imperium workers. As a form of class consciousness, its central idea is that blue collar work takes a distinctive form and is productive in a way that

the work of other classes is not. As a form of gender consciousness it implies such work is for men, not women.

Like Yoshino's merchant seaman, Halle's factory workers tuned into the consciousness and politics of how physical their work is and the surveillance they are under, but away from the refinery they tuned into their interests as homeowners and providers.

Class awareness also manifests itself in Americans' willingness to attribute class rank to others. When presented with mini-biographies or vignettes (as in Coleman and Rainwater 1978), people have the ability to calculate their own and others' social positions. More important for our purposes here, they give greater weight to differences in education, occupation, and income than to other "facts" woven into the vignettes—the hypothetical person's race, gender, marital status, and age.

Objective Class and Subjective Class

Americans, for the most part, express identities that are quite congruent with their objective circumstances. Figures 1.1 through 1.3 reveal for employed persons clear, strong relationships between subjective class and each major class indicator—family income, current occupation, and education.[11] Multivariate analyses in subsequent figures and tables show that each factor contributes even when the other two (and other relevant factors) are held constant.

Figure 1.1 shows the sharp differences among the subjective-class identifications of six income groups. Among employed Americans in families with incomes under $20,000 per year, 20 percent identified as middle class. Middle class identification rose with income, but most people in families with an income under $50,000 identified with the working class. At $50,000, the majority identified with the middle class, two-thirds of those with annual incomes between $75,000 and $100,000 did so, and in families with annual incomes $100,000 and over, three-fourths saw themselves as middle class and most of the rest identified as upper class. Only in that top income category did a significant fraction see themselves as upper class.

Figure 1.2 shifts attention to the subjective-class placements of people in different occupations. To classify occupations, I started with the oft-used Erikson-Goldthorpe (1992) class scheme. It distinguishes a "salariat" of professionals and managers, other white collar employees, self-employed entrepreneurs, farmers, skilled blue collar workers, unskilled blue collar workers, and low-wage service workers. Optionally the scheme separates upper and lower professionals: physicians, attorneys, engineers, and so on, are the upper professionals, and schoolteachers, nurses, social workers, and so on, are the lower. The prevalence of unions for many of the lower professions suggests that they might be open to a working class identity that would be

Figure 1.1   Class Identification of Employed Persons Age Twenty-Five and Older, by Family Income

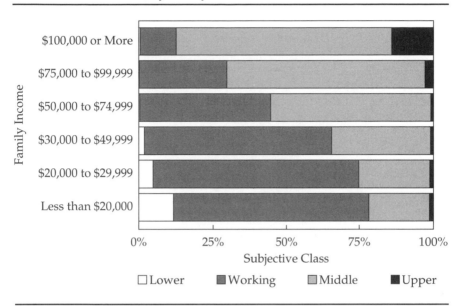

Source: General Social Survey (GSS), 2000 to 2004.

harder for upper professionals to embrace. To this scheme I add two distinctions. First, following Hout, Brooks, and Manza (1995), I separate professionals and managers ("professional I" in figure 1.2). Second, I distinguish between the self-employed nonprofessionals who would be classified as white collar based on their occupation and those who would be blue collar in order to separate the impact of employment status better (self-employed, white collar and self-employed, blue collar in figure 1.2). Figure 1.2 ranks these ten classes from highest percentage middle class to lowest.

Strong majorities of upper professionals, managers, and white collar self-employed identified with the middle and upper classes: 71 percent of the top professionals said middle class and 9 percent said upper class; 59 percent of white collar self-employed said middle class and 13 percent upper class; and 59 percent of managers said middle class, with 5 percent saying upper class. Lower professionals were more closely divided, but a majority—55 percent—identify with the middle class. Majorities of employed people from all other classes identify with the working class. Other white collar workers split 42 percent middle class and 51 percent working class. The blue collar categories—including self-employed blue collar workers—had strong to very strong working class majorities. Two-thirds of skilled and unskilled blue collar workers identify with the working class; another 6 percent of unskilled blue collar workers identify with the lower class.

Figure 1.2   Class Identification of Employed Persons Age Twenty-Five and Older, by Occupation

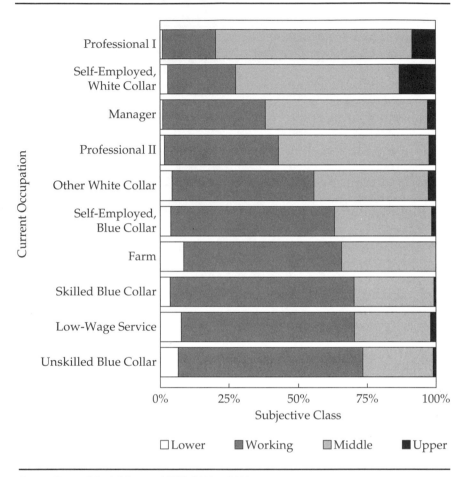

Source: General Social Survey (GSS), 2000 to 2004.

Low-wage service workers were very similar to the unskilled blue collar workers at 63 percent working class and 8 percent lower class.

These relationships are all based on people's own current occupations. Janeen Baxter (1994) found that married women tend to give more weight to their husband's occupation than their own when answering subjective-class questions. However, when I substituted husband's occupation for the occupation of married women and redid figure 1.2, there was no substantively interesting difference.[12] The biggest difference was in the number of cases available for analysis: the substitution increased the number of valid cases from 4,768 to 5,180. The largest change in subjective class was an

Figure 1.3   Class Identification of Employed Persons Age Twenty-Five
and Older, by Education

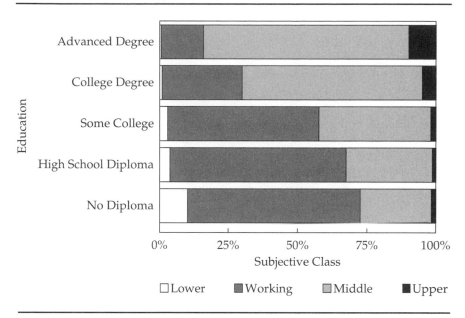

Source: General Social Survey (GSS), 2000 to 2004.

increase in middle class identification among low-wage service workers,
from 27 percent to 30 percent.

Figure 1.3 shifts our attention to education. College graduates identified
with the middle class; less-educated people identified with the working
class. Moving from highest to lowest education, we see that among people
with a degree beyond the bachelor's 75 percent identified with the middle
class and another 10 percent with the upper class; 67 percent of those for
whom BA was their highest degree thought of themselves as middle class;
41 percent of people with some college but no degree thought of themselves
as middle class; 29 percent of high school graduates identified with the middle class; and only 23 percent of high school dropouts thought of themselves
as middle class. Working class identification pretty much complemented
the middle class identification, though 10 percent of high school dropouts
actually viewed themselves as lower class.

These three charts show that Americans not only recognize the class
labels but know how to use them as social scientists would. Each figure portrays a strong statistical relationship. Two comparisons that use the GSS's
subjective income question—"Compared with American families in general, would you say your family income is far below average, below average, average, above average, or far above average?"—establish the strength

of these relationships. We would reasonably expect answers to the more specific subjective-income question to track family income more closely than the answers to subjective class. And that is what the data show. In a statistical model that summarizes the relationship in figure 1.1 with a single coefficient, we get a value of 1.57; applying the same model to the subjective income data, we get a value of 1.95.[13] The relationship between family income and subjective class is 81 percent as strong as the relationship between family income and subjective income.

We can just as reasonably expect that education and occupation will relate more closely to subjective class than to subjective income, once we control for actual income in multivariate statistical models. So my second comparison involves the coefficients for income, occupation, and education in association with subjective class and subjective income. The results are shown in table 1.2. As in the bivariate model, the association between family income and subjective income exceeds that for subjective class. The main effect of education on subjective class is twice its value for subjective income; the add-on effect of an advanced degree—important for understanding subjective class—is not even statistically significant in the subjective income equation. The coefficients for most occupations are larger in the class column than in the income column. The exceptions are the significant coefficients for the self-employed blue collar and skilled blue collar categories; people in those two occupations are further above unskilled blue collar workers in subjective income than in subjective class.

Ambiguity and Ambivalence

To this point I have debunked the claim that Americans deny class by showing that fewer than 3 percent explicitly deny class by refusing or failing to answer class questions and by confirming that a significant fraction of American adults identify with the working class. Furthermore, I have established that they put meaning into their choices by identifying with class labels that correspond to their objective circumstances. The case cannot rest there. It has been made before (Jackman and Jackman 1983; Wright 1997) and failed to convince class deniers (Clark and Lipset 1991; Kingston 2000). Significant variation in class identities that correlates with objective criteria is insufficient to prove that class is salient for Americans because the correlates are said to be indeterminate (Kingston 2000, 100) and the variation is said to be inconsequential (Kingston 2000, 101–58). I take up the issue of determinacy in this section and the issue of consequence later in the chapter.

The link between objective and subjective class is clear when the objective-class elements—income, occupation, and education—are all at their highest or lowest values. Ninety-six percent of professionals and managers with an advanced degree and family income over $110,000 identify with the middle (75 percent) or upper class (21 percent). At the other extreme, 81 percent of unskilled blue collar employees with no high school diploma and a family

Table 1.2   **Net Effects of Objective Variables on Subjective Social Class and Subjective Income Among Employed Persons Age Twenty-Five and Older**

Objective Variable	Dependent Variable	
	Subjective Class	Subjective Income
Family income (ratio-scale)	1.318*	1.786*
	(.068)	(.087)
Occupation		
Professional I	1.103*	.704*
	(.168)	(.172)
Professional II	.404*	.102
	(.159)	(.143)
Manager	.604*	.461*
	(.124)	(.142)
Other white collar	.308*	.321*
	(.149)	(.146)
Self-employed, white collar	1.017*	.671*
	(.208)	(.206)
Self-employed, blue collar	.282	.459*
	(.228)	(.220)
Skilled blue collar	−.065	.422*
	(.145)	(.142)
Unskilled blue collar	0	0
	—	—
Low-wage service	.200	−.102
	(.164)	(.150)
Farm	.165	−.613
	(.426)	(.434)
Education		
Main	.302*	.147*
	(.060)	(.047)
Advanced degree	.348*	.218
	(.142)	(.160)
Number of cases	4,332	2,876

Source: General Social Survey (GSS), 2000 to 2004.
Note: The GSS design calls for skipping the subjective income question for a random one-third of respondents, yielding fewer cases for analysis. Intercepts were suppressed to save space.
* Statistically significant at conventional level ($p < .05$).

income less than $20,000 identify as working (56 percent) or lower (25 percent) class.[14] Some people get mixed class signals because their income, occupation, and education do not line up—a condition Hodge and Treiman (1968) called "status inconsistency." People become ambivalent about their subjective class because, objectively, they are in more than one; forced to choose by the way most survey questions are posed, some pick middle class and others pick working class. Other people have an income, occupation, and education at the boundary between working and middle class. For them, their subjective class is ambiguous. People near the class border disagree on which class they are in; the percentage identifying with the working class comes close to the percentage identifying with the middle class, and objective class fails to determine subjective class. Both the ambivalence of status inconsistency and the ambiguity of being near the class border can be problems for class analysis, depending on their prevalence.

Status inconsistency arises because income, occupation, and education correlate, but not perfectly. A person's income depends on education and occupation, to be sure, but also on factors like employment status, gender, racial ancestry, marital status, spouse's earnings, local economic conditions, wealth, talent, pluck, and luck.[15] So inconsistencies arise and create class ambivalence.

Status inconsistency is probably not quite as prevalent now as it was in 1964 when the data Hodge and Treiman used were collected. Changes in the economy have eradicated some of the inconsistencies. Earnings inequality rose significantly and did so in a way that modestly reduced status inconsistency. The association between education and earnings climbed through the 1970s and 1980s (see, for example, Card and DiNardo 2002). Industrial changes made high-paying, low-status jobs much harder to come by, especially for high school dropouts (Fischer and Hout 2006, ch. 5). Marriage partners have increasingly similar educations (Schwartz and Mare 2005). And women's rising educational attainments have increased not only their own earnings but their chances of matching a higher-earning husband (DiPrete and Buchmann 2006). Statistical models (not shown) indicate that family income gaps among occupations and educational categories grew bigger from 1980 onward.[16] These trends have resolved some of the complexities that Americans contend with when weighing their social class identification.

To gain some insight into how status inconsistency works out in the contemporary setting, figure 1.4 shows middle and upper class identification by income, occupation, and education among employed people in 2004.[17] The patterns reflect the consequences of both status inconsistency and living on the class border. People with a consistently high or low status agreed on a class identity. Workers in low-status occupations who had a low family income identified with the working and lower classes by at least a two-to-one margin—that is, two-thirds or more were working or lower class, and one-third or fewer were middle or upper class. In a complementary way, three-fourths or more of upper professionals, managers, and white collar self-employed in families with an income of $75,000 or more identified with the middle and upper classes. Status inconsistency led to subjective-class ambiguity (in the form of expected percentages closer to 50 percent);

Figure 1.4   Identification of Employed Persons Age Twenty-Five or Older with the Middle or Upper Class, by Family Income, Occupation, and Education

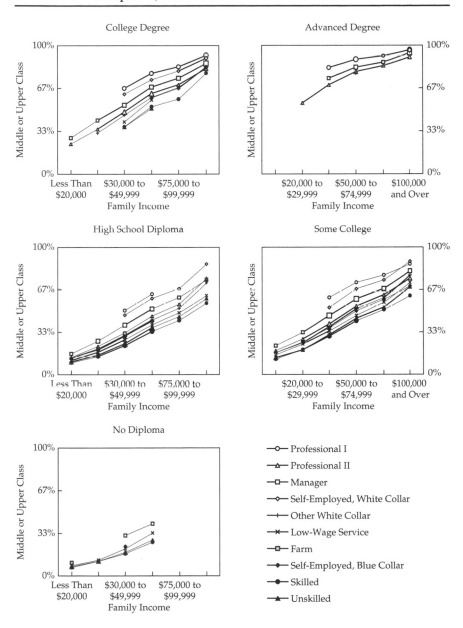

Source: Statistical model using data from General Social Survey (GSS), 2000 to 2004.
Note: Larger symbols and darker lines indicate more frequent combinations; small symbols and light lines indicate rare combinations; unobserved combinations are left off the chart.

it rose as income rose for lower status workers and as income fell for high-status employees and entrepreneurs. Middle status employees of all incomes split their identifications. Lower professionals, routine white collar workers, and blue collar self-employed split their identifications more closely unless their income fell below $40,000 (in which case strong majorities agreed they were working or lower class) or rose above $75,000 (in which case strong majorities agreed they were middle class).

Thus, the nearly even split of Americans into the middle and working classes reflects the balance of consistently high and consistently low status class locations, ambivalence stemming from status inconsistency, and ambiguity about the borderline that separates the working class from the middle class among people like high school graduates with average incomes and routine jobs who might fall on either side of the line.

What does this say about whether objective class determines subjective class? In the purely statistical sense, these are strong relationships, and most analysts would characterize the range of expected outcomes from near 10 percent to well over 90 percent middle class as very large. But expected percentages between 33 percent and 67 percent leave the door open a crack to those who would argue for the "classless" conclusion. The prevalence of clear class outcomes relative to ambivalent or ambiguous outcomes might close that door if clear class positions predominate. If we can agree that it is a clear class outcome when those who can be expected to identify as middle or upper class outnumber those we expect not to by a ratio of two-to-one, and when they in turn are outnumbered by that same two-to-one ratio, then we can calculate how many American adults are in clear class positions and how many are in ambivalent or ambiguous ones.[18] Among working people, 61 percent are in clear class positions—their expected percentages under this simple statistical model are either less than one-third or greater than two-thirds—and 39 percent are in ambivalent or ambiguous positions. Combining employed and non-employed adults reveals more ambivalence and ambiguity: 58 percent of all adults are in clear class positions, and 42 percent are in ambivalent or ambiguous positions. Retired people's tendency to identify more strongly with the middle class than we would otherwise expect accounts for the lower clarity in the total population.[19]

Adding criteria that many Americans consider relevant to class placement—homeownership, residence in certain neighborhoods, union membership—and some that a few consider relevant—marriage, children, church membership, leisure pursuits—improves the fit of statistical models to data but also yields more ways to detect ambivalent class signals—college graduates in poor neighborhoods, for example, or low-income homeowners. In other words, the longer the list of relevant factors, the more possibilities for the inconsistencies that make choosing a class hard for people. And by most indications, Americans use a rather long list. Recall Yoshino's merchant seaman and Halle's working men: they actually invoked dual identities—working class on the job and middle class elsewhere. The GSS question does not give people the opportunity to choose more than one. So different people resolve it differently in the interview, yielding ambiguity. When I elaborated the statistical model to include all the factors above, I once again found that 61 percent of employed people were in clear class positions, and 39 percent were in ambivalent or ambiguous ones.

The final consideration is whether people in clear class positions actually identify as the model predicts they will. They do by a four-to-one margin. Among employed people in a clear working class position, 79 percent identify as either working class (71 percent) or lower class (8 percent). Among employed people in clear middle class positions, 86 percent identify with either the middle class (77 percent) or the upper class (9 percent). When class is harder to predict, the split is much closer to even: 47 percent middle class and 53 percent working class (less than 1 percent each upper and lower class).[20]

Taken together, these results amount to more evidence than most other studies yield that objective class affects subjective class. The evidence accumulated in this analysis yields a clearer picture of how objective class affects subjective class and why class is occasionally ambiguous and why some Americans might be objectively ambivalent about their class position.

Competing Identities

Post-class advocates such as Jan Pakulski (2005) argue that other aspects of modern life offer Americans choices about their identities that compete with their class position. The distraction of marital, religious, racial, and regional identities blunts the impact of class in American life. A full canvass to determine whether this is a reasonable assessment of contemporary American society and culture is beyond the scope of this chapter. But among the argument's key hypotheses is the idea that people are becoming less responsive to their objective-class position in forming their sense of their place in society and in making important choices. I consider four hypotheses that would have to be true for the post-class thesis to make sense:

1. The net effect of objective class after statistically controlling for competing identities is notably smaller than the gross effect of objective class by itself.

2. The net effect of objective class after statistically controlling for competing identities is notably smaller than the net effects of some of the competing variables.

3. The effect of objective class is notably weaker for people with strong competing identities—for example, as Southerners, parents, or religious people—than it is in general.

4. The effect of objective class on subjective class has declined since the 1970s.

If these hypotheses are confirmed, the argument that competing identities blunt the effects of objective class on subjective class will be strengthened. If the hypotheses are rejected, the post-class case will be seriously weakened and the perspective that held sway at the conference—that Americans understand class and its implications for describing American inequality—will be strengthened.

If competing identities were blunting the effects of class, then either other identities would matter more than objective class in the analysis of subjective class or adding those factors to the model would reduce my estimates of objective-class differences in subjective social class. Substantial differences between the coefficients in the gross and net columns in table 1.3 would confirm this first hypothesis. The evidence contradicts this first hypothesis. The net effects of education and family income are actually slightly larger than they appear to be without controls; the net effect of education is 8 percent bigger than its gross effect, and the net effect of family income is 6 percent bigger than its gross effect. The effect of occupation is a little harder to discern because it is the combination of nine coefficients. In previous research, my colleagues and I introduced a useful statistic, κ, for these kinds of situations; κ equals the standard deviation of the occupational coefficients (see Hout, Brooks, and Manza 1995). In the gross column, the κ for occupation is .356; in the net column it is .335. Thus, competing identities were not blunting the impact of objective class.

The evidence clearly negates the second hypothesis as well. Income, occupation, and education all have much bigger effects than any of the competing identities. Racial ancestry, for example, forms powerful identities in the United States. Furthermore, African Americans are significantly less likely to voice a middle class identity than whites; 35 percent of African Americans versus 54 percent of whites say they are middle or upper class. Yet all of that difference is attributable to racial differences in objective-class variables. The coefficient for being African American in a model that predicts class from nothing but racial categories is −.770 (its standard error is .090), and it perfectly reproduces the observed nineteen-percentage-point difference between African Americans and whites.[21] In the net effects model the coefficient for being African American is a trivial −.096 (its standard error is .104), which corresponds to an adjusted difference between African Americans and whites of just 2 percent (at the means of all other variables).

Most other competing identities also show gross differences that disappear when objective-class measures are statistically controlled. Married people are more middle class than single people in the cross-section, but the net difference is insignificant. Parents with children at home are more middle class than other Americans in the cross-section, but not within objective-

Table 1.3   Net Effects on Employed Persons Age Twenty-Five and Older, of Objective Variables on Subjective Social Class Alone and with Sociodemographic Controls

Objective Variable	Objective Only	With Controls
Family income (ratio-scale)		
Main effect	.957*	1.017*
	(.061)	(.069)
Top code	.467*	.353*
	(.169)	(.170)
Occupation		
Professional I	1.065*	1.019*
	(.167)	(.170)
Professional II	.356*	.326*
	(.128)	(.130)
Manager	.583*	.558*
	(.101)	(.105)
Other white collar	.314*	.277*
	(.104)	(.105)
Self-employed, white collar	.766*	.597*
	(.174)	(.179)
Self-employed, blue collar	.263	.210
	(.173)	(.177)
Skilled blue collar	−.260*	−.282*
	(.127)	(.127)
Less-skilled blue collar	0	0
	—	—
Low-wage service	.192	.198
	(.108)	(.116)
Farm	.328	.237
	(.340)	(.346)
Education		
Main effect	.233*	.253*
	(.047)	(.051)
Advanced degree	.593*	.453*
	(.145)	(.149)
Number of cases	6,424	6,424

Source: General Social Survey (GSS), 2000 to 2004.
Note: The additional variables are racial ancestry, gender, marital status, age, region, religion, and attendance at religious services.
* Statistically significant at conventional level ($p < .05$).

Table 1.4   **Net Effects of Objective Variables on Subjective Social Class for All Employed Adults and for Select Subpopulations: Persons Age Twenty-Five and Older**

Class Variable	Employed	African American	Southern	Parent	Religious
Family income (ratio-scale)					
Main	1.253*	.750*	1.006*	1.110*	1.171*
Top code	−.036	−.157	.281	.368*	.350*
Occupation[a]					
Professional I	.714	.801	.826	.678	.754
Professional II	.022	.021	.022	.019	.014
Manager	.264	.294	.306	.255	.223
Other white collar	−.056	−.064	−.063	−.057	−.077
Self-employed, white collar	.370	.443	.444	.375	.606
Self-employed, blue collar	−.168	−.176	−.194	−.164	−.181
Skilled blue collar	−.487	−.559	−.573	−.465	−.307
Unskilled blue collar	−.391	−.431	−.457	−.385	−.446
Low-wage service	−.146	−.205	−.176	−.141	−.226
Farm	−.123	−.125	−.134	−.116	−.359
κ	.343*	.389*	.400*	.331*	.387*
Education					
Main	.298*	−.187	.328*	.370*	.324*
Advanced degree	.335*	.925*	.411*	.253	.467*
Number of cases	4,279	549	1,524	3,103	1,469

Source: General Social Survey (GSS), 2000 to 2004.
Note: The other variables in each model are racial ancestry, gender, marital status, parenthood, age, region, religion, and attendance at religious services.
[a] Due to norming, standard errors for separate occupational groups are not available.
* Statistically significant at conventional level (p < .05).

class categories. Religious people are more middle class than people with no religion, but only Jews are more middle class than would be expected based on their objective-class characteristics. Conservative Christians and Catholics are significantly *less* middle class than their objective-class characteristics imply. The strongest effect among the control variables is for age, and Pakulski does not address it as an important competing identity.

The third hypothesis refers to variation in class effects across subpopulations. The logic is that some identities are strong enough to override objective class. If true, that would show up as a weaker relationship between objective and subjective class for groups with strong identities. Table 1.4 compares all employed adults age twenty-five and over, with four sub-

Table 1.5   Net Effects on Employed Persons Age Twenty-Five and
Older, of Objective Variables on Subjective Social Class for
All Years and by Decade

Class Variable	All Years	1973 to 1978	1980 to 1989	1990 to 1998	2000 to 2004
Family income (ratio-scale)					
Main	1.055*	.885*	1.089*	1.031*	1.255*
	(.043)	(.103)	(.072)	(.081)	(.087)
Top code	.164*	.104	.223	.181	−.034
	(.080)	(.198)	(.132)	(.148)	(.179)
Number of cases	21,142	3,508	6,530	6,824	4,279

Source: General Social Survey (GSS), 1973 to 2004.
Note: The other variables in each model are education, occupation, employment status, racial ancestry, gender, marital status, parenthood, age, region, religion, attendance at religious services, and decade.
* Statistically significant at conventional level ($p < .05$).

populations defined by a strong competing identification: African Americans, Southerners, parents, and religious Americans.[22] The African American population is the most distinct. Income differences are only about three-fourths as consequential for African Americans as for others, and only advanced degrees affect blacks. Occupational distinctions are about 16 percent more important for African Americans (and Southerners and religious people). In the other three subpopulations, objective class is as strong as, or stronger than, it is for all employed people taken together. Thus, the long history of exclusion levels distinctions among African Americans, but there is no evidence that other identities are strong enough to cancel class distinction. Even in the black population, class distinctions are strong and significant; the effects of income and education are just weaker for African Americans.

The last hypothesis addresses change over time. Presumably the post-class changes are relatively recent, so we should see them emerge over time. In fact, the opposite occurred: racial and other disparities in subjective-class identification declined after the 1970s, while the effect of income increased. Table 1.5 shows income coefficients for all GSS years combined and for each decade. The effect of family income on middle and upper class identification is 42 percent greater in the current decade than it was in the 1970s.[23]

The rising effect of income was somewhat offset by falling effects of occupation (between the 1970s and 1980s) and education (since the 1990s). Figure 1.5 shows κ values (the standardized index introduced before) for each decade. According to this metric, the income effect rose 33 percent while the occupation and education effects fell by 28 and 24 percent, respectively.

Figure 1.5   Estimated Effects on Employed Persons Age Twenty-Five and Older of Education, Occupation, Family Income, Religion, Racial Ancestry, and Marital Status on Middle Class Identification by Year

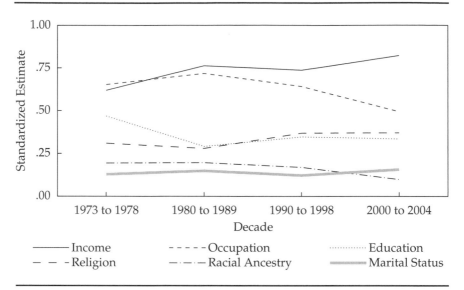

Source: Statistical model using data from General Social Survey (GSS), 1973 to 2004.
Note: Standardized estimates are κ values for regression coefficients in the table 1A.1.

The effect of racial ancestry, barely significant in the 1970s, was only half as big by 2004 (and no longer statistically significant). The effects of marital status and religion are not as strong as those of income and education; nor have they changed significantly since the 1970s.

Thus, although the relative weights of income, occupation, and education shifted over the last thirty years, they remain the most important factors in class identification. In the balance between sociological conceptions of class as the source of livelihood and economic ideas about the efficacy of money itself, money is clearly the factor on the rise. The myriad changes over the last thirty years make it hard to say what has recalibrated the class equation in favor of income. Two candidates come to mind. First, the decline of public goods may have put more families on their own account, as it were. That is, with fewer public goods to share, families now buy for themselves the goods and services they desire, such as private security services, private education, and private transportation. Second, employment security and substandard employment (Kalleberg, Reskin, and Hudson 2000) may be undermining the efficacy of occupation as a feature of identity. If more people are underemployed, or at least think they are, then they may identify with a job they no longer (or do not yet) hold.

Lifestyle, Attitudes, and Well Being

The final criterion for gauging the relevance of subjective social class is its consequences. Causal claims are beyond the scope of this inquiry, but the cross-sectional survey data in the GSS can establish some interesting associations. Mostly I view class as the independent variable and the others as dependent variables in the discussion—except for homeownership, which I see as contributing to the subjective-class identity, not following from it. I begin with lifestyle because it is most relevant to figuring out how class works. Then I move on to political behaviors and attitudes, confidence in institutions, worldview, and subjective well being. The results are shown in table 1.6.

Lifestyle and Subjective Social Class

The cornerstone of the middle class lifestyle is homeownership, especially from the working man's point of view (Halle 1984). Homeownership hovered at around 63 percent of American households from 1965 to 1990, then rose five percentage points to 68 percent by 2005 (U.S. Census Bureau 2006, table 14). The GSS estimated that 66 percent of people twenty-five years old or older owned their place of residence in the period 2000 to 2004. Middle class homeownership (72 percent) was fifteen percentage points higher than that of the working class (57 percent) and thirty-three percentage points higher than lower class homeownership (39 percent).

The language that parents use to talk to their children and how much talk there is in a family has become an important issue in class analysis thanks to Annette Lareau's *Unequal Childhoods* (2003). In 1990 the GSS asked a question that taps into these concerns: "A child should never be allowed to talk back to his parents, or else he will lose respect for them." Working class (64 percent) and lower class (63 percent) adults were significantly more likely to agree with this proposition than middle class (52 percent) and upper class (36 percent) adults were.[24]

Class goes with musical taste and leisure pursuits in most rich countries (Katz-Gerro 2002). For Americans, hunting, fishing, going to auto races, and listening to country music are working class pursuits and preferences; classical music is a middle and upper class preference. The differences in the first half of this decade were modest—all these things were done or preferred by less than half of all classes—but statistically significant.

Class politics deserves a whole chapter of its own (see Manza and Brooks, this volume), but a couple of contrasts show that subjective-class differences mirror objective ones. The biggest difference between middle class and working class Americans was in voter turnout (seventeen percentage points). The partisan divide was greatest in Republican identification (ten points). George W. Bush's margin in the 2000 election (six points) would

Table 1.6   Selected Attitudes and Behaviors of Persons Age Twenty-Five and Older, by Subjective Social Class

	Lower	Working	Middle	Upper	Middle-Working
Lifestyle					
Own home	39%	57%	72%	74%	15%
Talking back to parents led to disrespect (1990)	63	64	52	36	−12
Went hunting or fishing (1993)	36	41	30	33	−12
Went to auto race (1993)	10	22	10	10	−11
Went to classical music concert (1993)	5	11	23	39	11
Country music: like very much (1993)	30	29	19	19	−10
Classical music: like very much (1993)	9	14	22	46	8
Politics					
Voted in 2000	37	55	73	87	17
Voted for George W. Bush	34	50	56	57	6
Republican identification	14	23	33	42	10
Independent identification	46	42	34	29	−8
Democratic identification	40	35	33	29	−2
Supports legal abortion (six of six items)	27	29	40	42	11
Spending (government in Washington spends too little on:)					
Social Security	75	69	56	45	−13
Halting rising crime rate	64	64	54	51	−9
Child care	70	64	56	60	−8
Improving nation's health	80	78	73	71	−4
Mass transit	38	33	41	51	7
Redistribution					
Differences in income too large (1996, 2000)	74	72	63	47	−9
Government: no action on inequality	11	17	26	39	9
Government: should redistribute incomes	52	30	25	17	−5
Government should reduce income gap (1990 to 1996)	53	34	26	17	−9
Taxes on the rich are too low (1996)	61	42	37	12	−5
Companies: profits to workers, then investors (1991)	90	88	74	59	−13
Okay if some get rich (1993)	54	55	61	72	6

(continued)

Table 1.6   *Continued*

	Lower	Working	Middle	Upper	Middle-Working
Confidence in institutions					
Labor unions	13	15	12	15	−3
Banks	21	24	32	36	8
Major companies	14	19	28	45	10
Scientific community	30	38	49	54	11
Worldview					
World is good (2000, 2002)	16	30	36	45	6
People are helpful	35	42	53	55	12
People try to be fair	32	44	61	57	17
People can be trusted	14	30	43	38	13
Well being					
Very happy	16	28	37	42	9
Health excellent	11	25	37	48	12
Very satisfied with work	30	44	54	60	10
Satisfied with finances	9	19	43	58	24
Standard of living will improve	48	67	76	81	9

Source: General Social Survey (GSS), 2000 to 2004, except where noted.

have been larger had it not been for the abortion issue: middle class Americans supported legal abortion more than working class Americans did, holding down class voting.

Most social spending issues did not split along class lines, but there were five issues that showed significant class differences. The largest was social security. Three-fourths of the lower class (75 percent), 69 percent of the working class, 56 percent of the middle class, and 45 percent of the upper class supported spending more on social security. The working class supported more spending for halting the rising crime rate, child care, and improving the nation's health.[25] The middle class favored more spending for mass transit (even though the lower class was most likely to use it).

In 1996 and again in 2000, the GSS asked whether "income differences . . . are too large." A majority of Americans agreed that they were: 74, 72, 63, and 47 percent of the lower, working, middle, and upper class, respectively. The GSS asks a complicated question about whether the government should do something about inequality:

Some people think that the government in Washington ought to reduce the income differences between the rich and the poor, perhaps by raising the taxes of wealthy families or by giving income assistance to the poor. Others think that the government should not concern itself with reducing this income difference between the rich and the poor. Here is a card with a scale from 1 to 7. Think of a score of 1 as meaning that the government ought to reduce the income differences between rich and poor, and a score of 7 meaning that the government should not concern itself with reducing income differences. What score between 1 and 7 comes closest to the way you feel?

Middle class (26 percent) and upper class (39 percent) adults favored no government action significantly more than working class (17 percent) and lower class (11 percent) adults did. At the other end of the scale, 52 percent of lower class and 30 percent of middle class adults chose the strongest government action position, as compared to 25 percent of middle class and 17 percent of upper class people. Average scores on the seven-point scale (with "government should not concern itself" equal to 7) by class were 2.8, 3.6, 4.0, and 4.8 for the lower, working, middle, and upper classes, respectively. Asked more simply between 1990 and 1996, "It is the responsibility of the government to reduce the differences in income between people with high incomes and those with low incomes," the class gap was similar. The idea of raising taxes on the rich was popular among the lower class, but even the working class was skeptical about raising taxes on anyone.

Classes also divided sharply over what profitable companies should do with their money. The 1991 GSS posed the proposition: "Corporations should pay more of their profits to workers and less to shareholders." A majority of Americans of all classes agreed, surprisingly. The margin of agreement fell as class rose: 90 percent of lower class and 88 percent of working class people agreed, 74 percent of middle class people did, and even 59 percent of the upper class agreed.

In 1993 the GSS asked a normative question about inequality: "People should be allowed to accumulate as much wealth as they can even if some make millions while others live in poverty." The majority of all classes supported that principle, and it differed only modestly (but significantly) by class.

The low ebb of confidence in labor unions has even spread to the lower and working classes. The GSS asks about confidence in "people running" a number of major institutions, including labor unions. Classes did not differ significantly from the overall average of 14 percent having "a great deal" of confidence in labor leaders, though, presumably, the reason why they lacked confidence might have differed by class. Confidence in the people running banks, major companies, and the scientific community rose significantly with rising social class.

The GSS asks people about their view of the world and human nature over many years.[26] The longest-running question is: "Where would you place yourself on a scale from 1 to 7 where 1 means 'The world is basically filled with evil and sin' and 7 means 'There is much goodness in the world that hints at God's goodness'."

Lower and working class Americans saw more sin and less goodness than middle and upper class people did. Among people with no religious preference, the answers were mostly similar, but the working class gave significantly fewer sanguine answers: only 23 percent of working class, unchurched Americans said the world is good. The lower and working classes also took a more dyspeptic view of human interaction. Significantly fewer lower and working class people viewed people as helpful, fair, or trustworthy. The working and middle classes were furthest apart on whether people try to be fair.

Income increases happiness (Hout 2003); these results show that happiness also rises with subjective class: 9 percent more middle class than working class people were very happy. Subjective health also improved with social class status—from 11 percent excellent among the lower class to 25 percent for the working class to 37 percent of the middle class and 48 percent of the upper class. The majority of the lower and working classes were not satisfied with their work, while the majority of the middle and upper classes were satisfied. Satisfaction with finances rose steadily with class, from 9 percent to 19 percent to 43 percent to 58 percent very satisfied among the lower, working, middle, and upper classes, respectively. Yet majorities of all but the lower class were optimistic about the prospect of their standard of living improving. Apparently, however, the sky is the limit, as the tendency to see improvement in the future was greatest for those already at the top.

This canvass of behaviors and attitudes identified thirty-six items on which subjective social class was a statistically significant divider.[27] The difference between the middle and working classes ranged from just 4 percent on health care spending to twenty-four points on satisfaction with family finances. Finding that subjective social class matters for such a broad range of socially meaningful distinctions implies that subjective social class is itself socially meaningful. Some of the differences can be explained using multivariate models and a list of objective-class factors (most notably income, occupation, and education); others cannot. But the simple differences here strengthen the case that class in general and subjective social class in particular organize Americans' sense of their place in society and constrain their behavior, interests, and attitudes.

Conclusions

Class works as an expression of people's sense of where they fit in the rank order from privilege to poverty in the United States. Nearly every American recognizes social class terms. Most use ranking terms that do not necessarily include "working class" when they are not prompted by interviewers, yet they know what surveys mean if the proffered categories include it. Most significantly, Americans are familiar enough with class terminology to place themselves more or less where experts would put them in the upper, middle, working, and lower class scheme that most surveys offer them.

About one American in three does not have a clear objective-class position. Some receive mixed class signals from inconsistencies between their income, occupation, and education. Objective indicators have become more consistent in the last twenty years, but income, occupation, and education are still only somewhat correlated. Others occupy an objective class that combines middle class and working class features in one job. Living in a mixed-class household in which one adult holds a working class job and another does middle class work further complicates some people's task of placing themselves, since most of us feel some constraint to assign one subjective class to our whole family.[28] Further complicating matters, class borders are vague. Respondent and analyst alike have difficulty saying precisely where the middle class–working class line is. Nonetheless, class ambivalence and class ambiguity do not mean that subjective class is a bad concept.

These and other patterns reported here support the conclusion that "class counts." Most of the data here replicate, using the 2000 to 2004 GSS, patterns found in the older GSS in Wright (1997) and other data sets (for example, Hodge and Treiman 1968; Jackman and Jackman 1983). My contribution is to update and reframe some very general empirical regularities. Among my novel findings are the way objective-class indicators explain differences in subjective social class among important segments of the population. Their lower incomes and higher prevalence of blue collar jobs explain why African Americans identify more with the working class, just as higher incomes and more education explain why married and religious people are more middle class. But other things, notably age, homeownership, and union membership, remain important factors in subjective-class identification, even after statistically controlling for income, occupation, and education. Thus, even though my results are a bitter pill for those who deny class, they may challenge some class analysts too.

Post-class speculations fare the worst in this analysis. None of the changes that supposedly made the current era different from the 1970s actually occurred. In fact, the trend to greater inequality and the growing links between education and income, education and residence, and education and marriage (for evidence on all three, see Fischer and Hout 2006) intensified the relationships among objective-class indicators and resolved some subjective-class ambiguities over the last thirty or so years. There is no evidence that competing identities rival class in people's calculus of where they go in society's order.

Appendix

Table 1A.1   **Logistic Regression Coefficients for Models of Middle or Upper Class Identification**

Variable	Gross	Net	Working	Black	South	Parent	Religious
Education							
Main	.232	.245	.300	−.083	.204	.247	.205
	(.047)	(.052)	(.065)	(.117)	(.080)	(.079)	(.078)
Advanced	.601	.463	.324	.990	.287	.746	.573
degree	(.143)	(.147)	(.167)	(.460)	(.266)	(.301)	(.260)
Occupation							
Professional I	1.082	1.022	1.140	.739	1.122	.803	1.115
	(.170)	(.173)	(.200)	(.340)	(.260)	(.291)	(.251)
Professional II	.373	.338	.413	−.586	.581	.086	.347
	(.131)	(.133)	(.174)	(.355)	(.218)	(.204)	(.191)
Manager	.580	.555	.637	−.142	.689	.391	.547
	(.104)	(.107)	(.144)	(.311)	(.198)	(.194)	(.187)
Other white	.326	.290	.317	−.789	.354	.252	.247
collar	(.106)	(.108)	(.163)	(.337)	(.191)	(.196)	(.179)
Self-employed,	.802	.624	.759	1.229	.812	.357	.771
white collar	(.176)	(.182)	(.196)	(.585)	(.296)	(.301)	(.277)
Self-employed,	.290	.233	.223	.095	.257	−.104	.199
blue collar	(.175)	(.179)	(.241)	(.394)	(.278)	(.260)	(.265)
Skilled blue	−.251	−.276	−.115	−1.203	−.110	−.221	−.062
collar	(.130)	(.130)	(.170)	(.367)	(.202)	(.235)	(.201)
Unskilled	.000	.000	.000	.000	.000	.000	.000
blue collar	—	—	—	—	—	—	—
Low-wage	.211	.223	.229	−.117	.415	.325	.029
service	(.110)	(.118)	(.181)	(.218)	(.218)	(.212)	(.192)
Farm	.342	.230	.232	1.277	.784	.206	.227
	(.341)	(.351)	(.465)	(.580)	(.600)	(.581)	(.525)
Family income	.961	1.032	1.253	.750	1.006	1.110	1.171
(log)	(.061)	(.069)	(.087)	(.196)	(.121)	(.129)	(.117)
Income	.459	.346	−.036	−.157	.281	.368	.350
top-coded	(.174)	(.174)	(.181)	(.533)	(.314)	(.285)	(.314)
Employment status							
Unemployed	.183	.226		.141	.697	.000	.022
	(.182)	(.188)		(.462)	(.331)	(.383)	(.361)
Retired	1.423	.734		1.203	.685	.434	.809
	(.095)	(.122)		(.331)	(.202)	(.496)	(.197)
At home	.647	.532		.657	.434	.422	.420
	(.125)	(.122)		(.239)	(.210)	(.159)	(.182)
Other	.000	.000		.000	.000	.000	.000
	—	—		—	—	—	—

(continued)

Table 1A.1   *Continued*

Variable	Gross	Net	Working	Black	South	Parent	Religious
Racial ancestry							
Black		−.096	−.257		−.124	−.079	−.006
		(.104)	(.146)		(.154)	(.184)	(.158)
Latino		−.240	−.139	−.070	−.421	−.230	−.359
		(.141)	(.179)	(.376)	(.211)	(.223)	(.222)
Other		.000	.000	.000	.000	.000	.000
		—	—	—	—	—	—
Woman		−.030	−.112	.267	−.079	−.222	.074
		(.075)	(.091)	(.194)	(.101)	(.127)	(.115)
Marital status							
Married once		−.113	−.168	.201	−.088	.225	−.144
		(.100)	(.128)	(.257)	(.156)	(.239)	(.178)
Remarried		−.112	−.086	.167	−.129	.386	−.024
		(.128)	(.157)	(.341)	(.185)	(.269)	(.233)
Widowed		.299	.313	.401	.417	.155	.388
		(.156)	(.225)	(.344)	(.248)	(.423)	(.267)
Divorced		−.090	−.069	−.053	−.008	.289	−.084
		(.097)	(.120)	(.250)	(.172)	(.288)	(.197)
Never married		.000	.000	.000	.000	.000	.000
		—	—	—	—	—	—
Children at home		−.136	−.026	−.384	−.291		−.043
		(.085)	(.098)	(.228)	(.144)		(.132)
Religion							
Conservative Protestant		−.291	−.368	−.094	−.080	−.130	−1.145
		(.111)	(.152)	(.264)	(.223)	(.197)	(.483)
Mainline Protestant		.071	−.009	.353	.355	.334	−.671
		(.112)	(.140)	(.318)	(.235)	(.204)	(.491)
Catholic		−.206	−.307	.145	.273	−.134	−.914
		(.109)	(.132)	(.370)	(.226)	(.190)	(.468)
Jewish		.846	.947		.686	1.438	
		(.270)	(.416)		(.462)	(.548)	
Other religion		−.044	.007	−.423	.128	−.332	−.886
		(.180)	(.214)	(.603)	(.346)	(.408)	(.494)
No religion		.000	.000	.000	.000	.000	.000
		—	—	—	—	—	—
Attendance at services		.040	.079	−.082	.028	.054	−.018
		(.023)	(.033)	(.058)	(.042)	(.042)	(.039)

Table 1A.1   Continued

Variable	Gross	Net	Working	Black	South	Parent	Religious
Region							
Northeast		.000	.000	.000		.000	.000
		—	—	—		—	—
Midwest		−.048	.062	.307		−.255	.009
		(.118)	(.129)	(.285)		(.194)	(.188)
South		.077	.107	.134		−.220	.018
		(.121)	(.142)	(.238)		(.192)	(.180)
Mountain		−.026	.036			−.130	−.089
		(.151)	(.161)			(.280)	(.233)
Pacific		−.040	−.100	.186		.020	−.309
		(.144)	(.166)	(.239)		(.207)	(.213)
Age group							
Twenty-five to twenty-nine		.000	.000	.000	.000	.000	.000
		—	—	—	—	—	—
Thirty to thirty-four		.352	.285	.204	.306	.245	.501
		(.131)	(.142)	(.254)	(.178)	(.178)	(.207)
Thirty-five to thirty-nine		.247	.222	.051	.257	.104	−.114
		(.118)	(.129)	(.307)	(.197)	(.185)	(.232)
Forty to forty-four		.218	.150	.100	.003	.050	.071
		(.129)	(.150)	(.348)	(.200)	(.215)	(.227)
Forty-five to forty-nine		.535	.470	.612	.445	.412	.300
		(.146)	(.162)	(.335)	(.187)	(.224)	(.231)
Fifty to fifty-four		.360	.360	.380	.284	.552	.202
		(.124)	(.146)	(.364)	(.207)	(.270)	(.227)
Fifty-five to fifty-nine		.365	.338	−.184	.355	−.150	.363
		(.172)	(.200)	(.529)	(.232)	(.461)	(.263)
Sixty to sixty-four		.725	.773	.004	.661	.877	.663
		(.191)	(.234)	(.553)	(.296)	(.516)	(.281)
Sixty-five to sixty-nine		.766	.552	.048	.671	.398	.412
		(.174)	(.257)	(.529)	(.282)	(.599)	(.296)
Seventy to seventy-four		1.083	1.504	.490	.877	1.741	.895
		(.201)	(.387)	(.523)	(.329)	(.752)	(.325)
Seventy-five and older		1.066	.246	−.194	.876	1.044	.911
		(.175)	(.477)	(.480)	(.274)	(.870)	(.313)
Intercept	−4.715	−5.091	−6.119	−3.356	−5.038	−5.535	−4.449
	(.224)	(.286)	(.352)	(.865)	(.448)	(.619)	(.629)
Number of cases	6,309	6,309	4,238	880	2,278	2,072	2,297

Source: General Social Surveys (GSS), 2000 to 2004.

Table 1A.2   Logistic Regression Coefficients for Models of Middle or Upper Class Identification for All Periods and by Decade: Persons Age Twenty-Five and Older, 1973 to 2004

Variable	All Periods	1973 to 1978	1980 to 1989	1990 to 1998	2000 to 2004
Education					
Main	.405	.444	.468	.422	.245
	(.022)	(.045)	(.037)	(.035)	(.052)
Advanced	.214	.079	.186	.152	.463
degree	(.072)	(.204)	(.143)	(.134)	(.147)
Occupation					
Professional I	.960	1.336	.755	.914	1.022
	(.073)	(.198)	(.127)	(.122)	(.173)
Professional II	.391	.645	.303	.317	.338
	(.051)	(.115)	(.088)	(.093)	(.133)
Manager	.690	1.138	.656	.582	.555
	(.050)	(.147)	(.088)	(.083)	(.107)
Other	.359	.515	.402	.191	.290
white collar	(.045)	(.104)	(.078)	(.079)	(.108)
Self-employed,	.815	1.091	.709	.818	.624
white collar	(.074)	(.149)	(.123)	(.132)	(.182)
Self-employed,	.155	.208	.108	.071	.233
blue collar	(.071)	(.180)	(.118)	(.113)	(.179)
Skilled	−.062	.156	.011	−.179	−.276
blue collar	(.051)	(.115)	(.089)	(.091)	(.130)
Unskilled blue	.000	.000	.000	.000	.000
collar	—	—	—	—	—
Low-wage	.252	.361	.131	.262	.223
service	(.052)	(.111)	(.087)	(.103)	(.118)
Farm	−.005	−.001	−.010	−.002	.230
	(.101)	(.160)	(.165)	(.204)	(.351)
Family income	.909	.771	.922	.917	1.032
(log)	(.034)	(.068)	(.056)	(.066)	(.069)
Income top-coded	.397	.290	.500	.350	.346
	(.073)	(.174)	(.125)	(.134)	(.174)
Employment status					
Unemployed	.081	−.102	.111	.042	.226
	(.091)	(.169)	(.180)	(.159)	(.188)
Retired	.600	.525	.571	.584	.734
	(.053)	(.127)	(.096)	(.099)	(.122)
At home	.676	.766	.629	.736	.532
	(.043)	(.081)	(.079)	(.078)	(.122)
Other	.000	.000	.000	.000	.000
	—	—	—	—	—

Table 1A.2   *Continued*

Variable	All Periods	1973 to 1978	1980 to 1989	1990 to 1998	2000 to 2004
Racial ancestry					
Black	−.344	−.411	−.429	−.415	−.096
	(.051)	(.120)	(.089)	(.089)	(.104)
Latino	−.207	−.413	−.025	−.213	−.240
	(.063)	(.173)	(.113)	(.122)	(.141)
Other	.000	.000	.000	.000	.000
	—	—	—	—	—
Woman	−.050	−.059	−.003	−.086	−.030
	(.033)	(.079)	(.057)	(.054)	(.075)
Marital status					
Married once	−.143	−.138	−.215	−.103	−.113
	(.050)	(.126)	(.093)	(.084)	(.100)
Remarried	−.157	−.225	−.154	−.166	−.112
	(.062)	(.143)	(.105)	(.111)	(.128)
Widowed	.208	.114	.213	.162	.299
	(.066)	(.167)	(.115)	(.121)	(.156)
Divorced	−.068	.076	.007	−.155	−.090
	(.050)	(.137)	(.096)	(.082)	(.097)
Never married	.000	.000	.000	.000	.000
	—	—	—	—	—
Children at home	−.120	.030	−.170	−.144	−.136
	(.038)	(.078)	(.064)	(.074)	(.085)
Religion					
Conservative Protestant	−.262	−.145	−.323	−.228	−.291
	(.061)	(.137)	(.110)	(.111)	(.111)
Mainline Protestant	.003	.215	−.135	.002	.071
	(.052)	(.122)	(.098)	(.102)	(.112)
Catholic	−.078	.129	−.223	.054	−.206
	(.054)	(.127)	(.104)	(.101)	(.109)
Jewish	.745	.840	.546	.921	.846
	(.112)	(.252)	(.201)	(.190)	(.270)
Other religion	−.026	.212	−.069	−.015	−.044
	(.095)	(.320)	(.173)	(.173)	(.180)
No religion	.000	.000	.000	.000	.000
	—	—	—	—	—
Attendance at service	.062	.032	.088	.064	.040
	(.010)	(.024)	(.017)	(.017)	(.023)

(continued)

Table 1A.2   *Continued*

Variable	All Periods	1973 to 1978	1980 to 1989	1990 to 1998	2000 to 2004
Region					
Northeast	.000	.000	.000	.000	.000
	—	—	—	—	—
Midwest	.005	.031	−.006	.056	−.048
	(.053)	(.101)	(.078)	(.093)	(.118)
South	.140	.240	.177	.094	.077
	(.051)	(.101)	(.080)	(.079)	(.121)
Mountain	.016	.082	.040	.011	−.026
	(.090)	(.150)	(.168)	(.156)	(.151)
Pacific	.010	−.042	.059	.022	−.040
	(.064)	(.126)	(.093)	(.099)	(.144)
Age group					
Twenty-five to	.000	.000	.000	.000	.000
twenty-nine	—	—	—	—	—
Thirty to	.143	.176	.179	−.021	.352
thirty-four	(.052)	(.114)	(.086)	(.102)	(.131)
Thirty-five to	.137	−.059	.204	.112	.247
thirty-nine	(.050)	(.113)	(.091)	(.095)	(.118)
Forty to	.104	.032	.193	.014	.218
forty-four	(.055)	(.121)	(.102)	(.104)	(.129)
Forty-five to	.229	.268	.258	.010	.535
forty-nine	(.062)	(.134)	(.117)	(.107)	(.146)
Fifty to	.256	.198	.331	.216	.360
fifty-four	(.058)	(.127)	(.106)	(.121)	(.124)
Fifty-five to	.376	.356	.543	.315	.365
fifty-nine	(.066)	(.134)	(.122)	(.122)	(.172)
Sixty to	.619	.421	.772	.620	.725
sixty-four	(.072)	(.156)	(.121)	(.148)	(.191)
Sixty-five to	.887	.603	1.136	.961	.766
sixty-nine	(.076)	(.172)	(.132)	(.161)	(.174)
Seventy to	1.127	.988	1.298	1.142	1.083
seventy-four	(.089)	(.183)	(.163)	(.162)	(.201)
Seventy-five	1.294	1.542	1.310	1.388	1.066
and older	(.088)	(.194)	(.148)	(.178)	(.175)
Decade					
1973 to 1978	.304				
	(.054)				
1980 to 1989	.241				
	(.049)				
1990 to 1998	.089				
	(.039)				
2000 to 2004	.000				
	—				

Table 1A.2   *Continued*

Variable	All Periods	1973 to 1978	1980 to 1989	1990 to 1998	2000 to 2004
Intercept	−4.928	−4.464	−4.807	−4.764	−5.091
	(.162)	(.302)	(.248)	(.291)	(.286)
Number of cases	32,678	6,102	10,244	10,023	6,309

Source: General Social Surveys (GSS), 1973 to 2004.

I thank Neil Fligstein, Michèle Lamont, Annette Lareau, Jeff Manza, Erik Olin Wright, and two anonymous referees for their comments. Neither funders nor colleagues are responsible for the conclusions, opinions, or errors in this chapter.

Notes

1. On birthweight, see Conley, Strully, and Bennett (2003); on mortality, see Williams and Collins (1995), Carpiano, Link, and Phelan, this volume; on age at marriage, see Blau, Kahn, and Waldfogel (2000); on neighborhood segregation by income, see Fischer et al. (2004); on eating out, see Cohen (1998); on language, see Lamont (1992).

2. See Clark and Lipset (1991) for the original question, Goldthorpe and Marshall (1992) and Hout, Brooks, and Manza (1993) for rebuttals, and Pakulski and Waters (1996), Wright (1996), and Manza and Brooks (1996) for another round of debate.

3. This rephrases (with slight modification) Christopher Jencks's (1991) rendering of the issue. So too does the following attribution of them as characteristic of sociologists, economists, and non-academics.

4. Evidence for these assertions comes from Baldassare (personal communication, June 9, 2006) and my own analysis of the General Social Survey (GSS).

5. Education and occupation are sociological "where the money comes from" measures; income is an economist's "how much?" measure.

6. Beginning in 1948, the American National Election Studies have drawn a representative sample of adults eligible to vote in years that have national elections in the United States. Originally the interviews were face-to-face, ninety-minute interviews that combined forced choice and open-ended questions (see Campbell, Converse, and Miller 1960). Since then, panels have been used in some years, phone interviews in some, and mail-back questionnaires in others. Sample sizes have ranged from 662 in 1948 to 2,485 in 1992, with an average close to 1,500.
   The General Social Survey has, since 1972, conducted face-to-face interviews with representative samples of English-speaking adults on a wide array of

subjects. For the first twenty-two years, the GSS was fielded almost every year; the size of the main samples averaged 1,500 interviews. (Oversamples of African Americans made 1982 and 1987 bigger.) Since 1994, the GSS has been fielded in even-numbered years, with sample sizes averaging 2,850 interviews. Beginning in 2006, interviews were in Spanish as well as English.

7. The range of positive answers—from 61 percent to 75 percent—is wider than the ANES's margin of error, so the association between answer and year is statistically significant. But there is no discernible trend. The high point was 1960, and it was followed by the two lowest points in 1964 and 1968; the second-highest point was reached in 1988. The 2004 ANES did not include this question.

8. There is no significant trend in the answers.

9. Our 1991 survey focused on class in the United States and probably had more prompts in the questions leading up to the open-ended class question than the Hodge and Treiman (1968) survey did. (I do not have the Hodge and Treiman questionnaire, so I cannot say for sure.) Another possibility, though somewhat remote considering the lack of change in answers to forced-choice questions, is that the working class label became more prominent between 1964 and 1991.

10. Despite the rich mix of labels that Roger Hodge was able to invoke.

11. GSS is the data source for these figures. People under twenty-five years of age are excluded because a significant and nonrandom portion of the eighteen- to twenty-four-year-old group is out of the sample because they are still in school. Since the excluded students are likely to be the most successful members of their cohorts in the long run, their absence biases what we see as the eighteen- to twenty-four-year-old group.

12. I made the substitution only if the husband was currently living with the wife and currently working.

13. To reduce the relationship to a single coefficient, I transformed family income first to adjust for inflation (as in figure 1.1); then I recoded low incomes so that all incomes below $15,000 were treated as if they were $15,000 (scatterplots showed a flat relationship at the very lowest incomes); and finally, I took the natural logarithm of the numbers at that point. The logarithmic transformation is fairly standard practice in research of this kind. It is sometimes called a ratio-scale transformation because in the log-scale the difference between $15,000 and $30,000 is the same as the difference between $30,000 and $60,000 or between $45,000 and $90,000. In the same way, other ratios (say five, as in $10,000 to $50,000 and $25,000 to $125,000) produce the constant differences on the logarithmic scale. Scatterplots of the percentage middle class by family income showed a pattern that is consistent with this ratio-scale treatment. I then used the transformed income measure as an independent variable in an ordered logistic regression model. That model has special assumptions (see Long 1997) that I did not test here because I was mostly interested in a convenient summary measure. I doubt that the relative effects would be different if another model had been the basis of comparison.

14. Unless otherwise noted, all calculations refer to people twenty-five years and older in the 2000 to 2004 GSS. Sampling weights were used to adjust for the complex design in 2004.

15. I could cite any number of authorities here, including Jencks et al. (1972), Fischer et al. (1996), and Keister (2005), but this is best thought of as the professional consensus about family incomes. For while scholars might debate how much weight to give each item, it is fair to say that few, if any, sociologists, economists, and demographers would argue against this list.

16. Following Harding et al. (2004), I analyzed annual family, not personal, income. The coefficients indicate that the absolute contribution of occupation and education to inequality in income grew. However, the R-square, a statistic that indicates how much of the family income variance is "explained" by occupation and education, did not increase over the last twenty-five years. It would have, all else being equal, but in fact the income inequality within the big classes I use here increased even as the differences among the income categories were increasing. The R-square gauges the proportional contribution of education and occupation to the total inequality—and because the parts and the whole grew at a roughly equal pace, the R-square stayed the same.

17. I used logistic regression to model the percentage identifying with the middle or upper class because a Wald test rejected the key assumption of the ordered logistic regression model—that all independent variables affect each subjective-class contrast identically—when the list of independent variables grew beyond the three objective class variables in table 1.2. So I switched to logistic regression and focused on the contrast that is key to most discussions—that on the border between middle and working class identification. The dependent variable equals one if the person identifies with the middle or upper class and zero if the person identifies with the working or lower class. I expanded the list of independent variables to include employment status and year of survey and used weights to compensate for design features in the 2004 survey. See documentation on the sampling strategies at "SDA: Survey Documentation and Analysis," http://sda.berkeley.edu (click on General Social Survey cumulative file and follow links to the sampling design). The expected percentages in figure 1.4 pertain to employed people in 2004.

18. I do not have a criterion for distinguishing ambivalent from ambiguous positions.

19. Retirees' answers probably reflect their worklife income, which we have no measure of, as well as their current income. Retirees also tend to have more home equity and other financial resources than working people do (Keister 2005). They might be considering their assets too.

20. Note that almost all the upper and lower class identification arose in class positions that were either clearly above or clearly below the middle class–working class border.

21. The transformation of logits into probabilities is not linear, but a rule of thumb aids interpretation: 5 percent, 10 percent, and 25 percent are close to −3, −2, and −1 on the logit scale, 50 percent is exactly zero on the logit scale, and 75 percent, 90 percent, and 95 percent are close to 1, 2, and 3 on the logit scale.

22. "Employed" includes full- and part-time work but excludes being on strike, furlough, paid or unpaid leave, and so on. "African American" is based on the respondent's own assessment of his or her race. "Southerners" live in the

Census Bureau's South region: Maryland, Washington, D.C., Virginia, North Carolina, South Carolina, Georgia, Florida, Alabama, Mississippi, Tennessee, Kentucky, Louisiana, Arkansas, Texas, and Oklahoma. "Parents" have at least one child of their own (of any age, not necessarily living at home), and "religious people" are those who answered yes to the question: "Are you a strong [the respondent's religion or denomination, filled in by the interviewer]?"

23. Technical issues make comparing logistic regression coefficients difficult. The fundamental underidentification of the logit model makes it impossible to isolate the effect of changing variance in underlying class identification from change in the impact of income. It could be that the effect of income was constant but the latent variance of class identification decreased by 40 percent. That seems unlikely on its face, since the 1970s to the present decade has been a time of rising, not falling, inequality. If it is nonetheless true that the latent variance decreased, then it would proportionally affect all other variables in the equation as well. That would make the flat lines in figure 1.5 incline downward and the downward-sloping lines even steeper.

24. The differences were as big for nonparents as for parents.

25. That is the premise of the question even though the crime rate does not actually rise every year.

26. Most questions were discontinued after the 1994 survey; one was included in the 1996 to 2002 surveys.

27. Table 1.6 shows thirty-eight items. The class differences are not statistically significant for Democratic Party identification and confidence in people running unions.

28. We do not have enough evidence on this interesting subject, but what we have is consistent with this idea (see Baxter 1994).

References

Baxter, Janeen. 1994. "Is Husband's Class Enough? Class Location and Class Identity in the United States, Norway, Sweden, and Australia." *American Sociological Review* 59(2): 220–35.

Blau, Francine, Lawrence M. Kahn, and Jane Waldfogel. 2000. "Understanding Young Women's Marriage Decisions: The Role of Labor and Marriage Market Conditions." *Industrial and Labor Relations Review* 53(4): 624–47.

Campbell, Angus, Phillip Converse, and Warren Miller. 1960. *The American Voter.* Chicago, Ill.: University of Chicago Press.

Card, David, and John DiNardo. 2002. "Skill-Biased Technological Change and Rising Wage Inequality: Some Problems and Puzzles." *Journal of Labor Economics* 20(4): 733–83.

Centers, Richard, 1949. *The Psychology of Social Classes.* Princeton, N.J.: Princeton University Press.

Clark, Terry Nichols, and Seymour Martin Lipset. 1991. "Are Social Classes Dying?" *International Sociology* 6(4): 397–410.

Cohen, Philip N. 1998. "Replacing Housework in the Service Economy: Gender, Class, and Race-Ethnicity in Service Spending." *Gender and Society* 12(2): 219–31.

Coleman, Richard P., and Lee Rainwater. 1978. *Social Standing in America.* New York: Basic Books.

Conley, Dalton, Kate W. Strully, and Neil Bennett. 2003. *The Starting Gate: Birth Weight and Life Changes.* Berkeley, Calif.: University of California Press.

DiPrete, Thomas A., and Claudia Buchmann. 2006. "Gender-Specific Trends in the Value of Education and the Emerging Gender Gap in College Completion." *Demography* 43(1): 1–24.

Downs, Anthony. 1957. *An Economic Theory of Democracy.* New York: Harper & Row.

Erikson, Robert, and John H. Goldthorpe. 1992. *The Constant Flux: Comparative Analysis of Social Mobility in Industrial Societies.* Oxford: Clarendon Press.

Fischer, Claude S., and Michael Hout. 2006. *Century of Difference.* New York: Russell Sage Foundation.

Fischer, Claude S., Gretchen Stockmayer, Jon Stiles, and Michael Hout. 2004. "Distinguishing the Geographical Levels and Social Dimensions of U.S. Metropolitan Segregation, 1960–2000." *Demography* 41(1): 37–59.

Fischer, Claude S., Michael Hout, Martín Sánchez Jankowski, Samuel R. Lucas, Ann Swidler, and Kim Voss. 1996. *Inequality by Design.* Princeton, N.J.: Princeton University Press.

Goldthorpe, John H., and Gordon Marshall. 1992. "The Promising Future of Class Analysis." *Sociology* 26(3): 381–400.

Halle, David, 1984. *America's Working Man.* Chicago, Ill.: University of Chicago Press.

Harding, David, Christopher Jencks, Leonard M. Lopoo, and Susan E. Mayer. 2004. "The Changing Effect of Family Background on the Incomes of American Adults." In *Unequal Chances: Family Background and Economic Success,* edited by Samuel Bowles, Herbert Gintis, and Melissa Osborne. New York and Princeton, N.J.: Russell Sage and Princeton University Press.

Hodge, Robert W., and Donald J. Treiman. 1968. "Class Identification in the United States." *American Journal of Sociology* 73(5): 535–47.

Hout, Michael. 2003. "Money and Morale: How Inequality Is Affecting How Americans Feel About Themselves and Others." Working paper. New York: Russell Sage Foundation.

Hout, Michael, Clem Brooks, and Jeff Manza. 1993. "The Persistence of Classes in Postindustrial Societies." *International Sociology* 8(3): 259–77.

———. 1995. "The Democratic Class Struggle in U.S. Presidential Elections, 1948–1992." *American Sociological Review* 60(6): 805–28.

Hout, Michael, Erik Olin Wright, and Martín Sánchez Jankowski. 1992. "Class Structure and Class Consciousness Survey." Data file. Ann Arbor, Mich.: University of Michigan, Institute for Social Research, Inter-University Consortium for Political and Social Research (ICPSR). Accessed at http://www.icpsr.umich.edu.

Jackman, Mary R., and David W. Jackman, 1983. *Class Awareness in the United States.* Berkeley, Calif.: University of California Press.

Jencks, Christopher, 1991. "Is the Underclass Growing?" In *The Urban Underclass,* edited by Christopher Jencks and Paul E. Peterson. Washington: Brookings Institution Press.

Jencks, Christopher, with Marshall Smith, Henry Ackland, Mary Jo Bane, David Cohen, Herbert Gintis, Barbara Heyns, and Stephan Michelson. 1972. *Inequality.* New York: Basic Books.

Kalleberg, Arne, Barbara Reskin, and Ken Hudson. 2000. "Bad Jobs in America." *American Sociological Review* 65(2): 256–78.

Katz-Gerro, Tally. 2002. "Highbrow Cultural Consumption and Class Distinction in Italy, Israel, Germany, Sweden, and the United States." *Social Forces* 81 (September): 207–29.

Keister, Lisa. 2005. *Getting Rich: America's New Rich and How They Got That Way.* Cambridge: Cambridge University Press.

Kingston, Paul W. 2000. *The Classless Society.* Stanford, Calif.: Stanford University Press.

Lamont, Michèle. 1992. *Money, Morals, and Manners.* Chicago, Ill.: University of Chicago Press.

———. 2000. *The Dignity of Working Men.* Cambridge, Mass.: Harvard University Press.

Lareau, Annette. 2003. *Unequal Childhoods: Class, Race, and Family Life.* Berkeley, Calif.: University of California Press.

Lockwood, David. 1966. "Sources of Variation in Working-Class Images of Society." *Sociological Review* 14(3): 249–67.

Long, J. Scott. 1997. *Regression Models for Limited Dependent Variables.* Thousand Oaks, Calif.: Sage Publications.

Manza, Jeff, and Clem Brooks. 1996. "Does Class Analysis Still Have Anything to Contribute to the Study of Politics?" *Theory and Society* 25(5): 717–24.

Pakulski, Jan, 2005. "Foundations of a Post-Class Analysis." In *Approaches to Class Analysis,* edited by Erik Olin Wright. Cambridge: Cambridge University Press.

Pakulski, Jan, and Malcolm Waters. 1996. "The Reshaping and Dissolution of Class." *Theory and Society* 25(5): 667–91.

Schwartz, Christine, and Robert D. Mare. 2005. "Trends in Educational Assortative Marriage from 1940 to 2003." *Demography* 42(4): 621–46.

U.S. Census Bureau. 2006. "Housing Vacancies and Homeownership." Housing Vacancy Survey Series H-111 reports. Washington: U.S. Census Bureau. Accessed at http://www.census.gov/hhes/www/housing/hvs/hvs.html.

Warner, W. Lloyd, Marchia Meeker, and Kenneth Eells. 1960. *Social Class in America.* New York: Harper & Row.

Weeden, Kim, and David B. Grusky. 2005. "The Case for a New Class Map?" *American Journal of Sociology* 111(1): 141–212.

Weininger, Elliot B. 2005. "Foundations of Pierre Bourdieu's Class Analysis." In *Approaches to Class Analysis,* edited by Erik Olin Wright. Cambridge: Cambridge University Press.

Williams, David R., and Chiquita Collins. 1995. "U.S. Socioeconomic and Racial Differences in Health: Patterns and Explanations." *Annual Review of Sociology* 21: 349–86.

Wright, Erik Olin. 1996. "The Continuing Relevance of Class Analysis." *Theory and Society* 25(5): 697–716.

———. 1997. *Class Counts.* Cambridge: Cambridge University Press.

———. 2005a. "If 'Class' Is the Answer, What Is the Question?" In *Approaches to Class Analysis,* edited by Erik Olin Wright. Cambridge: Cambridge University Press.

———. 2005b. "Foundations of a Neo-Marxist Class Analysis." In *Approaches to Class Analysis,* edited by Erik Olin Wright. Cambridge: Cambridge University Press.

Yoshino, I. Roger. 1959. "The Stereotype of the Negro and His High-Priced Car." *Sociology and Social Research* 44(November–December): 114.

Chapter 2

Are There Social Classes? A Framework for Testing Sociology's Favorite Concept

DAVID B. GRUSKY AND KIM A. WEEDEN

T HE STUDY of inequality is plagued by a surplus of measurement paradigms based variously on socioeconomic or prestige scales, income or earnings reports, and Weberian, neo-Marxian, or Durkheimian class schemes. The chapters in this volume reveal quite strikingly this embarrassment of riches, with some contributors characterizing inequality in terms of aggregate occupational categories (Manza and Brooks, Lareau and Weininger), others treating income or education as more fundamental metrics (Lacy and Harris, McCall), and yet others focusing on the subjective classes with which individuals identify (Hout). Most often, scholars choose a measurement paradigm not on the basis of scientific criteria, but rather as a matter of faith or as a symbolic badge of affiliation with a discipline, subfield, or favored scholar (for a similar critique, see Bollen, Glanville, and Stecklov 2001, 163; Duncan et al. 2002; Hout and Hauser 1992). This affiliative effect accounts, for example, for the great regularity with which economists "decide" to analyze labor markets in terms of income or earnings, while sociologists "decide" to analyze much the same phenomena in terms of class or socioeconomic standing. Frequently, these decisions take place without much attention to the discarded alternatives, so much so that many economists treat the study of income inequality as synonymous with the study of inequality itself (see, for example, Sen 2006), just as many sociologists assume that the study of class inequality exhausts the study of inequality.

The purpose of this chapter is to develop a framework for subjecting such extra-empirical decisions to empirical test. Although our framework could be used to test a variety of measurement approaches, we concentrate here on assessing the viability of class models. This is an appropriate starting point because the class model has long dominated sociological models of life chances (Breen 2005), health, illness, and mortality (Robert and House 2000), political attitudes and outcomes (Svallfors 2006), lifestyles and consumption practices (Lareau 2003), and many other social behaviors (Weeden 2002). If socioeconomic and related scales reigned supreme in the 1960s and 1970s, it is the class scheme that has come to be dominant since the 1980s. The ubiquity of the class control within sociology led Paul DiMaggio (2001, 542) to conclude that measures of social class are modern day "crack troops in the war on unexplained variance."

The class concept remains, then, a core commitment within sociology, yet arguably its influence has been waning in recent years. It is not merely that postmodernists continue to argue that the class concept is rooted historically in the early industrial period and is less useful in understanding the structure of contemporary inequality (see, for example, Pakulski 2005). Additionally, standard class categories (such as professional, manager, clerical, craft) are gradually being displaced by measurements of income, earnings, or education in conventional quantitative analyses of social behavior. This movement away from class models has not, to our knowledge, been driven by new empirical results that have shown that class no longer captures the structure of inequality all that well (see Kingston 2000). If in the past sociologists defaulted to class models without much empirical foundation, now they are turning away from such models with just as little empirical justification.

It is striking how little interest there has been in adjudicating among competing measurement traditions. The decision to privilege one tradition over another is often treated as a matter of taste that hardly requires defense. In those relatively rare cases when measurement decisions are defended, the tendency is to resort to non-empirical criteria, such as tradition or theory, in waging that defense. The class and socioeconomic concepts, for example, are often defended by simply referring to their provenance in the literature or by rehearsing long-standing and untested claims that social classes or socioeconomic scales represent the underlying variables that define interests, life chances, or life conditions. To be sure, some scholars have examined empirically the relative merits of different types of occupational scales (Hauser and Warren 1997), while others have likewise offered putative tests of the class concept (see Evans and Mills 1998, 2000; Hout, Brooks, and Manza 1993; Halaby and Weakliem 1993; Evans 1992). These tests fall well short, as we show here, of a convincing adjudication among competing measurement approaches.

The premise of our chapter is that discipline-specific preferences for particular measurement approaches, including the class concept, can and should be converted from purely metaphysical commitments to testable claims about the structure of the inequality space and how it is changing. We develop a modeling framework that allows scholars to determine whether conventional measurements of income, socioeconomic status, or social class adequately characterize the multidimensional space of inequality. This framework also allows us to monitor trends in the extent to which inequality takes on a particular structural form; and to quantify the effects of inequality (once it is adequately characterized) on individual-level outcomes of interest such as attitudes or demographic outcomes. Although we hope ultimately to deploy this framework, here we merely describe it.

As will become clear, our goal is not to advance or promote any particular class model (such as Marxian, Weberian, or micro-class), but to develop methods that make it possible to subject class models of all kinds to convincing empirical test. We therefore reject the standard presumption, illustrated throughout the chapters of this volume, that measurement choices may be justified by simply proffering a definition that appears to motivate them. We instead accept at face value all the various and sundry definitions of class on offer and ask how such definitions might be evaluated. The conventional definition-based legitimation of measurement decisions should be replaced, we argue, with an empirical legitimation that requires analysts to demonstrate that their preferred measure in fact adequately captures the structure of inequality.

Two complementary analytic approaches form the centerpiece of our framework: a "pure" approach that makes no reference to the consequences of class, and an "effect-calibrated" approach that builds in such consequences quite explicitly. In the pure approach, the objective is to examine whether conventional measurement schemes (socioeconomic, class-based, income-based) can account for the multidimensional space of inequality, where the latter is defined by endowments (education, work experience), working conditions (authority, autonomy, form of employment contract), and rewards (income, wealth). The multidimensional models that we develop will allow scholars to distinguish between gradational, class-based, and disorganized forms of inequality. If a class form emerges, scholars can further determine how many classes are necessary to characterize the space adequately and whether those classes correspond to detailed occupations (the micro-class solution), aggregations of detailed occupations (the big-class solution), or more heterogeneous constellations of positions at the site of production (the "postmodern" solution).

This approach allows scholars to answer fundamental questions about trends in inequality. Is inequality increasingly taking on a class form? Are particular social classes (such as the professional-managerial class) becoming especially coherent and well formed? Is the middle class breaking down? Is a true working class or underclass developing in the late industrial context? Are the various inequality dimensions instead becoming less tightly associated and more postmodern in form (see, for example, Pakulski 2005)? These questions entail a shift in focus from monitoring trends in the amount of inequality to monitoring trends in the shape and form of inequality. The latter trends are critical in understanding how inequality is experienced. If the well-known rise in income inequality has been coupled with a tightening of the association between income and other dimensions of inequality, it follows that the disadvantaged are doubly losing out, not just because they are ever more distant from the advantaged but also because they are increasingly likely to be disadvantaged in many overlapping ways (income, wealth, risk of unemployment).

In our effect-calibrated analyses, we ask whether gradational scales or class categories have true emergent effects on social behaviors, where "emergent effects" refers to those that cannot be reductively explained in terms of selection (the nonrandom recruitment of individuals into classes), the underlying job conditions that define classes (including the form of employment contract), or job rewards (including class-specific profiles of income). These analyses address whether particular types of class schemes perform especially well in explaining social outcomes (attitudes, political behavior, and lifestyles) and whether nonclass measurement approaches (income and SES) can outperform class models. We do not develop models that tease out the particular mechanisms through which such class effects might arise. The logically prior step, we argue, is to determine whether there are any effects to explain and hence any need to identify mechanisms behind them. Indeed, just as scholars of neighborhood effects led off by testing for contextual effects before turning to mechanisms (Sampson, Morenoff, and Gannon-Rowley 2002; Sobel 2003), so too class analysts should begin by testing for the simple existence of class effects. It is strange that such tests have to date been overlooked.

The first line of analysis thus represents the structure of inequality without taking into account its effects on dependent variables ("pure" operationalizations), whereas the second line of analysis develops representations that do take into account such effects ("effect-calibrated" operationalizations). We review each approach in turn.

Pure Operationalizations

Inevitably, all measurement models are predicated on *some* pre-empirical decisions, and good science is all about making those decisions as transparent as possible and locating them at such a primitive level that they are as uncontroversial as possible. By current convention, a scholar is obligated at most to justify his or her adoption of a particular type of class scheme (Weberian, Marxian, micro-class), a particular type of scale (Duncan SEI, prestige), or a particular type of earnings report (hourly wages, annual wages). There is no corresponding obligation to justify the decision to privilege one family of measurement approaches (such as social class) over another (such as earnings report).

How might we attempt such a justification? The first step, we argue, is to define the "inequality space" as a multivariate distribution of variables (income, wealth, authority) that index the structure of advantage and disadvantage. The task of specifying the underlying dimensions of advantage and disadvantage has generated much discussion among sociologists, economists, and philosophers (see Bourdieu 1984; Grusky and Ku 2008; Nussbaum 2006). These literatures reveal some amount of agreement on the importance of three families of variables: "investments and endowments" (I) refers to personality attributes, human capital, formal and vocational schooling, and all forms of experience; "working conditions" (C) refers to the type of employment contract (salary, wage, self-employed), union status, labor market type (formal, informal), and job authority, autonomy, and complexity; and "rewards" (R) refers to earnings, investment income, program income, and wealth. This list of variables omits some important dimensions but is comprehensive enough to shift the burden of proof to those skeptics who believe that adding yet more variables would lead to fundamental changes in the underlying structure of inequality.

The virtue of building our measurement approach in terms of the inequality space is not that doing so eliminates pre-empirical considerations. The foregoing list of dimensions defining our inequality space instead reflects and specifies our assumptions about what matters for life chances. By committing to a particular inequality space, these assumptions about the dimensions that govern life chances are directly revealed, and there is no longer any need to glean those assumptions indirectly from some operational commitment to a particular scale or class scheme.

The many available scales or class schemes can then be understood as different ways of simplifying the multidimensional space defined by these underlying dimensions. We may ask, for example, whether earnings reports, detailed occupations, or socioeconomic scales can represent adequately the structure of this multidimensional space. These models of inequality, now construed as hypotheses about the inequality space, can be tested with confirmatory latent-class models, as described later. The latent-class framework also allows us to assess whether individuals cluster into classes that combine dimensions in ways that are not well described by conventional class models.

This framework is viable because of three statistical advances in latent-class modeling: the development of models for mixed-mode data that combine continuous and categorical indicators (see, for example, Magidson and Vermunt 2002); the associated development of models that constrain the underlying classes to be scaled or ordered (see Croon 2002); and programming enhancements that make it possible to estimate models with many more parameters than was previously feasible (see Hagenaars and McCutcheon

2002, appendix C). The analyses that we propose are tractable because latent-class models for mixed-mode data obviate the need to discretize continuous variables and thus allow them to be treated parsimoniously.

We describe the latent-class approach in more technical terms later. The less technically inclined reader need merely appreciate that this approach allows us to assess whether conventional measurement models adequately characterize how individuals are distributed across the multidimensional inequality space.

Until relatively recently, latent-class models for continuous and categorical indicators developed along quite separate tracks, making it difficult to carry out analyses that combined the two scale types. However, these two tracks have now been joined (see Vermunt and Magidson 2002), with the resulting latent-class model for mixed-mode data represented as follows:

$$f\left(\mathbf{y}_i/\theta\right)\sum_{k=1}^{K}\pi_k\prod_{j=1}^{J}f_k\left(y_{ij}/\theta_{jk}\right) \tag{2.1}$$

In this model, $\mathbf{y}_i$ denotes the respondent's scores on the manifest variables (the variables defining the inequality space), K is the number of postulated latent classes, π_k refers to the probability of belonging to the kth latent class (thus indexing latent-class size), J denotes the total number of manifest variables, and j is a particular manifest variable. The distribution of $\mathbf{y}_i$ is a function of the model parameters of θ, a function that takes the form of a mixture of class-specific densities ($f_k(y_{ij}/\theta_{jk})$). We must also specify the appropriate univariate distribution for each element y_{ij} of $\mathbf{y}_i$. For continuous y_{ij}, the natural choice is the univariate normal, whereas for discrete nominal or ordinal variables it is the (restricted) multinomial.

The manifest variables are assumed to be independent within latent classes. That is, we do not assume that all class members have identical scores on the manifest variables, but we do assume that, whenever a class member has a score that deviates from the class mean, this deviation does not convey any information on the likelihood of deviating on any of the other variables. The assumption of local independence can be relaxed, but we insist on it because it captures a main constraint embodied in the class hypothesis.

The utility of this approach may be illustrated by representing a simplified case in which the multidimensional space is defined by only three individual-level variables, such as income, education, and authority. We have further simplified our illustrative figures by representing just three big classes (aggregations of detailed occupations) and six micro classes (detailed occupations). We might postulate, for example, that the inequality space resolves into three classes: professionals and managers, routine nonmanual workers, and manual workers. The micro-class hypothesis might be represented by the competing claim that the professional-managerial class is best subdivided into separate professional and managerial classes, the routine nonmanual class is best subdivided into separate sales and clerical classes, and the manual class is best subdivided into separate craft and operative classes. As it is usually understood, the micro-class approach implies far finer distinctions than the foregoing (see, for example, Weeden and Grusky 2005a, 2005b, 2006), but our simplified example illustrates the type of analysis that might be undertaken. In the figures that follow, big-class membership is signified by three symbols (square, triangle, circle), and micro-class membership within each big class is signified by shades of these symbols (light, dark).

This framework may be used to define several measurement models and to assess the extent to which the structure of the inequality space is consistent with those models. In all cases, our measurement models are best regarded as ideal types, with the question being whether the structure of inequality is becoming more or less consistent with such ideal types. We review here seven illustrative questions that may be taken on within this general framework.

1. Can standard big-class or micro-class models capture the association in the inequality space? The rise of multidimensionalism within economics has led to much fretting about the difficulty of parsimoniously characterizing the structure of inequality (Sen 1997). We have argued elsewhere that class models long favored by sociologists may provide the parsimonious solution to multidimensionalism that economists seek (Grusky and Kanbur 2006; Grusky and Weeden 2007). After all, class models make multidimensionality tractable by characterizing it in terms of a relatively small number of categories, each representing a distinct combination of endowments, working conditions, and rewards. The class of "craft workers," for example, has historically been made up of individuals with moderate educational investments (secondary school credentials), considerable occupation-specific investments in human capital (vocational and on-the-job training), average income, relatively high job security, middling social honor and prestige, and quite limited authority and autonomy. The underclass, by contrast, has been represented as a rather different package of endowments, conditions, and rewards. Although many definitions of the underclass have been offered, members are usually understood to have limited educational investments (secondary school dropouts), sporadic participation in the (legal) labor market, exceedingly low income from wages, limited opportunities for on-the-job training and virtually no authority or autonomy during (brief) bouts of employment, and much social denigration and exclusion. It is likewise possible to define other social classes as characteristic sets of endowments, working conditions, and rewards.

This type of class model is conventionally treated as an assumption, but here we treat it as a hypothesis that can be tested by forcing the latent classes of equation 2.1 to be perfectly defined by class membership. If such a constraint holds, it implies that the inequality space has a relatively low dimensionality—indeed, a dimensionality no more or less than the number

Figure 2.1   Big-Class Regime

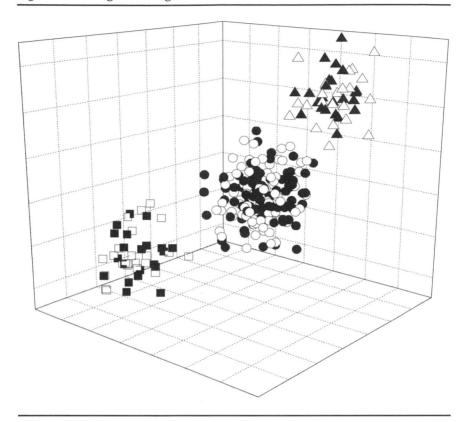

Source: Authors' compilation.

of postulated classes. The big-class solution, for example, implies that the underlying dimensions are independent of one another within each big class and hence that subdividing into micro classes is unnecessary (see figure 2.1). By contrast, the independence constraint is clearly violated in figure 2.2, meaning that further subdivision into micro classes is now required. Although our earlier research suggests that micro-class models are likely to outperform big-class models in the bivariate context (Weeden and Grusky 2005a, 2005b), we have not yet attempted a comprehensive evaluation of micro-class models in the context of the full multidimensional space.

   2. *Are class models becoming more or less viable?* The latent-class approach may also be applied to address long-standing debates about trends in the shape of inequality. Is the takeoff in income inequality accompanied by the rise of well-defined social classes? Or are such classes instead breaking down? Is the labor market increasingly fracturing into separate occupational markets

Figure 2.2   Micro-Class Regime

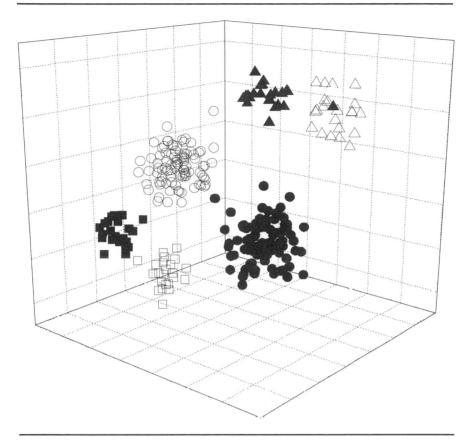

Source: Authors' compilation.

(see, for example, Barley 1995)? Or is the labor market becoming increasingly "post-occupational" in form (see Casey 1995)? Are all forms of structure at the site of production, big-class and micro-class alike, withering away (Hall 2001)? The disciplines of economics and even sociology have fixated on the dramatic trends in income inequality over the last thirty years and largely ignored such questions. This fixation, while understandable, has diverted attention from the equally important question of whether the various dimensions of economic and non-economic inequality are coming together in ways that make the inequality space an increasingly classlike affair.

3. *Is the division of labor still central to the structure of inequality?* The long-standing presumption among sociologists has been that inequality is best measured at the "site of production" (see, for example, Parkin 1979). This presumption underlies class models that are defined by occupation (micro-class models), aggregations of occupations (big-class models), or

various job-level variables (authority, autonomy). We may distinguish such conventional site-of-production models from those that stress the centrality of either premarket endowments (such as education) or extra-market rewards (such as wealth). For example, John Meyer (2008) has suggested that class models are quaint artifacts of our early industrial past, artifacts to which scholars continue to cling even as "education classes" have come to capture the most fundamental cleavages of contemporary inequality (see also Brooks 2006; Pakulski and Waters 2001). We may test this hypothesis by forcing the latent classes of equation 2.1 to be perfectly determined by educational categories (high school dropout, high school graduate, college attendance, college graduate). Although a highly constrained model of this sort is not likely to fit well, it may provide over time an increasingly good approximation of the inequality space. We might likewise fit hybrid models that represent the inequality space as the combination of site-of-production cleavages (such as occupations) and qualification-based cleavages (such as education).

4. *Does poverty take on a class form?* The same logic can be adapted to assess whether class models adequately characterize that portion of the inequality space populated by the most disadvantaged workers (see Grusky and Weeden 2006).[1] Although many class analysts analyze only the paid labor force and thus define away the disadvantaged, it is surely worth testing more encompassing measurement approaches. It is conventional, for example, to distinguish between three disadvantaged classes: an "underclass" of individuals who are poorly attached to the labor force; a "formal sector" of poor workers who have a more substantial but still precarious attachment to low-wage laboring and service employment; and an "informal sector" of poor workers who subsist through an equally precarious attachment to self-employment in the laboring and service sector (for example, street vendors).[2] There are naturally many other class models of poverty and disadvantage that might also be assessed (Wilson 2006). We wish only to suggest that poverty classes can and should be subjected to the same empirical verification as class schemes pertaining to the nonpoverty population.

5. *Is the inequality space adequately represented by models that scale detailed occupations?* In figures 2.1 and 2.2, we represent a class structure that cannot be understood in simple gradational terms, as some classes are formed by combining high values on one dimension with low values on another. The gradationalist challenge to conventional class models involves the more aggressive claim that big classes or micro classes can be scaled on one or more dimensions (see figure 2.3). We can test for such a structure by estimating scale values for the manifest classes or, less restrictively, by imposing ordinality constraints on them (see Croon 2002; Rost 1988). This test for gradationalism is fundamental because it takes on the claim that all forms of advantage are increasingly concentrating at the top of the class structure and all forms of disadvantage are increasingly concentrating at the bottom of the class structure. Although there is much research on how particular

Figure 2.3   Gradational Micro-Class Regime

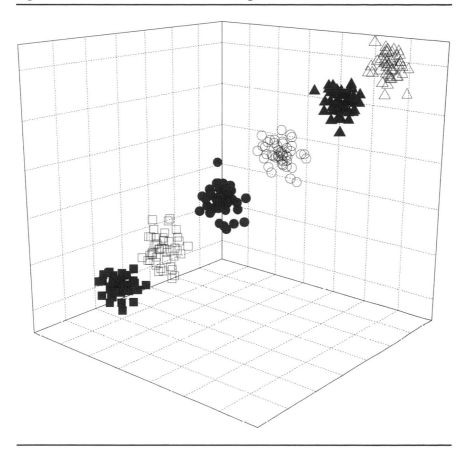

Source: Authors' compilation.

dimensions of inequality (such as income) are changing, we do not know whether late industrialism has also brought on a form of crystallization in which the inequality dimensions themselves are coming together to create a more purely gradational structure to inequality.

We can also test whether these freely estimated scale values closely reproduce the famous socioeconomic gradient (see, for example, Bourdieu 1984; Hauser and Warren 1997; Nakao and Treas 1994). The socioeconomic index is in fact a particular type of class model that treats all detailed occupations with the same socioeconomic score as a micro class and also presumes that such socioeconomic scores adequately represent inequality in all the dimensions that the postulated inequality space encompasses. If this very strong constraint fails, scholars who insist on a gradational solution can still fall back

Figure 2.4   Fractal Individualized Inequality

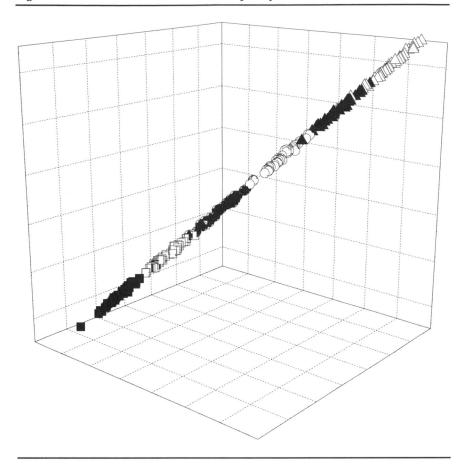

Source: Authors' compilation.

on the estimated (rather than constrained) scale values for micro classes. These estimated scale values, which constitute the optimal occupation-based scaling of the inequality space, may serve as a replacement for conventional socioeconomic scores.

6. *Does inequality take on a fractal character?* Although the regimes of figures 2.2 and 2.3 are inconsistent with standard big-class models, they express the class concept in revised form by allowing for ungraded (figure 2.2) or graded (figure 2.3) micro classes. By contrast, figure 2.4 represents a case in which the class concept itself must be rejected because, no matter the level of disaggregation, the underlying inequality variables continue to covary with one another. This ideal type may be understood as an extreme micro-class solution in which the diagonal of figure 2.3 thins out to the point where each individual becomes a class unto himself or herself. We refer to this solu-

Figure 2.5   Disorganized Inequality

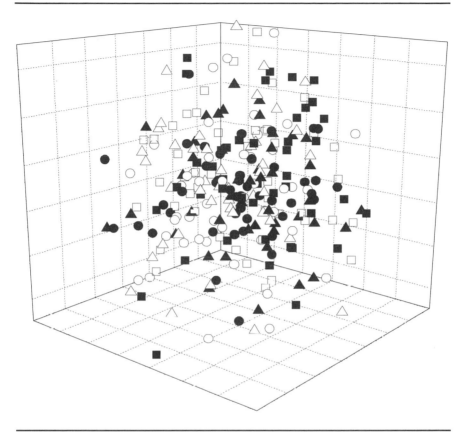

Source: Authors' compilation.

tion as fractal because the same gradational solution is apparent at each and every level of disaggregation. The economist should recognize this solution as consistent with the claim that income is a master variable, that it perfectly signals all other individual-level measures of inequality, and that no higher-level class organization therefore appears. Obviously, this ideal type would never be empirically realized in such extreme form, but it is nonetheless important to ask whether the simple economic model comes closer to being realized in some societies or time periods than in others.

7. *Is inequality becoming increasingly disorganized?* The regime of figure 2.5, unlike that of figure 2.4, does not allow the underlying individual-level variables to covary. This may be understood as a "one class" solution or, equivalently, a nonclass regime. Although there is much inequality under this specification, it takes a uniquely structureless form in which the independence assumption holds throughout multidimensional space, not just

within a given latent class. Again, it is unlikely that such extreme disorganization will ever be realized, but the ideal type represents a form of inequality that some postmodernists (Pakulski 2005; Pakulski and Waters 2001) argue is emerging. If they are correct, it means that the growth in income inequality is at least counterbalanced by a decline in the association between income and other forms of inequality.

We cannot claim to have exhausted the many ideal-typical forms that either class-based or classless inequality regimes might assume. Rather, we wish merely to stress the importance of developing a methodology for characterizing the form as well as the extent of inequality, a task that takes on special importance once the multidimensionality of inequality is appreciated. If properly elaborated, our approach also can provide a comprehensive framework for comparative multidimensional analyses of inequality, one that will allow us to consider not just cross-societal differences in the amount of inequality but also cross-societal differences in how that inequality is expressed and organized. Moreover, this approach will allow us to test long-standing—and long-untested—assumptions about the structure of inequality that are in part embedded in disciplinary divides.

Effect-Calibrated Operationalizations

The "pure" analyses described here can yield new insights into the underlying structure of inequality, how that structure is changing over time, and the relative power of competing measurement paradigms in representing such inequality. How might defenders of the income paradigm, the socioeconomic paradigm, or the class analytic paradigm react if it were shown that their preferred measurement approach does not represent the inequality space all that well? The standard response, we suspect, would be to counter that these paradigms were devised merely to capture those features of the inequality space that are consequential for social behavior (such as mobility, voting, or consumption), not to represent the structure of that space in its entirety (see Goldthorpe and McKnight 2006). If we wish, then, to convince others that measurement decisions should be founded on empirical considerations, we need to examine not just the underlying structure of the inequality space but also how a person's location within that structure affects a wide range of dependent variables.

It follows that a convincing empirical case for any particular measurement device must be forged on the twin claim that it provides a parsimonious account of the multidimensional space of inequality and that it has net effects on attitudes and practices that are not reducible to the effects of the constituent dimensions of the inequality space. The first claim is addressed with the latent-class analyses described in the preceding section. The second claim, to which we turn now, can be addressed by estimating class, income, or socioeconomic effects in the context of more comprehensive controls and more convincing specifications than have yet been attempted. In this second line of analysis, we consider whether classes or socioeconomic scales have true emergent effects on behaviors and attitudes rather than effects that could be explained in terms of the endowments, working conditions, or rewards with which such classes or socioeconomic scales are defined.[3]

It is striking that sociologists increasingly use class or socioeconomic models out of tradition, convenience, or habit rather than any strong conviction that these models capture the mechanisms through which inequality exerts its effects. There are three main lines of argument that appear to inform this contemporary loss of faith in the class realist position. First, postmodern and poststructural scholars have argued that social class has lost whatever power it once had, partly because other identities (such as race and gender) have become more prominent and "squeezed out" class-based identities (see, for example, Bradley 1996), but also because identity formation in the postmodern world is so atomized and individualized that all structural bases of social behavior become irrelevant (see Hall 2001), or because the institutions that once represented class interests (such as political parties and unions) have developed into new forms that are less class-based (see, for example, Clark and Lipset 2001; see also Hechter 2004). Regardless of the particular form of the argument, the expectation is that "emergent effects" of classes have become less prominent over the past quarter-century or more.

The second, and by far more common, line of anti-class argumentation questions not whether strong class effects will appear in conventional quantitative models, but rather whether such effects should be attributed to true class-based processes and mechanisms. The claim here is that the net class effects that routinely appear in quantitative models are generated entirely by selective processes (see Meyer 2008), with the implication that these effects would disappear if the variables on which selection occurs could be fully controlled. The service class in the Erikson and Goldthorpe (1992) scheme, for example, might appear to be more tolerant of alternative lifestyles merely because its incumbents are especially likely to have attended elite colleges where social tolerance is preached. Although selection-based arguments of this sort are ubiquitous, what has been lacking is a test of them that rests on comprehensive individual-level models that correct as convincingly as possible for such selective processes.

The third main line of anti-class argumentation comes from a more surprising source. In recent years, John Goldthorpe (2000) and Richard Breen (2005) have sought to refashion class analysis on rational action foundations, yet their efforts have had the perverse and unintended effect of undermining all but a purely nominalist rationale for class analysis. These authors have argued that classes index the "form of regulation of employment" (such as salaried or short-term contract), with this underlying variable presumed to affect how workers understand their interests and thus settle on particular beliefs, practices, or courses of action. This interpretation implies that the class concept is in the end superfluous because the true causal effect is not exerted by the class per se but by an underlying variable that class membership signals (the "form of regulation of employment"). The obvious question is whether anything is gained by pushing a nominalist analysis through a class fulcrum in this fashion. Why not abandon the pretense of class altogether and simply measure at the job level the various working conditions that classes putatively signal?

It follows that the realist case for class requires that scholars demonstrate net class effects in the context of a model that not only eliminates selection effects but also purges the effects of those working conditions (such as employment form) and job rewards (such as income) that may govern the calculation of interests. If such an analysis reveals that classes have no net effects, we can conclude that the class concept is superfluous and that the variables constituting the inequality space should be directly used in quantitative modeling.

We suspect that such tests will instead indicate that the class concept has merit and that class analysts have nothing to fear. Why might net effects of class be detected even with such rigorous controls? The standard argument in this regard is that classes constitute particular "packages" of rewards and working conditions that, in combination, lead to an *emergent* logic of the situation, a logic that then governs social action. The underclass, for instance, may be understood as a combination of negative conditions (intermittent labor force participation, limited education, low income) that, taken together, engender a sense of futility, despondency, or learned helplessness that is more profound than what would be expected from a model that simply allows for independent effects of each constituent class condition. To be sure, a committed reductionist might counter that we need merely include the appropriate set of interactions between the constituent variables, but insofar as classes define the relevant packages of interacting conditions, this objection becomes an unduly complicated way of sidestepping the reality of classes.

The argument for a net class effect also rests on the claim that class-defined packages of conditions are associated with distinctive cultures that take on a life of their own and thus independently shape behavior and attitudes. At minimum, class cultures may be understood as "rules of thumb" that encode best-practice behavioral responses to the working conditions that classes entail, with these rules then allowing class members to forgo optimizing calculations themselves and to rely instead on economical shortcuts to best practices (see, for example, Goldthorpe 2000). More ambitiously, it is sometimes argued that truly maladaptive class cultures emerge, such as a "culture of poverty" that filters information in unduly cynical ways and engenders an excessive sense of futility and despondency (see Wilson 2006). It is notable that in either case classes play a role in empirical models of inequality that is similar to the role of neighborhoods in the neighborhood effects literature. Namely, classes are expected to have net effects on a wide range of behaviors, interests, and attitudes that are not reducible to mere selection or to constituent working conditions.

We have assumed to this point that the main coefficients of interest are the true causal effects of contemporaneous class on attitudes, behaviors, lifestyles, health, fertility, and the host of other demographic dependent variables that sociologists and other social scientists routinely analyze. Although much of quantitative sociology relies on such measures of contemporaneous class, there is also continuing interest in treating class of origin as a "parental background" variable. This type of measurement allows scholars to assess the extent to which life chances vary by social origins and hence opportunities are unequally distributed. Because many economists and philosophers now work within the "capabilities approach" (see, for example, Sen 1997), the emerging fashion is to treat reward-based measures of inequality, such as income, as affected by differential tastes (including tastes for leisure or consumption) and hence reflective of preferences as well as true inequality. Within this tradition, measures of opportunity or "capability" are featured because, by contrast, they speak to inequalities that predate the operation of tastes or preferences. This line of reasoning implies that a comprehensive test of the class concept entails assessing its usefulness in representing origins as well as destinations (Grusky and Weeden 2006).

Is there any reason to believe that scholars need the class concept to measure origins? Although we think that there is, it is again the case that social scientists have simply defaulted to class-based measurements of origins without providing even minimally satisfactory evidence that they add anything beyond a reductive model resting on separate measurements of parental endowments, working conditions, and rewards (see Hauser 1973). The conventional, if untested, view is that such a reductive model falls short because parents transmit information, skills, networks, and tastes that reflect not just their education or income but also their class position (Grusky and Weeden 2002). The children of sociologists, for example, are more likely to themselves become sociologists because they know about and aspire to such a role, have special access to high-quality information about how to train for such a role, have special access to the human capital that will assist them in preparing for such a role, and have special access to social networks that may also provide some small advantage in securing such a role. It will not suffice, therefore, to simply fit a "parental income" effect in models of income determination, given that the children of sociologists will disproportionately follow income trajectories that are specific to sociologists rather than the larger group of workers with sociology-sized family incomes (see, for example, Grusky and Weeden 2006).

The challenge, then, is to offer convincing evidence that class effects are not reducible to investments and endowments that drive selection into particular classes or reducible to rewards that constitute a set of background conditions in terms of which interests are gauged and behaviors selected. We also require models that will allow us to estimate the net effects of class, income, or socioeconomic status in both the contemporaneous and intergenerational context.

The obvious starting point for this task is the usual array of general linear models in which the link function (such as linear or logistic) differs by the type of measurement for the outcome variable. The following model, for example, may be used to assess whether there are net effects of class, income, or socioeconomic status on (binary) vote choice:

$$Y_i = \alpha + X_i\beta + I_i\delta + C_i\varphi + \varepsilon_i, \tag{2.2}$$

where Y_i is the logit of vote choice, X_i is a vector of variables measuring the social and demographic "causes" of voting (such as age, sex, race), I_i is a vector of endowments (such as education, labor market experience), working conditions (such as firm tenure, union membership, self-employment status), and rewards (such as income) that together define the inequality space, C_i includes the dummy variables pertaining to the categories of the preferred class scheme, and ε_i is an error term. If we wish instead to condition on a socioeconomic index, doing so of course requires the further constraint that the class effects (on C_i) are consistent with a socioeconomic gradient. The effects of family background on outcomes could also be represented within the context of equation 2.2 by converting I_i and C_i into measurements for the parents rather than for the children (and Y_i would now presumably pertain to income or some other career outcome). The resulting models would differ from conventional status attainment models because they would contain far more measures of the underlying inequality space (see Hauser 1973; for more details, see Grusky and Weeden 2006).

There are two ways in which such analyses might lead to the conclusion that class or socioeconomic measurement (via C_i) should be preferred relative to a purely reductive strategy in which inequality is represented in terms of an individual-level vector of endowments, working conditions, and job rewards (I_i). First, the fit statistic for the model of equation 2.2 may be superior to that for a trimmed model that eliminates C_i, implying that there are true emergent effects of class or socioeconomic status. This conclusion rests merely on establishing that the effects of C_i, taken together, are substantial enough to be preferred by BIC (for a Bayesian) or a standard F-test or likelihood-ratio contrast (for a classicist).[4] Of course, if the models show that both class and reductive measures have net effects, sociologists would be well advised to adopt hybrid models of inequality rather than relying on class or socioeconomic status alone.

Even in the absence of such emergent effects, the results may still support a second, nominalist rationale for class or socioeconomic operationalizations. If the model of equation 2.2 shows that simple class or socioeconomic measures can account for the vast majority of individual-level effects, we might still justify conventional sociological practice as a relatively inexpensive, albeit imperfect, approach to measuring inequality. We can assess whether conventional schemes can capture much of the effects of inequality by contrasting the fit statistic for the model of equation 2.2 against that of a model that eliminates elements of X_i. If the trimmed model performs well (using, for example, a BIC criterion), we can conclude that class or socioeconomic measures are (potentially) justifiable for reasons of parsimony or convenience.

Conclusions

The spectacular rise in income inequality has reinvigorated inequality research and generated one of the most prominent research literatures in contemporary social science. This literature has focused almost exclusively on trends in the *amount* of inequality and has all but ignored possible changes in the *form* of inequality. We are accordingly left with many unasked and unanswered questions: Is inequality increasingly taking on a class form? Are social classes disappearing even as income inequality is growing? Is there a simple gradational structure to inequality? Or are many individuals in ambiguous situations that combine advantage and disadvantage in complicated ways?

The foregoing questions will continue to be ignored insofar as measurement choices remain largely determined by disciplinary ties or by commitments to certain theoretical schools. These commitments appear to be as strong as ever: the class analyst presumes classes and studies inequality through a class lens; the economist presumes gradationalism and studies inequality through a gradational lens (income inequality); and the stratification scholar presumes "socioeconomic" inequality and studies inequality through a socioeconomic lens. Although some scholars reject conventions of this sort, they nonetheless remain very much the norm.

We have proposed here a two-pronged modeling framework that converts such disciplinary assumptions into testable hypotheses. The first part of this framework allows us to test whether conventional simplifications of the multidimensional inequality space are empirically tenable. These simplifications, which are ultimately assumptions about the form and structure of inequality, are best treated as hypotheses that can then be subjected to test. If this descriptive task has been given short shrift in the past, it is largely because the necessary methods have not been available, not because of any shortage of fundamental questions about the form of inequality (see Grusky and Kanbur 2006; Kanbur 2001). We have shown that a latent-class framework provides a potentially useful methodological foundation for a new research agenda on the shape and form of inequality.

The second part of our framework addresses the causal effects of class and other measures of inequality. In individual-level models of all kinds, scholars typically include measures of social class, income, or socioeconomic status as covariates, either because of an intrinsic interest in the effects of such variables or merely as a means of securing unbiased estimates of other effects with which these measures are associated. These covariates routinely appear, for example, in models of health (Robert and House 2000), mortality (Martikainen, Valkonen, and Martelin 2001), marriage and cohabitation (Smock 2000), fertility (Bollen, Glanville, and Stecklov 2001), divorce (White and Rogers 2000), migration (Iceland, Sharpe, and Steinmetz 2003), political behavior (Hout and Moodie 2007), attitudes (DiMaggio 2001), and lifestyles and consumption practices (Chan and Goldthorpe 2005).[5] In some cases, the availability of particular inequality measures dictates the choice of a measurement approach, but clearly there are also large and seemingly unjustifiable effects of discipline, type of dependent variable, and research camp on the preferred measure of inequality.

The class model, long the mainstay of sociological research, is becoming less popular within many subfields. If the sociological model of class is to survive, it is doubtful that it will happen because economists and other social scientists suddenly decide to mimic the research practices of sociologists or to read the famous treatises on class and status provided by Marx, Weber, and their followers. Rather, a compelling *empirical* defense of the payoff to class or socioeconomic models is required, without which we can expect economists and other social scientists to continue to privilege individualistic models and thereby dismiss or ignore the sociological legacy. Obviously, it would be harmful to the discipline of sociology if its premier measurement choice were superseded by other approaches, but of course the only legitimate scientific question is whether such a loss would lead to less powerful accounts of the structure of inequality.

This is an opportune time to intervene in such measurement debates because many economists are themselves coming to doubt the adequacy of the "income paradigm" and are actively shopping for multidimensional or categorical alternatives to conventional income reports (Bourguignon 2006; Duclos, Esteban, and Ray 2004; Sahn and Younger, forthcoming; Sen 2006). Are class models a viable multidimensional alternative to the income paradigm? If a strong empirical case for class models is made, we think such models may develop a renewed following. There is, to be sure, no guarantee that class or socioeconomic models will pass this empirical test. If they do fail, sociologists had best face up to this result now and jettison that part of the discipline's intellectual history that proves to be an empirical dead-end. It is no longer tenable to merely duck the question.

The research reported here was supported with discretionary funds from Stanford University and Cornell University. We are grateful for the comments of Annette Lareau, Dalton Conley, anonymous reviewers, and the conference participants.

Notes

1. In theory, we could also test hypotheses about the most advantaged regions of the inequality space, although survey data are typically too sparse in such regions to make definitive tests possible.

2. If the poverty space is further differentiated by geography, it might be necessary to distinguish urban and rural variants of each of the foregoing three classes, thus yielding a six-class solution. This type of model may be understood as a hybrid specification in which classes are defined both within the site of production and outside it (via geography).

3. The case for socioeconomic scales rests implicitly on the presence of contextual effects. When a socioeconomic scale is used, the assumption is that occupations with the same status form a "class" and that the contextual effects of such classes follow a simple socioeconomic gradient (see Hodge 1981). Although advocates of classes and socioeconomic scales must therefore be prepared to defend the concept of contextual effects, advocates of income or earnings scales need not (because the latter scales are measured at the individual level).

4. The variables in I_i will likely be highly intercorrelated, but this is unproblematic because such variables are only serving as controls (and hence their independent effects need not be distinguished).

5. It has long been suspected that inequality has equally profound effects on macro-level outcomes (economic output, terrorism, revolution), but here the evidence is more mixed and the debates more contentious (see, for example, Krueger and Malečková 2003).

References

Barley, Stephen. 1995. "The Technician as an Occupational Archetype: A Case for Bringing Work into Organizational Studies." Working paper, Stanford University.
Bollen, Kenneth A., Jennifer L. Glanville, and Guy Stecklov. 2001. "Socioeconomic Status and Class in Studies of Fertility and Health in Developing Countries." *Annual Review of Sociology* 27: 153–85.
Bourdieu, Pierre. 1984. *Distinction: A Social Critique of the Judgment of Taste*, translated by Richard Nice. New York: Cambridge University Press.
Bourguignon, François. 2006. "From Income to Endowments: The Difficult Task of Expanding the Income Poverty Paradigm." In *Poverty and Inequality*, edited by David B. Grusky and Ravi Kanbur. Stanford, Calif.: Stanford University Press.
Bradley, Harriet. 1996. *Fractured Identities: Changing Patterns of Inequality.* Cambridge: Polity Press.

Breen, Richard. 2005. "Foundations of a Neo-Weberian Class Analysis." In *Approaches to Class Analysis,* edited by Erik Olin Wright. Cambridge: Cambridge University Press.

Brooks, David. 2006. "Bobos in Paradise." In *The Inequality Reader: Contemporary and Foundational Readings in Race, Class, and Gender,* edited by David B. Grusky and Szonja Szelényi. Boulder, Colo.: Westview Press.

Casey, Catherine. 1995. *Work, Self, and Society.* London: Routledge.

Chan, Tak Wing, and John H. Goldthorpe. 2005. "The Social Stratification of Theatre, Dance, and Cinema Attendance." *Cultural Trends* 14 (September 2005): 194–212.

Clark, Terry Nichols, and Seymour Martin Lipset. 2001. *The Breakdown of Class Politics: A Debate on Post-Industrial Stratification.* Washington and Baltimore, Md.: Woodrow Wilson Center Press and Johns Hopkins University Press.

Croon, Marcel. 2002. "Ordering the Classes." In *Applied Latent Class Analysis,* edited by Jacques A. Hagenaars and Allan L. McCutcheon. Cambridge: Cambridge University Press.

DiMaggio, Paul J. 2001. "Social Stratification, Life Style, Social Cognition, and Social Participation." In *Social Stratification: Class, Race, and Gender in Sociological Perspective,* 2nd edition, edited by David B. Grusky. Boulder, Colo.: Westview Press.

Duclos, Jean-Yves, Joan Maria Esteban, and Dabraj Ray. 2004. "Polarization: Concepts, Measurement, Estimation." *Econometrica* 74(6): 1737–72.

Duncan, Greg G., Mary C. Daly, Peggy McDonough, and David R. Williams. 2002. "Optimal Indicators of Socioeconomic Status for Health Research." *American Journal of Public Health* 92(7): 1151–7.

Erikson, Robert, and John H. Goldthorpe. 1992. *The Constant Flux: A Study of Class Mobility in Industrial Societies.* New York: Clarendon Press.

Evans, Geoffrey. 1992. "Testing the Validity of the Goldthorpe Class Schema." *European Sociological Review* 8(3): 211–32.

Evans, Geoffrey, and Colin Mills. 1998. "Identifying Class Structure: A Latent Class Analysis of the Criterion-Related and Construct Validity of the Goldthorpe Class Schema." *European Sociological Review* 14(1): 87–106.

———. 2000. "In Search of the Wage Labor/Service Contract: New Evidence on the Validity of the Goldthorpe Class Scheme." *British Journal of Sociology* 51(4): 641–61.

Goldthorpe, John H. 2000. *On Sociology: Numbers, Narrative, and the Integration of Research and Theory.* New York: Oxford University Press.

Goldthorpe, John H., and Abigail McKnight. 2006. "The Economic Basis of Social Class." In *Mobility and Inequality: Frontiers of Research in Sociology and Economics,* edited by Stephen L. Morgan, David B. Grusky, and Gary S. Fields. Stanford, Calif.: Stanford University Press.

Grusky, David B., and Ravi Kanbur. 2006. "Conceptual Ferment in Poverty and Inequality Measurement: The View from Economics and Sociology." In *Poverty and Inequality,* edited by David B. Grusky and Ravi Kanbur. Stanford, Calif.: Stanford University Press.

Grusky, David B. and Manwai C. Ku. 2008. "Gloom, Doom, and Inequality." In *Social Stratification: Class, Race, and Gender in Sociological Perspective,* 3rd ed., edited by David B. Grusky. Boulder, Colo.: Westview Press.

Grusky, David B., and Kim A. Weeden. 2002. "Class Analysis and the Heavy Weight of Convention." *Acta Sociologica* 45(3): 229–36.

————. 2006. "Does the Sociological Approach to Studying Social Mobility Have a Future?" In *Mobility and Inequality: Frontiers of Research in Sociology and Economics,* edited by Stephen L. Morgan, David B. Grusky, and Gary S. Fields. Stanford, Calif.: Stanford University Press.

————. 2007. "Measuring Poverty: The Case for a Sociological Approach." In *The Many Dimensions of Poverty,* edited by Nanak Kakwani and Jacques Silber. Hampshire, UK: Palgrave Macmillan.

Hagenaars, Jacques A., and Allan L. McCutcheon, editors. 2002. *Applied Latent Class Analysis.* Cambridge: Cambridge University Press.

Halaby, Charles, and David Weakliem. 1993. "Ownership and Authority in the Earnings Function: Nonnested Tests of Alternative Specifications." *American Sociological Review* 58(1): 16–30.

Hall, Stuart. 2001. "The Meaning of New Times." In *Social Stratification: Class, Race, and Gender in Sociological Perspective,* 2nd ed., edited by David B. Grusky. Boulder, Colo.: Westview Press.

Hauser, Robert M. 1973. "Disaggregating a Social Psychological Model of Educational Attainment." In *Structural Equation Models in the Social Sciences,* edited by Arthur S. Goldberger and Otis D. Duncan. New York: Seminar Press.

Hauser, Robert M., and John Robert Warren. 1997. "Socioeconomic Indexes of Occupational Status: A Review, Update, and Critique." In *Sociological Methodology,* edited by Adrian Raftery. Cambridge, Mass.: Blackwell.

Hechter, Michael. 2004. "From Class to Culture." *American Journal of Sociology* 110(2): 400–45.

Hodge, Roger W. 1981. "The Measurement of Occupational Status." *Social Science Research* 10(December): 396–415.

Hout, Michael, and Robert M. Hauser. 1992. "Hierarchy and Symmetry in Occupational Mobility." *European Sociological Review* 8(December): 239–66.

Hout, Michael, and Benjamin Moodie. 2007. "The Realignment of U.S. Presidential Voting, 1948–2004." In *The Inequality Reader: Contemporary and Foundational Readings in Race, Class, and Gender,* edited by David B. Grusky and Szonja Szelényi. Boulder, Colo.: Westview Press.

Hout, Michael, Clem Brooks, and Jeff Manza. 1993. "The Persistence of Classes in Postindustrial Societies." *International Sociology* 8(3): 259–77.

Iceland, John, Cicely Sharpe, and Erika Steinmetz. 2003. "Class Differences in African American Residential Patterns in U.S. Metropolitan Areas: 1990–2000." U.S. Census Bureau. Paper presented to the Population Association of America meetings, Minneapolis, Minn., May 1–3, 2003.

Kanbur, Ravi. 2001. "Economic Policy, Distribution, and Poverty: The Nature of Disagreements." *World Development* 29(6): 1083–94.

Kingston, Paul W. 2000. *The Classless Society.* Stanford, Calif.: Stanford University Press.

Krueger, Alan B., and Jitka Malečková. 2003. "Education, Poverty, Political Violence, and Terrorism: Is There a Causal Connection?" *Journal of Economic Perspectives* 17(4): 119–44.

Lareau, Annette. 2003. *Unequal Childhoods: Class, Race, and Family Life.* Berkeley and Los Angeles, Calif.: University of California Press.

Magidson, Jay, and Jeroen K. Vermunt. 2002. *Latent Class Models.* Boston, Mass.: Statistical Innovations.

Martikainen, P., T. Valkonen, and T. Martelin. 2001. "Change in Male and Female Life Expectancy by Social Class: Decomposition by Age and Cause of Death in Finland, 1971–1995." *Journal of Epidemiology and Community Health* 55(7): 494–99.

Meyer, John W. 2008. "The Evolution of Modern Stratification Systems." In *Social Stratification: Class, Race, and Gender in Sociological Perspective*, 3rd ed., edited by David B. Grusky, Manwai Candy Ku, and Szonja Szelényi. Boulder, Colo.: Westview Press.

Nakao, Keiko, and Judith Treas. 1994. "Updating Occupational Prestige and Socioeconomic Status Scores: How the New Measures Measure Up." In *Sociological Methodology, 1994*, edited by Peter Marsden. Oxford: Basil Blackwell for the American Sociological Association.

Nussbaum, Martha. 2006. "Poverty and Human Functioning: Capabilities as Fundamental Entitlements." In *Poverty and Inequality*, edited by David B. Grusky and Ravi Kanbur. Stanford, Calif.: Stanford University Press.

Pakulski, Jan. 2005. "Foundations of a Post-Class Analysis." In *Approaches to Class Analysis*, edited by Erik Olin Wright. Cambridge: Cambridge University Press.

Pakulski, Jan, and Malcolm Waters. 2001. "The Death of Class." In *Social Stratification: Class, Race, and Gender in Sociological Perspective*, 2nd ed., edited by David B. Grusky. Boulder, Colo.: Westview Press.

Parkin, Frank. 1979. *Marxism and Class Theory: A Bourgeois Critique*. New York: Columbia University Press.

Robert, Stephanie A., and James S. House. 2000. "Socioeconomic Inequalities in Health: Integrating Individual-, Community-, and Societal-Level Theory and Research." In *Handbook of Social Studies in Health and Medicine*, edited by Gary L. Albrecht, Ray Fitzpatrick, and Susan C. Scrimshaw. Thousand Oaks, Calif.: Sage Publications.

Rost, Jurgen. 1988. "Rating Scale Analysis with Latent Class Models." *Psychometrika* 53(3): 327–48.

Sahn, David E., and Stephen D. Younger. Forthcoming. "Changes in Inequality and Poverty in Latin America: Looking Beyond Income." *Journal of Applied Economics*.

Sampson, Robert J., Jeffrey D. Morenoff, and Thomas Gannon-Rowley. 2002. "Assessing Neighborhood Effects: Social Processes and New Directions in Research." *Annual Review of Sociology* 28: 443–78.

Sen, Amartya. 1997. *On Economic Inequality*. Oxford: Oxford University Press.

———. 2006. "Concepts and Measures." In *Poverty and Inequality*, edited by David B. Grusky and Ravi Kanbur. Stanford, Calif.: Stanford University Press.

Smock, Pamela J. 2000. "Cohabitation in the United States: An Appraisal of Research Themes, Findings, and Implications." *Annual Review of Sociology* 26: 1–20.

Sobel, Michael E. 2003. "What Do Randomized Studies of Housing Mobility Reveal? Causal Inference in the Face of Interference." Working paper, Columbia University.

Svallfors, Stefan. 2006. *The Moral Economy of Class: Class and Attitudes in Comparative Perspective*. Stanford, Calif.: Stanford University Press.

Vermunt, Jeroen K., and Jay Magidson. 2002. "Latent Class Cluster Analysis." In *Applied Latent Class Analysis*, edited by Jacques A. Hagenaars and Allan L. McCutcheon. Cambridge: Cambridge University Press.

Weeden, Kim A. 2002. "Why Do Some Occupations Pay More Than Others? Social Closure and Earnings Inequality in the United States." *American Journal of Sociology* 108(1): 55–101.

Weeden, Kim A., and David B. Grusky. 2005a. "The Case for a New Class Map." *American Journal of Sociology* 111(1): 141–212.

———. 2005b. "Are There Any Big Classes at All?" In *Research in Social Stratification and Mobility*, vol. 22, *The Shape of Social Inequality: Stratification and Ethnicity in Comparative Perspective*, edited by David Bills. Amsterdam: Elsevier.

———. 2006. "Is Inequality Becoming Less Organized?" Unpublished paper, Cornell University, Department of Sociology.

White, Lynn, and Stacy J. Rogers. 2000. "Economic Circumstances and Family Outcomes: A Review of the 1990s." *Journal of Marriage and the Family* 62(4): 1035.

Wilson, William Julius. 2006. "Social Theory and the Concept of 'Underclass.' " In *Poverty and Inequality*, edited by David B. Grusky and Ravi Kanbur. Stanford, Calif.: Stanford University Press.

PART II

SOCIAL CLASS IN DAILY LIFE: HOW DOES IT WORK?

Chapter 3

Education-Based Meritocracy: The Barriers to Its Realization

JOHN GOLDTHORPE AND MICHELLE JACKSON

T HE IDEA of "meritocracy" originates in sociological fantasy—that is, in Michael Young's remarkable piece of social science fiction, *The Rise of the Meritocracy*, which was first published in 1958.

In this book, the recent history of British society is recounted from the standpoint of 2033. The narrator describes how a meritocracy was created in Britain in the late twentieth century as a work of enlightenment. Merit, defined as "IQ plus effort," was taken to be expressed primarily through educational attainment. A strict relationship was then established between such attainment and the social positions that individuals obtained. The educational elite formed the governmental elite and assumed responsibility for using their exceptional abilities in the best interests of society at large. However, the narrator's main concern is with the increasing discontent generated by the operation of meritocracy. Indeed, he tells how, at the time of his writing, the lower classes, encouraged by certain dissident elements within the elite, are in open rebellion against the meritocratic order. He expresses his confidence that the rebellion will fail, since the lower classes, being deprived of their more able members by several generations of meritocratic social selection, could never again be anything more than "a rabble," and as a loyal member of the elite, he looks forward to verifying this prediction "when I stand next May listening to the speeches from the great rostrum at Peterloo" (Young 1958, 190). But a concluding editorial note explains that at Peterloo the author of the work we have read unfortunately perished in what was apparently the massacre that ended the "rule of the cleverest" in Britain— and without even having had the opportunity to correct his proofs.[1]

93

Michael Young meant his fantasy to serve as a warning. He was disturbed by how postwar governments in Britain were interpreting the purposes of the Education Act of 1944. The 1944 act established "secondary education for all." It was intended to give all children a greater opportunity to realize their academic potential and develop their abilities, whatever form or level these might take. But, Young believed, the act was being increasingly used in a purely instrumental fashion—that is, as a basis for the social selection of children for different, and invidiously distinguished, types of education and, in turn, for different grades of employment with differing levels of reward. And further, he feared that a consequence of such selection in the name of "merit" was the creation of a new kind of social stratification that would be no less extreme and at the same time psychologically yet more punitive than that which already existed. In a supposed meritocracy, those who did badly would tend to be regarded by others—and might even come to regard themselves—as being not merely unfortunate but as in fact having deserved no better.

The Rise of the Meritocracy was a notable success. It attracted wide and generally sympathetic attention. Young's warning seems to have been well understood. It is therefore all the more remarkable to find that, within little more than a decade of the book's publication, the term "meritocracy" was being widely used, in social commentary and debate, in a way that, for Young, must have been highly disturbing—that is, without any ironic or critical connotation but rather in an essentially positive sense. This rapid transvaluation of the concept seems to be attributable primarily to its adoption during the 1970s by a group of American intellectuals who were of what might be described as a "cold-war liberal" persuasion, among whom Daniel Bell (1972, 1973) was perhaps the most influential figure.

For Bell, it was evident that, in the modern world, meritocracy—and indeed, education-based meritocracy—was a functional imperative. "The post-industrial society," he wrote, "is, in its logic, a meritocracy" (Bell 1972, 30; see also Bell 1973, 454). High-level qualifications are essential if individuals are to meet the present-day requirements of professional and managerial employment. Economic and social efficiency demand that key positions should no longer be obtained merely as a result of birth and family. Rather, the prime criterion of social selection has to be educated talent as this is demonstrated through formal qualifications: achievement necessarily replaces ascription.[2]

Further, however, Bell seeks to uphold the idea of meritocracy from a normative as well as a functionalist standpoint. In the new social order, differences in educational and in turn occupational attainment inevitably form the main basis of class stratification. Nevertheless, Bell maintains, it is possible for the inequalities in income and wealth that thus arise to be provided with a moral grounding. Not only do class inequalities serve as incentives for individuals to disclose, develop, and utilize their abilities, but further, under appropriate conditions, high rewards can be regarded as being quite fairly earned or, in other words, as being "merited." What is necessary is to create a broad equality of opportunity for educational attainment through the expansion and reform of educational institutions. Insofar as this is achieved, a meritocracy can be something more than a mere technocracy: it can become what Bell calls a "just" meritocracy. Given equality of educational opportunity, differences in the rewards deriving from subsequent achievements in occupational life can be seen as largely reflecting individuals' application and effort, and thus as having their own inherent legitimacy.

For Bell and other liberals of similar persuasion, the idea of meritocracy was of key importance as a basis for countering egalitarian arguments that were more radical than they were themselves ready to uphold and that, indeed, they viewed as being dangerously "socialist" in inspiration: that is, arguments not just for greater equality of opportunity but also for greater equality in *outcomes,* which, as well as having various forms of populist expression, had also gained a powerful philosophical statement in John Rawls's *A Theory of Justice* (1971). What was found unacceptable in such arguments was that, in their preoccupation with social inequalities among different collectivities, such as social classes, they seriously neglected *individual differences,* and differences not just in natural endowments but also in such respects as readiness to take up opportunities, to work at the acquisition of skills and competencies, to deploy them diligently, and in general to "make an effort" (see Bell 1972, 53–59; 1973, 440–55). The theory of a just meritocracy, it was believed, could serve to underpin the class inequalities that radicals wished to call into question, and it could do so in terms *both* of individuals' differing societal contributions *and* of due rewards for the display of qualities that were ultimately of a moral character.[3]

In other words, then, exactly the ideas that Michael Young had sought to warn against were reasserted: that in modern societies the educational system can, and indeed *must,* serve as the primary determinant of merit, and that an appeal to merit can in turn provide justification for the differentiation of rewards obtained in labor markets and the wider social inequalities that follow.

Subsequently, it should be added, the positive conception of meritocracy that resulted from the American reception of the term moved back to Europe. In the more recent past it has in fact become an important element in the ideology of various center-left political parties, following the lead given in Britain by New Labour. Meritocracy, or more precisely, education-based meritocracy, represents an apparently "progressive" goal that center-left parties can pursue, but one that does not entail any radically redistributive policy measures—that is, measures that could appear threatening to the "median voter" electoral strategies that these parties see as essential to their success.

Significantly, in one of his last publications before his death, Michael Young (2001) returned to the issue of meritocracy and launched a forceful attack on Prime Minister Tony Blair for having "caught on to the word without realising the dangers of what he is advocating." Young again stressed the adverse psychological consequences that a (supposedly) meritocratic social order would bring by encouraging the self-satisfaction of those who have done well for themselves and, worse, the demoralization of those who have not. "It is hard indeed in a society that makes so much of merit to be judged as having none. No underclass has ever been left as morally naked as that." Rather than celebrating meritocracy, Young urged, New Labour would do better to drop the word from its political vocabulary and return to more genuine egalitarian commitments.[4]

All of the foregoing is by way of background. In what follows, our main concern is to examine the idea of education-based meritocracy (henceforward EBM), not primarily from the standpoint of its history or of its philosophical or ideological implications—though related issues will inevitably arise—but rather from the quite different and, we believe, neglected standpoint of its *sociological viability*. All else aside, is the creation of, or even significant progress toward, an EBM a feasible project within the context of modern market-based economies and societies? Or, more generally, is it possible for educational attainment to provide a new moral basis for the class inequalities that are inherent to such economies and societies?

Movement in the direction of an EBM could be said to require three main processes of social change:

1. The association between individuals' social origins and their educational attainment must increasingly reflect *only* their level of demonstrated academic ability as other factors that might prevent the full expression of this ability are removed or offset.

2. The association between individuals' educational attainment and the level of employment they eventually achieve must *strengthen* as qualifications acquired through education become of dominant importance in employers' selection procedures.

3. The association between educational attainment and level of employment must become of *similar* strength for individuals of all social origins as all other considerations in social selection, being irrelevant to the principles of an EBM, are discounted.

On this basis, we will now develop a twofold argument. First, at an empirical level, we will show that these processes of change are not in fact going ahead in the way that those who favor the idea of an EBM would wish to see, *and in large part on account of the powerfully countervailing force of social class*. In particular, we present evidence to indicate that individuals' class origins continue to exert a major influence on their educational attainment even when demonstrated academic ability is controlled; that individuals' educational attainment is not of increasing importance in determining their level of employment and thus the class positions that they eventually attain; and that the part played by education in this respect is not the same for individuals of all class origins.

The concept of class we use is one that has been developed over recent decades within a European theoretical tradition (Goldthorpe 2007, vol. 2; Goldthorpe, with Llewellyn and Payne 1987) and that is now widely applied, via the Erikson-Goldthorpe-Portocarero (EGP or CASMIN) class schema, in European research on educational inequalities and social mobility (Breen 2004; Breen et al. 2007; Erikson and Goldthorpe 1992; Erikson, Goldthorpe, and Portocarero 1979).[5] Class is treated as a form of stratification that arises out of the social relations of economic life, and more specifically, class positions are seen as being determined by the employment relations in which individuals are involved and, in the case of employees, by the differing forms of their employment contracts. It should be noted that class, as thus understood, is conceptually quite distinct from social status (Chan and Goldthorpe 2007), and also from synthetic notions of "socioeconomic status" as widely used in American stratification research. Our empirical findings come chiefly from several different lines of research in which we are ourselves currently engaged, together with various colleagues. This research is restricted to modern British society, but by referring to a range of other work, we are able to provide ample indication that results of the kind we report are by no means specific to Britain.

Second, at a theoretical level, we set out reasons for believing that the general lack of movement toward an EBM is not attributable to difficulties of a merely transient kind that might be expected to weaken simply with the passage of time. Rather, we argue, the barriers that stand in the way of the realization of an EBM are ones that could be overcome only through political intervention of a quite radical kind or that must be accepted as integral to all societies with class structures deriving from the operation of free-market economies.

Social Origins, Academic Ability, and Educational Attainment

If an EBM is in the making, then any association that exists between individuals' social origins and their educational attainment should, to a steadily increasing degree, reflect only their demonstrated academic ability. We examine whether or not such a process of change is in operation in the case of one crucial educational transition that arises in England and Wales. This is the transition that may be made by students, at around age sixteen, to 'A-level' courses—the courses that typically need to be taken to secure university entry—as against the alternatives of leaving full-time education for the labor

Figure 3.1   Regression of Transition to A-Level Work on Academic Performance for Students from Three Different Class Backgrounds, 1974

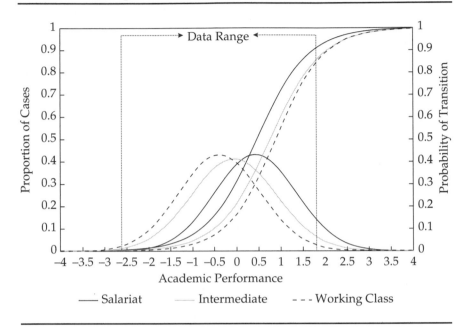

Academic Performance

——— Salariat   ——— Intermediate   - - - Working Class

Source: Authors' calculations from National Child Development Study (NCDS) data set.
Note: N = 4,323.

market or staying on in school or college to take less academic, more vocational courses (or some combination of these two latter possibilities).

In figure 3.1, we show a set of results derived from analyses of the data of the National Child Development Study (NCDS), a cohort study based on all children born in Britain in one week in 1958, who thus reached age sixteen in 1974.[6] This figure may best be understood by looking first at the three bell-shaped distributions. These are the distributions of demonstrated academic ability—that is, the actual academic performance—of students from three different social class backgrounds. They are based on (standardized and normalized) grades obtained in public examinations in English and mathematics taken at around age sixteen.[7] The distributions overlap a good deal, but students of salariat (professional or managerial) background show the highest levels of performance overall, followed by those of intermediate-class background, and then by those of working class background. These distributions can be taken as expressing what may be called "primary" effects in class differentials in educational attainment (see Boudon 1974):

that is, effects that stem from the fact that children of more-advantaged class backgrounds tend on average to do better in school than children from less-advantaged backgrounds on account, one may suppose, of a complex interplay of sociocultural and genetic factors.

We turn now to the three S-shaped curves. These derive from binomial logistic regression analyses in which academic performance—as indicated by the bell curves—is the explanatory variable in relation to the transition (or nontransition) to A-level courses. The S-curves thus show, separately for students from each of the three classes, their estimated probabilities of opting for A-level courses (the vertical axis) at each point on the performance axis (the horizontal axis). What is chiefly notable is that the curve for students of salariat origin always lies above that for students of intermediate-class origin, which in turn always lies above that for students of working class origin.

In other words, in 1974 students of more-advantaged class origins were more likely to take up A-level courses than were those of less-advantaged origins *at all levels of previously demonstrated ability.* The presence of such "secondary" effects in class differentials does therefore indicate that, at this time, class background—through whatever mechanisms—played a significant part in children's educational careers and thus in their eventual educational attainment *over and above* the influence it exerted on their actual performance at any particular stage. That is to say, an EBM was still some way off.

To investigate whether this situation has changed, we can turn to the results of identical analyses we have carried out using data from the 2001 Youth Cohort Study (YCS), a survey commissioned by the Department of Education and Skills and based on a probability sample of all young people in England and Wales who reached age sixteen in that year (see Jarvis, Exley, and Tipping 2005).

As can be seen from figure 3.2, the pattern of results that emerges is essentially the same as that shown in figure 3.1. In figure 3.2, the S-curves start on a steeper upward rise further to the left, because increasing proportions of students from all class backgrounds and at all levels of performance have gone on to A-level work. But the gaps between the curves are little changed. Thus, in 2001, as in 1974, the gap between the curves for students of salariat and working class backgrounds is at its widest—at some fifteen to twenty percentage points—at around, or a little above, the average level of performance.

In the light of these results, there is little reason to suppose that, over the last quarter of the twentieth century, demonstrated academic ability became of any greater importance, relative to class background, in determining the probability of students continuing to A-level courses. And insofar as secondary effects in class differentials in this crucial educational transition are found to persist, a lack of movement toward an EBM must in turn be implied. The ultimate distribution of educational attainment in the popu-

Figure 3.2   Regression of Transition to A-Level Work on Academic Performance for Students from Three Different Class Backgrounds, 2001

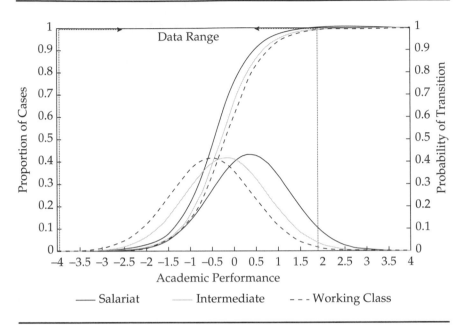

Source: Authors' calculations from Youth Cohort Study (YCS11) data set.
Note: N = 11,683.

lation will *not* reflect *only* academic performance. For students of less-advantaged class origins, the full realization of their academic potential will remain to some degree impeded.

Moreover, where data on differential educational attainment can be presented in the form of figures 3.1 and 3.2, it is in fact possible to move on to at least an approximate quantitative assessment of the relative importance of primary and secondary effects. Using a methodology that we have described in detail elsewhere (Erikson et al. 2005), we estimate (Jackson et al. 2007) that in the transition to A-level work over the period we cover secondary effects account for at least one-quarter, and possibly for up to as much as one-half, of class differentials, as these are conventionally measured by odds ratios.[8] In turn, we can calculate that if, for example, in 2001 an EBM *had* prevailed in England and Wales—that is, if only previously demonstrated ability (as we measure this) and not class background had determined the probability of continuation to A-level work—then even on our lowest estimate of the relative importance of secondary effects, 13 percent more students of intermediate-class background and 20 percent more students of working class background would have made this transition. In other words, not only is movement toward an EBM difficult to discern, but the gap between this ideal and the prevailing social reality remains substantial.

Finally, in this regard it should be noted that secondary effects in themselves are by no means a British peculiarity (for a review of relevant research, see Goldthorpe 2007, vol. 2, ch. 2), and results from several analyses similar to the analysis here have confirmed that their importance is far from negligible (for example, for Sweden, see Erikson 2007; for the Netherlands, see Kloosterman et al. 2007; for other studies, see EQUALSOC, n.d.). It may thus be taken that the barriers to the realization of an EBM to which this body of research points are quite generally present, even though it is possible that societies may differ in the actual extent to which in this regard they fall short of the requirements of an EBM.

Educational Attainment and Level of Employment

If a society is moving toward an EBM, then the association between individuals' educational attainment and the level of employment, and thus class position, that they eventually achieve should be steadily strengthening. To investigate whether a trend of this kind is in evidence in contemporary British society, we turn, first, to results from repeated cross-sectional analyses from the early 1970s through to the early 1990s based on the data set of the General Household Survey (GHS) (see also Jackson, Goldthorpe, and Mills 2005).[9]

Figure 3.3 shows coefficients, from multinomial logistic regression analyses, for the effects of educational qualifications on the chances of individuals being found in different classes of destination, with class of origin controlled. As can be seen, a seven-class version of the EGP schema is used, while educational qualifications are ordered according to an official seven-level classification that ranges from no qualifications to degree-level or equivalent.

The easiest way to understand the graphs presented is as follows. If education had *no* effect on class of destination, then all the points for different classes of destination would be piled up at zero, together with that for the reference class, I&II&IVa, which comprises the professional and managerial salariat plus employers. Correspondingly, the more these points are strung out to the left, the more difference education makes in regard to class of destination. As can be seen, education does indeed make a good deal of difference—the points *are* well strung out, and in a generally unsurprising way. For example, educational attainment clearly counts for more in determining the chances of someone ending up as an unskilled worker in class VIIa or VIIb rather than in the reference class than it does in determining the chances of someone ending up as a routine nonmanual worker in class III rather than in the reference class.

Figure 3.3   **Coefficients for the Partial Effects of Educational Qualifications on the Chances of Men and Women Age Twenty-Five to Fifty-Nine, Employed Full-Time, Being Found in Different Classes of Destination Relative to Being Found in Class I&II&IVa, with Class of Origin Controlled**

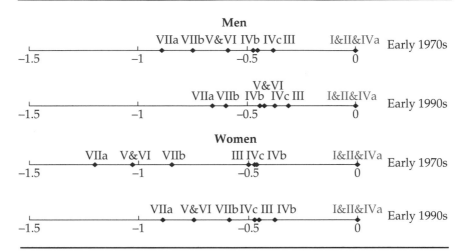

Source: Authors' compilations from General Household Study (GHS) data set.
Note: N = 38,614 men and 41,811 women.
Classes:
I&II&IVa—Professionals, managers, and employers
III—Routine nonmanual employees
IVb—Self-employed workers
IVc—Farmers
V&VI—Supervisors, technicians, and skilled manual workers
VIIa—Nonskilled manual workers
VIIb—Agricultural laborers

However, for present purposes, it is a further feature of the graphs that is of main significance: namely, that the points referring to destination classes are *less* strung out in the graphs for the 1990s than they are in the graphs for the 1970s. In other words, over the period covered the dependence of class position on educational attainment would appear not to be increasing but rather decreasing. Thus, if we were to translate from the log scale of the graphs into multiplicative terms, we would find that across this period the range of the estimated effects of education falls for men, from clearly above to clearly below a twofold effect, and for women from over a threefold effect to less than a two-and-a-half-fold one.

The analyses presented in figure 3.3 run only up to the early 1990s. To bring us more up-to-date and also to allow us to treat the issue that concerns

Figure 3.4   Coefficients for the Partial Effects of Educational Qualifications
on the Chances of Men and Women Employed Full-Time
Being Found in Different Classes of Destination Relative to
Being Found in Class I&II&IVa, with Class of Origin
Controlled

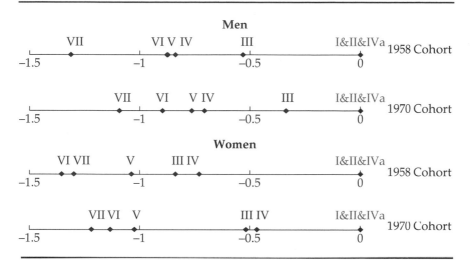

Source: Authors' compilations from National Child Development Study (NCDS) and British
Cohort Study 1970 (BCS70) data set.
Note: N = 6,123 men and 3,349 women.
Classes:
I&II&IVa—Professionals, managers, and employers
III—Routine nonmanual employees
IV—Self-employed workers
V—Supervisors and technicians
VI—Skilled manual workers
VII—Nonskilled manual workers and agricultural laborers

us in a different perspective, we can again turn to the data set of the NCDS,
relating to children born in 1958, taken together with that of a follow-up
study, the British Cohort Study 1970 (BCS70), which is based on all children
born in Britain in one week in that year.

In figure 3.4, we show graphs that have an essentially similar form to
those of figure 3.3—that is, they show coefficients, from multinomial logistic
regressions, for the effects of educational qualifications on individuals' class
positions, with their class of origin being controlled. The same educational
classification is used as in figure 3.3, but a somewhat different version of the
class schema—a six-category version rather than a seven-category one—has
to be applied. And further, since we are here working with birth cohort
rather than cross-sectional data, we are concerned with the class positions

that individuals had achieved at a particular age: age thirty-three for respondents in the NCDS (sweep of 1991) and age thirty for respondents in the BCS70 (sweep of 2000).[10]

Notwithstanding these differences, what is chiefly notable about the graphs of figure 3.4 is that they reveal essentially the same features as do those of figure 3.3. The points for the different destination classes are well strung out to the left, and in a sequence of a kind we might expect, but there is no indication that the level of individuals' educational qualifications is of increasing importance over time for the classes in which they are found. If anything, the contrary conclusion is again suggested. For men at least, the range of the estimated effects of education is clearly *lower* for those in the 1970 cohort than for those in the 1958 cohort—falling, in multiplicative terms, from almost a fourfold to around a threefold effect—and a similar decline for women also shows up, although the difference here falls just short of statistical significance.[11]

Once more, then, our empirical results must lead to the conclusion that in contemporary British society the realization of an EBM is not in fact under way. Whether we analyze repeated cross-sectional or birth cohort data, we find no evidence that the association between educational attainment and class position is strengthening in the way that would follow from the development of an EBM. In turn, then, there is little reason to believe that educational qualifications are becoming increasingly dominant in processes of social selection within labor markets and production units. In their personnel policies, employers appear not to be acting as the unswerving agents of an EBM. They are not, it seems, progressively increasing the weight that they give to the formal qualifications of employees, or potential employees, and to the exclusion of their other attributes.

Moreover, we would add that, although the results we report may strike some readers as counterintuitive and perhaps lead them to suspect that, if valid, they apply only to Britain, there are in fact no good grounds for taking such a view. Results of a broadly similar kind to those presented here—that is, results indicating a declining or at least an unchanging association between education and class position attained—have of late been reported for most other advanced societies for which relevant analyses have been undertaken (for European societies, see Breen and Luijkx 2004).

Educational Attainment and Level of Employment Across Social Origins

We come finally to the question of the strength of the association between educational attainment and level of employment for individuals of differing social origins. The results presented in the previous section show that, for individuals of all class origins, the association between education and level of employment, as indicated by class position, has certainly not strengthened over recent decades. But now we must ask whether this association differs in its strength *across* class origins. In an EBM, it should obviously not do so. Individuals' education should determine their class destinations to the same (quite dominant) extent, whatever their class origins might be. Qualifications should have the same "payoff" for individuals of all class origins alike.

An issue that arises in this regard is that of whether, in the three-way relationship between class origins, educational attainment, and class destinations, there is an interaction effect. In fact, such an effect has been shown for many national cases through loglinear analyses of appropriate three-way contingency tables. However, this effect has then usually been interpreted in a way that, for present purposes at least, is not the most pertinent.

Figure 3.5 shows the three-way relationship in question, and the interpretation of the interaction effect so far most commonly given is that indicated by arrow A: that is, the strength of the origin-destination (OD) association is taken to vary with level of education (E). And given the interaction parameters that are typically returned, it can then further be said that the origin-destination association tends to be *weaker* the *higher* the level of education attained. For example, Michael Hout (1988) has reported that among American university graduates, the association between origins and destinations completely disappears: all of the association between O and D occurs at lower educational levels (for France, see Vallet 2004; for Sweden, see Breen and Jonsson 2007). The idea behind this interpretation of the OED interaction is that those individuals who attain higher levels of education are thus able to enter segments of the labor market in which, because of the technical demands of the work involved, selection does tend to be predominantly meritocratic—that is, education-based—and social background, in itself, counts for little.

However, an alternative interpretation can be suggested. Following arrow B in figure 3.5, we might say that the strength of the ED association varies with O. And if this interpretation is taken, then the interaction parameters typically returned would allow us to say that the association between education and class of destination tends to be *weaker* the *more advantaged* the class of origin. Here the underlying idea is the following. For children from less-advantaged backgrounds, whether or not they do well educationally is likely to be quite crucial for their chances of upward mobility, but for children from more-advantaged backgrounds, other resources may be available to help them maintain their parents' position even if their educational attainment is only modest (see Goldthorpe 2007, vol. 2, ch. 7).[12]

Furthermore, if we move from the loglinear modeling of contingency tables to a logistic regression approach, then conditioning on O rather than

Figure 3.5   Two Interpretations of the Interaction Effect in the OED Relationship

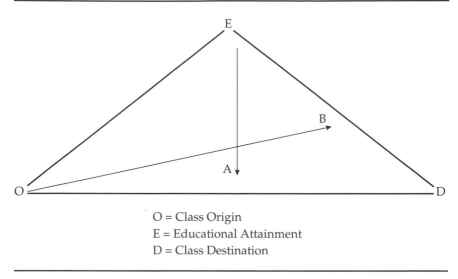

O = Class Origin
E = Educational Attainment
D = Class Destination

Source: Authors' compilation.

on E would seem the more natural way of treating the interaction (see Cox 1984). D is the dependent variable, and O and E are the explanatory variables, with O being treated as an "intrinsic" variable that is given (individuals cannot change their class origins) and E as the "treatment" variable on which individuals could in principle take a different value to that they actually have. (Individuals' educational attainment could be different depending on opportunities or choice.) So we then ask how the effect of E on D varies across different levels of O.

We have followed such a regression approach, using once more the General Household Survey data set—which gives us the advantage of relatively large numbers—in order to investigate the part played by education in access to the professional and managerial salariat (rather than the non-salariat, excluding the self-employed) in Britain in the mid-1970s and during the period 1989 to 1992. We find, first of all, that having a high-level qualification—a degree or the equivalent—was in fact somewhat *less* predictive of access to the salariat by the 1990s than it was in the 1970s: in other words, we confirm our finding from our previous use of the GHS and the two birth cohort studies of a probably declining effect of education on class position attained. Second, however, we also find that, during both time periods, the importance for access to the salariat of having a degree was *less* for individuals who were born into the salariat than it was for individuals who originated outside the salariat. In other words, education is more important

Figure 3.6   **Estimated Probabilities of Entering the Salariat (Rather Than the Nonsalariat, Excluding the Self-Employed) for Individuals of Differing Levels of Qualification and Class Origins**

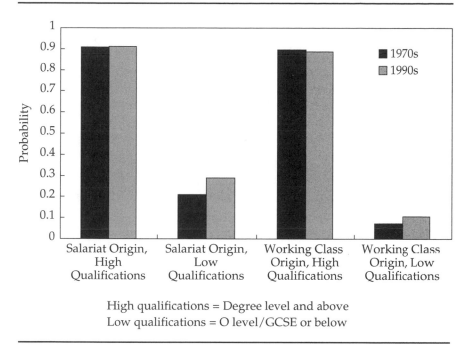

High qualifications = Degree level and above
Low qualifications = O level/GCSE or below

Source: Authors' compilation from General Household Surveys (GHS) data set.
Note: N = 71,074.

for intergenerational *upward mobility into* the salariat than it is for intergenerational *immobility within* the salariat.

In figure 3.6, we show some probabilities estimated under our logistic regression models when all control variables are held constant at their mean values.[13] It can be seen that individuals with degree-level qualifications have around a 90 percent chance of entering the salariat, regardless of whether they are of salariat origin or not, and that there is little difference in this respect between the 1970s and the 1990s. However, for individuals with relatively low educational attainment—those with no more than lower secondary qualifications—*their* chances of gaining access to the salariat do clearly differ according to their class origins. And it is further revealed that while poorly qualified individuals of salariat origin still had almost a 20 percent chance of being themselves found in the salariat in the 1970s, this rose to as much as a 35 percent chance in the 1990s.[14]

Once more, then, insofar as any change is apparent, it is clearly not in the direction of an EBM. Upward mobility into the salariat does appear to be largely mediated through high-level qualifications, according to the principles of an EBM. But education is less important in maintaining inter-generational stability within the salariat—or, we might say, low educational attainment does not bring about the amount of *downward* mobility out of the salariat that an EBM would require. And at least up to the 1990s, this "deficit" in downward mobility would appear, if anything, to have been increasing.

Alternative Explanations of the Empirical Findings

In the foregoing, we have sought to show empirically that three processes of change essential to the creation of an EBM are not in fact evident in present-day Britain—nor, it would seem, in most other advanced societies. By way of conclusion, we turn to the question of how, in general terms, this situation is to be explained.

One possible line of argument would be to the effect that progress toward EBMs is no more than stalled. Barriers may stand in the way of their realization, but these are ones of a largely contingent kind that sooner or later will be overcome—by the fact that, as Bell would have it, modern, postindustrial societies are meritocracies in their functional logic. An opposing line of argument, however, would regard the barriers to EBMs as being of a more deeply rooted kind: that is, ones that could be overcome only by forceful political intervention or, indeed, ones that have to be regarded as integral to any society with a market economy and in turn a class structure. Consequently, these barriers cannot be expected to disappear simply with the passage of time. In what follows we try to spell out how these two rival arguments might be developed in relation to each of the three processes of change we have identified as crucial to the development of an EBM and to indicate why we believe that it is the second explanatory approach that is in general the more convincing.

To begin with social origins, academic ability and educational attainment, and, more specifically, the problem of persisting secondary effects in class differentials in such attainment, an argument might run on the following lines. The failure of students from less-advantaged backgrounds—and the failure of working class students especially—to take up opportunities for translating their ability into qualifications in the same way as do students from more-advantaged backgrounds reflects a low level of aspirations and, related to this, an inadequate appreciation of the economic returns that education brings. But, the argument would continue, such difficulties are to be seen as only transient ones. In time—through, say, various "demonstration effects"—these students will form more rational expectations of the returns to education, and their educational aspirations will thus rise.[15]

However, in contrast to this, secondary effects could in fact be seen as the outcome of action that is already of a quite rational kind. For students from less-advantaged backgrounds, taking up more ambitious educational options typically entails *a greater degree of risk*, in terms of potential costs and benefits, than it does for students from more-advantaged backgrounds. It is therefore entirely rational for, say, working class students to require a relatively high probability of success as a condition for pursuing more ambitious options, and their previous academic performance is the obvious indicator of this probability (for elaboration of this argument, see Breen and Goldthorpe 1997; Breen and Yaish 2006; Goldthorpe 1996; for an evaluation of related evidence, see Goldthorpe 2007, vol. 2, ch. 4). It is in this way that secondary effects are chiefly to be explained, and the further implication then is that eliminating such effects will call for something more fundamental than change simply at the level of expectations and aspirations. It will be necessary, through appropriate policy measures, to reduce the inequalities in class conditions—in economic security, stability, and prospects— that create differential risk for young people in exploiting educational opportunities up to the full limits of their ability.[16] In other words, it will be necessary to return to what Michael Young saw as more genuine egalitarian commitments than those embodied in the idea of meritocracy, and in opposition to which, as we have noted, the "positive" version of meritocracy was developed.[17]

Second, as regards the apparently persisting tendency for employers to attach importance to attributes of employees or potential employees other than their educational qualifications, a functionalist position might be developed on such lines as these. For employers to act in ways that ignore the increasing requirement for formally warranted knowledge and skills in a modern economy has to be understood as merely a reflection of "traditional" attitudes or of various prejudices or biases on their part, and of a kind that cannot be indefinitely sustained. Given the rational and highly competitive character of modern economic life, employers who persist in applying non-meritocratic criteria in their personnel policies are unlikely to flourish or indeed survive.

In this case, the counterargument would turn on two main points. First, as forcefully maintained by Friedrich Hayek (1960, 1976), in a free-market economy it must rest with employers, and only with employers, to determine what counts as merit—or at least as productive value—in the case of their employees.[18] And second, in present-day economies employers may often in fact have good reasons for *not always* giving formal qualifications an overriding role in their selection procedures.

In earlier work (Jackson, Goldthorpe, and Mills 2005), we have drawn on content analyses of several thousand job advertisements (see also Jackson 2002, 2007) in order to show that the attributes of individuals to which employers attach greatest weight do indeed vary, widely but quite intelligibly, with the type of employment for which they are recruiting. And we have also shown (in further analyses of GHS data) that the more important qualifications are *in general* for access to a particular class of destination, the more variation there is in the importance of qualifications for access to different occupational subgroups *within* that class. Thus, while entry into the salariat does on average call for higher levels of qualification than entry into other classes, professional positions within the salariat are clearly more demanding of such qualifications than are managerial positions, and managerial positions in production and transport are more demanding than those in sales and personal services. There would, moreover, seem little reason for questioning the judgment that employers seemingly make that in certain positions cognitive or technical abilities of the kind most readily certified by formal qualifications are likely to be of less relevance—at least above some threshold level—than are various other attributes: for example, social and communication skills, general savoir faire, and a range of personal characteristics, whether of a physical, psychological, or subcultural kind, that involve "looking good and sounding right" (see Warhurst and Nickson 2001).

Moreover, insofar as employers do choose to focus on other attributes of employees or potential employees aside from their formal qualifications, this is not a tendency that would appear open to "correction" via public policy aimed at the promotion of an EBM. To return to Hayek's point, it is difficult in a liberal-democratic society to see not only how the imposition of any single criterion of merit, such as educational attainment, could be justified, but how it could in any event be achieved. "Merit," at least in the context of labor markets and production units, can be no more than whatever particular employers may deem it to be.[19]

Finally, then, as regards the greater part played by education in upward mobility into the salariat than in maintaining immobility within this class, it might once again be held that, even if this effect appears stable for the moment, it is still a residue of an earlier period. At one time, the argument would go, more-advantaged families could fairly readily protect their educationally less able or undermotivated children against any radical déclassement through such nonmeritocratic means as nepotism, patronage, "contacts," and so on, but in the context of modern, "knowledge-intensive" economies such strategies are outmoded and must eventually lose their effectiveness.

However, the alternative view here follows directly from what we have already said. As shown in figure 3.6, obtaining high-level qualifications is indeed the surest way for children of salariat origins to maintain their parents' position. But as also shown in figure 3.6, even if these children do not do well educationally, they still have some chances—far better than those of children of working class origins—of entering the salariat themselves. And this, we would suggest, is because they are more likely to have other attributes that are of productive value—in particular, the "soft skills" and personal characteristics that employers are looking for in the kinds of work that have more "high-touch" than "high-tech" requirements. In other words, in this respect too, as well as that of educational attainment, the children of the salariat have a clear "edge" over the children of the working class. And it needs further to be recognized that despite all the talk of the knowledge-intensiveness of modern economies, it is in fact in the service sector, especially the personal services sector, rather than the science-based sector that the growth of employment at all levels tends at the present time to be strongest. Modern economies thus provide widening rather than narrowing opportunities for individuals who can meet employers' requirements for attributes of a kind less likely to have been learned in schools and colleges than acquired simply through socialization within appropriate family, community, and peer-group contexts.[20]

Moreover, it is difficult, again, to see on what basis any change in this situation might be sought or indeed proposed. The question of whether attributes acquired outside of education can be truly regarded as reflecting "merit" is not likely to be a matter of much concern to employers. And insofar as educationally underachieving children from advantaged class backgrounds are still protected against downward mobility by their general socialization, this does not involve practices, whether on the part of these children or their parents, that could be considered in any sense illegitimate.

Conclusions

The idea of education-based meritocracy may well continue to have appeal for some social commentators and party ideologues, although it would now appear to be attracting increasing criticism from those who, like Michael Young himself, find it philosophically problematic and morally questionable (see especially Barry 2005). But, however controversies over meritocracy may develop at a normative level, there is, we would maintain, little empirical basis for believing that modern societies are being transformed into EBMs, or indeed are likely to be so transformed. Some movement toward a more genuine equality of educational opportunity might be achieved that would be consistent with the realization of an EBM—although it would be equally consistent with the realization of more radical egalitarian principles under which education would be viewed in more than a merely instrumental light. And the kinds of policy intervention necessary to eliminate even secondary effects in class differentials in educational attainment—let alone those necessary to tackle the deeper problem of primary effects—would be likely to take proponents of an EBM precisely in the "socialist" direction they so clearly wish to avoid.

Furthermore, even if educational attainment did come more closely to reflect academic potential as well as demonstrated ability, other barriers to the emergence of an EBM would remain, and these are barriers that would appear to lie beyond the reach of public policy in any form, at least within the context of free-market liberal democracies. In particular, the crucial role that has to be given to employers, rather than to governments and the state, in deciding what importance should attach to educational attainment in processes of social selection in labor markets and production units means that such selection is in fact likely to proceed according to a wide variety of criteria. In turn, it is likely that some of these criteria will be ones that could not be very plausibly linked to individual merit under any description, such as those, in the case we have taken, that favor attributes that are far less the result of ability and effort than of the happenstance of socialization, but that are nonetheless of real productive value to employers in certain economic sectors.

Our main conclusion, then, is that the idea of an EBM is likely to remain in large part merely utopian or dystopian, according to sociopolitical taste. For those who share in the beliefs and values that led Michael Young, half a century ago, to expose the psychological dangers of the idea of meritocracy in his brilliant fantasy, this conclusion will be a welcome one—even though they will be aware that many dangers remain from continued misguided attempts to pursue meritocracy. However, a further implication is that for those who would wish to see prevailing economic and social inequalities provided with some form of moral grounding, the efforts of the American liberals of the 1970s must be recognized as steadily losing in persuasive force. If such inequalities are to be given some further legitimation than that supplied in classical liberalism—that is, as the often arbitrary and essentially amoral consequences of acceptance of the overriding value of liberty—then some other basis than that of educationally achieved merit will need to be discovered.

We are grateful to Jane Roberts for help in data preparation and to Gunn Birkelund, Robert Erikson, David Grusky, Sandy Jencks, and participants in the EQUALSOC conference at Mannheim, December 2005, for useful comments. While this chapter was being prepared, Michelle Jackson held an Economic and Social Research Council (ESRC) research fellowship within the "Understanding Population Trends and Processes" research program.

Notes

1.   Readers unfamiliar with the details of British social history may wish to know that the original "Peterloo" massacre occurred on August 16, 1819—four years after the battle of Waterloo—when a crowd of over fifty thousand, gathered at St. Peter's Fields, Manchester, to hear radical speakers campaigning for universal manhood suffrage and the repeal of the Corn Laws, was charged by cavalry of the local militia. Eleven people were killed and over four hundred injured.

2. In arguing thus, Bell was to a large extent simply attaching the idea of "meritocracy" to lines of thinking already quite current in American sociology; see, for example, Parsons (1960, chs. 3, 4; 1967, chs. 4, 15) and Blau and Duncan (1967, ch. 12).

3. Some tension may, however, be observed in Bell's position in that at certain points (for example, Bell 1973, 453) he stresses the importance of individual demonstrations of competence in occupational roles as against mere "credentialism," while in general still maintaining that educational institutions, and especially the universities, are the key institutions of postindustrial societies. It is also important to note that Bell supposes that the classical liberal view of the market "as the arbiter of differential reward, based on scarcity or demand," is now becoming outmoded "as economic decisions become politicized and the market replaced by social decisions"—and that, as a consequence, economic inequality will decrease (451). In this, as in other respects, Bell's "venture in social forecasting" was not very successful.

4. It may also be noted that in an American edition of *The Rise of the Meritocracy*, Young (1994) took the opportunity in his preface to note and deplore American misperceptions of the point of the book; see also Briggs (2001).

5. It is a feature of the class schema that it can be used in different, more or less elaborated, versions depending on the analytical task at hand and also depending, more importantly perhaps, on the quantity and quality of the data available. As will be seen, in the analyses that follow several different versions are used. In each case, descriptive class labels are provided. Readers wishing for further information on the construction of the classes of the schema and for the results of various validation exercises may consult the sources cited in the text.

6. For further details on this research, see Jackson et al. (2007). For information on the NCDS and other British cohort studies, see the website of the Centre for Longitudinal Studies, http://www.cls.ioe.ac.uk.

7. We concentrate on these grades because, while students can, and do, take examinations in widely differing numbers and varieties of subjects, almost all take English and mathematics. Moreover, grades achieved in these subjects can be shown to correlate quite highly with those achieved overall. We here work with the most basic, three-class version of the EGP schema in order to maintain adequate numbers within each class.

8. Our methodology exploits the fact that normal and logistic curves of the kinds used in figures 3.1 and 3.2 to show class-specific levels of academic performance and transition propensities (given performance) can be (numerically) integrated. This allows us to make counterfactual analyses, substituting the performance or transition curve of one class for that of another, which in turn provides a basis on which the relative importance of primary and secondary effects can be determined, although, for reasons we set out, with some important qualifications.

9. These analyses cannot be continued to a later date since, unfortunately, after 1992 the GHS no longer collected any information on respondents' social origins.

10. It is usually supposed in mobility research that by their early thirties men have reached a stage of "occupational maturity," following which the probability of further change in occupation of a kind that would also imply a change in class position falls off rather sharply. But this age range is more problematic in the case of women, since many are likely to be in the stage of active motherhood, at which time, if not out of the labor market, they may take employment at a lower level than that in which they were previously engaged.

11. It may be noted that the effects of education appear generally stronger in figure 3.4 than in figure 3.3. This is likely to result in part from the more restricted reference category used in figure 3.4—the salariat rather than the salariat plus employers. But, further, the cross-sectional data on which figure 3.3 is based cover many individuals who were born in the earlier decades of the twentieth century, and we would think it very probable that educational attainment did play a greater part in determining the class positions of those born in the second half of the century, if only because of the previously very low variance in such attainment. Recognition of this point does not, however, detract from our argument that there is little evidence of a *continuing* increase, up to the present, in the strength of the association between educational qualifications and class position.

12. Low ED associations tend also to arise with children of the petty bourgeoisie— small employers and self-employed workers—as well as with those of the salariat, since in this case there is the possibility of the direct intergenerational transmission of the family business or of capital deriving from it. It should be added here that the two interpretations of the OED interaction are not incompatible—both are indeed based on the same interaction parameters— and so it is not surprising to find that some authors shift between them. For example, Hout (1988, 1388) at one point notes that "the log-odds on a higher-status destination versus a lower-status one rise sharply with origin status among workers who lack a college degree."

13. The full results from the regression models from which the probabilities shown in figure 3.6 derive are available from the authors on request.

14. This change is driven by the generally weakening effect of education on class destinations, not by a strengthening of the main effects of class origin or of the interaction term.

15. Arguments on these lines are advanced in Britain by New Labour politicians and some of their economic advisers when, for example, they seek to downplay the effects of rising costs on the readiness of (qualified) students of working class background to enter university.

16. We recognize the possibility that, in different educational systems, secondary effects may be created in other ways that would call for different policy responses: for example, in the American case (see Lareau and Weininger, this volume), through more-advantaged parents interfering more often and more forcefully with teachers and administrators than less-advantaged parents are able or ready to do in order to influence decisions affecting their children.

17. And of course from this same egalitarian standpoint measures designed to reduce primary effects too—such as high-quality preschool programs for

children from disadvantaged backgrounds—would likewise be given priority over any celebration of meritocracy (see Barry 2005, pt. 3).

18. American liberals, it should be noted, were greatly perturbed by Hayek's critique of meritocracy in that it was made not from a standpoint that could be denigrated as "socialist" but rather from that of classic European liberalism. See, for example, the despairing essay of Irving Kristol (1970) and Hayek's ruthlessly honest reply (Hayek 1976, 73–74).

19. The societies that have perhaps come closest to being EBMs were the postwar communist societies of Eastern and Central Europe that operated "command" economies and whose governments were able, at least in principle, to closely coordinate educational and manpower policy. But how functionally efficient this system was is, of course, open to serious question, and exceptions to meritocracy in these societies, most obviously in the case of children of the nomenklatura, must also be noted.

20. More detailed analyses that we have undertaken show that children of salariat origin with low educational qualifications who nonetheless gain access to the salariat are disproportionately found, by around a factor of two, in managerial positions in services. Those children of working class origin with low qualifications who enter the salariat are also disproportionately found in these same positions to a similar degree but, as we know from figure 3.6, constitute a far smaller minority.

References

Barry, Brian. 2005. *Why Social Justice Matters.* Cambridge: Polity Press.

Bell, Daniel. 1972. "On Meritocracy and Inequality." *The Public Interest* 29: 29–68.

———. 1973. *The Coming of Postindustrial Society.* New York: Basic Books.

Blau, Peter M., and Otis Dudley Duncan. 1967. *The American Occupational Structure.* New York: Wiley & Sons.

Boudon, Raymond. 1974. *Education, Opportunity, and Social Inequality.* New York: Wiley & Sons.

Breen, Richard, editor. 2004. *Social Mobility in Europe.* Oxford: Oxford University Press.

Breen, Richard, and John H. Goldthorpe. 1997. "Explaining Educational Differentials: Towards a Formal Rational Action Theory." *Rationality and Society* 9(3): 275–305.

Breen, Richard, and Jan O. Jonsson. 2007. "Explaining Change in Social Fluidity: Educational Equalization and Educational Expansion in Twentieth-Century Sweden." *American Journal of Sociology* 112(May): 1775–810.

Breen, Richard, and Ruud Luijkx. 2004. "Conclusions." In *Social Mobility in Europe,* edited by Richard Breen. Oxford: Oxford University Press.

Breen, Richard, and Meir Yaish. 2006. "Testing the Breen-Goldthorpe Model of Educational Decision-Making." In *Mobility and Inequality: Frontiers of Research in Sociology and Economics,* edited by Stephen L. Morgan, David B. Grusky, and Gary S. Fields. Stanford, Calif.: Stanford University Press.

Breen, Richard, Ruud Luijkx, Walter Muller, and Reinhard Pollak. 2007. "Long-Term Trends in Educational Inequality in Europe: Class Inequalities and Gender." Paper presented to the Brno meeting of ISA Research Committee 28 (Social Stratification and Mobility), May 24–27, 2007.

Briggs, Asa. 2001. *Michael Young, Social Entrepreneur.* Basingstoke, UK: Palgrave.

Chan, Tak Wing, and John H. Goldthorpe. 2007. "Class and Status: The Conceptual Distinction and Its Empirical Relevance." *American Sociological Review* 72(4): 512–32.

Cox, David R. 1984. "Interaction." *International Statistical Review* 52(1): 1–31.

EQUALSOC, EU Framework 6 Network of Excellence. n.d. "Primary and Secondary Effects in Educational Attainment in Five European Countries." Accessed at http://users.ox.ac.uk/~trin0292/index.htm.

Erikson, Robert. 2007. "Social Selection in Stockholm Schools: Primary and Secondary Effects on the Transition to Upper Secondary Education." In *From Origin to Destination: Trends and Mechanisms in Social Stratification Research*, edited by Stefani Scherer, Reinhard Pollak, Gunnar Otte, and Markus Gangl. Frankfurt am Main and New York: Campus.

Erikson, Robert, and John H. Goldthorpe. 1992. *The Constant Flux: A Study of Class Mobility in Industrial Societies.* Oxford: Clarendon Press.

Erikson, Robert, John H. Goldthorpe, and Lucienne Portocarero. 1979. "Intergenerational Class Mobility in Three Western European Societies: England, France, and Sweden." *British Journal of Sociology* 30(4): 415–41.

Erikson, Robert, John H. Goldthorpe, Michelle Jackson, Meir Yaish, and David R. Cox. 2005. "On Class Differentials in Educational Attainment." *Proceedings of the National Academy of Sciences* 102: 9730–33.

Goldthorpe, John H. 1996. "Class Analysis and the Reorientation of Class Theory: The Case of Persisting Differentials in Educational Attainment." *British Journal of Sociology* 47(3): 481–505.

———. 2007. *On Sociology*, 2nd ed., 2 vols. Stanford, Calif.: Stanford University Press.

Goldthorpe, John H., with Catriona Llewellyn and Clive Payne. 1987. *Social Mobility and Class Structure in Modern Britain*, 2nd ed. Oxford: Clarendon Press.

Hayek, Friedrich. 1960. *The Constitution of Liberty.* London: Routledge.

———. 1976. *Law, Legislation, and Liberty*, 3 vols. London: Routledge.

Hout, Michael. 1988. "More Universalism, Less Structural Mobility: The American Occupational Structure in the 1980s." *American Journal of Sociology* 93(6): 1358–400.

Jackson, Michelle. 2002. "Explaining Class Mobility: Meritocracy, Education, and Employers." Ph.D. thesis, University of Oxford.

———. 2007. "How Far Merit Selection? Social Stratification and the Labour Market." *British Journal of Sociology* 58(3): 367–90.

Jackson, Michelle, John H. Goldthorpe, and Colin Mills. 2005. "Education, Employers, and Class Mobility." *Research in Social Stratification and Mobility* 23: 3–34.

Jackson, Michelle, Robert Erikson, John H. Goldthorpe, and Meir Yaish. 2007. "Primary and Secondary Effects in Class Differentials in Educational Attainment: The Transition to A-Level Courses in England and Wales." *Acta Sociologica* 50(3): 211–29.

Jarvis, Lindsey, Sonia Exley, and Sarah Tipping. 2005. *Youth Cohort Study: Survey of Sixteen-Year-Olds (Cohort 11, Sweep 1): Technical Report.* London: Department for Education and Skills.

Kloosterman, Rianne, Paul de Graaf, Stijn Ruiter, and Gerbert Kraaykamp. 2007. "Parental Education and the Transition to Higher Secondary Education: A Comparison of Primary and Secondary Effects (for Five Cohorts of Dutch Pupils, 1965–1999)." Paper presented to the Brno meeting of ISA Research Committee 28 (Social Stratification and Mobility), May 24–27, 2007.

Kristol, Irving. 1970. "When Virtue Loses All Her Loveliness: Some Reflections on Capitalism and 'The Free Society.' " *The Public Interest* 21: 3–15.

Parsons, Talcott. 1960. *Structure and Process in Modern Societies.* Glencoe, Ill.: Free Press.

———. 1967. *Sociological Theory and Modern Society.* New York: Free Press.

Rawls, John. 1971. *A Theory of Justice.* Cambridge, Mass.: Harvard University Press.

Vallet, Louis-André. 2004. "Change in Intergenerational Mobility in France from the 1970s to the 1990s and Its Explanation: An Analysis Following the CASMIN Approach." In *Social Mobility in Europe,* edited by Richard Breen. Oxford: Oxford University Press.

Warhurst, Chris, and Dennis Nickson. 2001. *Looking Good, Sounding Right: Style Counseling in the New Economy.* London: Industrial Society.

Young, Michael. 1958. *The Rise of the Meritocracy.* Harmondsworth, UK: Penguin.

———. 1994. "Preface." In *The Rise of the Meritocracy* (U.S. edition). New York: Transaction Books.

———. 2001. "Down with Meritocracy." *The Guardian,* June 29, 2001. Accessed at http://www.guardian.co.uk/politics/2001/jun/29/comment.

Chapter 4

Class and the Transition to Adulthood

ANNETTE LAREAU AND ELLIOT B. WEININGER

A MERICANS TEND to believe that schools are the best option for overcoming patterns of social inequity: education is a pathway for social mobility. Social scientific research, however, has demonstrated repeatedly that this view of education as a simple leveler of social privilege is unsustainable. For example, studies have established that college access, enrollment, and graduation are linked to various dimensions of stratification, including social class and race.[1] The mechanisms that drive these associations remain poorly understood, however. The search for better conceptual and empirical tools for explaining the relationship between education and inequality has led researchers to construct models that attempt to formalize the decisions faced by adolescents at different stages of their educational trajectories (see, for example, Breen and Goldthorpe 1997; Morgan 2005). These studies focus on the key points at which individuals commit to one of multiple possible educational paths. The transition from secondary schooling to higher education—that is, from high school to college—is frequently modeled. Researchers suggest that students formulate the decisions involved in this transition by weighing such factors as their ability to succeed in college, the potential labor market payoffs to success, and their capacity to make the necessary financial investment in higher education and absorb the associated opportunity costs. In many of these studies, the models typically assume this decisionmaking to be a rational process (at least in the aggregate) and an *individualistic* one. Information is collected and evaluated, and then deliberate choices are made by what are assumed to be isolated high school students.[2]

118

Faced with such models, it is necessary to ask how closely these assumptions approximate real-life conditions. In particular, it is important to examine whether and how students gain access to the concrete, detailed information that would enable them to transform the aspiration to attend college into a reality.[3] Additionally, it is necessary to take account of the role that parents—as the most proximate source of such information—play in the process. Journalistic reports document a growing level of parental involvement in all facets of children's education, even at the college level (where we now find references to "helicopter parents," who continually hover above their children [Will 2005]). In turn, parental involvement in education has been documented to be linked to parents' social class position (Lareau 2000; Reay 1998). Thus, there is reason to suspect that the confluence of social class and family life may have an impact on the decisionmaking process itself.[4]

In this chapter, we draw on follow-up interviews with the families originally analyzed in Annette Lareau's book *Unequal Childhoods* (2003) to evaluate how transition decisions—and especially, the choice of whether to attend college after high school—are actually made. These data enable us to examine the views and behaviors of a set of families after the children have exited high school and to assess these recent reports in light of family members' earlier views and behaviors. We use the data to address in detail the question of who makes educational decisions and how the process unfolds. Our focus is on the involvement of key adults. We suggest the following general points:

- The college application process is best conceptualized as a family affair, rather than an individual affair, for some (but not all) students. In our small sample, we found considerable social class differences in the direct involvement of "significant others" in the process of identifying and selecting a future path. In the course of developing their educational plans and making educational decisions, working class and poor students tended to rely on assistance from teachers and guidance counselors; their parents viewed the provision of this kind of help as a responsibility of "the school." By contrast, for middle class students, the process was typically a familial one: it was the student and parents together who mapped alternative courses of action and then selected among them. Although counselors and teachers (along with tutors and other professionals) played a part, the role of middle class parents, and especially mothers, was substantial. Parents frequently were deeply involved in organizing college visits, reading ancillary materials, helping with the college essay, and monitoring the entire process.

- College aspirations, relatively high grades, boundless energy, and determination were insufficient in some instances to produce an acceptance at a local college. Rather, a thorough understanding of the higher education system, and particularly the status hierarchy, was a crucial factor in structuring the application process. We present evidence of one student who desperately aspired to attend college but lacked sufficient informal information to negotiate central aspects of the application process. Despite a considerable investment of time and energy, she failed to be accepted by a four-year college. Hence, parents' informal knowledge of the educational system, which is clearly higher in middle class families, as well as parents' conceptions of their proper role in schooling, appeared to be key.

- The contrasting roles of parents in the transition to college are highly consistent with the findings presented in *Unequal Childhoods*, particularly the claim that there are class-specific cultural orientations to child rearing. Differences in parental involvement in the transition out of high school appear to be an extension of the child rearing styles used when the children were much younger. Thus, middle class parents' heavy participation reflects an orientation to "concerted cultivation"—that is, to the active fostering of children's talents and skills. Working class and poor parents' lesser involvement reflects an orientation to the "accomplishment of natural growth"—that is, to the proposition that children must be cared for and protected, but that they will then develop and thrive spontaneously. Since the transition to college is a complex process with many steps, and since young people can benefit from the guidance and assistance of adults, middle class youth whose parents helped to customize the process with countless hours of involvement had significant advantages over equally devoted parents in working class and poor families who turned over responsibility for education to the school. Put differently, informal cultural knowledge of the higher education system, dispositions to intervene in schooling, and other cultural resources could, when shrewdly activated, become forms of cultural capital for some of the youth in our study. In this respect, our findings parallel those of Goldthorpe and Jackson (this volume) on the salience of informal knowledge, habits, and styles of self-presentation for various outcomes.

We therefore argue that deep-seated, relatively stable, class-specific child rearing dispositions persist over the course of children's early lives, resulting in a distinct pattern of relations between families and educational institutions. These differences are significant. Key educational decisions—and in particular, the question of higher education—entail substantial work: information must be gathered and evaluated on course-taking options, students' likelihood of success, college enrollment requirements, and the available options if students encounter difficulties in educational institutions. The informal cultural knowledge of middle class parents, as well as middle class parents' conception of their role in child rearing, can sometimes become forms of advantages, or forms of cultural capital, in the stratification system. By contrast, parents of working class and poor students may fervently want their children to experience educational success, but their relative lack of detailed knowledge of educational institutions, as well as their role in child rearing and in supervising schooling, can lead family members to turn responsibility for the college-choice process over to the student and the school. Thus, above and beyond questions of financial resources and children's "academic ability," the stratification system on which higher education is based is one in which individuals have unequal levels of the key cultural resources that facilitate the development of a customized educational career. Hence, the *process* through which young people decide about their educational futures—particularly the transformation of hopes and dreams of educational success into high school persistence and college applications—may be a source of ongoing inequality.

In what follows, we first describe the data sets on which our analysis is based and recount the core premise of *Unequal Childhoods.* Then, to provide a sense of the time, energy, expense, and expertise involved in making decisions about postsecondary education, we briefly describe the typical steps in the college application process. Next, we present a detailed comparison of the college transitions made by Tara Carroll, a girl from a poor family, and Stacey Marshall, a middle class girl; this comparison encapsulates many of the relevant differences we found. We supplement this comparison with discussions of the transitions out of high school made by each of the children from *Unequal Childhoods.* We conclude with some thoughts on the implications of the participating families' experiences for our understanding of educational decisionmaking in general, and of the transition to college in particular.

Our study has formidable limitations. Our data only provide the perspectives of parents, siblings, and young adults; we do not have any school observations or interviews with school officials. This omission is significant: we cannot independently confirm or assess the portraits drawn by family members or clarify key events. In addition, there is ample literature to suggest that school officials are a critical part of the college transition process and that the transition to college experience varies across schools (Bloom 2006; Cookson and Persell 1985; McDonough 1997; Stevens 2007; Weis 2007). While all research is partial and incomplete, the lack of information from schools limits our understanding of a critical part of the picture. Still, longitudinal ethnographic studies are rare (Burawoy 2003). In addition, most studies focus only on the perspective of either the student or the parent. In this instance, the vantage points of parents, a sibling, and the students offer key insights into the college application process.

Table 4.1   Distribution of Children in the Study by Social Class and Race

Social Class	White	Black	Total
Middle class[a]	Melanie Handlon Garrett Tallinger (subsample total = 18)	Stacey Marshall Alexander Williams (subsample total = 18)	(sample total = 36)
Working class[b]	Wendy Driver Billy Yanelli (subsample total = 14)	Tyrec Taylor Jessica Irwin[d] (subsample total = 12)	(sample total = 26)
Poor[c]	Katie Brindle Mark Greeley (subsample total = 12)	Tara Carroll Harold McAllister (subsample total = 14)	(sample total = 26)
Total	(subsample total = 44)	(subsample total = 44)	(sample total = 88)

Source: Authors' compilation.
[a] Middle class children are those who live in a household in which at least one parent is employed in a position that either entails substantial managerial authority or centrally draws on highly complex, educationally certified (college-level) skills.
[b] Working class children are those who live in a household in which neither parent is employed in a middle class position, and at least one parent is employed in a position that has little or no managerial authority and does not draw on highly complex, educationally certified skills. This category includes lower-level white collar workers.
[c] Poor children are those who live in a household in which parents receive public assistance and do not participate in the labor force on a regular, continuous basis.
[d] Interracial girl: black father and white mother.

Methodology

The analysis is based on longitudinal ethnographic data collected during re-interviews with twelve young adults and their families, conducted approximately ten years after their participation in a study of variations in family life and children's activities.[5] The families were white and African American; some lived in a large northeastern city and others in the suburbs of that city. Table 4.1 presents a breakdown of the race and class of the twelve adolescents discussed here, along with data on the participants in the larger study. (The definition of social class is also provided in table 4.1.) Nine of the twelve families were recruited from the classrooms of two public schools, one located in the city and one in the suburbs, where Lareau and a multiracial team of research assistants had done observations. The boy and the girl from the two black middle class families and the boy from the poor white family came from other sites. Most original observations and interviews took place between 1993 and 1995; the re-interviews took place between 2003 and 2005.

During the original study, the research assistants and Lareau took turns visiting the participating families daily, for a total of about twenty visits per family, often in the space of one month. The observations were not limited to the home. Fieldworkers followed the children and parents as they took part in school activities, church services and events, organized play, kin visits, and medical appointments. Most field observations lasted about three hours; sometimes, depending on the event (for example, an out-of-town funeral, a special extended-family event, a long shopping trip), they lasted much longer. In most cases, there was one overnight visit. Team members often carried tape recorders and used the audiotapes for reference in writing up field notes. Families were paid $350 for their participation; payments typically were made at the end of the course of visits. Unquestionably, the presence of researchers altered family dynamics, especially at first. Over time, however, signs of adjustment emerged (for example, yelling and cursing increased on the third day and again on the tenth). The children especially seemed to find participating in the project enjoyable. They reported it made them feel "special."

For ten years following completion of the study, Lareau kept in touch with almost all of the families by sending an annual holiday card with $5 tucked inside for the child who had participated in the study. When the children graduated from high school, she heard from some of the families and was invited to a few parties. Between 2003 and 2005, she located all twelve families and conducted two-hour, separate interviews with each of the target children, now nineteen to twenty-one years old, as well as separate interviews with their mothers, fathers, and siblings. One family had moved to a southern community; Lareau flew there to conduct the interviews. Three people declined to be interviewed (Mr. and Mrs. Williams and Katie Brindle's estranged husband). The young people were paid $75 for the interview; family members were paid $50. The interviews were tape-recorded and transcribed. All names are pseudonyms. The names of the colleges that the youth attended have been switched with those of colleges with comparable levels of selectiveness and similar character.[6]

Cultural Orientations to Child Rearing

On the basis of the original observational and interview data, *Unequal Childhoods* argues that a great deal of parental behavior is driven by cultural repertoires that vary sharply across social classes but not across racial groups. Middle class child rearing, the book asserts, generally conforms to the logic of *concerted cultivation,* according to which parents view it as their duty to actively foster the development of their children's potential skills and talents. By contrast, the book notes, working class and poor child rearing conforms to a logic of the *accomplishment of natural growth,* according to which parents assume that if they provide their children with love, feed and clothe them, and keep them safe, the children will grow and thrive spontaneously.

Lareau examined how these contrasting cultural orientations operate in three domains of everyday life. In the area of time use, she found that middle class children are enrolled in numerous age-specific leisure activities that are believed to transmit important life skills, while their working class and poor counterparts are generally granted autonomy in the use of leisure time. In the area of language use, middle class parents generally emphasize the development of verbal reasoning, frequently drawing their children into conversation and offering them chances to negotiate, whereas working class and poor parents are more likely to use directives when conversing with their children, to engage in brief exchanges of information, and to rely more on physical discipline than on negotiation. Lastly, in the area of institutional contacts, middle class parents generally consider it appropriate to closely monitor the behavior of institutional agents (such as teachers and other school officials) and to intervene on behalf of their children if they deem that their children's best interests are not being served, whereas working class parents consider these agents' authority and responsibility to be broad and not open to challenge.

In this chapter, we narrow the focus to one domain of everyday life—contacts between families and key institutions—and draw on the follow-up data to assess the extent to which the two cultural orientations to child rearing at the center of *Unequal Childhoods* have persisted through time. Our first goal is to determine whether notions of concerted cultivation and the accomplishment of natural growth aptly characterized parental behavior as the children were making the transition out of high school.

Jumping Through the Hoops: Preparing for and Applying to College

In studies of students' negotiations of educational institutions, including the transition to college, researchers tend to focus on the characteristics of the system itself (Kinzie et al. 2004), the unequal demographic representation of various groups (Hossler, Braxton, and Coopersmith 1989; Hurtado et al. 1997; Walpole 2003), or the educational characteristics of students who do or do not apply to college (Higher Education Research Institute 2004, 2005). Less attention is paid to the ever-changing standards for admission to college and the resources that students draw on in complying with these standards (but see McDonough 1997; Horvat 1996). Yet the college admission process is very complex, and much more complex than it was thirty years ago (Kinzie et al. 2004). Thus, before discussing how the youth in our study negotiated the college application process, we provide a short exposition of the process of preparing for and applying to college. As the discussion makes clear, colleges differ in their requirements, deadlines are inflexible yet highly variable across institutions, and considerable informal knowledge is needed to gauge the best "fit" between the educational performance of the student, the student's personal preferences, and the selectivity of the college.

The criteria for admission to colleges and universities are complex. For example, as table 4.2 shows, the University of California (a public system) requires incoming students to have taken fifteen yearlong courses in seven different subject areas.[7] Seven of these courses must have been completed during the student's junior or senior years of high school. There are also distribution regulations that limit which courses may be used to fulfill certain requirements. For example, two years of Spanish and one year of French will not fulfill the requirement for a foreign language and a college preparatory elective. There are also important differences in requirements across universities. The University of Maryland, for example, requires three (rather than two) years of history or social science and three (rather than two) years of science. It does not, however, require a year of art or a year of a college preparatory elective. The College Board (2006) website encourages students to apply to five to eight colleges.

Following this advice requires that students critically assess their academic records, gain detailed information about the application criteria for each school, and be able to assess the probability of their own admission. Students who anticipate applying to five to eight colleges must contend with the different admission dates, admission criteria, application fees, and other unique characteristics of each school. In addition, they must plan ahead and take a broad range of college preparatory courses so that they will be able to meet the colleges' specific course requirements.

There are many elements to the college application process (see tables 4A.1 and 4A.2). All college applications entail paying fees and meeting deadlines, but the amount of the fees and the dates of the deadlines vary by school. Even though there is now a "common application" form, most colleges and universities that use it (and many do not) also require the student to submit a supplemental application. Most require an essay. Applications for financial aid require input from parents as well as students. Students who intend to go to college also must sign up for, pay for, and take a standardized achievement test such as the SAT or ACT. Many, but not all, students buy at least one book or software program to prepare for the SAT; some students take prep courses or use private tutors. College visits also are complex, as table 4A.3's twenty-five-point list of what to do during a visit shows. Many of the steps, such as arranging an overnight stay in a dorm or planning a way to attend all of the necessary meetings during a single visit, require elaborate organizational skills; it would be difficult for many adolescents to complete these tasks without adult aid (Bloom 2006). The follow-up interviews suggest that the quantity of adult assistance as well as the degree to which the assistance is customized to the student's needs varies across schools as well as families, as the next section makes clear.

Table 4.2 Admission Requirements for the University of California

A	History and social science	Two years required	Must include one year of world history, cultures, and geography; and one year of U.S. history or one-half year of U.S. history and one-half year of civics or American government.
B	English	Four years required	Four years of college preparatory English classes that include frequent and regular writing and reading of classic and modern literature. No more than one year of ESL-type courses can be used to meet this requirement.
C	Mathematics	Three years required; four years recommended	Three years of college preparatory mathematics classes that include the topics covered in elementary and advanced algebra and two- and three-dimensional geometry. Approved integrated math courses may be used to fulfill part or all of this requirement, as may math courses taken in seventh and eighth grade that the high school accepts as equivalent to its own math courses.
D	Laboratory science	Two years required; three years recommended	Two years of a laboratory science providing fundamental knowledge in two of these three core disciplines: biology, chemistry, and physics. Advanced laboratory science classes that have biology, chemistry, or physics as prerequisites and offer substantial additional material may be used to fulfill this requirement. The final two years of an approved three-year integrated science program may be used to fulfill this requirement.
E	Language other than English	Two years required; three years recommended	Two years of the same language other than English. Courses should emphasize speaking and understanding and include instruction in grammar, vocabulary, reading, composition, and culture. Courses in languages other than English taken in seventh and eighth grades may be used to fulfill part of this requirement if the high school accepts them as equivalent to its own courses.
F	Visual and performing arts	One year required	A single yearlong approved arts course from a single VPA discipline: dance, drama/theater, music, or visual art.
G	College preparatory elective	One year (two semesters)	In addition to the courses listed above, courses chosen from the following areas: visual and performing arts (non-introductory-level courses), history, social science, English, advanced mathematics, laboratory science, and language other than English (a third year in the language used for the language requirement or two years of another language).

The applicant must complete fifteen yearlong high school courses. At least seven of these fifteen yearlong courses must be taken in the last two years of high school.

Source: University of California Office of Admissions, accessed at http://www.universityofcalifornia.edu/admissions.

Class and the Transition to Adulthood

If the educational research models are correct, then students' negotiation of the transition to higher education can be conceptualized as an individual process. Since students are on the cusp of adulthood and, in many instances, pressing for increased autonomy, this approach could be a useful one. Yet there are also signs in the literature that at earlier points in children's educational careers class differences in parent involvement have surfaced (Brantlinger 2003; Lareau 2000; Reay 1998). In addition, as the previous section makes clear, even if everything goes smoothly, the process of applying to college is complex. If a student encounters trouble, for example, in securing a promised letter of recommendation, or gets a low grade in a key course, then the assistance of adults might be particularly helpful in keeping him or her on track (Deil-Amen 2007). In this section, we compare two young African American women who each aspired to a medical career. Tara Carroll grew up in a poor family and dreamed of becoming a nurse. Stacey Marshall grew up in a middle class family and hoped to become a pediatrician. Tara was raised by her grandmother when she was younger and later moved in with her mother (her father was in prison). Stacey's biological parents had raised her since birth. Both young women had a sibling who was approximately two years older. The careers they aspired to required a science background. During middle school, both had struggled with math; neither young woman was naturally gifted in the subject.

Comparing Tara's and Stacey's transitions from high school shows that the differences in parental interventions in education observed when the children were younger have persisted. For example, in keeping with the cultural logic of the accomplishment of natural growth, Tara's mother placed the responsibility for applying to college on her daughter.

> Well, I let Tara make her choices. She told me what she wanted to do, and I let her do it. I should have participated more, yes, but because of my [work] schedule, I couldn't. . . . I should have participated more and pushed a little more. You know, get on the Internet and find scholarships, utilize that. Get her to write and sell herself more. You have to do essays to participate for scholarships. I should have been a little bit more pushy that way.

Although she had a car, and all of the schools Tara was interested in were within a one-hour drive of their home, Tara's mother did not visit any. The visits that Tara experienced were arranged at the "health academy" in her public high school. Tara's mother also did not recall ever having seen an application. Tara filled out the forms at school, with assistance from teachers: "Every college that she applied to, all I saw was the letters, yea or nay, and that was hurtful for her—everybody kept turning her down." Her mother also lacked basic information about crucial aspects of Tara's education: "I wish I could find that letter. All I remember is that [her GPA] was above average. I don't know exactly what it was. I think it was around a B."

Tara's knowledge was limited too. As a senior, she had to ask her counselor what a "3.4" meant:

> I had went to my counselor, his name was Mr. Bradley, and he did my GPA, like combined my averages, like, add[ed] up all my grades. . . . I remember, it was close to a 3.5 or it was like a 3.4. [I said] something like, "Well, what's that?" He was like, "That's a B." So I knew I did good overall [in] high school.

Tara's combined SAT scores totaled 690. She applied to six or seven colleges, including a number of schools whose representatives had made visits to her high school. In addition to assistance from teachers, Tara received advice from an aunt who had graduated from college. Still, she was unable to overcome some of the challenges the applications posed:

> I only got one recommendation. I didn't know a lot of teachers in there, um, but I had one teacher I really liked. Her name was Ms. Thomas. She gave me a letter of recommendation. . . . I had to get one more, but I couldn't. I tried to get one from my counselors, my counselor, but he came up with an excuse, like, um [*she changes her voice*], "You know, I got a lot of people to do, and I got to take time," some ol' excuse, and he had to see if he had time. And I was supposed to get one more, and that was from my English teacher . . . his name was Mr. Rogers. He was the head coordinator of my [school within a school] health academy. But he never got around to writin' it. He just kept saying, "Remind me, remind me, remind me." And I never got a chance to get that letter of recommendation from him, so I only had one.

Tara applied to colleges where the median SAT scores were 100 to 300 points above her own scores. She was rejected everywhere. She went to community college "as a last resort" to pursue her hope of becoming a nurse. She enrolled in an anatomy and physiology course but soon found that she did not like the instructor. Although she went to the instructor's office hours, she still did not understand the material, did not feel comfortable asking questions, and did not know that she could have sought help from an adviser. She simply stopped going to class. Since she did not formally drop the course, she failed it and will have to take it again. She says she is "taking a break from school" but hopes to go back in the future. Put differently, although Tara had relatively high grades and a fervent desire to attend college and had energetically visited colleges and filled out numerous applications, her college search failed to yield admission to a four-year college because of her lack of informal knowledge about the higher education system and the fact that she applied to schools that were quite selective (reflecting her high aspirations). Both she and her mother found the process to be "hurtful."

Middle class parents, especially mothers, generally have active roles in the college application process. Often parents guide their children every step of the way. For example, Stacey Marshall's experience with college applications was quite different from Tara's. From the beginning, Stacey received considerable adult support. Middle class parents, having gone to college themselves and having sought out detailed information from their social networks, generally feel comfortable providing their children with informal advice on academic matters. Stacey's mother worked in the computer industry and had a master's degree. In addition, she had long been committed to an especially active form of concerted cultivation. She reported that she had "kept tabs with the teacher" all through her daughter's primary and secondary education: "I was then and remained through high school kind of a visible parent in the school district, letting them know that I was watching what was going on."

Stacey's mother was concerned about her daughter's desire to be a premed student because she was aware that math was not Stacey's strong suit:

> She had the traumatic experience near the end of the [fifth-grade] year where she had gotten what I believe was her very first C. . . . Math has haunted her ever since. [*Pauses.*] Even now, there is this insecurity, this feeling that "I can't do it," which in my mind puts a damper on that desire to go into medicine, because she's got to deal with that math.

Nor, in her mother's opinion, had Stacey chosen to enroll in sufficiently challenging classes in high school: "Stacey was always a B-plus student with the ability to be A-minus, [who] never wanted to accept a challenge to go for a more challenging class. She did stick with the sciences. The counselor and I forced her into that."[8]

Indeed, Stacey's mother actively sought ways to further the development of her daughter's natural sciences skills. She mentioned, for example, that the summer before Stacey's senior year she and her husband had spent "a lot of money" (at least $1,500) to have Stacey attend a ten-day "young people in science" program suggested by a high school microbiology teacher.

After Stacey grew three inches in a single summer and was no longer competitive in gymnastics, she was persuaded to play basketball for her middle school. She became a basketball star in high school. During her senior year, she was recruited by Ivy League schools. Her combined SAT scores were 1060, and her grades were a B average. Although Stacey desperately wanted to go to Columbia and the basketball program there would have helped her gain admission, her parents told her the financial aid gap (over $15,000 per year) was too large and that therefore she could not go. (Privately, she reported still feeling "bitter" about her parents' unilateral decision.) Her mother worked hard to collect extensive information about the acceptance policies of various colleges; she guided her daughter to colleges that she thought would be a good fit for Stacey and that also reflected her daughter's desire not to be too far from home. Ultimately, Stacey was admitted to a selective state university three hours from home; as a member of the women's basketball team, she was given a full scholarship.[9]

During Stacey's freshman year, her parents continued to play the same sort of active role they had taken throughout the college application process. Her mother helped her select courses strategically: "I said, 'Look, you have got to get out of calculus. Because first semester you don't want your GPA to get too low, because then you can never dig yourself out of it.' And so she was calling me about 'what should I take?' "

Her mother's advice concerned both the immediate decision and, more importantly, the resources Stacey needed to use to make effective decisions in general:

> She emailed me first, and then she called me one night at eleven o'clock. And it was like, "Well, I can take the cinema course." I said, "*Stacey.*" [*Laughs.*] I said, "Do you know anything about this? Do they even give you a description?" [She said,] "Wellllllll, no, not really." But she . . . was on the computer; she could see that there were seats in this class; the time was right. I said, "Sometimes you can be jumping out of the frying pan into the fire. This course may have an interesting name, but, one, it sounds like, yeah, you'd be watching movies, but two, you'll probably be writing about [them]. You have these other courses where you will be writing. You are telling me that you don't like to write." She said, "Well, I don't know. I guess I see your point."

Stacey's mother continued:

> "In the meantime, you have an academic adviser. . . ." I really stressed with her that *she* needed to establish communication with those people. I said, "You need to call Alesha. Call Alesha, set up an appointment, and *go to talk to her.* Talk to her about your major. And see what advice she can give to you. That is what she is getting paid for."

Indeed, in some ways, her mother appeared to be trying to teach Stacey to be less dependent:

> I think that she was used to, throughout school, to me making a call or talking to a teacher as part of my parental responsibility. A couple of times I got emails from her while she was at college with questions like, "What should I do?" or, "What do you think?" And as the year wore on, there were some things that I would say, "Look, Stacey, this is *your* responsibility. I can't go and talk to this professor. This is college. [Stacey's university] doesn't even send me your grades. [*Laughs.*] They won't tell me anything. . . ."

Stacey Marshall clearly benefited from her mother's informal guidance. Although it is uncertain whether she will be able to successfully pursue her university's premed curriculum, it is much more likely that Stacey will graduate from college than it is that Tara will, although both are attached to the idea.

To summarize, comparing Tara Carroll's experiences with Stacey Marshall's suggests that middle class children have more informational resources at their disposal as they negotiate college than do working class and poor youth. Also, the comparison reveals a striking similarity in the overall cultural logic of child rearing that parents followed when their children were in fourth grade and when their children were in high school, even though the problems and concerns shifted considerably.

Natural Growth Continues

Many students, particularly those of working class and poor origins, do not attend college. A significant number, particularly in urban communities, drop out of high school. Since Lareau's study drew on this population, it is not surprising that a number of the youth in her study struggled in high school. A number dropped out. Some graduated from high school and attempted to start, but quickly stopped, attending community college. Their mothers and fathers were extremely concerned about their educational progress. But since parents generally defined education as the school's responsibility, parents played much less of a role in critically overseeing or intervening in their children's high school experiences than did middle class parents. When mothers did try to intervene, they reported that they were unable to alter the course of events. Put differently, in *Unequal Childhoods*, Lareau reported that working class and poor families spent scarce resources taking care of children and keeping them safe. Unlike the middle class parents, the working class and poor parents did not see it as their duty to continuously develop their children's talents and skills. Interviews conducted ten years later revealed continuity with these earlier patterns (see table 4.3).

Overall, parents continued to try to keep their children safe and to protect them. Parents (many of whom were high school dropouts) continued to cede responsibility for education to the school and, in addition, to the children themselves. Unlike middle class parents, the less-privileged parents did not micro-manage core aspects of the school experience. Nor did they seem to possess potentially important informal knowledge, such as the academic status hierarchy of their local public high schools. In the case of Katie Brindle, a white girl from a poor background, this apparent lack of information had long-term consequences. When Katie was about to enter high school, her mother's primary concern was her daughter's safety. Her mother did not want Katie to go across town to attend a school in a different neighborhood. This more distant school was much more highly ranked academically than the one that her mother directed her daughter to attend, although it is unclear whether either she or Katie knew this. Katie recalled that she had "wanted to go to Lincoln High. But my mom said I could only take the Washington or Franklin [choices] because they were in the neighborhood."

Table 4.3 Continuities in Class Differences in Concerted Cultivation and Natural Growth

Social Class	White		African American	
	Garrett Tallinger	Melanie Handlon	Alexander Williams	Stacey Marshall
Middle class students	Did elaborate college search. Admitted to Ivy League schools, but chose Villanova, a small Catholic college with a good basketball program; on basketball scholarship. Father guides course selection.	Applied to colleges, but was rejected by top choices; did not want to attend the school that did offer admittance. Her mother was embarrassed by Melanie's decision not to attend college. Attends cosmetology school.	Did elaborate college search, with college visits; admitted to Columbia University medical school program as an undergraduate. Mother gives college advice.	Did elaborate college search, with college visits; admitted to the University of Maryland. Mother helps select courses and gives college advice.
Working class students	Billy Yanelli	Wendy Driver	Tyrec Taylor	Jessica Irwin (bi-racial)
	Dropped out of high school; obtained a GED.	High school graduate; accepted by small Catholic college, but decided not to attend.	High school graduate; never took the SAT.	High school graduate; received solicitations from dozens of colleges owing to PSAT scores in

Does not know anyone attending college.	Mother extremely disappointed by Wendy's decision not to attend college.	1300s. Attends Temple University.	
Father helped with job acquisition; father intervened when drug test violation threatened job retention.	College search handled by high school; parents did not know SAT scores or that application fees were nonrefundable.	Mother wants Tyrec to become a lawyer; will help him "apply for a loan" for college.	
		Started at community college but stopped.	

	Mark Greeley	Katie Brindle	Harold McAllister	Tara Carroll
Poor students	Dropped out of high school; wants to work "in computers."	Dropped out of high school. Cleans houses full-time with mother.	Dropped out of high school; works as a waiter in a chain restaurant.	High school graduate; currently works taking care of disabled adults
	Mother pressured Mark to take GED course; he did so, but did not take certification exam.	With help of eighth-grade teacher, admitted to public magnet high school.	Denial of opportunity to play basketball in high school a major life disappointment (coach wanted him to play football instead; Harold refused).	Superficial college search with little parental input; some college visits and all applications overseen by high school personnel; applied to many colleges, but not admitted to any.
	Complained of police harassment.	Mother nixed the most academic and prestigious school because of bad neighborhood; wanted her to stay closer to home.		Enrolled in community college; failed a key class; hopes to return.

Source: Authors' compilation.

Saying that she was "wild" and that there was nothing her mother could have done to change that, Katie reported that she "never really went to high school." Her teenage years were punctuated by truancy, fighting, alcohol, and drugs. At age seventeen, she became pregnant, dropped out of school, and gave birth to a daughter, who is now being raised mainly by Katie's sister. As with many working class and poor youth in the study, she has received substantial assistance from her family. Her mother found her a job and got up with the baby at night when Katie was recovering from the cesarean section surgery. Her sister often took care of the baby and, when Katie was "running the streets," offered to raise the child. Her mother and sister also gave her gifts of cash and food. Katie hopes to get a GED one day; in the meantime, she works with her mother cleaning houses.

An orientation to schooling similar to the Brindles' was evident in other poor and working class families. Parents showed love and concern for their children in many different ways, but since they did not define their proper role as including the management of school careers, they had limited information about the options available to their children. For example, the Greeleys, another poverty-level white family, relied on school personnel for guidance when Mark, their eldest son, was ready for high school. As one of the few whites in an inner-city middle school, Mark had had a difficult time, frequently getting into fights. His mother explained that in selecting a high school for Mark, she "went by the word of his [middle school] school counselor, who said that this would be a great school for him. It's smaller, no one has issues, no one has problems." The school, however, did not prove to be a good choice. Mark was again one of the few white students, and he again had problems. Although he later transferred to a different high school, he became increasingly disengaged and eventually dropped out.

As Mark's problems were escalating, his mother attempted to intercede. She called "the school" to find out what she could do. This effort proved futile:

> I called the school. And I asked them, what, what—you know, "My son doesn't wanna come to school—what legal—what can I do legally?" There's nothing I can do when he's seventeen—if he don't wanna go, he don't have to go. It's just that simple. They can quit when they're sixteen, but you have to have the parents' permission, and he has to have a job. But, you know, he just didn't go to school the last month, and then he was seventeen. So . . . there's nothin' that I could've made him do.

Mark dropped out of high school when he was sixteen. He got a job stocking grocery shelves at night for $10 an hour. At the time of the follow-up interview, he lived at home, and his mother frequently drove him to work.

All three of Ms. Greeley's children have scored high enough on standard IQ tests to qualify for school-based gifted programs. (A teacher recommended that Mark be tested, and Ms. Greeley then had his siblings tested as well.) Nevertheless, none of the Greeley children have done well academically, although Mark's sister is likely to graduate from high school. Their mother noted ruefully that

> Pammy was one hundred forty-something [IQ score], and Rick was one hundred forty-something. But none of them did nothing with it. I think if situations . . . I don't know—I just believe that it's because of circumstances and situations and environment. They didn't flourish, you know, they didn't flourish. I mean, it might be the same anywhere. [But] I think if schools were different and they had different opportunities to go to better schools—they didn't. Unfortunately, when you're poor, you have to go to the neighborhood school, you know. They didn't have—there was no choices of going anywhere else—you have to go to the neighborhood school.

Ms. Greeley's reliance on school officials when making key decisions concerning her children's schooling, coupled with her sense of powerlessness in the face of negative events, was typical of working class and poor parents in the study, and it closely echoed the sensibility that was apparent among them some ten years earlier—namely, the supposition that responsibility for their children's education was properly relegated to educators.

Also striking is the case of Harold McAllister. An African American child from a poor family, Harold grew up in a housing project. When asked whether anyone had discussed the possibility of his pursuing his education beyond high school, Harold indicated that in ninth grade he had been in a college-oriented school:

> Like ninth grade, I was in the magnet charter, that was like the top charter—in the school they do all college-bound work. So I was cool. The magnet was in just like math and science, that's their true, like, subjects, math and science. So I was cool with that, but like my attendance wasn't that good, though.

Harold's late arrivals eventually led to his being dismissed from the school:

> So they kind of kicked me out [of] that charter and put me into another charter. The other charter, the work was easier, so I started, you know how you just start chillin' more, so if I could have stayed in [the] magnet, I would have been cool. The work was harder, but that was, like, on my pace. It gave me a challenge.

Harold received Cs and Bs at his new school, with an occasional D. His academic record was shaped in part by a sports-related setback. An avid and talented athlete, he loved basketball, but he had the build of a football player (five-eleven and 240 pounds). The same teacher coached the football and basketball teams. Worried about his knees, Harold refused to try out for the football team (which "stunk"). Despite his formidable basketball talent, Harold was not selected for the basketball team. He was convinced that the coach made that decision because he was angry about Harold's lack of desire to play football. Harold was devastated. After an appeal to the school's principal proved unsuccessful, Harold chose another school and planned to transfer, but that move never materialized:

> LAREAU: And what was involved in transferring?
> HAROLD: Paperwork. . . . Because I had, I knew like a couple of players on their basketball team. I played with them in my city league. . . . I've never been a problem child, you know, like my grades were average or above-average, so what was the reason for them to not let me transfer there?
> LAREAU: And when did you talk to your dad about it?
> HAROLD: Like, some nights after, like, I'd have a basketball game, and we'd win, like, easily with, like, all of us playing together. I'm like, hey, we can do this in high school too, though. He used to say something, but, like, I knew . . . he didn't really care about basketball [laughs], like, he never played basketball. He was boxing and, like, that's it.
> LAREAU: And did you talk about it with anybody else at that time besides your dad?
> HAROLD: My mom sometimes. Like, I just, I didn't, I just felt the vibe . . . um, I don't know how to say it, though, um. I talked to my mom a lot, but, not a lot, but, like, sometimes, though. But, like, nothing ever happened, though.

In the end, Harold got a job busing dishes at a suburban restaurant. He worked the 4:00 PM to midnight shift. During the interview, he explained that he "just started working to get my mind off of basketball." Although he had to take four buses and the trip lasted two hours, he liked the job and soon switched to a full-time schedule. He planned to work full-time and attend high school full-time. Around this time his mother moved in with her daughter, and Harold, who said he could not "deal with all those females," took up residence with his father. His school attendance again became spotty because he frequently overslept after having gotten home very late from his job. Traditionally, Harold's mother had woken him up in time to go to school; his father did not. In the spring of his senior year, Harold dropped out. His mother was outraged:

> He had a nice time in there, he was progressing good. He was—he didn't play sports in school. He played sports outside of school. But when we moved, we moved in . . . April, he had two more months of school and graduate, and Harold didn't graduate. I was mad. [Voice rising.] All he had to do was graduate, two months, April, May, and June.

Unlike the middle class parents in the study, Harold's mother did not create a customized and individualized school career for her son. Instead, like Ms. Greeley, Ms. McAllister depended on educators to use their professional expertise to do this. And like Ms. Greeley, Ms. McAllister felt intensely frustrated by and powerless in the face of the events leading up to her son's decision to drop out.

In all, three of the four youth from poor backgrounds dropped out of high school (Tara Carroll was the exception), and one of the four working class youth (Billy Yanelli) did so. Of those who graduated, all expressed a desire to go to college. Only one did; the others were diverted by various life events. For instance, Wendy Driver, a white working class young woman, attended a private Catholic high school after not being admitted to any of the more desirable public high schools. Her paternal grandfather paid her tuition. Although Wendy struggled academically, the school counselors helped her apply to college. She was accepted at a small Catholic college with a program for students with learning disabilities. After high school graduation, however, she told her mother and stepfather that she would not attend. She reported being worried that she could not manage the work and thought that she "would fail," especially since her girlfriends who were already in college, and who had been much better students in high school than she was, were struggling. Her parents offered other explanations. Her stepfather felt that Wendy wanted to be with her boyfriend (soon to become her husband). Her mother felt that the college, a ninety-minute drive away, seemed too far from home; Wendy had no experience being away from home. In December of what would have been her freshman year of college, she became pregnant: "It wasn't a planned pregnancy. We were being careful and everything. I was taking birth control. It just happened. I was scared of course. He was scared because he didn't know what we were going to do."

Abortion was out of the question, and although her mother "was shocked at first," she became supportive. Over the objections of Wendy's boyfriend's mother, the two married immediately, in a small ceremony. A year later, they had a large formal wedding and reception. Before she had the baby, Wendy briefly explored attending the local community college, but then abandoned the idea when she found out that she would have to take remedial non-credit courses (and be "the only white girl" in the classroom). Today she is a full-time homemaker; her husband is in the Navy. Wendy hopes someday to have a child care business in her home. In the meantime, her step-father routinely drives to her house (a three-hour trip) to bring her and the baby home for visits. She and her husband are now expecting a second (planned) child. Wendy's mother, while continuing to be disappointed by her daughter's failure to attend college, has provided substantial psychological, economic, and social support for Wendy and her family.

Tyrec Taylor, a young man from an African American working class family, attended three different high schools and came extremely close to dropping out. After a disastrous junior year that included two juvenile arrests, Tyrec's mother pleaded with his father to take out a large loan ($6,000) to cover tuition at a private school. He did, and Tyrec attended and graduated. Tyrec said that he felt he was "supposed to go to college," but he never took many college preparatory classes or the SATs. Nor did he apply to college. He completed one remedial noncredit English course at a community college. He has not returned to school since that time.

Of the eight working class and poor students in the study, only Jessica Irwin, who was biracial, enrolled in a four-year college. Jessica's parents were more highly educated than the parents of the other working class and poor students: her father had attended college, and her mother had graduated from college.[10] Nevertheless, with respect to their daughter's educational career, the Irwins followed the natural growth approach. Jessica's grade point average (94) and SAT scores (1310) generated "tons and tons of mail" from colleges that hoped to recruit her. Also, many of the colleges recruiting students categorized her as African American. Jessica's parents drove her to schools for visits, but their primary concern was how her college career would be financed. Her college search process did not have the breadth and depth of those carried out by the middle class children and their families. Although she had wanted to attend Carnegie Mellon, Jessica's parents vetoed this choice once they learned the tuition. They were unaware that the financial aid packages of private schools can be large enough to wholly or almost wholly offset the high tuition rates. Nor were they aware that a nearby elite private university offers full scholarships for twenty young people from the Irwins' home city each year. Jessica ended up attending a small public university. The full scholarship that she received pleased both her and her parents. She received high grades at college and planned to major in art.

Concerted Cultivation Continues

Not all of the middle class adolescents went to college. But in every case, their parents took an extremely active role in their transition out of high school; such parental actions are rarely accounted for in the current models of educational transitions. Mothers in particular did not hesitate to intervene. For example, the mother of Garrett Tallinger, a white middle class young man, reported:

MS. TALLINGER: In talking to the guidance people, I said, "I think he's capable of honors [enrolling in the honors courses]. But obviously you-all need to decide that. . . ." One of the things I did know was that the more competitive colleges look at what is available in a high school, and if you're not taking the most rigorous of what's available, that's a strike against you in terms of their evaluating your transcript. And so I wanted Garrett, as is true with all my kids, I want them to take the most rigorous [courses] that they're possibly capable of taking.
LAREAU: And how did you know that?
MS. TALLINGER: Well, from friends who work in admissions offices. I mean, a very good friend used to work in admissions. And she said, "It's very important." And actually then talking to some other parents that had taken their

daughter on a tour of Yale and Duke. He told a funny story of visiting at Duke, and the question to the person guiding the admissions discussions . . . the question from the student was, "Well, is it better to take honors calculus and get a B or take regular calculus and get an A?" He says, "It's better to take honors calculus and get an A." [*Laughs.*]

For many middle class parents in the study, friends' experiences with the college admission process proved to be an important source of information.

Garrett did enroll in rigorous high school courses, including AP economics, AP calculus, AP English literature, and two years of both physics and history. His weighted grade point average was 4.26 (which he believes is equivalent to an unweighted average of 3.78). In guiding their son's school career, the Tallingers tapped multiple resources, including the expertise of school personnel. For example, it was Garrett's ninth grade math teacher who facilitated his entrance into the highest levels of math, including AP calculus. Nevertheless, Garrett's mother took steps promptly anytime she felt that her son's best interests were not being fully served by the school. Thus, when a scheduling problem threatened to prevent Garrett from taking college preparatory courses in both math and English, she quickly intervened:

> I did have to go fight about his schedule, because they went into this new scheduling system, and if he wanted to take the AP English and AP calculus, they were given at the same time. I was like, "C'mon, this is not—you gotta figure something out. I mean, I can't believe Garrett's the only person this is impacting. You have to figure a way for these kids to maximize their opportunities, and they have to switch things around." So that I did fight for.

Ms. Tallinger's efforts to directly manage Garrett's education closely resembled her behavior, and that of other middle class parents, some ten years earlier, when the children were in elementary school.

Garrett paid close attention to the college application process. In the follow-up interview, he described his behavior in explicitly calculative terms. He considered his first SAT scores disgraceful:

> The first time I hated my score. I got a ten-sixty, I . . . ten-thirty, ten-sixty? I was embarrassed, real embarrassed. So I took it again [and] got . . . I can't remember what I got the second time, but . . . 'cause I remember you can mix and match. Like you take your best verbal and your best math. My mix-and-match, I got eleven-ninety.

Even this score he felt was not a good measure of his true ability: "And I know I'm better than that. My goal was to get a twelve hundred, so, ten shy."

Choosing a college also required making calculations and strategizing. As recent articles in the *Chronicle of Higher Education* (White 2005) and books such as *College Unranked* (Thacker 2005) suggest, the college search process often involves a huge investment of time and energy for both parents and children from the middle class. Garrett considered many different colleges, at different collegiate sports division levels: Stanford, Columbia, Princeton, Memphis, Boston University, North Carolina State, Davidson, and Villanova. The gap in financial aid precluded his attending Princeton or Columbia. In the end he went to Villanova on a full basketball scholarship.

For Alexander Williams, an African American middle class young man, college visits began during sophomore year of high school. By the time he made his final choice, he had visited Duke, Columbia, Dartmouth, Brandeis, Georgetown, Haverford, Northwestern, and a few others. During the follow-up interview, he recalled being annoyed that he had had to spend his spring break in junior year visiting campuses: "I didn't want to go to visit colleges on my spring break," he said, but then quickly added, "No, it was fun." He applied early-decision to Columbia, which meant that he was committed to going if he got admitted. With an A average and SAT scores of 1350, he was reasonably confident. He explained: "I didn't apply anywhere else, and if I hadn't gotten in, I would have had about a week and a half to apply everywhere else." His father had not been enthusiastic about this strategy: "I think that my mom was pretty sure I would get in; my dad was wondering why I hadn't applied anywhere else." Put differently, compared to Tara Carroll's mother, Alexander's mother had considerable informal knowledge about the higher education system, was aware of his skills, and guided him through the process ("my mom was pretty sure I would get in"). In other cases, the middle class students visited and toured many schools but, after narrowing their preferences, applied to a small number of potential colleges.

Even after their children have begun their college careers, middle class parents often remain deeply involved. The Tallingers reported that they speak with Garrett frequently and give him advice. During the follow-up interview, his father offered this example:

> He called us the end of last semester when it was time to register for this fall's semester, and he said he was going to get up and get out of business school—he wanted to be a teacher. And it surprised me a little bit. I didn't have anything against it; I was supportive. I told him, "Do what you want, whatever makes you happy." . . . I said, "Garrett, you just need to realize that . . ."—his high school coach, who he idolizes, who's been a high school teacher now for twenty years or something . . . I mean, you know he makes probably high fifty thousands or sixty thousand dollars a year and will probably never make a whole lot more than that. He has a great life, loves his life. So I said, "You just need to be aware of that." He kind of went, "Oh, really?" [Chuckles.] I said, "Yeah." 'Cause he's just unaware of these kinds of things. . . . It was on a Thursday, so on Friday afternoon he called and said, "Well, I'm in the business school." So he stayed in the business school.

By providing their son with regular input during his college career, Mr. and Ms. Tallinger helped Garrett align his short-term educational choices with his long-term goals. Other middle class parents in the study saw themselves as being so central to their children's postsecondary school career that they often used the term "we" during the follow-up interviews. Ms. Handlon, for instance, in reporting with embarrassment that her daughter Melanie (a white middle class young woman) had dropped out of community college, said, "We only made it one semester."[11] This pattern of parental involvement is not unique to the young people in this study. As one college administrator notes, "The 'helicopter parent,' or hovering parent who repeatedly tries to intervene and manage his or her child's life, seems to be a growing phenomenon on many campuses" (White 2005).[12]

Conclusions

In this chapter, we have taken up the question of how families from different class locations negotiate children's transition out of high school. We began by noting that in much current research, this transition is construed in terms of choices made by the isolated individuals of statistical decision theory (or, at most, by generic "students and their parents"). The key decisionmaking parameters of these models include the potential returns to additional schooling, students' academic abilities, and their available resources. We suggested that these models might usefully be juxtaposed with empirical data on the decisionmaking process as it actually occurs.

Our central finding is that substantial class differences exist in the role played by the family, and in particular by parents. In our ethnographic data, parental involvement is an overwhelmingly middle class phenomenon. Moreover, it takes numerous forms. Middle class parents may help their children formulate effective strategies while they are still in high school (for example, by overseeing the choice of appropriate courses), help them evaluate their individual academic strengths and weaknesses, and help them realistically assess the costs and benefits of specific courses of action (including not just whether to attend college but also, for example, what to major in once there). Thus, if, as Stephen Morgan (2005) has asserted, high school decisionmakers are confronted with considerable uncertainty with respect to these crucial factors, then our data suggest that parental involvement may help them reduce this ambiguity. However, it is important to recognize that middle class parental involvement often goes beyond providing advice to include, at times, directly interceding to ensure that their children's interests (as perceived) are well served. These interventions can take the form of speaking with high school counselors about course selection, complaining to school officials when AP course schedules conflict, working closely with their children—sentence by sentence—on college essays, planning (and funding) a large number of visits to potential colleges, and other actions. Indeed, the heavy involvement of middle class parents in the complex and long-term process of preparing for and applying to college is one of our most notable findings. To varying degrees, middle class parents and their children form a collective in which concerted action on the part of each family member is carefully directed toward a shared goal over the course of a child's high school career.

Among working class and poor children, by contrast, parental involvement appears to be substantially rarer. Parents do not typically see it as part of their job to monitor the minutiae of their children's educational careers or to play a central role in making or helping their children make key decisions about their post–high school path. Thus, these parents usually do not try to help their children evaluate the potential long-term implications of their high school course selection or assess their career interests in light of their academic strengths and weaknesses. Nor did we document any conversations in working class or poor families that were comparable to the one between Garrett Tallinger and his father concerning the long-term financial payoff to a particular college program, or even to college attendance in general. Additionally, most did not have experience with the college application process themselves, and neither could they draw on the cumulative experience of a network of college-educated friends; therefore, they could not serve their children as a significant source of information. Consequently, working class and poor children are more likely to rely exclusively on teachers, counselors, and school officials for assistance when making key decisions. Moreover, direct interventions in schooling by working class or poor parents are rare; when they do occur, as with Mark Greeley's mother, they are less likely to be successful.

Working class and poor parents are no less deeply committed, however, to the well being of their children than are middle class parents. The less-privileged parents in the study helped their children frequently and in many ways. They babysat, paid car insurance, supplied transportation to and from work sites, set up job interviews, and provided other crucial emotional and financial support. Some of the working class and poor parents championed college, and some were deeply disappointed that their children did not, in the end, attend. Nevertheless, compared with middle class parents, their enthusiastic "pushing" typically was less informed and less useful in enabling their children to navigate the complexities involved in pursuing higher education.

The portrait that emerges from these data is strikingly consistent with the one presented in *Unequal Childhoods*. In particular, class-specific cultural orientations to child rearing retain their purchase on family behavior—at least in the area of relations to institutions—approximately ten years after the original data collection took place. Thus, the behavior of middle class parents in managing their children's high school career and transition into college can be viewed straightforwardly as an extension of the same "concerted cultivation" child rearing strategy they practiced earlier. Similarly, the propensity of working class and poor parents to assume that their children's education is the responsibility of professional educators constitutes an extension of the "accomplishment of natural growth" approach. This indicates that the cultural dispositions identified in *Unequal Childhoods* are highly durable.

We conclude by pointing out that these dispositions have profound consequences when they come into contact with the standards of gatekeeping institutions such as colleges. The ability to negotiate the (absurdly) complex process of applying to college is enhanced dramatically by the presence of parents whose informal knowledge covers the myriad factors involved (the costs, the entry requirements, the strengths and weaknesses and status of potential schools) and who are inclined to involve themselves deeply in their children's institutional lives. As such, we maintain that this knowledge, and the associated dispositions, may be viewed as a form of "cultural capital"—one that is clearly implicated in the long-term persistence of class inequality. As the other chapters in this book demonstrate, the importance of class can be seen in a number of spheres, including health (Carpiano, Link, and Phelan), politics (Manza and Brooks), and identity (Lacy and Harris). Analyzing the role of cultural processes in these spheres, and the ways in which cultural resources can become forms of cultural capital, is an important task for the future.

Appendix

Table 4A.1   What to Do Junior Year of High School so You Get into the College of Your Choice

Junior year: year of tests and driver's license. Because of that license, you'll have more freedom than you've ever had before. Enjoy it. But don't forget about your grades. This year is crucial—maybe the most important of your high school career. It's the year you'll be taking the PSAT and SAT; the year you'll start to take real leadership in your extra-curricular activities; the year you'll start thinking more seriously about what colleges you'd like to attend.

Junior Fall
- If your extracurricular activities have elections at the end of the year, shoot for leadership roles.
- Sign up for the PSAT. You should take it in October. Make sure to take a practice test before taking the real thing.
- Start thinking about college. Go over your transcript with your guidance counselor and come up with a preliminary list of colleges you might want to attend based on your high school resume and your interests.
- Also start to think about financial aid. Get to know how it works, what you have to do, and what kind of financial aid you might need.

Junior Winter
- Decide when you want to take the SAT and register for the test. If you haven't taken at least two SAT II Subject Tests, plan when to take those tests as well.

(continued)

Table 4A.1   *Continued*

- Go over your PSAT results to determine your strengths and weaknesses. Think about whether you'd like to take an SAT test prep course.
- Start whittling down your college choices. Come up with a list of 10–15 schools that you're interested in based on their location, size, reputation, and the strength of the academic departments that you're interested in.
- Start thinking about what you want to do in the summer.

Junior Spring
- Prepare for the SAT. You may want to do this on your own, though many people nowadays take an SAT Prep Course.
- Start visiting colleges. Get a feel for the colleges you're interested in. Stay with a friend at the schools if possible, or just visit with your parents and take a tour.
- Study hard for AP Exams. Good results on the test will provide you with college credit and give you a significant leg up on other students applying to colleges.
- Try to get top positions in your extracurricular activities for your senior year.
- Decide on an enriching, challenging summer program, internship, or job.

Junior Summer
- Have fun! Give everything you've got to your summer activity. Remember, your summer employer, teacher, or mentor could be someone who writes one of your letters of recommendation.
- Continue visiting colleges.
- Start requesting your high school resume before your senior year starts. The sooner you get a head start on applications and your college essays, the better.
- You'll receive your SAT scores during the summer. If you're scores are what you wanted, great! If not, you may want to register to take them again early Senior year and sign up for an SAT Test Prep Course.

Source: About.com, accessed at http://collegeapps.about.com/od/yourhighschoolresume/a/checklist_frosh.htm.

Table 4A.2   College Application Calendar

College applications can seem overwhelming at first glance. What needs to be done, and when? Use this calendar to get a bird's-eye view of the college application process.

Summer Before Senior Year
  Visit colleges that interest you. Call ahead for the campus tour schedule.
    Schedule an on-campus interview with an admissions representative.
  Finalize your list of colleges. Be sure your list includes "safe" schools as well as "reach" and "realistic" schools. Request college applications and informational packets. Organize materials into separate files by college.
  Keep a college calendar of all admission deadlines.
  If you plan on competing in Division I or Division II college sports and want to be eligible to be recruited by colleges, you must register with the NCAA Initial Eligibility Clearinghouse.

Table 4A.2   *Continued*

If you took AP® Exams in May, you will receive your AP Grade Reports in July.
Register early for fall SAT® tests.

September

Your counselor will play a big role in helping you get into college, so keep him or
her informed. Meet to talk about your college plans and review your transcript.

Get started on your applications right away if you plan to apply through an
Early Decision or Early Action program. Deadlines for early applications
tend to fall in October or November.

Start working on your college essays. Write essays that focus on your experiences
and make you stand out from the crowd.

Update your "resume"—your list of accomplishments, involvements, and work
experiences—with your senior year activities. Your resume will help you
complete your applications and essays.

October

Ask your counselor, teachers, and coaches, or employers for letters of recommendation. Give them plenty of time to meet your deadlines and make sure to
provide them with stamped and addressed envelopes.

Take SAT tests. Make sure your scores are sent to each of your colleges.

If you are applying under an Early Decision or Early Action program, be sure
to get all forms in as soon as possible. Applying online might be the right
option for you.

November

Submit early decision and early action applications on time.

Work hard at completing your college essays. Proofread them rigorously for
mistakes.

Follow up with your teachers to ensure that letters of recommendation are sent
on time to meet your deadlines.

Mail applications as early as possible for colleges with "rolling" deadlines
(admission decisions are made as applications are received).

Take SAT tests. Make sure your scores are sent to each one of your colleges.

December

Try to wrap up college applications before winter break. Make copies of each
application before you send it.

Take SAT tests. Make sure your scores are sent to each one of your colleges.

Early Decision and Early Application responses arrive this month.

January

Early Decision and Early Application responses arrive this month.

Some colleges include your first-semester grades as part of your application
folder. This is called the mid-year grade report. Have your counselor send
your grades to colleges that require them.

February

Contact your colleges and confirm that all necessary application materials have
been received.

Don't get senioritis! Colleges want to see strong second half grades.

(continued)

Table 4A.2   *Continued*

March

    Some admissions decisions arrive this month. Read everything you receive carefully, as some of it may require action on your part.

April

    Most admissions decisions and financial aid award letters arrive this month. Read everything you receive carefully, as some of it may require action on your part.

    Make a final decision, and mail the enrollment form and deposit check to the school you select before May 1 (the enrollment deadline for most schools).

    Notify each of the schools to which you were accepted that you will not be attending in writing so that your spot can be freed up for another student.

    On the waiting list? Contact the admissions office and let them know of your continued interest in the college and update them on your spring semester grades and activities.

May

    AP Exams are administered. In 2003, AP Exams are scheduled for May 5–9 and May 12–16. Make sure your AP Grade Report is sent to your college.

    Study hard for final exams. Most admission offers are contingent on your final grades.

    Thank your counselor, teachers, coaches, and anyone else who wrote you recommendations or otherwise helped with your college applications.

June

    Have your counselor send your final transcript to your college choice.

    If you plan on competing in Division I or Division II college sports, have your counselor send your final transcript to the NCAA Initial Eligibility Clearinghouse.

Summer

    Make travel plans. Book early for the best prices.

    Finalize your housing plans.

    Shop for items you will need in college.

    Make sure to sign up for first-year orientation.

    Plan your first-semester courses with an eye toward eventually selecting your college major.

Source: "College Application Calendar," copyright © 2008 The College Board, accessed at http://www.collegeboard.com. Reproduced with permission.

Table 4A.3   Campus Visit Checklist: Make the Most of Your Trip

Here are things you shouldn't miss while visiting a college. Take a look at this list before planning campus trips to make sure that you allow enough time on each campus to get a sense of what the school—and the life of its students—is really like.

1. Take a campus tour.
2. Have an interview with admissions officer.
3. Get business cards and names of people you meet for future contacts.
4. Pick up financial aid forms.

Table 4A.3   *Continued*

5. Participate in a group information session at the admissions office.
6. Sit in on a class of a subject that interests you.
7. Talk to a professor in your chosen major or in a subject that interests you.
8. Talk to coaches of sports in which you might participate. Talk to a student or counselor in the career center.
9. Spend the night in a dorm.
10. Read the student newspaper.
11. Try to find other student publications—department newsletters, alternative newspapers, literary reviews.
12. Scan bulletin boards to see what day-to-day student life is like.
13. Eat in the cafeteria.
14. Ask a student why he/she chose this college.
15. Wander around the campus by yourself.
16. Read for a little while in the library and see what it's like.
17. Search for your favorite book in the library.
18. Ask a student what he/she hates about the college.
19. Ask a student what he/she loves about the college.
20. Browse in the college bookstore.
21. Walk or drive around the community surrounding the campus.
22. Ask a student what he/she does on weekends.
23. Listen to the college's radio station.
24. Try to see a dorm that you didn't see on the tour.
25. Imagine yourself attending this college for four years.

Source: "Campus Visit Checklist," copyright © 2008 The College Board, accessed at http://www.collegeboard.com. Reproduced with permission.

We are grateful to the Spencer Foundation for its generous support of this research, as well as to Temple University, the Maryland Population Research Center, and Sociology Department at the University of Maryland. Annette Lareau also gratefully acknowledges the Center for the Advanced Study of the Behavioral Sciences. Erin McNamara Horvat, Demie Kurz, Pamela Barnhouse Walters, and Cecilia Ridgeway provided helpful feedback on an earlier version, as did audiences at UCLA, CUNY Graduate Center, Northwestern University, and the University of Maryland. Kathy Mooney provided invaluable editorial assistance. Responsibility for any errors or omissions, of course, rests with the authors and not the sponsoring agencies.

Notes

1. Research indicates the existence of substantial differences in the high school experiences of and the transition to college for children of differing positions in the social class structure (Karen 2002; Karen and Dougherty 2005; McDonough 1997; Stevens 2007). For example, the National Center for Education Statistics (NCES) (2005) found that college students whose parents had a high school education or less ("first-generation college students") were "significantly handicapped" in core aspects of the college experience. They were more likely to

attend less academically selective institutions, they completed fewer credit hours, they worked for pay significantly more hours, and they were less involved in extracurricular activities than students whose parents held a BA degree or higher. Kevin Dougherty and Gregory Kienzl (2006, 452) report that community college students from higher socioeconomic backgrounds are significantly more likely to transfer from two-year to four-year colleges than students from less-privileged backgrounds, in part because of advantages "in precollege academic preparation and educational aspirations." Patricia McDonough (1997) examines differences in the "organizational habitus" with which schools prepare and guide students through the choice of colleges. Important resources for the college search process, such as Internet access, also are unequally distributed in the population (Clark and Gorski 2002), but little attention has been focused on how this shapes the transition to college.

2.   For a partial exception to this approach, see Morgan (2005). For a contrast to the atomistic approach, see McDonough (1997) and Souza (2003).

3.   The higher education literature, especially the "college choice" literature, is voluminous. A full review of it is outside the bounds of this chapter. For general discussion of the admission process, see Kinzie et al. (2004), Karen (2002), Karen and Dougherty (2005), and the 2004 and 2005 reports by the Higher Education Research Institute at the University of California at Los Angeles. For a discussion of race and higher education, see, among others, Allen (1992), Allen, Bonous-Hammerth, and Teranishi (2002), Bowen and Bok (1998), and Hurtado et al. (1997). For a discussion of the expectation that all students should go to college, see Rosenbaum (2001). For literature on the increasing commodification of higher education and the application process, see McDonough (1994) and the thoughtful essays by higher education administrators in Thacker (2005). For the crucial role of education in gaining access to the labor market and fostering social mobility, see, among others, Hout (1988), Karen and Dougherty (2005), and Mishel, Bernstein, and Allegretto (2006). For reports showing how first-generation college students generally have less favorable college experiences than students whose parents are college graduates, see NCES (2001a, 2001b, 2005); see also Rosenbaum, Deil-Amen, and Person (2006). For discussions of students who do not go to college, see NCES (2004), and on the inferior value of a GED and a high school diploma, see Murnane, Willet, and Boudett (1995).

4.   In this respect, this chapter is similar in spirit, though certainly not in method, to Grodsky and Jones (2007).

5.   See Burawoy (2003) and Weis (2004) for more information on longitudinal ethnography.

6.   In the spring of 2006, if the young people were enrolled in college—and most were not—they would have been in the final stretch of their senior year.

7.   We have chosen the University of California because it is a large public system that, in previous decades, was considered a leader in the field of higher education. The requirements for the University of California are quite similar to those for the schools that the students in this study attended (if they went to college), but as we note, each college was idiosyncratic.

8. Stacey's mother regretted that she did not force her daughter to take more AP and honors classes: "I kick myself for that. I think that she would have gotten in more writing and more reading. She was a kid who hated to read. She's at a college that is very challenging. . . . I think that she is challenged."

9. Children do not, of course, always conform to their parents' wishes. Stacey's older sister Fern, who also played basketball, chose a selective public university with an excellent basketball team that was located in a relatively rural location. Her mother was vociferously opposed to the choice because she thought, given her daughter's temperament, she would be better off in an urban setting. Fern found the basketball coach to be very difficult. (Her mother wrote a letter to school officials complaining about the treatment the coach was giving her team.) Fern transferred at the end of her freshman year to a school close to home. Not wanting to sit out a year, per NCAA rules, she transferred from a Division 1 school to a lower division. She liked that school much better; with a major in business, she was planning to get an MBA. On variations among siblings, see Conley (this volume).

10. Jessica Irwin's father worked in a closely supervised technical job; her mother was a babysitter. They lived in a very small apartment. In the original study, they were classified as working class on the basis of their occupational characteristics and because the study did not include a lower middle class category. The family was asked to participate in part because Jessica was the highest-achieving child in the urban classroom where the observations were conducted, and her parents exhibited the most middle class characteristics in their family-school relationship. In the intervening years, her parents have been socially mobile. They purchased a house, and Ms. Irwin got her teaching credential. She began as a classroom aide but eventually was given her own classroom. Mr. Irwin left his job to start a business in computers; he is self-employed.

11. Melanie Handlon worked for a while in a coffee shop and then went to cosmetology school. Her case highlights the important variability within class; see Lacy and Harris (this volume) for an additional discussion of this issue.

12. According to *The Chronicle of Higher Education*, the University of Vermont has hired "parent bouncers" to help keep parents away from their children at college orientations and to allow them to make their course selections without parental input (Will 2005).

References

Allen, Walter R. 1992. "The Color of Success: African-American College Student Outcomes at Predominantly White and Historically Black Public Colleges and Universities." *Harvard Educational Review* 62(Spring): 26–44.

Allen, Walter R., Marguerite Bonous-Hammerth, and Robert Teranishi. 2002. " 'Stony the Road We Trod': The Black Struggle for Higher Education in California." Los Angeles, Calif.: CHOICES, University of California (February). Accessed at http://www.choices.gseis.ucla.edu/reports/Stony%20Road%20Full.pdf.

Bloom, Janice. 2006. "Bridges and Barriers: Social Class and the Transition to College." Ph.D. dissertation, City University of New York, Program in Urban Education.

Bowen, William G., and Derek Bok. 1998. *The Shape of the River: Long-Term Consequences of Considering Race in College and University Admissions.* Princeton, N.J.: Princeton University Press.

Brantlinger, Ellen. 2003. *Dividing Classes: How the Middle Class Negotiates and Rationalizes School Advantage.* New York: Routledge Falmer.

Breen, Richard, and John Goldthorpe. 1997. "Explaining Educational Differentials: Towards a Formal Rational Action Theory." *Rationality and Society* 9(3): 275–305.

Burawoy, Michael. 2003. "Revisits: An Outline of a Theory of Reflexive Ethnography." *American Sociological Review* 68(5): 645–79.

Clark, Christine, and Paul Gorski. 2002. "Multicultural Education and the Digital Divide: Focus on Socioeconomic Class Background." *Multicultural Perspectives* 4(3): 25–36.

College Board. 2006. "College Application Calendar." Accessed at http://www.collegeboard.com/article/0,3868,5-25-0-23626,00html.

Cookson, Peter W., Jr., and Caroline Hodges Persell. 1985. *Preparing for Power: America's Elite Boarding Schools.* New York: Basic Books.

Deil-Amen, Regina. 2007. "When Aspirations Meet Reality for Low-Income Minority High School Students in Their Transition to College." Paper presented to the American Sociological Association annual meeting. New York, August 13, 2007.

Dougherty, Kevin J., and Gregory S. Kienzl. 2006. "It's Not Enough to Get Through the Open Door: Inequalities by Social Background in Transfer from Community Colleges to Four-Year Colleges." *Teachers College Record* 108(March): 452–87.

Grodsky, Eric, and Melanie T. Jones. 2007. "Real and Imagined Barriers to College Entry: Perceptions of Cost." *Social Science Research* 36(2): 745–66.

Higher Education Research Institute. 2004. *The 2003 Your First College Year (YFCY) Survey: Exploring the Academic and Personal Experiences of College Students.* Los Angeles, Calif.: University of California.

———. 2005. *The American Freshman: National Norms for Fall, 2005: Thirty-Five-Year Trends.* Los Angeles, Calif.: University of California.

Horvat, Erin McNamara. 1996. "African American Girls and Decisionmaking in Social Context." Ph.D. diss., University of California at Los Angeles.

Hossler, Don, John Braxton, and Georgia Coopersmith. 1989. "Understanding College Choice." In *Higher Education Handbook of Theory and Research,* edited by John C. Smart. New York: Agathon Press.

Hout, Michael. 1988. "More Universalism, Less Structural Mobility: The American Occupational Structure in the 1980s." *American Journal of Sociology* 93(3): 1358–400.

Hurtado, Sylvia, Karen Kurotsuchi Inkelas, Charlotte Briggs, and Byung-Shik Rhee. 1997. "Differences in College Access and Choice Among Racial-Ethnic Groups: Identifying Continuing Barriers." *Research in Higher Education* 38(1): 43–75.

Karen, David. 2002. "Changes in Access to Higher Education in the United States: 1980–1992." *Sociology of Education* 75(3): 191–210.

Karen, David, and Kevin J. Dougherty. 2005. "Necessary but Not Sufficient: Higher Education as a Strategy of Social Mobility." In *Higher Education and the Color Line: College Access, Racial Equity, and Social Change,* edited by Gary Orfield, Patricia Marin, and Catherine L. Horn. Cambridge, Mass.: Harvard Education Press.

Kinzie, Jillian, Megan Palmer, John Hayek, Don Hossler, Stacy A. Jacob, and Heather Cummings. 2004. *Fifty Years of College Choice: Social, Political, and Institutional Influences on the Decision-Making Process.* Lumina Foundation for Education

New Agenda Series 5(3). Accessed at http://www.luminafoundation.org/publications/Hossler.pdf.

Lareau, Annette. 2000. *Home Advantage: Social Class and Parental Intervention in Elementary Education,* 2nd ed. Lanham, Md.: Rowman and Littlefield.

———. 2003. *Unequal Childhoods: Class, Race, and Family Life.* Berkeley, Calif.: University of California Press.

McDonough, Patricia 1994. "Buying and Selling Higher Education: The Social Construction of the College Applicant." *Journal of Higher Education* 65(4): 427–46.

———. 1997. *Choosing Colleges: How Social Class and Schools Structure Opportunity.* Albany: State University of New York Press.

Mishel, Lawrence, Jared Bernstein, and Sylvia Allegretto. 2006. *The State of Working America 2006–2007.* Washington: Economic Policy Institute.

Morgan, Stephen. 2005. *On the Edge of Commitment: Educational Attainment and Race in the United States.* Stanford, Calif.: Stanford University Press.

Murnane, Richard J., John B. Willet, and Kathryn Boudett. 1995. "Do High School Dropouts Benefit from Obtaining a GED?" *Educational Evaluation and Policy Analysis* 17(2): 133–47.

National Center for Education Statistics (NCES). 2001a. *Students Whose Parents Did Not Go to College: Postsecondary Access, Persistence, and Attainment.* NCES 2001–126 by Susan Choy. Washington: U.S. Department of Education.

———. 2001b. *The Condition of Education, 2001.* Washington: U.S. Department of Education.

———. 2004. *Dropout Rates in the United States: 2001.* NCES 2005–046. Washington: U.S. Department of Education.

———. 2005. *First-Generation Students in Postsecondary Education: A Look at Their College Transcripts.* NCES 2005–171 by Xianglei Chen and C. Dennis Carroll. Washington: U.S. Department of Education.

Reay, Diane. 1998. *Class Work: Mothers' Involvement in Their Children's Primary Schooling.* London: University College London.

Rosenbaum, James E. 2001. *Beyond College for All: Career Paths of the Forgotten Half.* New York: Russell Sage Foundation.

Rosenbaum, James E., Regina Deil-Amen, and Ann E. Person. 2006. *After Admission: From College Access to College Success.* New York: Russell Sage Foundation.

Souza, Elizabeth. 2003. "Middle-Class Families and the Transition to College." Ph.D. dissertation, University of Massachusetts at Amherst, Department of Sociology.

Stevens, Mitchell. 2007. *Creating a Class: College Admissions and the Education of Elites.* Cambridge, Mass.: Harvard University Press.

Thacker, Lloyd, editor. 2005. *College Unranked: Ending the College Admissions Frenzy.* Cambridge, Mass.: Harvard University Press.

Walpole, MaryBeth. 2003. "Socioeconomic Status and College: How SES Affects College Experiences and Outcomes." *Review of Higher Education* 27(1): 45–73.

Weis, Lois. 2004. *Class Reunion: The Remaking of the American White Working Class.* London: Routledge.

———, editor. 2007. *The Way Class Works: Readings on Family, School, and the Economy.* London: Routledge.

White, Wendy S. 2005. "Students, Parents, Colleges: Drawing the Lines." *Chronicle of Higher Education* 52(17): B16.

Will, Eric. 2005. "Parent Trap." *Chronicle of Higher Education* 51(46): A4.

Chapter 5

Breaking the Class Monolith: Understanding Class Differences in Black Adolescents' Attachment to Racial Identity

KARYN LACY AND ANGEL L. HARRIS

SCHOLARS HAVE long debated the relative importance of social class as a key indicator of social distinctiveness (Bourdieu 1984; Clark and Lipset 1991; Clark, Lipset, and Rempel 1993; Hout, Brooks, and Manza 1993; Kingston 2000; Lamont 1992, 2000; Pakulski 1993; Wilson 1979, 1987). A burgeoning research agenda within this subfield of social stratification is concerned with assessing the impact of social class in the everyday lives of families (Gecas 1979; Hansen 2005; Hochschild 1989; Lareau 2003; Rubin 1976). Many of these studies demonstrate that social class shapes parental socialization strategies. They show that parents differ by social class in terms of the norms and values they seek to help children internalize. Specifically, working class and middle class children are taught by their parents to think about life differently. Melvin Kohn and Carmi Schooler (1983) discovered that working class parents value an authoritarian approach to parenting, while middle class parents value a nonconformist approach. After engaging in intensive ethnographic observation of poor, working class, and middle class white and black families, Annette Lareau (2003) established that poor or working class and middle class parents do not merely *value* different types of parenting styles; they actually engage different parenting strategies as they socialize their children, the effect of which is to foster a sense of entitlement among the middle class children and a sense of constraint among working class and poor children.

Studies conducted by Kohn and Schooler (1983) and Lareau (2003) show that these disparate class dispositions matter enormously in the larger social world. Middle class parents give their children an edge over working class and poor children when they socialize them to interact with adults as equals and to negotiate mainstream institutions. Yet, in their explicit attention to class, these scholars often downplay the role of race in the daily lives of families. Drawing primarily on the socialization experience of a middle class black boy in her sample, Alexander, Lareau reports that racial identity is important to the middle class black parents in her study. However, she does not expand on what parents mean by the concept or depict in much detail how they would balance nurturing a positive black racial identity alongside the considerable effort required to instill a middle class disposition in their children. Lareau argues that Alexander's parents sought to protect him from racism, but "race did not appear to shape the dominant cultural logic of child rearing in Alexander's family or in other families in the study" (Lareau 2003, 133).

Another line of research suggests that parents differ by race in terms of certain values and norms they impart to their children. Although parents from every racial group practice some form of race socialization, proponents of this perspective argue that black parents face an additional burden with respect to their children's socialization (Bowman and Howard 1985; Cose 1993; Hughes 2003; Peters 1985; Tatum 1997; Thomas and Speight 1999; Thornton et al. 1990). According to this perspective, black parents must teach their children how to negotiate interactions in the larger white society and they must also educate them about black culture and lifestyles. The process by which black parents emphasize knowledge of black culture in conjunction with the importance of learning strategies to cope with racial discrimination in mainstream society is known as *racial socialization* (Constantine and Blackmon 2002; Demo and Hughes 1990; Hughes and Johnson 2001; Lesane-Brown et al. 2005). As a result of this racial preparation and development, black children begin to perceive themselves as members of a black community (Coard et al. 2004). Proponents of this perspective conclude that how parents choose to socialize a black child racially has implications for the child's long-term attachment to a positive black racial identity (Hughes and Chen 1997). Numerous studies on race socialization show that children who possess a positive racial identity are better prepared to deal with prejudice, stigmatization, and discrimination and less likely to experience underachievement in school (Bowman and Howard 1985; Oyserman et al. 2003; Thomas and Speight 1999).

While all blacks face a threat of discrimination or racial stereotyping that they must learn to cope with, they may not all respond to this pressure similarly. A positive racial identity is posited to be especially salient among middle class black parents. Middle class blacks report more discrimination than do poor blacks and are generally less optimistic about racial progress than the black working class or poor (on the racial attitudes of middle class blacks, see Feagin and Sikes 1994; Hochschild 1995; Sigelman and Tuch 1997; Young 1999). There is growing evidence to suggest that middle class blacks seek connections to other blacks as a buffer against the demands of living or working in mainstream society (Benjamin 1991; Graham 1999; Lacy 2004; Neckerman, Carter, and Lee 1999). Thus, given their routine interactions in predominantly white settings, racial socialization beliefs and practices may be more prevalent among the black middle class than they are among the black lower classes.[1]

At the same time, there is reason to believe that the race socialization practices of black parents may vary not only *across* social classes, but also *within* the black middle class, a phenomenon neglected by both class socialization and race socialization scholars. In a qualitative study of the parenting strategies of middle class blacks in three middle class suburbs of Washington, D.C., Karyn Lacy (2007) shows that different groups of middle class blacks think differently about how to socialize their children. Upper middle class blacks create gradations between their group and middle class blacks who live close by in neighboring subdivisions, and this dichotomy shapes their perceptions about how best to socialize their children. Middle class blacks employ a different strategy, drawing distinctions against the black poor, and it is concern with maintaining this boundary that informs their parenting strategies. Lacy's work suggests that treating middle class blacks as one broad, undifferentiated category obscures the heterogeneity within this group. However, we do not know whether her findings are unique to the population she studied or if the differences she identified in parenting strategies would replicate among a broader sample of blacks. Moreover, Lacy does not assess the extent to which parents' beliefs about race are actually adopted by their children.

It is surprising that social scientists have produced so few studies that merge these two informative literatures on class and racial socialization.[2] Assessing the impact of black parents' class position and their racial beliefs and practices on their children's racial identity is critical to a proper understanding of how class and race work within black families. At stake is whether black children from different social class backgrounds are equally prepared for the demands of mainstream society. Consistent with the racial socialization literature, being prepared in this context means that parents have socialized their children to understand and appreciate black culture and taught them how to deal effectively with discrimination in mainstream society as it arises.[3] Despite the posited importance of variation in racial identity by social class, little attention has been devoted to class differences in racial socialization (for an exception, see Lacy 2004, 2007). In general, race socialization studies tend to underplay class variation in the kinds of racial socialization strategies that black parents adopt (but see Hughes and Chen 1997; Thornton et al. 1990). Scholars who have explored this relationship find no difference in black parental socialization by social class when it is operationalized as income (Hill 1997; Thornton et al. 1990).

In this study, we examine the effect of parents' social class and racial socialization beliefs and practices on black adolescents' attachment to their racial identity. We argue that we can elaborate on existing models of racial and class socialization by investigating the following research questions. First, do the racial socialization beliefs and practices of black parents vary by social class? Second, does the racial identity of black adolescents vary by social class? And third, does parents' social class have an effect on youths' racial identity independent of the effect of parental socialization? Thus, we assess whether merging the class and race socialization literatures provides new insight into the relationship between parental racial socialization and black youths' attachment to racial identity. Our findings contribute to the ongoing debate about the salience of social class in American society. Specifically, we show that there are meaningful differences by social class in the parenting strategies of blacks, both across class and within a single-class category—the middle class—and furthermore, that parents' beliefs do bear on youths' developing racial identity.

To explore these questions, we divide the black middle class into finer gradations. This strategy allows us to draw comparisons in two ways: according to conventional wisdom through analysis of comparisons of the well-known dichotomy between the black middle class and the black poor; and according to new wisdom through analysis of comparisons between three distinct groups of black middle class people—the lower middle class, the middle class, and the upper middle class.

Our initial step is to determine whether there really are notable differences in the racial socialization practices of poor and middle class blacks. We then explore whether drawing internal comparisons between the black lower middle class, middle class, and upper middle class is a more useful way to understand race socialization practices; in this analysis, we uncover intra-class differences that would be otherwise missed if the black middle class were defined as a single unified group. Similar to class socialization theorists who have determined that parents in different class categories teach their children to think differently about upward mobility and the potential for occupational success, we examine whether social class informs parents' practices around race and preparation for negotiating mainstream society. Our next step is to investigate the extent to which parents' racial beliefs and practices are actually internalized by their children. We conclude by assessing whether social class has an independent effect on youths' black racial identity, net of parental race socialization.

It is important to note that there may be clear and meaningful differences between parents who hold college degrees and those who do not, and that these differences in educational attainment could bear on parents' racial socialization practices. College is one of the few public spaces where individuals are encouraged to talk about race. In recent years, many colleges have incorporated a race requirement into the core curriculum; students must take a "race course" in order to graduate. For these reasons, measuring social class in terms of income alone may not capture significant mechanisms associated with parents' racial socialization beliefs and practices. Simply giving more material resources to parents does not necessarily mean they will privilege the need to be knowledgeable about black culture or to learn to cope with racial discrimination as beliefs important enough to transfer to their children. However, their college experiences with other racial and ethnic groups and their participation in college courses where race is debated may compel them to do so. To be sure, higher income is generally good for overall child well being, but it does not necessarily follow that parents with greater economic resources are more likely to take a hands-on approach to nurturing their children's racial identity. We argue that educational attainment—and more specifically, college attendance—is positively correlated with deeply held concerns about racial socialization.

Examining the Link Between Social Class and Racial Identity

This study explores the effect of social class on parental socialization and on youths' attachment to a black racial identity. The top panel of figure 5.1 portrays the theoretical model in which social class is mediated by parental racial socialization. The assumption is that parents in different social class positions socialize their children differently with regard to race and that this results in social class variation in racial identity among the youths. The bottom panel of the figure portrays the empirical model; it shows how we operationalize social class, racial socialization, and racial identity. The dotted arrow illustrates the primary focus of this study: assessing the presence of an independent effect of social class on youths' racial identity. If black children in higher social class positions feel more positively about their race than their less-advantaged counterparts, net of how they are racially socialized, this would indicate the salience of social class in American society.

Methods

We rely on data from the Maryland Adolescence Development in Context Study (MADICS) to explore the role of social class in the development of youths' racial identity. The MADICS is a longitudinal study involving interviews with 1,407 black (66 percent) and white (34 percent) families.

Figure 5.1   Theoretical and Empirical Models for the Link Between Social Class and Racial Identity

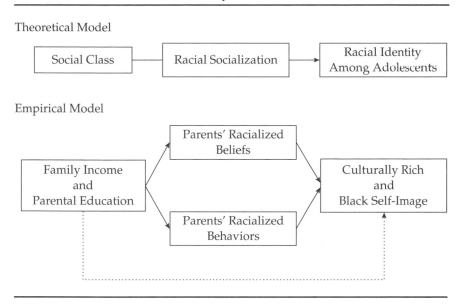

Theoretical Model

| Social Class | — | Racial Socialization | ➔ | Racial Identity Among Adolescents |

Empirical Model

Source: Authors' compilation.

The sample contains slightly fewer girls (49 percent) than boys (51 percent). The data were collected by the Gender and Academic Research Program (GARP) at the University of Michigan in five waves beginning in 1991, when the target youths (1,407) entered seventh grade. Data were collected via face-to-face interviews and self-administered questionnaires from both parents and youths. Interviews lasted an average of one hour and fifteen minutes. This process was repeated when the target youths were in grades eight (1,004) and eleven (954). A final interview was conducted three years after the youths had graduated from high school.[4] The highest attrition rates occurred between grades seven and eight; only 3 percent of the sample was lost between grades eight and eleven. Therefore, it is unlikely that sample attrition is the result of students dropping out of high school. Also, in supplemental analyses not shown, blacks were *not* more likely to leave the study than whites; the proportion of whites and blacks within the sample remained the same for each wave.

The GARP used a stratified sampling procedure to select from the approximately five thousand adolescents in Prince George's County who entered middle school during the 1991 school year. Located on the southern tip of Maryland and about a twenty-minute drive from Washington, D.C., Prince George's County is majority-black and disproportionately middle class. Scholars and journalists write frequently about Prince George's County because it is the only county in the country in which the median income continued to rise as the county's black population increased. But this upward tick in median income is not spread evenly across the county: the inner-suburban communities closest to the Washington border contain high concentrations of poor and lower middle class residents. Therefore, youths from low income, middle class, and upper middle class families are all included in our sample. The MADICS contains a proportional representation of families from each of the county's twenty-three junior high schools. In this study, we include only black respondents who were present in the first three waves of the MADICS and completed the racial identity scales (n = 519). The mean family income reported by parents in 1990 ranged from $45,000 to $49,000. The mean family income for whites ($50,000 to $54,999) was significantly higher than that for blacks ($40,000 to $44,999).

Although the MADICS is primarily used by psychologists and was collected for the purposes of understanding the processes behind the psychological determinants of behavior and developmental trajectories during adolescence, it is well suited to the goal of this study. Typically, scholars interview either parents *or* their children. But the wide variety of measures collected for both parents and youth in the MADICS provide ample data to assess social class differences in the impact of parents' racial socialization on youths using a longitudinal approach. Through this process, we examine directly the impact of parents' beliefs and practices on their children. Here, too, we explore differences across class categories, this time among the youths. In short, the MADICS has the necessary quality and breadth to address the goals of this study. One unfortunate limitation of the MADICS is that it was not designed to draw inferences regarding a national population of black adolescents. However, to our knowledge, no theoretical model posits that the underlying causal mechanisms by which social class influences black youths' racial identity vary by region.

To assess whether parents' racial beliefs and socialization practices vary by class, we construct dummy variables based on income gradations as our first proxy for class: lower middle class, $30,000 to 49,999 (mean = .23); middle class, $50,000 to 74,999 (mean = .24); and upper middle class, $75,000 or greater (mean = .28). Families with income ranging from $0 to $29,999 (mean = .25) serve as the reference group. We construct a dummy variable based on educational attainment as our second proxy for class: those who have earned a four-year college degree or higher and those who have not. Our indicators are consistent with a move among some inequality scholars who advocate for independent rather than composite measures of social class. In a critique of the widely embraced Duncan SEI measure, Robert Hauser and John Warren (1997) argue that not only does a social class composite divided into single measures allow researchers to select the measures most suitable for their research question, but that composite measures may produce erroneous conclusions. We avoid this pitfall by decomposing our measures of social class.

We assess two dimensions of parents' racial socialization: parents' beliefs about race and their behaviors around race. To measure parents' beliefs about race, respondents were asked about the importance of their own racial background to the daily life of their family (mean = 2.96, on a 4-point scale); the degree to which they believe blacks are supportive of one another (mean = 2.75); the extent to which they believe black people have a rich culture (mean = 3.30); and whether being black has affected the goals they set for their children (mean = .22, on a 0-to-1 scale). These variables reveal how parents *think* about what it means to be black. To understand whether parents' racial socialization practices or behaviors vary by social class, we relied on a second set of measures. Respondents were asked about the frequency with which they celebrate days connected to blackness or black culture (mean = 3.04 on 5-point scale); participate in community activities with other blacks (mean = 3.13); discuss race with their child (mean = 3.59); and talk to their child about racial discrimination (mean = 2.93, on a 6-point scale). The first two indicators in this second group of variables reveal what parents actually *do* to show their children what it means to be black. The latter indicators show how much discussions of race are a part of the child's family experience. Table 5.1 presents the means and standard deviations for each of these variables.

Since our primary interest is the salience of adolescents' black racial identity, we rely on two measures that reflect the transfer of racial beliefs and practices from parent to child: the degree to which adolescents believe that blacks have a rich culture and the importance of a black self-image. The first measure taps into the youths' collective identity, that is, the belief that they share a rich culture with other blacks. Youths were asked the same questions that were posed to their parents: Do you believe that people of your race have a rich culture? Do you believe that you have meaningful traditions because of your race? The second measure is an index designed to assess the youths' individual identity by gauging how positively they feel about being black. Specifically, youths were asked the degree to which they believe being black is an important part of their self-image; have a strong attachment to other blacks; believe being black is an important reflection of who they are; and believe being black matters little for how they feel about themselves (reverse-coded). We also assess the impact of black adolescents' friendship networks on their identity by the proportion of their friends who are black.

Findings

Our first research question—whether parents' racial beliefs and socialization practices vary by class—is addressed in table 5.2. The top panel examines whether class differences exist in parents' racial *beliefs*. In model 1,

Table 5.1 Means, Standard Deviations, and Descriptions for Variables Used in the Analysis

Variables	Description	Metric	Mean (Standard Deviation)	Alpha
Youth outcome measures (grade 11)				
Culturally rich	(a) People of my race-ethnicity have a culturally rich heritage; (b) I have meaningful traditions because of my race-ethnicity.	1 = Not at all 5 = Extremely true	2.99 (1.12)	.698
Black self-image	(a) In general, being black is an important part of my self-image; (b) I have a strong attachment to other black people; (c) being black is an important reflection of who I am; (d) overall, being black has very little to do with how I feel about myself.[a]	1 = Strongly disagree 5 = Strongly agree	3.49 (.73)	.629
Parent beliefs about race (youth in grade 8)				
Importance of race	How important is your racial background to the daily life of your family?	1 = Not at all 4 = Very	2.96 (1.20)	—
Supportive	People of your race are very supportive of each other.	1 = Not at all 4 = Very	2.75 (.85)	—
Culturally rich	How true are the following? (a) People of your race have a culturally rich heritage; (b) you have meaningful traditions because of your race.	1 = Not at all 4 = Very	3.30 (.78)	.697
Race affects goals (grade 7)	Has being black affected the goals you have for (child)?	0 = No 1 = Yes	.22 (.41)	—
Parent behaviors around race (youth in grade 8)				
Celebrate days	How often do you celebrate any special days connected to your racial background?	1 = Almost never 5 = Almost always	3.04 (1.17)	—

			Mean (SD)	α
Participate in activities	How often do you participate in community activities with people of your racial background?	1 = Almost never 5 = Almost always	3.13 (1.24)	—
Talk about being black (grade 7)	How often do you talk in the family about being black?	1 = Never 5 = Very often	3.59 (1.40)	—
Talk about discrimination	How often do you talk to (child) about how much discrimination (he or she) may face because of (his or her) race?	1 = Almost never 6 = Almost every day	2.93 (1.53)	—
Peers (grade 7)				
Proportion of friends who are black	(Youth's response to) How many of the friends you spend most of your time with are black?	1 = None of them 5 = All of them	3.94 (.88)	—
Youth's self-perception				
Self-confidence	Are you very good at (a) figuring out problems and planning how to solve them; (b) carrying out the plans you make for solving problems; (c) bouncing back quickly from bad experiences; (d) learning from your mistakes? (e) Are you pretty sure about yourself?	1 = Almost never 5 = Almost always	4.04 (.62)	.740
Social class (assessed from parents)				
$0 to $29,999	Based on total family income	0 = No 1 = Yes	.25 (.43)	—
$30,000 to $49,999	Based on total family income	0 = No 1 = Yes	.23 (.42)	—
$50,000 to $74,999	Based on total family income	0 = No 1 = Yes	.24 (.43)	—
$75,000 and over	Based on total family income	0 = No 1 = Yes	.28 (.45)	—
BA/BS or higher	Proportion of parents with a BA/BS degree or higher	0 = No 1 = Yes	.36 (.48)	—

Source: Maryland Adolescence Development in Context Study (MADICS), 1991, 1995.
[a] Item is reverse-coded.

Table 5.2 Social Class Differences in Parents' Racial Beliefs and Socialization Practices

	Importance of Race to Daily Life			People of Race Are Supportive			Culturally Rich			Race Affects Goals Set for Youth		
	(1)	(2)	(3)	(1)	(2)	(3)	(1)	(2)	(3)	(1)	(2)	(3)
Income ($0 to $29,999 omitted)												
$30,000 to $49,999	.323 (.173)	—	.278 (.173)	-.106 (.122)	—	-.118 (.123)	.198 (.114)	—	.146 (.112)	1.452	—	1.269
$50,000 to $74,999	.185 (.183)	—	.057 (.189)	-.059 (.129)	—	-.090 (.133)	.359** (.120)	—	.219 (.121)	2.812**	—	1.983
$75,000 or more	.340 (.196)	—	.202 (.202)	.134 (.138)	—	.099 (.143)	.434*** (.128)	—	.281* (.130)	3.681**	—	2.540*
Education (less than BA/BS omitted)												
BA/BS or higher	—	.308** (.112)	.302** (.118)	—	.089 (.080)	.077 (.084)	—	.387*** (.072)	.342*** (.075)	—	2.639***	2.264***
Constant	2.794*** (.143)	2.889*** (.103)	2.758*** (.143)	2.829*** (.101)	2.771*** (.073)	2.820*** (.101)	3.052*** (.094)	3.130*** (.066)	3.011*** (.093)	—	—	—
Odds ratio, chi-squared (df)									11.98, 6	18.47, 3	23.86, 7	—
R-squared	.014	.019	.027	.014	.004	.015	.032	.060	.071	—	—	—

	Celebrate Days Connected to Race			Participate in Activities			Talk About Being Black			Talk About Discrimination		
	(1)	(2)	(3)	(1)	(2)	(3)	(1)	(2)	(3)	(1)	(2)	(3)
Income ($0 to $29,999 omitted)												
$30,000 to $49,999	.215	—	.218	.219	—	.145	.358	—	.286	.089	—	.045
	(.169)		(.170)	(.177)		(.175)	(.202)		(.201)	(.222)		(.222)
$50,000 to $74,999	.068	—	.077	.351	—	.149	.672**	—	.478*	.111	—	-.015
	(.178)		(.184)	(.187)		(.190)	(.213)		(.218)	(.234)		(.241)
$75,000 or more	.183	—	.193	.596**	—	.370	.727**	—	.518*	.290	—	.151
	(.191)		(.198)	(.201)		(.205)	(.231)		(.236)	(.252)		(.260)
Education (less than BA/BS omitted)												
BA/BS or higher	—	-.008	-.022	—	.549***	.499***	—	.566***	.476***	—	.325*	.314*
		(.110)	(.115)		(.114)	(.119)		(.130)	(.136)		(.145)	(.152)
Constant	2.855***	2.983***	2.858***	2.822***	2.867***	2.764***	2.997***	3.176***	2.944***	2.938***	2.914***	2.902***
	(.141)	(.101)	(.142)	(.147)	(.104)	(.145)	(.169)	(.118)	(.167)	(.184)	(.131)	(.184)
R-squared	.013	.003	.014	.021	.047	.055	.038	.051	.062	.005	.012	.014

Source: Maryland Adolescence Development in Context Study (MADICS), 1991, 1995.
Note: All models are net of family structure and sex. Number of observations range from 487 to 502.
*p < .05; **p < .01; ***p < .001 (two-tailed tests)

where social class is measured as income, there are no differences among the parents in terms of the importance they attach to race in their everyday lives or the perception that blacks are supportive of one another. But a higher class position is associated with stronger beliefs about the richness of black culture and the importance of race in setting goals for children. Both middle class and upper middle class parents strongly agree that blacks have a rich culture. Indeed, these beliefs are most salient among upper middle class blacks. Moreover, middle class blacks are nearly three times as likely as the black lower class to believe that race affects how they think about their child's development (odds ratio = 2.81), while upper middle class blacks are nearly four times as likely as the black lower classes to hold this view (odds ratio = 3.68).

Model 2 shows this link when social class is measured using parental education. Education mediates the relationship between social class and three of the four racial beliefs. Specifically, relative to blacks without a four-year college degree, college graduates attribute greater importance to race in daily life and greater richness to black culture, and they are more than twice as likely to report that their race affects the goals they set for their children. Model 3 shows that these findings are similar when both income and parental education are controlled. Although income has an effect on blacks' belief that they have a rich cultural tradition in model 1, model 3 shows that all of the effect for middle class blacks is explained by educational attainment, as is much of the effect for upper middle class blacks. Similarly, with regard to the belief that race factors into goals parents set for their children, educational attainment accounts for all of the effect among middle class blacks and for part of the effect among upper middle class blacks. Thus, in terms of their beliefs about race, middle class blacks, upper middle class blacks, and blacks with a four-year college degree hold stronger beliefs about the richness of black culture and the importance of considering race when setting goals for children than their less-advantaged counterparts.

In the bottom panel of table 5.2, we focus on parental socialization *practices* and assess whether parents' racial socialization practices vary by class. Models for the first outcome show no variation by social class in the frequency with which blacks celebrate holidays associated with their race. The second and third outcomes show that upper middle class parents interact more with other blacks and that discussions about being black occur more frequently within middle class and upper middle class families. Relative to parents with less than a four-year college degree, college graduates interact more with other blacks within their communities, talk more with their families about being black, and discuss racial discrimination more with their children. Thus, blacks who have a college degree feel stronger about the centrality of race than those who have not completed a four-year college degree. The findings for model 3 are also displayed in figure 5.2.

Figure 5.2   Social Class Differences in Parents' Racial Beliefs and Socialization Practices

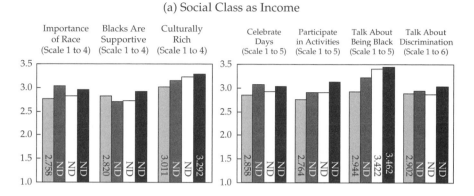

(a) Social Class as Income

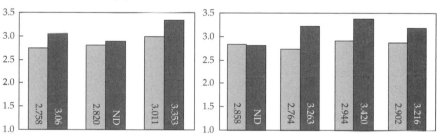

(b) Social Class as Parental Education

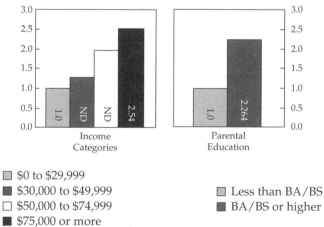

(c) Race Affects Goals Parents Set for Child (0 – No, 1 – Yes): Odds Ratios

☐ $0 to $29,999
■ $30,000 to $49,999
☐ $50,000 to $74,999
■ $75,000 or more

☐ Less than BA/BS
■ BA/BS or higher

Source: Authors' compilation.
Note: Numbers are from model 3 in table 5.2 for each outcome. ND = no difference.

Table 5.3 Youths' Beliefs About Having a Rich Culture on Social Class, Parents' Racial Beliefs and Behaviors, and Proportion of Black Peers

	Culturally Rich								
	Models with Social Class as Income				Models with Social Class as Parents' Education				
	Social Class +	Parents' Beliefs	Parents' Behaviors +	Proportion of Black Peers	Social Class +	Parents' Beliefs	Parents' Behaviors +	Proportion of Black Peers	Full Model
Income ($0 to $29,999 omitted)									
$30,000 to $49,999	.429** (.166)	.341* (.166)	.311† (.168)	.300† (.168)	—	—	—	—	.288† (.169)
$50,000 to $74,999	.585*** (.174)	.484** (.176)	.416* (.180)	.398* (.181)	—	—	—	—	.362* (.184)
$75,000 or more	.748*** (.187)	.616*** (.191)	.582** (.194)	.578** (.194)	—	—	—	—	.543** (.197)
Education (less than BA/BS omitted)									
BA/BS or higher	—	—	—	—	.318** (.109)	.210† (.112)	.186 (.115)	.177 (.116)	.120 (.119)
Parents' beliefs about race									
Importance of race	—	.114* (.046)	.076 (.051)	.078 (.051)	—	.114* (.046)	.076 (.051)	.076 (.051)	.076 (.051)
Supportive	—	-.004	.011	.012	—	-.003	.014	.017	.016

	(1)	(2)	(3)	(4)	(5)	(6)	(7)	(8)	(9)
(variable name cut off; SE only)	(.068)	(.071)	(.071)	(.071)	(.068)	(.070)	(.071)	(.071)	(.071)
Culturally rich	.126† (.075)	.094 (.078)	.094 (.079)	.095 (.079)	.129† (.076)	.094 (.079)	.094 (.080)	.095 (.079)	.083 (.079)
Race affects goals	.119 (.132)	.061 (.135)	.075 (.135)	.075 (.135)	.139 (.133)	.081 (.136)	.095 (.136)	.095 (.136)	.064 (.136)
Parents' behaviors around race									
Celebrate days	—	-.018 (.050)	-.007 (.051)	—	—	-.015 (.051)	-.006 (.051)	—	-.001 (.051)
Participate in activities	—	-.018 (.047)	-.019 (.047)	—	—	-.017 (.048)	-.017 (.048)	—	-.026 (.048)
Talk about race	—	.110* (.045)	.106* (.045)	—	—	.115** (.045)	.109* (.045)	—	.104* (.045)
Talk about discrimination	—	.010 (.038)	.009 (.038)	—	—	.007 (.038)	.008 (.038)	—	.006 (.038)
Youth measure									
Proportion of black peers	—	—	-.022 (.061)	—	—	—	-.005 (.060)	—	-.016 (.061)
Constant	1.605*** (.361)	.893* (.434)	.806 (.446)	.898 (.511)	1.900*** (.350)	1.121** (.427)	1.000* (.440)	1.009* (.504)	.920 (.512)
R-squared	.075	.113	.128	.133	.058	.097	.114	.119	.135

Source: Maryland Adolescence Development in Context Study (MADICS), 1991, 1995.

Note: All models are net of youth's self-confidence, family structure, and sex. Number of observations is 449.

†p < .10; *p < .05; **p < .01; ***p < .001 (two-tailed tests)

Table 5.3 presents findings from the analysis of the impact of black parents' racial beliefs and socialization practices on one component of their children's black racial identity—whether the adolescents believe that blacks have a rich cultural heritage. The first model, which addresses the second research question, shows that family income is positively related with black adolescents' beliefs about their rich cultural heritage. In fact, these beliefs are more strongly held by black adolescents as black families ascend the class ladder. Findings for the next model, which includes parents' beliefs about race, show that parents' beliefs about the importance of race in the daily life of their family explain some, though not much, of the effect of income on youths' beliefs about blacks having a rich culture. The effect remains present across all income categories. Interestingly, the transferal of parents' beliefs as to whether blacks have a rich culture to their children is only marginally significant. With regard to parents' socialization practices, only one measure has an effect on whether youths believe they have a rich cultural tradition: the frequency with which their parents talk in the family setting about being black. Discussing race leads to slight declines in income effects across all income groups. Also, parents' beliefs about the importance of race are expressed by talking to their children about being black. The effect of income for the lower middle class is reduced to marginal significance when talk about race is controlled. We find no effect of black friends on youths' perception that blacks have a rich cultural tradition.

We repeat these analyses using parents' education rather than their income as the measure for social class. These results are presented in the right-hand columns of table 5.3. Education is positively related with youths' perception that blacks have a rich culture, though the effect of education is not as large as that of income. Similar to the previous set of models, parents' beliefs about the importance of race in the daily lives of their family explains most of this effect; the main effect of education reduces to marginal significance. However, controlling for the frequency of family discussion about race leads the effect of education to become nonsignificant.

In summary, when social class is operationalized in terms of parental income, it remains a significant explanation for youths' beliefs about black culture even after we account for the parental racial socialization measures. That is to say, income has a greater effect on adolescents' beliefs about blacks having a rich culture than how they are socialized by their parents to understand race. Black middle class and upper middle class adolescents feel strongly that blacks have a rich cultural tradition independent of how their parents socialize them racially.

In table 5.4, we present findings for the impact of black parents' racial beliefs and socialization practices on a different measure of their children's black racial identity—adolescents' black self-image. In the first four models, we use income as our measure of social class. Among all class groupings, parents' income is important for adolescents' black self-image (see model 1) and remains important even after we include the race socialization measures in our models (models 2 to 4). The extent to which parents talk about race has a marginal effect on youths' black self-image (model 3). Also, adolescents' proportion of black peers is more important for their black self-image than either parents' racial beliefs or behaviors (model 4), which was not the case for youths' perceptions about the richness of black culture in table 5.3. Finally, the last set of models shows that parents' educational attainment does not influence adolescents' black self-image.

Conclusions

Our study used attitudinal data collected from a social survey of black parents and their children in two distinct waves to examine whether the racial socialization beliefs and practices of parents vary by social class and the effect of parents' social class on the salience of a black racial identity among their children. The study's results illustrate the critical role that social class plays in black families' attachment to a racial identity. We draw three conclusions from our analysis.

First, we discovered that there are both inter-class and intra-class differences in racial socialization practices. When considered together as a group, middle class black parents differ from the black lower class on only a few variables: the extent to which they believe blacks are culturally rich, whether race affect the goals they set for their children, and the frequency of their discussions about being black. Importantly, the lower middle class is indistinguishable from the black poor on each of the parental socialization measures. But when the black middle class is divided into gradations, intra-class differences emerge. Generally, strong beliefs about race and the importance of demonstrating through practices what it means to be black increase with class. This finding allows us to extend both the class and race socialization models. Black parents differ in their racial beliefs and practices. Just as middle class black and white parents believe that socializing their children into a middle class orientation through activities, language, and networks is an important component of their development (Lareau 2003), middle class and upper middle class black parents feel more strongly than the black lower classes that socializing their children racially through certain racial beliefs and practices is important for their development.

Second, we find that class operates differently when we control for a second measure of social class—parents' educational attainment. The income effect of class on two parental socialization measures, "culturally rich" and "goal-setting," disappears. All of the difference between the black middle class and the black poor is explained by educational attainment. Education is important across more of the parental racial attitude and belief outcomes than income. Additionally, controlling for educational attainment produces two important effects that would be missed if social class were operationalized solely with income: college-educated blacks feel more strongly

Table 5.4   Youths' Black Self-Image on Social Class, Parents' Racial Beliefs and Behaviors, and Proportion of Black Peers

	Black Self-Image								
	Models with Social Class as Income				Models with Social Class as Parents' Education				Full Model
	Social Class +	Parents' Beliefs +	Parents' Behaviors +	Proportion of Black Peers	Social Class +	Parents' Beliefs	Parents' Behaviors +	Proportion of Black Peers	
Income ($0 to $29,999 omitted)									
$30,000 to $49,999	.274** (.104)	.231* (.104)	.234* (.105)	.210* (.105)	—	—	—	—	.210* (.105)
$50,000 to $74,999	.283** (.109)	.230* (.110)	.225* (.112)	.238* (.112)	—	—	—	—	.240* (.114)
$75,000 or more	.364*** (.117)	.315** (.119)	.317** (.121)	.309** (.120)	—	—	—	—	.311** (.123)
Education (less than BA/BS omitted)									
BA/BS or higher	—	—	—	—	.052 (.068)	.007 (.071)	.004 (.073)	.030 (.073)	-.007 (.075)
Parents' beliefs about race									
Importance of race	—	.067* (.029)	.062* (.032)	.055† (.032)	—	.071* (.029)	.064* (.032)	.055† (.032)	.055† (.032)
Supportive	—	-.052 (.042)	-.049 (.043)	-.039 (.043)	—	-.057 (.042)	-.053 (.043)	-.042 (.043)	-.039 (.043)
Culturally rich	—	.057 (.048)	.062 (.050)	.054 (.049)	—	.072 (.048)	.072 (.050)	.062 (.050)	.055 (.050)

	(1)	(2)	(3)	(4)	(5)	(6)	(7)	(8)	(9)
Race affects goals	—	-.041	-.049	-.047	—	-.022	-.032	-.033	-.046
		(.082)	(.083)	(.082)		(.082)	(.083)	(.083)	(.083)
Parents' behaviors around race									
Celebrate days	—	—	-.011	-.016	—	—	-.010	-.015	-.017
			(.031)	(.030)			(.031)	(.031)	(.031)
Participate in activities	—	—	-.023	-.022	—	—	-.019	-.019	-.021
			(.029)	(.029)			(.029)	(.029)	(.029)
Talk about race	—	—	.049+	.048+	—	—	.054*	.052+	.049+
			(.027)	(.027)			(.027)	(.027)	(.027)
Talk about discrimination	—	—	-.032	-.025	—	—	-.033	-.026	-.025
			(.023)	(.023)			(.023)	(.023)	(.023)
Youth measure									
Proportion of black peers	—	—	—	.100**	—	—	—	.105**	.087*
				(.038)				(.038)	(.038)
Constant	2.940***	2.675***	2.727***	2.309***	3.099***	2.767***	2.811***	2.380***	2.307***
	(.228)	(.273)	(.280)	(.321)	(.223)	(.271)	(.278)	(.318)	(.321)
R-squared	.054	.087	.102	.115	.033	.072	.087	.102	.115

Source: Maryland Adolescence Development in Context Study (MADICS), 1991, 1995.
Note: All models are net of youth's self-confidence, family structure, and sex. Number of observations is 494.
+p < .10; *p < .05; **p < .01; ***p < .001 (two-tailed tests)

about the importance of race in their daily lives and they talk more frequently with their children about the discrimination they could face than do those who are not college graduates. These findings point to the importance of defining social class through a series of single indicators rather than a composite measure. Thus, results from this study build on the study by Michael Thornton and his colleagues (1990) of socialization practices among a socioeconomically diverse group of black parents. Thornton et al. find no effect when social class is measured as income, but they report an effect when social class is measured as education.

How do we explain these class-based differences in parental socialization beliefs and practices? Why do upper middle class, middle class, and highly educated black parents hold such strong beliefs about racial socialization? One possible explanation is that high-income and highly educated black people experience race differently than other blacks do. These blacks often work in predominantly white environments where they must conform to mainstream cultural standards in order to move through the ranks of their industry or organization. Paradoxically, having to master white cultural norms and negotiate interactions with white coworkers may lead blacks to place a high value on black culture and being black. This interpretation is consistent with the literature on the experiences of middle class blacks in which blacks report their frustrated attempts to "fit in" in the corporate world, the ongoing discrimination they face in their daily lives, and their disbelief that conditions will improve dramatically for black people in the near future (Anderson 1999; Bell and Nkomo 2003; Cose 1993; Feagin and Sikes 1994; Hochschild 1995; Sigelman and Welch 1991; Young 1999).

Why do the racial beliefs and practices of the black lower middle class not differ substantively from those of the black poor? As Mary Pattillo-McCoy (1999) shows in her book *Black Picket Fences*, there are many similarities in the social conditions of lower middle class and poor blacks. For example, lower middle class black adolescents in the Chicago neighborhood Pattillo-McCoy studied go out of their way to align themselves with poor blacks—the group that sets the tone for what it means to be black in their community. She suggests that black adolescents who are close to poor blacks spatially tend to share values and beliefs with them, even though they are lower middle class. In their neighborhood setting, being middle class means walking the line between a rigid middle class lifestyle and the lure of a seductive lower class lifestyle. "'Middle class' might include wearing baggy jeans or rapping along to an explicit song about rough sex and gunplay, but Groveland youth perform these styles simultaneously with participating in the church youth group or going off to college" (Pattillo-McCoy 1999, 214). Lower middle class black parents' socialization beliefs and practices are indistinguishable from those of poor blacks because people who are close to poor blacks on the class ladder tend to share with them certain attitudes about the relevance of racial socialization, while those furthest from poor blacks on the class ladder may form a different conception.

Third, we examined whether parents' racial socialization beliefs and practices bear on their children's attachment to a black racial identity. We find that income trumps parents' socialization beliefs and practices in terms of affecting black adolescents' views of their cultural heritage and racial self-image. While education is the best predictor of parents' racial attitudes and practices, family income is a more consistently important predictor of black adolescents' beliefs, and only a tiny portion of the income effect is explained away by parental socialization.

Thus, social class operates not only through the racial socialization practices of parents to have an impact on youths' identity but also has an independent effect on youths' racial identity. Adolescents in higher social class categories demonstrate greater attachment to racial identity; they feel more positively about being black than do their less-advantaged counterparts despite their parents' beliefs or practices regarding race.[5] This could mean that a higher social class position provides added preparation for negotiating the black and white worlds that youths will encounter when they become adults. That is, the class advantages identified by class socialization scholars may serve as an additional resource available to upper middle class and middle class black children to help them grapple effectively with racism.

Moreover, when racial identity is operationalized as "black self-image," the number of a child's friends who are black has a significant effect on his or her attachment to a racial identity. Clearly, there is something about growing up in a middle class or upper middle class family that encourages black youth to feel good about being black. Could it be, as Michael Hout and Mary Pattillo speculated, that income itself has a positive effect on black self-image? We live in a materialistic and status-conscious society, and given the historic association of black and poor, this outcome is not so far-fetched. Being able to reject the stigma of poverty, visibly and publicly, with material wealth may indeed be a powerful accomplishment. Idealistic teenagers are young enough to firmly believe that this strategy will work for them in the long run. These privileged youth may also be in a better position than the black lower class to grapple with discrimination they are likely to face in the larger white society once they become adults.

Taken together, our findings demonstrate the power of social class in affecting the racial identity of adolescents and provide a useful corrective to theories that emphasize the power of parents in socializing youths. Why do parents' racial beliefs and behaviors not matter more for adolescents' black self-image? Teenagers are at an age when they seek to sever ties with their parents in symbolic ways. When it comes to their presentation of self, adolescents care more about what their friends think than they do about what their parents think. The psychologist Beverly Daniel Tatum (1997) sums up this sentiment in her book *Why Are All the Black Kids Sitting Together in the Cafeteria?* She writes:

> In adolescence . . . finding the answer to questions such as, "What does it mean to be a young black person? How should I act? What should I do?" is particularly important. And although Black fathers, mothers, aunts, and uncles may hold the answers by offering themselves as role models, they hold little appeal for most adolescents. The last thing many fourteen-year-olds want to do is grow up to be like their parents. It is the peer group, the kids in the cafeteria, who hold the answers to these questions. They know how to be black. They have absorbed the stereotypical images of Black youth in the popular culture and are reflecting those images in their self-presentation (60).

Some readers may argue that all adolescents look to their teenage peers, not their parents, for direction about how to construct and maintain their identity as a teen. In this way, black adolescents would not differ from their white counterparts. Presumably, parents' beliefs might carry more weight among youth when they have grown past adolescence and become young adults. Future research should assess whether parents' beliefs matter more to their children after the children reach adulthood.

Readers may also question our use of the variable "culturally rich." The MADICS does not specify what is meant by "cultural heritage" or "cultural tradition." It is possible that middle class and upper middle class parents and children understand these terms differently than the black lower class does. Whereas among the upper classes the term "culture" may invoke images of jazz, art, or other forms of "high" culture, among the lower classes the term may conjure up equally favorable attachments to hip hop culture. Future research should sort out precisely what parents and adolescents envision when they hear the term "culture."

Class affects one's educational opportunities, determines where one will work, influences where one will live, and, as we have shown, shapes the racial beliefs and practices of parents and their impact on their black adolescents' attachment to their racial identity. Subsequent studies will need to explore these intra-class patterns in more detail in order to fully understand their implications. As Frank Furstenberg (2006, 2) laments:

> We have stopped measuring altogether the finer grade distinctions of growing up with differential resources . . . we certainly understand that affluence and education make a huge difference. Yet [social scientists] view economic status as a continuum that defies qualitatively finer breakdowns. . . . Just as we have come to recognize the hazards of lumping together all Hispanics or Asians . . . we need a more nuanced understanding of what difference it makes to possess certain levels of income, education, and occupation.

This chapter is a step in that direction.

Notes

1. William Julius Wilson argues in *The Truly Disadvantaged* (1987) that poor blacks are concentrated in central cities, isolated from the white and black middle classes and their social institutions. His work established the now commonly held perception that poor, urban blacks do not have opportunities to interact routinely with whites. However, some scholars disagree that poor blacks (and racial minorities generally) are necessarily isolated from middle class people, institutions, and norms. Mario Luis Small (2004) shows that Latinos concentrated in a poor, residential neighborhood in Boston do have social connections to middle class people who live well beyond the boundaries of their impoverished community.

2. One possible explanation is that some social scientists believe that socialization has fallen out of favor as a legitimate field of study. Many of these scholars have transitioned into other subfields, such as the life course, arguing that a more expansive research domain is a better way to explain how behaviors are acquired, then change, over time. On this point, see Glen Elder (1994).

3. Some parents may perceive racial socialization as more critical for the development of adolescent children than younger children, a possibility Lareau considers (2002, 773). Diane Hughes and Lisa Chen (1997) find that parental messages centered on discrimination and prejudice increase with the child's age. In this case, as older children begin to move about independently in the larger world, parents intensify their racial socialization practices. But others find that even parents of elementary school children engage in racial socialization, talking to their children frequently about racial barriers and discrimination (Cose 1993; Coard et al. 2004).

4. There were also two post–high school waves conducted one and three years after the youths had graduated from high school. However, given that our focus is on adolescents, we use only the first three waves of the MADICS.

5. Research demonstrates that black children from upper middle class and middle class families possess higher levels of general self-esteem than their counterparts in the lower classes. This general self-esteem could inform youths' black racial identity. We thank Mike Hout and Mary Pattillo for bringing this point to our attention. We control for general self-esteem and find no significant effect of this variable on our measures of racial identity. It is possible that our measures do not capture the beliefs and practices most affected by general self-esteem.

References

Anderson, Elijah. 1999. "The Social Situation of the Black Executive." In *The Cultural Territories of Race: Black and White Boundaries*, edited by Michele Lamont. Chicago, Ill.: University of Chicago Press.

Bell, Ella, and Stella Nkomo. 2003. *Our Separate Ways: Black and White Women and the Struggle for Black Identity*. Boston, Mass.: Harvard Business School Press.

Benjamin, Lois. 1991. *The Black Elite: Facing the Color Line in the Twilight of the Twentieth Century.* Chicago, Ill.: Nelson-Hall.

Bourdieu, Pierre. 1984. *Distinction: A Social Critique of the Judgment of Taste.* Cambridge, Mass.: Harvard University Press.

Bowman, Philip, and Cleopatra Howard. 1985. "Race-Related Socialization, Motivation, and Academic Achievement: A Study of Black Youths in Three-Generation Families." *Journal of the American Academy of Child Psychiatry* 24(2): 134–41.

Clark, Terry, and Seymour Lipset. 1991. "Are Social Classes Dying?" *International Sociology* 6(4): 397–410.

Clark, Terry, Seymour Lipset, and Michael Rempel. 1993. "The Declining Political Significance of Social Class." *International Sociology* 8(3): 293–326.

Coard, Stephanie, Scyatta Wallace, Howard Stevenson, and Lori Brotman. 2004. "Towards Culturally Relevant Preventive Interventions: The Consideration of Racial Socialization in Parent Training with African-American Families." *Journal of Child and Family Studies* 13(3): 277–93.

Constantine, Madonna, and Sha'kema Blackmon. 2002. "Black Adolescents' Racial Socialization Experiences: Their Relations to Home, School, and Peer Self-Esteem." *Journal of Black Studies* 32(3): 322–35.

Cose, Ellis. 1993. *The Rage of a Privileged Class.* New York: HarperCollins.

Demo, David, and Michael Hughes. 1990. "Socialization and Racial Identity Among Black Americans." *Social Psychology Quarterly* 53(4): 364–74.

Elder, Glen. 1994. "Time, Human Agency, and Social Change: Perspectives on the Life Course." *Social Psychology Quarterly* 57(1): 4–15.

Feagin, Joe, and Melvin Sikes. 1994. *Living with Racism: The Black Middle-Class Experience.* Boston, Mass.: Beacon Press.

Furstenberg, Frank. 2006. "Diverging Development: The Not-So-Invisible Hand of Social Class in the United States." Paper presented to the Society for Research on Adolescence, March 2006.

Gecas, Viktor. 1979. "The Influence of Social Class on Socialization." In *Contemporary Theories About the Family,* edited by Wesley Burr, Reuben Hill, F. Ivan Nye, and Ira Reiss. New York: Free Press.

Graham, Lawrence. 1999. *Our Kind of People.* New York: HarperCollins.

Hansen, Karen. 2005. *Not-So-Nuclear Families: Class, Gender, and Networks of Care.* New Brunswick, N.J.: Rutgers University Press.

Hauser, Robert, and John Warren. 1997. "Socioeconomic Indexes for Occupations: A Review, Update, and Critique." *Sociological Methodology* 27: 177–298.

Hill, Nancy. 1997. "Does Parenting Differ Based on Social Class? African American Women's Perceived Socialization for Achievement." *American Journal of Community Psychology* 25(5): 675–97.

Hochschild, Arlie. 1989. *The Second Shift: Working Parents and the Revolution at Home.* New York: Viking.

Hochschild, Jennifer. 1995. *Facing Up to the American Dream.* Princeton, N.J.: Princeton University Press.

Hout, Michael, Clem Brooks, and Jeff Manza. 1993. "The Persistence of Classes in Post-Industrial Societies." *International Sociology* 8(3): 259–77.

Hughes, Diane. 2003. "Correlates of African American and Latino Parents' Messages to Children About Ethnicity and Race: A Comparative Study of Racial Socialization." *American Journal of Community Psychology* 31(1–2): 15–33.

Hughes, Diane, and Lisa Chen. 1997. "When and What Parents Tell Children About Race: An Examination of Race-Related Socialization Among African American Families." *Applied Developmental Science* 1(4): 200–14.

Hughes, Diane, and Deborah Johnson. 2001. "Correlates in Children's Experiences of Parents' Racial Socialization Behaviors." *Journal of Marriage and Family* 63(4): 981–95.

Kingston, Paul. 2000. *The Classless Society*. Stanford, Calif.: Stanford University Press.

Kohn, Melvin, and Carmi Schooler. 1983. *Work and Personality*. Norwood, N.J.: Ablex.

Lacy, Karyn. 2004. "Black Spaces, Black Places: Strategic Assimilation and Identity Construction in Middle-Class Suburbia." *Ethnic and Racial Studies* 27(6): 908–30.

———. 2007. *Blue-Chip Black: Race, Class, and Status in the New Black Middle Class*. Berkeley, Calif.: University of California Press.

Lamont, Michèle. 1992. *Money, Morals, and Manners*. Chicago, Ill.: University of Chicago Press.

———. 2000. *The Dignity of Working Men*. Cambridge, Mass.: Harvard University Press.

Lareau, Annette. 2002. "Invisible Inequality: Social Class and Child-Rearing in Black Families and White Families." *American Sociological Review* 67(5): 747–76.

———. 2003. *Unequal Childhoods*. Berkeley, Calif.: University of California Press.

Lesane-Brown, Chase, Tony Brown, Cleopatra Caldwell, and Robert Sellers. 2005. "The Comprehensive Race Socialization Inventory." *Journal of Black Studies* 36(2): 163–90.

Neckerman, Kathryn, Prudence Carter, and Jennifer Lee. 1999. "Segmented Assimilation and Minority Cultures of Mobility." *Ethnic and Racial Studies* 22(6): 946–65.

Oyserman, Daphna, Markus Kemmelmeier, Stephanie Fryberg, Hezi Brosh, and Tamera Hart-Johnson. 2003. "Racial-Ethnic Self-Schemas." *Social Psychology Quarterly* 66(4): 333–47.

Pakulski, Jan. 1993. "The Dying of Class or Marxist Class Theory?" *International Sociology* 8(3): 279–92.

Pattillo-McCoy, Mary. 1999. *Black Picket Fences*. Chicago, Ill.: University of Chicago Press.

Peters, Marie. 1985. "Racial Socialization of Young Black Children." In *Black Children*, edited by Harriette McAdoo and John McAdoo. Beverly Hills, Calif.: Sage Publications.

Rubin, Lillian. 1976. *Worlds of Pain: Life in the Working-Class Family*. New York: Basic Books.

Sigelman, Lee, and Steven Tuch. 1997. "Metastereotypes: Blacks' Perceptions of Whites' Stereotypes of Blacks." *Public Opinion Quarterly* 61(1): 87–101.

Sigelman, Lee, and Susan Welch. 1991. *Black Americans' Views of Racial Inequality: The Dream Deferred*. New York: Cambridge University Press.

Small, Mario Luis. 2004. *Villa Victoria: The Transformation of Social Capital in a Boston Barrio*. Chicago, Ill.: University of Chicago Press.

Tatum, Beverly Daniel. 1997. *Why Are All the Black Kids Sitting Together in the Cafeteria and Other Conversations About Race*. New York: Basic Books.

Thomas, Anita, and Suzette Speight. 1999. "Racial Identity and Racial Socialization Attitudes of African American Parents." *Journal of Black Psychology* 25(2): 152–70.

Thornton, Michael, Linda Chatters, Robert Taylor, and Walter Allen. 1990. "Sociodemographic and Environmental Correlates of Racial Socialization by Black Parents." *Child Development* 61(2): 401–9.

Wilson, William Julius. 1979. *The Declining Significance of Race.* Chicago, Ill.: University of Chicago Press.

———. 1987. *The Truly Disadvantaged.* Chicago, Ill.: University of Chicago Press.

Young, Alford. 1999. "Navigating Race: Getting Ahead in the Lives of 'Rags to Riches' Young Black Men." In *Cultural Territories of Race*, edited by Michele Lamont. Chicago, Ill.: University of Chicago Press.

Chapter 6

Bringing Sibling Differences In: Enlarging Our Understanding of the Transmission of Advantage in Families

DALTON CONLEY

OW SIMILAR are the socioeconomic statuses of siblings, and what does this mean for class analysis and theory? In this chapter, I have multiple goals. First, I make the case that standard studies of family background (including the approaches used by John Goldthorpe, by David Grusky and Kim Weeden, and by other contributors to this volume) miss a crucial point: they fail to acknowledge that parents' resources are not distributed in an equal fashion to each child. Without this acknowledgment, their models remain incomplete and, at times, misleading. Drawing from the literature on the economics of the family, the life course model of status attainment, and qualitative empirical accounts from siblings of their own experiences, I draw out several competing models of the ways in which parents invest in their offspring over the life course and the expected norms for transfers that minimize sibling inequality.

Second, I turn to one aspect of the empirical analyses in sibling class resemblance. Specifically, I take up the question of how similar or different siblings turn out to be. Given the limitations of data sets, I cannot fully examine all of the issues that I suggest need attention. Still, I look at two important issues: changes in sibling resemblance across the life course (and in different measures of socioeconomic status) and differences in sibling resemblance by race and maternal education. I find that sibling correlations increase over the life course for children with highly educated mothers, but that a different pattern surfaces for children of mothers with less education. Differences between whites and blacks also surface.

Third, I suggest that the demonstration of significant variability in the experiences of siblings within one family should *not* be taken as evidence that the impact of family background is insignificant and unimportant. Quite to the contrary, I believe that family background consequences can be very important despite substantial sibling variability. But the family background influences can take different pathways across siblings. We need to be sensitive to how these variable sibling experiences work. I argue that family background is important, but that it is highly contingent and far more dependent on particular circumstances than researchers often acknowledge.

For the purposes of this chapter, I am proxying the "class" outcome or position of offspring (and of family of origin) by using the standard measures of socioeconomic status on which sociologists and economists have long relied, as well as some that are relatively new. Among the measures familiar to sociologists are maternal and filial education, occupational socioeconomic index (SEI) score, and income. (Net worth is, regrettably, absent from this analysis but is certainly implied to follow the same conceptual logic.) In addition to these proxies, I also analyze earnings (as distinct from income) and even physical status (the ratio of weight to height). Elsewhere, I have argued that such bodily capital should also be included in our conception of social class. The reader should keep in mind, however, that these measures are nothing more than proxies for an underlying concept of social class; in fact, in the epilogue to this volume, I make the case that social class is best understood as the dimension of social hierarchy that cannot be explicitly captured in measures of human or economic capital.

Background

The relationship of family background or socioeconomic status to the outcomes of offspring is one of the most central concerns of stratification research. Indeed, for nearly a century behavioral geneticists have used sibling correlations as measures of the effects of genes and shared environment on behavioral traits (Bouchard and McGue 2003), and for more than three decades sociologists have used sibling correlations as "omnibus measures" (Solon, Page, and Duncan 2000, 383) of the effects of family and community on socioeconomic outcomes (Warren, Hauser, and Sheridan 1999; Jencks et al. 1972; Solon et al. 1991). Yet, as Robert Hauser and William Sewell (1986) have written, "Nowhere has a research agenda of such substantive importance had to survive on such meager scraps of data" (quoted in Solon et al. 1991, 512). It is not just data that have been lacking. As Gary Becker and Nigel Tomes (1986) write, "While sociologists have taken the lead in estimating the impact of family background on a number of outcomes—most notably educational and occupational attainment—they have lacked a clear explication of an underlying behavioral model." This chapter tries to address both of these concerns by engaging with economic models of the family and integrating this literature with theories of class inheritance.

Sociological studies in social stratification examine the impact of parents' characteristics on children's life chances. The operating, if often implicit, assumption is that parents treat children similarly—indeed, almost identically—according to the models. There is also an important social norm in many American families to follow this approach to child investment (or, perhaps more accurately, at least to give lip service to it). Yet there is also considerable evidence that children believe that parents did not treat them equally. Also, shifts in employment, income, marital status, and so forth can lead to changes in parents' situations over time. Thus, children within the same family have a different experience of their parents. We can call this heterogeneity in family investment.[1]

With all these caveats, perhaps we should pose a relatively naive question: what are we seeing when we see a sibling resemblance or sibling discordance model? The often unspoken assumption is that a high degree of sibling resemblance reflects a more castelike society, one in which life chances are highly stratified. A low degree of sibling resemblance, by contrast, is taken to mean that a society is less ascriptive and more meritocratic. However, how accurately do sibling correlations (or parent-child correlations or mobility matrices, for that matter) represent the openness of a society and the impact of family background? The short answer is "not very accurately" after we open up the possibility of within-family heterogeneity in parental investment due to evolving family circumstances or parents' conscious or unconscious targeting of resources (not to mention sibling effects on one another or differing responses to familial investment in households with multiple offspring). Although it is trivially true that if there is a zero correlation between siblings (or between parent and child for that matter), family background can be said to have no impact, this is a descriptive account only. For example, it could be the case that family background matters enormously, but that within-family dynamics obscure this fact in sibling or parent-child associations of socioeconomic status.[2]

Envision the case of a two-child family in which the elder child is expected to sacrifice for the benefit of the younger sibling. If such a dynamic was widespread in a given society and resulted in downward mobility for the sacrificing sibling and upward mobility for the sibling who benefited from the sacrifice, we could observe a negative sibling correlation and a zero parent-child correlation (since the upwardly mobile offspring would be canceled out by the downwardly mobile one, assuming researchers would randomly survey one of the two). Negative assortative mating combined with specific child-parent socialization and investment patterns might also yield a zero (or negative) sibling (or parent-child) correlation

Figure 6.1   No Observed Family Effects 1: Birth Order

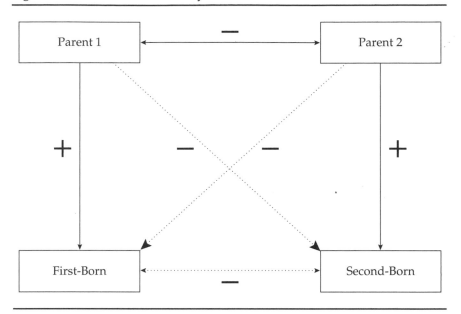

Source: Author's compilation.

when there are in fact quite strong background effects. This possibility is depicted graphically in figure 6.1.

   If such dynamics were systematically stratified by a measurable variable such as gender or birth position, then we could accurately describe the intra-family dynamics by observing correlations for within-family subgroups such as first-borns or boys (see figure 6.2, an example with respect to gender in a single-parent family). But if the way in which families generate outcomes among children is based on some unobservable factor—such as parental belief in child ability—then to the researcher the apparent result may be randomness and a potentially faulty observation that family background means little. In fact, what it would mean is that the family acts as a primary queuing mechanism for socioeconomic opportunity based on individual characteristics that we may think of as meritocratic or nonmeritocratic.

   By way of example, take the case of height and weight. Most researchers would argue that in an advanced, postindustrial knowledge economy, height and weight should matter little in terms of ability to perform most jobs. (Of course, such physical characteristics may be associated with and serve as proxies for relevant cognitive or noncognitive skills.) Figure 6.3 presents sibling correlations in height, weight, and body mass index (BMI—weight in kilograms divided by height in meters, squared). At just over .5, the correlation for brothers' height is similar to that typically measured for

Figure 6.2   No Observed Family Effects 2: Gender

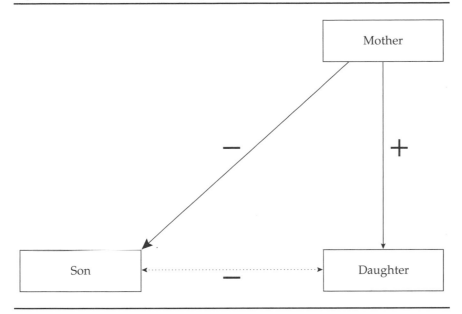

Source: Author's compilation.

Figure 6.3   Sibling Correlations in Physical Status: 1999 to 2001

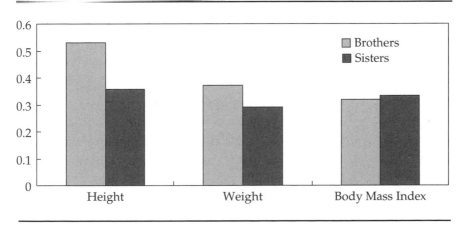

Source: Author's compilation from analysis of the Panel Study of Income Dynamics.

most measures of socioeconomic status (income, for example). This significant within-family variation on a "relatively" ascriptive characteristic such as height could, in theory, play a salient role in the stratification system. If schools and employers, for example, favored taller individuals, then this factor would generate sibling inequality and thus would appear to attenuate the effect of family background. In other words, if within-family variation in socioeconomic outcomes (that is, 1.0 minus the sibling correlation) were, in turn, explained by the within-family differences in height and weight, we might observe a low sibling correlation. This might give the false impression of a "meritocratic" society when social ascription was predominant. It would just happen to be the case that the basis of assignment cut within— as well as across—families. To take this case further, if the "discrimination" against shorter men took place primarily in the family home as the taller sibling received more parental investment, then this would be an important way in which family background influenced life chances but ended up driving *down* the sibling correlation. Likewise, if through differential nutritional investment the height difference (or any other difference, even in "ability") were generated by family dynamics, then sibling differences would reflect (rather than refute) background effects. The bottom line is that in order to make interpretive sense of sibling models, we must have a theory of whether, to what extent, and on what basis of assignment the family itself acts as a queuing mechanism for opportunity.

How to empirically resolve such ambivalent interpretations of sibling or parent-child associations? To know whether or not parental investment matters (and what types of investments count, if they do) we might randomly assign different resources to different sets of parents. For example, an experiment like Moving To Opportunity (MTO) randomly assigns families to a treatment group or a control group—where the odds of ending up in a low-poverty neighborhood with better schools is increased for the "treated." This is akin to providing parents with more resources of a particular type—namely, neighborhood quality is probably the quintessential common pool family resource. Likewise, the Negative Income Tax experiment altered the financial conditions of a randomly chosen treatment population. Other scholars have used lottery winners (who received variable amounts) (Imbens, Rubin, and Sacerdote 2001) or groups of Native Americans who received windfalls to investigate the impact of family income on offspring (Evans and Topoleski 2002). Susan Mayer (1997), most notably, has compared income from a variety of sources (some more exogenous than others) and come to the conclusion that income matters little in the life chances of children. None of these scholars, however, has examined the impact of exogenous increases of family financial resources on, for example, intergenerational income mobility or sibling correlations. Such studies would tell us much about what aspects of family background matter most and for which groups (assuming heterogenous treatment effects).

Meanwhile, to learn about differential investment patterns—for example, by SES—we would ideally make random assignments of parents to particular combinations of high- and low-ability offspring, which is obviously an impossibility. (Bruce Sacerdote [2004] examines the random assignment of Korean adoptees to families, but in this case child ability is unobserved.) In the absence of suitable or ethical experiments in this regard, the best way would be to find a viable instrumental variable (IV)—that is, a factor that affects one offspring's ability but is otherwise unrelated to the success of the other children in the family. If we could identify and measure such a factor, then we might be able to identify its impact on the family distribution of resources. That is, if an exogenous shock makes one child thrive (or fail), we can then measure the impact of that shock on parental investment in the other offspring. In other words, when one child is thriving, do parents invest more in that child or in her brother? (This strategy, of course, assumes adequate measurement of parental investment and no inter-sibling effects.)[3]

Given this apparent intractability of modeling the "true" causal pathways of family background, what are we to make of sibling correlations? The answer is simply that we can read a sibling correlation as a global effect of family background if we assume a model in which offspring are invested in equally (or in which any favoritism is at least randomly distributed) and in which siblings have only a mean-regressive effect on each other—that is, they tend to cause each other to be more alike than they would in each other's absence. This is not an entirely unreasonable assumption, but it is an assumption nonetheless. It is for researchers—both ethnographic and quantitative—to determine whether this assumption (and that of nonfavoritism) is accurate. What follows is a discussion of how we might indirectly test this assumption and what variations on it might mean for our understanding of the impact of family background on individual attainment.

Theoretical Debates About Sibling Resemblance

In a series of works, Becker and Tomes (1976, 1986) hold that parents have either child-neutral preferences, whereby they invest equally in both children, or child-equality preferences, whereby they invest differentially in children to equalize their ultimate status attainment.

In the former, parents follow an "efficiency" model—that is, they do not care about ultimate differences in outcomes between offspring that result from ability differences, and they merely provide the same investments in each; and over time innate ability is revealed. With uncertainty as to ability, this approach would maximize overall, average family attainment. However, from the point of view of a stratification researcher, since the returns to investing in a child with greater innate endowments are greater than those that result from marginal investment in a less-well-endowed child, parents may unwittingly act as transmission mechanisms for inequality despite equal investments. A more extreme version of this approach would have parents investing more in offspring who appear to display the most ability, since their parents' return on investment would putatively be highest for these children. And thus, from the point of view of maximizing the total returns from all offspring, this is even more efficient (assuming correct information about ability and returns) than investing equally in all children. However, this parenting strategy would produce an even more inequality-reinforcing result.

In the latter model—the "equalizing" paradigm—parents follow a "wealth" model and invest more in the human capital of their endowed child and make compensatory investments in the nonhuman capital (that is, wealth and income) of their less-endowed child. Thus, they try to maximize returns while at the same time acting like a government transfer program, by providing direct material support (as opposed to human capital investment) for the less-endowed children. Put crudely, they invest in the schooling of the smart ones and then transfer income or wealth to the dull ones.

A third alternative has parents less concerned about equalizing the ultimate wealth of their children and more concerned about equalizing the earnings of their children. In a series of studies on parental preference models, Jere Behrman, Robert Pollak, and Paul Taubman (1982, 1989) provide a "separable earnings-bequest" model as an alternative to Becker and Tomes's wealth model. Whereas in the wealth model parents are concerned with the combination of earnings and wealth of their children as indicative of their ultimate economic well being, in the separable earnings-bequest model parents view earnings and wealth as separate factors and attempt to maximize earnings over total income or wealth, since earnings are more socially valued than unearned income. These authors' analysis of fraternal white male twins shows that parents transfer wealth to their children equally but transfer resources to their children unequally so as to increase the earnings of their less-endowed offspring. In other words, they invest in exactly the opposite way as predicted by Becker and Tomes: they are inefficient, valuing equality so much as to invest more in the child who will generate a lower rate of return. In general, the (weak or strong) efficiency model would lead us to expect that siblings' social statuses diverge as differential ability—combined with either neutral (the weakly efficient model) or ability-reinforcing (the strongly efficient model) investment patterns—leads to cumulative differences over the life course.

There are other family dynamics that might result in a similar pattern of increasing divergence over the life course. For example, this might hold true if parental (and inter-sibling) influences are primarily made when offspring are children at home and decline in importance as children reach adult-hood. While sociological status attainment and life course models hold that earlier events and accomplishments structure later life events and accom-plishments (Blau and Duncan 1967), this is a stochastic process (a step-by-step progression with a random element introduced at each juncture—such as in a Markov chain process) in which additional (random) error is induced at each life course stage, thereby diluting the observed sibling correlation as individuals move outward from the educational system to job choice to earnings, income, and wealth accumulation. Along these lines, research by Christopher Jencks and his colleagues (1972) suggests that income is affected by many chance life events, or "luck." Following any of these theories, we would expect higher sibling correlations for education, followed by occupation (since this may, to a great extent, reflect the legacy of decisions and trade-offs made relatively early in adulthood), then by earnings, then by total family income (since this introduces sibling-specific dynamics within the marriage market as well), and finally by net worth (which typi-cally starts to vary most in later adulthood thanks to earlier investment deci-sions). Following these models, we provide alternative hypotheses:

Hypothesis 1: Sibling correlations are highest for education and increasingly less so for occupation, earnings, income, and wealth.

Hypothesis 2: Sibling correlations are highest under age thirty, lower by age forty, and lowest after age fifty.

Indeed, some recent research provides evidence of diverging sibling resemblance across the life course (Hauser and Wong 1999; Warren, Hauser, and Sheridan 2002). Rob Warren and his colleagues (2002) use longitudinal data from the Wisconsin Longitudinal Study (WLS) and find that siblings become less occupationally similar as they age.

However, if we believe that parents act more like a mini–welfare state and transfer resources to children in an iterative fashion in an attempt to maintain equality over the life course as they observe ability differences and as initial differences in success emerge, then we should observe the exact opposite pattern. That is, if we assume that there are multiple routes to eco-nomic success and it is the downstream economic measures (the ultimate rewards) that are equalized by parents rather than initial investments, we might hypothesize:

Hypothesis 1A: Sibling correlations for education, occupation, and earnings are not as high as sibling correlations for total income and wealth.

Hypothesis 2A: Sibling correlations under age thirty (on all measures) are lower than sibling correlations at age forty (on the same measures), which are lower than sibling correlations at age fifty (on the same measures).

Sibling Resemblance Across Population Subgroups

So far, the discussion based on the approaches of Becker and Tomes, on the one hand, and Behrman and his colleagues, on the other, has been working under the assumption of zero credit or capital constraints for investment in children. However, Becker and Tomes (1986) posit that *with* capital constraints, resource-constrained parents may not be able to optimally invest in their children's human capital. Such underinvestment may lead to higher degrees of sibling resemblance at lower incomes, since "high-ability children from poor families may receive the same low level of education as a sibling with lower academic ability, compressing their earnings compared with similarly different siblings from a prosperous family" (Mazumder and Levine 2003, 16).[4] Following this capital constraint model (which, like the parental preference model, assumes either equal investment or equal outcome norms among parents), we hypothesize:

Hypothesis 3: Sibling correlations among groups with fewer relative resources (large families, nonwhites, children of parents with lower educational attainment) are greater than sibling correlations among groups with greater relative resources (small families, whites, children of parents with higher educational attainment).

The alternative hypothesis to Becker and Tomes's (1986) theory is that among families that are disadvantaged we should observe greater sibling disparities (that is, lower correlations). This "strategic investment" model sees parental investment not as seeking to maximize the human capital (and earnings) of all children, or even to equalize them, but rather as seeking to maximize the human capital (and earnings) of the most endowed child, who promises the greatest returns on investment. This strategic investment model could result from one or both of two dynamics. First, opportunity-constrained parents may view status attainment as a "sticky" process with a stochastic element that varies with offspring ability—meaning that the error term for high-ability children is seen to be smaller than the error term for low-ability offspring, thus suggesting a greater chance of a return on investment. Second, such strategies may also be the most efficient route to the highest living standards for all offspring when parents expect cross-sibling subsidies in adulthood. That is, resource-constrained parents may feel compelled to follow the "strongly efficient" model and invest in the human capital of the best-endowed offspring, in the hope that this strategy will bring the highest possible returns and that, in time, that child will make wealth transfers to his or her less-endowed siblings. In this model, the parents are an engine of offspring income and wealth growth, and the children themselves are expected to act as the social transfer agents to ensure a degree of equality or insurance against gross, within-family economic status differences (perhaps enforced by informal norms or strong parental pressure).

Put another way, disadvantaged families may be behaving more efficiently (investing more in the offspring for whom they expect higher returns), thus reinforcing sibling differences. Whereas better-off families could be behaving inefficiently (investing more in the child for whom they expect lower returns), thus compensating—that is, trying to bring about more equity in the outcomes of their offspring. It is as if equality is a luxury good that only better-off families have the means to purchase. How could this difference emerge? There are two possibilities. First, if "success" is seen as a threshold, well-off families may (rightly) believe that their best-endowed children will certainly "make it" and then can invest in the higher-risk children. Second, if there is a declining marginal utility of child success, then parents who expect their children to be at different points along that curve may invest differentially to maximize total utility. In other words, the *differential* returns to investment may be steeper at the early part of the curve, where disadvantaged families' offspring are more likely to be operating, and flatter further out, where the offspring of advantaged families are more likely to be operating, making for different relative choices between siblings for the two hypothetical families.

Previous qualitative work (Conley 2004) has suggested that among disadvantaged households, sibling disparities tend to increase, since limited opportunities and resources may evince parenting strategies that accentuate sibling differences by directing family resources to the better-endowed sibling(s) for whom upward mobility is most likely. This research also suggested that parents in families that were well endowed with class resources (and were racially privileged as well) often invested more heavily in those offspring they saw as having the worst chances for success in the education system or labor market—in a compensatory fashion à la the separable earnings-bequest model (Behrman, Pollak, and Taubman 1989) or the child equality model of Becker and Tomes. Following these models, we posit an alternative hypothesis:

Hypothesis 3A: Sibling correlations among groups with fewer relative resources (larger families, nonwhites, children of parents with lower educational attainment) are not as great as sibling correlations among groups with greater relative resources (smaller families, whites, children of parents with higher educational attainment). This difference in correlations should be most distinct for education (where parental investments matter most) and perhaps occupational prestige and earnings, and less pronounced for total income and wealth (if indeed siblings engage in compensatory transfers).

We might also expect this outcome if the "price effect" of human capital investment trumps the "preference displacement effect." The preference displacement effect suggests that the budget constraint moves the earnings (and educational) possibility frontier closer to the origin, resulting in greater similarity among the offspring (similar to the Becker and Tomes model), since parents have minimal levels of investment they want to maintain among all their children. In contrast to this effect, the price effect suggests that when parents are budget-constrained—by virtue of low income and wealth or because of larger family size—their children are more likely to be eligible for student financial aid, which itself may vary with children's endowments (see Behrman, Pollak, and Taubman 1989). In other words, relying on outside financing accentuates endowment heterogeneity. This is really a public finance model of the strategic investment model at the family level.

Empirical Results and Implications

We are not the first to propose examining sibling correlations in social and economic status as a way of measuring the effect of measurable and unmeasurable family background characteristics (including shared environment and shared genes) and inter-sibling effects on socioeconomic outcomes. For example, Daphne Kuo and Robert Hauser (1995) analyze the Occupational Changes in a Generation (OCG) survey data and find that, for education, sibling differences (within-family variance components) among various age groups of black and white brothers range between 38 and 52 percent. Mary Corcoran and her colleagues (1990, 364) estimate a brother-brother correlation in permanent income of .45, using data from the Panel Study of Income Dynamics (PSID). Mazumder and Levine (2003) examine the National Longitudinal Survey (NLS) and the PSID and argue that between the 1960s and the 1970s the correlation in earnings between brothers rose from .26 to .45. Sibling resemblance in such other outcomes as welfare usage, education, and occupation follow similar patterns and are sensitive to the specification deployed, particularly for nonlinear measures. For example, a woman whose sister has received welfare is over three times more likely to receive it herself (a .66 versus .20 probability in their PSID sample).

When we reanalyze more recent waves of PSID data—in which the siblings are on average older and more stable economically—with a substantially larger sample size of person-years and sibling sets, we obtain similar estimates of the association between siblings on education, occupational prestige, earnings, and income (see figure 6.4). Parental preference models are challenged when we look to results across socioeconomic outcome measures in that sibling correlations in wealth remain lower than sibling correlations in income (as well as education and occupational prestige). Parental preference models would lead us to expect the opposite—that parents invest unequally in their children's education so as to efficiently

Figure 6.4   Sibling Correlations in Socioeconomic Outcomes

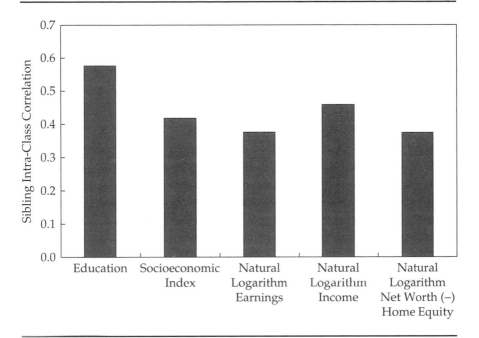

Source: Author's compilation from analysis of the Panel Study of Income Dynamics.

maximize the return on ability endowments, but then seek to equalize sibling economic status when it comes to nonhuman capital measures.

Our findings also lend some support to stratification and life course models in that we find that siblings resemble each other more on socioeconomic outcomes pertaining to earlier life events (those with less exposure to chance factors). However, when we analyze age effects directly (see figure 6.5), we find that siblings remain steady in their occupational resemblance, fluctuate in their earnings similarity, but tend to converge in income; this would not be expected given the theory of Jencks and his colleagues (1972) and others of declining sibling resemblance in income due to chance events. (We do not analyze wealth once we get into subgroups since it was surveyed relatively infrequently in the PSID and thus suffers from fewer person-years in the sample.) Rather, the findings of increasing sibling convergence in income could be due to a greater degree of measurement error for income earlier in the life course (of a classic errors-in-variables type), or it could be because of the emergent salience of shared genes. Alternatively, it could be due to an increase in direct inter-sibling effects in adulthood as siblings age (though this seems improbable thanks to relatively weak adult sibling relationships in American society), or it could be the result of

Figure 6.5   Sibling Correlations in Socioeconomic State, by Age

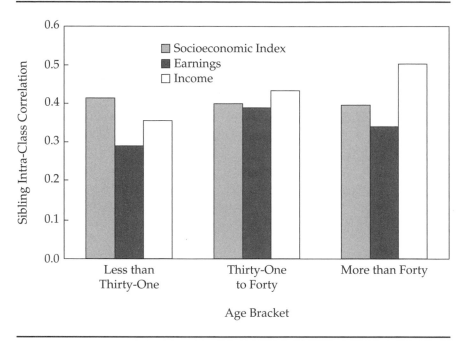

Source: Author's compilation from analysis of the Panel Study of Income Dynamics.

compensatory parental impacts later in life (though this also seems unlikely given norms of adult offspring economic independence). Most likely it is the effect of family background rearing its head in the marriage market (and with respect to marital stability). This is a feature of the stratification system that merits more attention, especially given the increased importance of multiple earnings in American families. At any rate, it suggests that if studies analyze economic correlations earlier in adulthood, they may be underestimating the degree of sibling similarity (and thus overstating the amount of income mobility) in the United States. This dynamic, as discussed later in this section, holds particularly true for blacks.

Our analyses further build on previous studies by exploring two questions regarding sibling convergence or divergence across the life course and across population subgroups; these results can be found in figures 6.6 and 6.7 (for a full discussion of these results, please see Conley and Glauber [2005]). Whereas Becker and Tomes (1986) predict and Mazumder and Levine (2003) find that siblings who have fewer economic resources tend to demonstrate greater concordance in their socioeconomic statuses, owing to budget constraints on optimal investment in well-endowed offspring, we find mixed evidence on this front. As shown in figure 6.6, sibling correlations in occu-

Figure 6.6   Sibling Correlations in Socioeconomic Measures
by Mother's Education

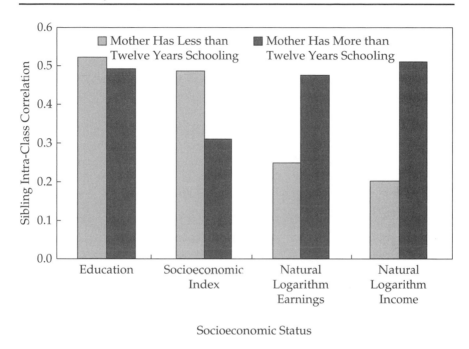

Source: Author's compilation from analysis of the Panel Study of Income Dynamics.

pation are indeed significantly higher for those whose mothers had lower educational attainment (lending support to their theories). However, the pattern for earnings and income is the opposite (confounding their expectations), while education correlations are not significantly different across mother's educational status.

Further complicating the picture, we report race effects in figure 6.7 such that black siblings resemble each other less on education, earnings, and income than nonblack siblings—obliquely supporting previous sociological work that has suggested weaker family effects for blacks vis-à-vis whites with respect to occupation and education because of the dynamics of discrimination and tokenism (see, for example, Blau and Duncan 1967; Featherman and Hauser 1978). (We say "obliquely" since the sign is opposite for SEI score, one of the very measures upon which these previous researchers have relied.)

The story gets even more confusing when we interact age with class background or race. When we break out income correlations over the life course by maternal education level (again a proxy for the SES of the family of origin), we find that the similarity in income among siblings with

Figure 6.7   Sibling Correlations in Socioeconomic Status (SES) Outcomes by Race

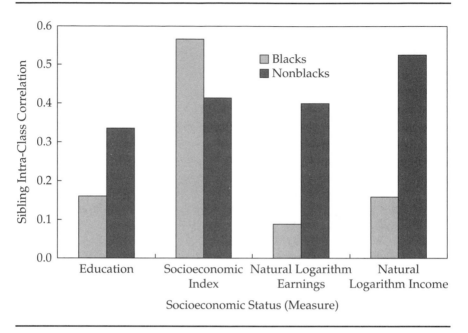

Source: Author's compilation from analysis of the Panel Study of Income Dynamics.

more highly educated mothers tends to increase with age, peaking at a figure of .537 for those age forty and older (while declining, insignificantly, over the life course among siblings born to mothers with less education, to a .329 level for the oldest group; see figure 6.8). This pattern offers a challenge to the Becker-Tomes prediction about resource group differences. But when we examine the interaction of life course and racial differences, we find that black siblings converge in income, whereas nonblack siblings do not converge in income as they age. Specifically, when we interact race and age in figure 6.9, we contradict previous findings that black siblings have weaker family effects. Indeed, among the oldest age group the black sibling correlation in income is a staggering .826—suggesting almost complete social reproduction in living standards by the fifth decade of life. (Although these results are statistically significant, we should keep in mind that this race-age analysis is based on a very small set of black siblings age forty or older.) When contrasted to the opposite age-class interaction effect whereby the more-advantaged group (as measured by maternal education at least) experiences income convergence while the less-advantaged group does not, these results suggest, but by no means prove, that the American stratification system functions differently for blacks and whites in a way that is not reducible to resource issues alone—a proposition that begs for future research.

Figure 6.8   Sibling Correlations in Income by Age and Class

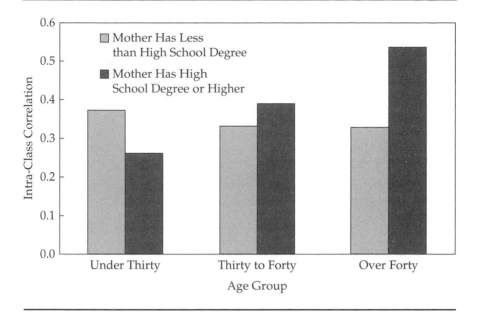

Source: Author's compilation from analysis of the Panel Study of Income Dynamics.

Conclusions

Though much more empirical work needs to be done, for now it is worth noting that researchers may get very different answers to the seemingly simple descriptive question about how much income (or SES) mobility there is in the United States depending on the age at which they measure economic status and the groups to which they are referring. Future researchers should perhaps refrain from using overall sibling correlations to make global assessments of the degree of openness in American society, since the answer appears to depend on the race-class group and age group under study. Furthermore, taken together, results could imply that the simple model of equal investment in offspring and mean-regressive sibling effects may not hold equally for all groups in society.

As mentioned, many researchers have tacitly or explicitly interpreted the sibling correlation as an omnibus measure of family background effects—that is, of the degree of ascription. In this vein, answering the questions of *when, where,* and *for what* measures sibling correlations are *low* is seen as a way to gain an indication of social openness in a particular time and a specific place for a particular measure of socioeconomic status. By contrast, we tend to lament high degrees of sibling resemblance as indicative of a more castelike system. However, such diagnoses may be premature. Envision the situation

Figure 6.9   Sibling Correlation in Income by Age and Race

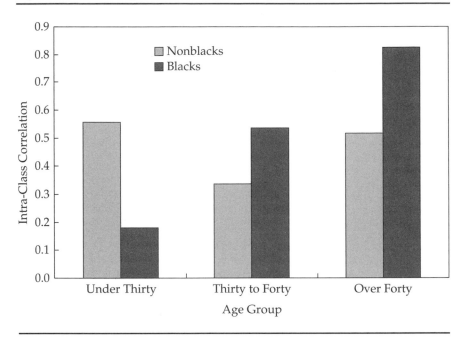

Source: Author's compilation from analysis of the Panel Study of Income Dynamics.

where there is an enormous amount of parent-child mobility; however, siblings move pair-wise away from their parents' status. For example, the two children of a manual worker both become doctors. From the point of view of sibling models, this scenario looks like a caste society (assuming the two children of the doctor end up similar in status as well). However, from the point of view of parent-child models, the picture is one of a completely open, fluid society with a high degree of mobility. Which is right? It is another instance of the blind men and the elephant. The ultimate lesson is that when we consider the family as a cauldron and not as a rubber stamp, then we should not take any one piece of information—sibling *or* parent-child correlations—as definitively indicative of the level of social ascription in a society.

In this chapter and elsewhere, we have already seen that the degree of sibling resemblance depends on the social conditions of the family—namely, its economic and social resources—not to mention unmeasured factors like the variance in ability and the cultural values of a given household with respect to inequality among its members. This should be clue enough that low sibling correlations do not necessarily mean that family background—or the family more generally—does not matter for class attainment. Rather, the family is a pivotal player in the assignment of social status and works not in a vacuum but in reaction to the resources within and the constraints and opportunities without.

A metaphor that may illustrate this relationship between the individual, the family, and society writ large is that of a three-level chessboard. At the first level is the individual, next is the family, and the top level is society. Envision a family where one sibling is recognized to be a musical prodigy from a young age and becomes the "star" of the household. Monetary and nonmonetary investment is directed to this talented child at the expense of her sister (perhaps owing to limited overall resources). For example, the parents pay for daily private piano lessons at the expense of a house in a better school district, so both sisters suffer a worse public education, but it matters more for the nonmusical sister. The parents' investments appear to pay off initially, as the musical sister gains admission to a prestigious conservatory. But classical music is what the economist Robert Frank calls a "winner take all" market in which the rewards for a few individuals at the very top are enormous but there is a steep drop to the next-best performers (think professional sports, too). So, despite incredible investment and support from the parents, this musically talented offspring ends up in the relatively low-status, low-pay position of a part-time music teacher to young children. Her sister, meanwhile, gets a regular college degree at the state university and works her way steadily up the corporate ladder. There is a high divergence in their earnings, and, ironically, it is the child who received less parental investment who economically outperforms the "golden child" in the end. Although there was a good fit between the talents of the musician offspring and the family's values (they invested in her after all), there was a poor fit between those two levels of the chessboard and what the economy tends to reward. Does this case mean that family or class background did not matter?

Alternatively, imagine a family where one child is a math genius; the parents, however, are sports nuts and do not value achievement in the area of quantitative reasoning and thus do not invest much in this particular child. She may or may not go on to outperform her siblings economically despite a lack of investment—given the high demand for math skills in the labor market. There is a good fit in this case between the individual's talents and what society rewards, but a poor fit between the individual and the family, as well as between the family and the society (and the latter poor fit may have disadvantaged *all* the offspring in the family). Did class or family background matter in this case? Or do both these cases illustrate why and how family background can often have very *little* impact in a three-dimensional space of social attainment? You decide.

Notes

1. Also, most researchers assume that the key family variables that have an impact are parents' actions, but this assumption neglects the real possibility

that siblings have an important impact on one another, including an impact on the life pathways taken by their siblings; stratification models need to take these sibling effects into consideration.

In fact, an IV (instrumental variable) strategy has been deployed in an attempt to identify inter-sibling reciprocal effects—a dynamic that has been repeatedly hypothesized but impossible, so far, to document. Hauser and Wong (1989) use friend's IQ as an IV to identify siblings' effects on one another's IQ. But this assumes that one's sibling's friend's IQ has no other effect on one's own IQ other than through sibling socialization. To the extent that this assumption is violated—through, for example, socialization between the friend and ego or through differential investment in each child by the parents based on their peer group—then the IV is invalid.

Birthweight might initially seem to provide a better instrument, given its individual nature (that is, the high degree of variation within families) and the associations it has been shown to have with socioeconomic outcomes (see, for example, Conley and Bennett 2000; Behrman and Rosenzweig 2004). However, parents may invest differentially in their children by estimating the rate of return according to birthweight. So it is unlikely that there will appear an instrument for inter-sibling effects that satisfies these two criteria; as a result, a fully specified model is by definition under-identified. (Moreover, if we add selective fertility—parity progression bias, that is, differences in the likelihood of going on to have more children—based on parental perceptions of whether they got a "winner" with the first child, then the problem of understanding social transmission within the family gets even more complicated.)

2. For a good example of how these processes can be modeled, see Behrman, Rosenzweig, and Taubman (1994).

3. We would not, however, have identification to examine the effect on actual outcomes, since that discounts the possibility of direct effects of siblings on each other.

4. Indeed, this is what Bhashkar Mazumder and David Levine (2003) find: lower correlations among high-income siblings in both the 1968 and 1979 waves of the Panel Study of Income Dynamics (PSID). However, when they split the sample along the median, they end up with only a maximum of 185 multiple sibling sets in an income group. (In the 1979 wave of the PSID, they have 1,086 cases from 901 families in all.) Even if these were all two-sibling sets, the maximum number of pairs for each income group would be 92—quite a small number. More important, however, is the fact that they do not split the sample based on the parental characteristics—as would be appropriate for the Becker-Tomes model—but rather by the incomes of the adult siblings themselves. This makes the sample split endogenous to their outcomes. In other words, what they may be observing could be a result of sibling decisions regarding trade-offs between equity and efficiency. If certain sibships value equality, they may sacrifice the attainment of the better-endowed sibling, bringing the overall mean down, but resulting in a higher correlation between siblings. By contrast, we split the sample by parental measures, which are at least temporally anterior to the sibling outcomes.

References

Becker, Gary S., and Nigel Tomes. 1976. "Child Endowments and the Quantity and Quality of Children." *Journal of Political Economy* 84(4, Part 2): S143–62.
———. 1986. "Human Capital and the Rise and Fall of Families." *Journal of Labor Economics* 4(3, Part 2): S1–39.
Behrman, Jere R., and Mark R. Rosenzweig. 2004. "The Returns to Birth Weight." *Review of Economics and Statistics* 86(2): 586–601.
Behrman, Jere R., Robert A. Pollak, and Paul Taubman. 1982. "Parental Preferences and Provision for Progeny." *Journal of Political Economy* 90(1): 52–73.
———. 1989. "Family Resources, Family Size, and Access to Financing for College Education." *Journal of Political Economy* 97(2): 398–419.
Behrman, Jere R., Mark R. Rosenzweig, and Paul Taubman. 1994. "Endowments and the Allocation of Schooling in the Family and in the Marriage Market: The Twins Experiment." *Journal of Political Economy* 102(6): 1131–74.
Blau, Peter, and Otis D. Duncan. 1967. *The American Occupational Structure.* New York: Free Press.
Bouchard, Thomas J., Jr. and Matt McGue. 2003. "Genetic and Environmental Influences on Human Psychological Differences." *Journal of Neurobiology* 54(1): 4–45.
Conley, Dalton. 2004. *The Pecking Order: Which Siblings Succeed and Why.* New York: Pantheon.
Conley, Dalton, and Neil G. Bennett. 2000. "Is Biology Destiny? Birth Weight and Life Chances." *American Sociological Review* 65(3): 458–67.
Conley, Dalton, and Rebecca Glauber. 2005. "Sibling Similarity and Difference in Socioeconomic Status: Life Course and Family Resource Effects." Working paper 11320. Cambridge, Mass.: National Bureau of Economic Research.
Corcoran, Mary, Roger Gordon, Deborah Laren, and Gary Solon. 1990. "Poverty and the Underclass: Effects of Family and Community Background on Economic Status." *American Economic Review* 80(2): 362–6.
Evans, William N., and Julie H. Topoleski. 2002. "The Social and Economic Impact of Native American Casinos." Working paper W9198. Cambridge, Mass.: National Bureau of Economic Research.
Featherman, David L., and Robert M. Hauser. 1978. *Opportunity and Change.* New York: Academic Press.
Hauser, Robert M., and William Sewell. 1986. "Family Effects in Simple Models of Education, Occupational Status, and Earnings: Findings from the Wisconsin and Kalamazoo Studies." *Journal of Labor Economics* 4(3, Part 2): S83–115.
Hauser, Robert, and Raymond Sin-Kwok Wong. 1989. "Sibling Resemblance and Intersibling Effects in Educational Attainment." *Sociology of Education* 62(3): 149–71.
Imbens, Guido W., Donald B. Rubin, and Bruce I. Sacerdote. 2001. "Estimating the Effect of Unearned Income on Labor Earnings, Savings, and Consumption: Evidence from a Survey of Lottery Players." *American Economic Review* 91(4): 778–94.
Jencks, Christopher S., Marshall Smith, Henry Acland, Mary Joe Bane, David Cohen, Herbert Gintis, Barbara Heyns, and Stephen Michelson. 1972. *Inequality: A Reassessment of the Effect of Family and Schooling in America.* New York: Basic Books.

Kuo, Hsiang-Hui Daphne, and Robert M. Hauser. 1995. "Trends in Family Effects on the Education of Black and White Brothers." *Sociology of Education* 68(2): 136–60.

Mayer, Susan. 1997. *What Money Can't Buy: Family Income and Children's Life Chances.* Cambridge, Mass.: Harvard University Press.

Mazumder, Bhashkar, and David I. Levine. 2003. "The Growing Importance of Family and Community: An Analysis of Changes in the Sibling Correlation in Earnings." Working paper 2003-24. Chicago, Ill.: Federal Reserve Bank.

Sacerdote, Bruce. 2004. "What Happens When We Randomly Assign Children to Families?" NBER Working Paper W10894.

Solon, Gary, Marianne E. Page, and Greg J. Duncan. 2000. "Correlations Between Neighboring Children in Their Subsequent Educational Attainment." *Review of Economics and Statistics* 82(3): 383–92.

Solon, Gary, Mary Corcoran, Roger Gordon, and Deborah Laren. 1991. "A Longitudinal Analysis of Sibling Correlation in Economic Status." *Journal of Human Resources* 26(3): 509–34.

Warren, John Robert, Robert M. Hauser, and Jennifer T. Sheridan. 2002. "Occupational Stratification Across the Life Course: Evidence from the Wisconsin Longitudinal Study." *American Sociological Review* 67(3): 432–55.

Chapter 7

Class and Politics

JEFF MANZA AND CLEM BROOKS

EXTBOOK MODELS of how class inequalities influence political processes and outcomes suggest a vast array of topics. There are class differences in political participation and citizen activism, as well as differences in partisanship and voting behavior. Classes have varying political capacities, especially if we compare class-related organizations such as business and trade associations versus unions or groups seeking to represent the poor. Political institutions often favor some classes over others. Tensions between the current global economy and national institutions and configurations of class power raise important questions; historical evidence suggests that both class inputs into the political system and redistributive policy outputs ebb and flow over long periods of time. Moving from the micro to the macro, from the local to the global, and across time and space, there is no shortage of suggestions about how class matters for the political life of democratic capitalist societies.

But all of these claims are neither uncontroversial nor uncontested. Class divisions as a source of electoral behavior or policy preferences have sometimes been said to be either modest or declining, with other factors providing more vital influence (Kingston 2000, chapter 6; for a review of this literature, see Brooks, Manza, and Bolzendahl 2003). The comparative welfare state literature presents a striking paradox for strong models of class politics: the nearly universal weakening of union strength coupled with increasing flows of global capital have not, surprisingly, produced much systematic evidence of welfare state retrenchment to date (Korpi 2003; Brooks and Manza 2007, ch. 3). Indeed, most of the evidence is just the opposite: although specific policies and eligibility rules in programs for health, sickness, unemployment insurance, and social assistance have changed, over-all spending levels have proven surprisingly resilient. These outcomes persist even as the social forces that brought the welfare state into existence in the first place have lost political influence.

Given such contradictory interpretations and results, it should come as little surprise that sorting out the relationship between "class" (however defined) and political outcomes is complicated. Several issues are especially pressing. First, class divisions may shape political outcomes, but so too do policy and political outcomes shape class politics—for example, the rise of the welfare state and the ways in which redistributive social policies have transformed the operation of labor markets and levels of inequality between groups. Class power from below was an important source of welfare state development in the first place, but today welfare state institutions empower lower classes and change the balance of class capacities. Second, studying variation in class politics is important. For example, research on class differences in political participation produce the intriguing result that in high-turnout countries there are few, if any, differences in turnout rates among classes, while in lower-turnout countries the class skew in participation grows. With the advent of truly compatible comparative data sets containing individual-level sociodemographic characteristics and information about respondents' attitudes and political behaviors and country-level data sets with information about policy outputs, we now have the tools to engage such comparative questions systematically (see, for example, Evans 1999; Svallfors 2006; Brooks and Manza 2007). But generalizing such findings into coherent theories and generalizations about class politics has proven difficult.

The goal of this chapter is to sort through some of the debates and evidence about class politics and to provide a coherent portrait of how and when class matters.[1] We take as our primary reference point contemporary American politics, although to understand the distinctiveness of class politics in the United States we will need to introduce a comparative perspective. As we shall see, there are a variety of ways in which the context of American politics both enables and frustrates class politics. For example, class divisions in voting behavior are relatively weaker than in a number of other affluent democracies, where strong unions and social democratic parties organize class interests in the electoral arena. But class differences in *political participation*—an oft-neglected aspect of how class locations shape political behavior—are far *greater* in the United States than in other countries. Further, the unique system of financing political campaigns in the United States provides another important avenue of class influence on politics not found elsewhere. Donations by wealthy individuals and corporate political action committees, with virtually no ceilings on candidate expenditures, are unique in the democratic world. And in recent decades vast and growing disparities in the sources of campaign financing highlight a key source of class influence on politics in the United States.

Questions about class politics are of both scholarly and public interest. There have been many recent and highly visible discussions of how rising levels of inequality influence American politics. A task force of the American Political Science Association, for example, has recently issued a substantial report declaring that "the voices of citizens with lower or moderate incomes are lost on the ears of inattentive public officials, while the advantaged roar with a clarity and consistency that policymakers readily hear and routinely follow" (Jacobs and Skocpol 2005, 1). Thomas Frank's best-selling 2004 book *What's the Matter with Kansas?* has also stirred a considerable debate. Frank identifies a decline of traditional class politics that he located in an emerging alignment of the white working class with the Republican Party. According to Frank, conservative politicians and strategists have successfully framed electoral contests around social issues such as abortion, gun control, and family values, encouraging working class voters to overlook (or misunderstand) their own economic interests (see also Roemer 1998). Several hard-hitting critiques of the Frank thesis have now appeared, showing that income groups remain as strongly aligned in the early twenty-first century as four decades ago (Bartels 2006; McCarty, Poole, and Rosenthal 2006). Other work employing occupational measures of class, including our own, finds a more mixed picture of "class realignment" that is not easily captured by the debate between Frank and his critics (see Hout, Brooks, and Manza 1995; Manza and Brooks 1999).

These examples suggest that the question of class and politics is a lively one. To discipline our narrative, we focus on several specific questions. We start with one of the core concerns of this volume: What are the mechanisms through which class divisions manifest themselves in contemporary American politics? Next, we turn to three specific empirical questions about class politics and recent trends: class differences in turnout and other forms of political participation; class voting; and class impacts on the financing of elections. We conclude the chapter with a few general observations about the continuing importance of the analysis of class divisions in American politics.

How Does Class Matter?

Why do classes differ politically? Analysts of class politics have often defined "class" in very different ways. The predominant components of class location identified elsewhere in this volume—income, wealth, education, occupation—vary in their impact on political behavior, as in other arenas of social life (Conley, this volume; Grusky and Weeden, this volume). Perhaps the common usage is to examine differences among income groups (Bartels 2006; McCarty, Poole, and Rosenthal 2006). Income groups share a common interest in certain kinds of public policies, such as taxes or social provision. But there are also a variety of reasons why current income may poorly

capture an individual's class location. Income groups have no common organizational anchor, and as Michael Hout notes in his chapter, current income
alone is a poor measure of long-term social standing and life chances (see also
Hout, Brooks, and Manza 1993). Education level is sometimes substituted
as a measure of class (Frank 2004), although individuals with the same level
of educational attainment also do not necessarily have any organizational
anchor connecting them outside of their occupational locations.

It is for these reasons that we believe occupation provides the most plausible basis for thinking about how specifically *class-related* political micro
processes and influences occur (cf. Grusky and Sorensen 1998). Workplace
settings provide the possibility of talking about politics and forging political
identities, and work also provides the springboard for membership in organizations where class politics are engaged: unions, professional associations,
business associations, and so forth. Moreover, even setting aside the asso-
ciational and network dimensions of class micro foundations, common
occupational locations tend to give incumbents a shared set of interests
connected by the level and type of assets they possess or control in labor
and capital markets (Wright 1985; Grusky and Sorensen 1998; Manza and
Brooks 1999).

However class is measured, debates center on how and why class location influences political behavior. The classical literatures identified both
individual-level mechanisms and organizational and institutional factors.
Focusing first on individual-level processes, three generations of scholarship
on class politics have proposed a set of mechanisms—economic interests,
social-psychological factors, and social networks—that provide a robust
tool-kit with which to analyze variation in class politics.

The most straightforward of the class models of voting behavior grew
out of the nineteenth-century assumptions—shared by proponents and
foes alike—that support for socialism derives from economic interests.
Working class voters would vote for socialist parties as a way of pursuing
their material interests, while bourgeois or upper middle class voters were
presumed to favor conservative parties that would protect their relative
economic advantages.[2] Economic models of voting behavior have been
considerably refined over the years. Analysts now distinguish between
retrospective and *prospective* evaluations of candidates, parties, and issues,
as well as between *egocentric* (one's own interests) and *sociotropic* (the well
being of the nation as a whole) evaluations.[3] Further, a number of important
elaborations focus on voters' class-based responses to economic factors.
Douglas Hibbs's (1987; Hibbs, Rivers, and Vasilatos 1982) pioneering work
on macroeconomic conditions and vote choice suggested one type of
class-specific application: working class voters prefer economic outcomes
in which unemployment is low, whereas middle class voters prefer a low-
inflation environment. And indeed, there is evidence that the Democrats
have sought to reduce unemployment while the Republicans have focused

on inflation (Alesina, Londregan, and Rosenthal 1989, 1993). Democratic presidents produce more income growth for poor families than rich families, while Republican presidents have sponsored larger gains for affluent families (Bartels 2004, 2008). Such evidence implies that parties tend to adjust their policy priorities accordingly in order to best serve their electoral constituencies (Haynes and Jacobs 1994).

A second, quite different set of mechanisms connecting class location to political behavior centers on the importance of subjective identification, or "group consciousness." Models of this sort extend the classical "Michigan School" (Campbell et al. 1960) approach to studying voting behavior by broadening the concept of group membership to focus on the degree to which people identify with, or develop positive affect toward, a particular group (or class). If *objective* group membership does not involve a *subjective* component, it can be expected to have less influence over attitudes and behavior. Working class voters will behave as the classical economic interest model predicts largely to the extent to which they view themselves as members of the working class (Centers 1949; Vanneman and Cannon 1987; see also Hout, this volume).

At the heart of the social-psychological mechanisms accounting for group-based political differences are conceptions of the "linked fate" of group members (Dawson 1994, ch. 4). In his important formulation of this argument in relation to African American political identities, Michael Dawson argues that a strong sense of linked fate helps to explain why remarkable levels of political solidarity persist among African Americans, with 90 percent or more regularly supporting Democratic presidential nominees, even as class divisions among African Americans have grown. On this account, middle class blacks see their own prospects as tied to the well being of all blacks because "the historical experiences of African Americans have resulted in a situation in which group interests have served as a useful proxy for self-interest" (Dawson 1994, 77; but cf. Pattillo, this volume). A similar logic can be applied to classes. Union membership, for example, strengthens class-linked voting behavior among the working class (Form 1995), while membership in upper class institutions likewise serves to strengthen conservative consciousness among the affluent (Domhoff 2006). But when members of particular classes see their primary interests as linked to racial, religious, or other non-class identities, class-based political behavior declines (Manza and Brooks 1999).

A large research literature has identified the processes of group identification in the United States that reduce the impact of class identification (Vanneman and Cannon 1987; Hout, this volume). The landmark statement of this position was developed by Seymour Martin Lipset (1960/1981), who postulated that cross-cutting cleavages reduce the impact of class divisions. At the center of the analysis of such cross-cutting cleavages in American politics today is the enduring power of racial identities and racial resentments (see, for example, Kinder and Sanders 1996; Gilens 1999). Numerous analysts have traced the weaknesses of working class identity to American racial divisions (for example, Wilson 2001). The relative strength of the religious cleavage in American society, in which high levels of competition in the religious marketplace and a denominational structure that cross-cuts the class divide, represents another constraint on the salience of class-based identities (Wuthnow 1988).[4] More contentious have been claims that moral and religious values undermine class identities, a widely believed but controversial thesis (see, for example, Frank 2004).

Hout's chapter in this volume presents mixed evidence about the extent of class identification in the United States today. He finds that for those individuals in objective working class locations *and* with subjective consciousness aligned with their lived experience, class cleavages are sharpened. Those working class respondents who perceive themselves as "middle class," however, are less likely to support redistributive social policies.

The third major factor connecting class location to individual political behavior concerns the role of social networks. Neighborhoods, workplaces, occupational groups, and organizations embed individuals within social networks that provide the basis for discussion that shapes their political attitudes and behavior. Social networks of family, friends, coworkers, and other members of social or civic organizations disseminate new beliefs or, alternatively, reinforce predispositions. Robert Huckfeldt and John Sprague (1995) demonstrate the importance of network-based information to voters' decisionmaking and voting behavior, arguing that such information is routinely transmitted through both strong ties (such as those to friends) and weak ties (for example, those between individuals acquainted solely through a common contact; for an application to class networks see Weakliem and Heath 1994). Related findings concern the impact of social mobility on political preferences. Lifelong social ties arising from individuals' class origins and current class location influence political behavior far more than those of mobile citizens (whose "destination" class is different than their family class). Nan De Graaf, Paul Nieuwbeerta, and Anthony Heath (1995) present evidence suggesting that the behavior of mobile individuals falls between those more typical of their class of origin and those of incumbents of their current class. These findings are important; one of the most robust arguments in favor of the decline of class politics is the breakup of once-solid working class communities and neighborhoods where identities and networks persisted over time (Pakulski and Waters 1996, ch. 5).

These three mechanisms—economic interests, group-based consciousness, and social networks—are neither mutually exclusive nor necessarily in conflict. Social networks can reinforce a sense of class-based consciousness; common economic interests may locate individuals in neighborhoods and communities and other non-class groups such as schools and churches. The analytical problem of separating out the respective influences of each is demanding, and few existing election data sets contain fully adequate measures to carry out appropriate tests. The American National Election Studies, for example, typically contain batteries of items about respondents' economic situation and social group identities but lacks detailed measures of respondents' social networks.

The probabilistic nature of the relationships between interests, identities, networks, and political behavior warrants further comment. A crucial general problem for class analysis is that class location—however defined—is not a sole or even necessarily primary influence on the attitudes and behavior of members of different classes. Some, or even many, working class voters may choose conservative parties for reasons that cannot be explained by their current class location (as is true for upper class left wing voters). For example, when a group of billionaires led by the father of Microsoft founder Bill Gates opposed the Bush administration's proposal to eliminate the estate tax, they could not be said to be acting out of material self-interest. Further, class location is itself subject to measurement error. We assign individuals in surveys to a class location even when they may have widely varying material assets (Grusky and Weeden, this volume). Misidentification attenuates our estimates of the linkage between class and behavior. Finally, because class cleavages vary significantly over time and across electoral contexts or polity, class analysts must pay close attention to the key question of magnitude in their investigations.[5]

Macro Processes

In addition to the micro mechanisms through which class location exerts influence on political life, the organizational and institutional context of class politics matters as well. Claims about weak or diminishing impacts of class at the level of micro-political behavior must be viewed alongside evidence of the persistent or even growing macro impacts of class. It is striking that in current scholarly discourses the leading "death of class" texts almost completely ignore the macro context to focus solely on micro evidence (see, for example, Kingston 2000). This is an important lacuna. Governments operate in national and global political economies in which class power through investment decisions provides a critical set of constraints on the distribution of outcomes and the making of public policy. Politics is never simply about individuals who participate and how they vote; interest groups, social movements, and political parties are also intimately connected to class forces. Although these organizational effects are challenging to measure, it is shortsighted to dismiss them from theory and research.

Let us briefly consider some of these points in more detail. The existence of organizations such as unions and business associations influences the political alignment of classes. Unions organize workers, not only at the point of production but also at the polls. In the United States, organizations

representing minority-group interests are especially important in organizing political action among subordinate groups, even if not explicitly
based on class interests (Rosenstone and Hansen 1993, ch. 6; Leighley
2001). At the top of the social hierarchy, the interest groups and institutions of the powerful—peak business associations and upper class
organizations—align upper class groups politically and exert disproportionate political influence (Domhoff 2006).

Political parties vary widely in the degree to which they seek to organize
on the basis of social cleavages such as class, but some common patterns can
be found. Institutional features of the electoral systems shape the number
and types of political parties and their general character (such as catchall
parties versus parties organized around specific cleavages) (see, for example,
Mair 1997). In the majoritarian two-party system in the United States, the
major parties have a strong incentive to be catchall parties that appeal across
the board to a wide array of groups, while in multiparty systems quite different electoral strategies will be common (Powell 2000).[6] Changes in class
structure change the incentives for parties as well. An instructive example
is the transformation of European social democratic parties from class-based
parties to parties that compete more broadly for middle class votes (see
Przeworski and Sprague 1986; Heath, Jowell, and Curtice 2001), although,
as we will suggest later, a similar dynamic has occurred in the class bases
of American parties.

A final set of macro factors influencing class politics are the feedback
processes through which class divisions are reinforced by policy outcomes
and politicians' strategic behavior. Policy outcomes themselves, particularly
over the long term, tend to influence the perceptions and preferences of
voters, and those that are skewed toward the benefit of some groups both
reflect the existence of significant cleavages in the political system and *reproduce* those differences. Once in office, parties reward their supporters and
attempt to make good on at least some of their campaign promises, thereby
responding in a manner that reinforces group-based loyalties.

It would go beyond the scope of the chapter to try to summarize all these
impacts (on the United States, see, for example, Weir 1998; Hacker 2002; for
comparative evidence, see, for example, Lijphart 1997; Hicks 1999; Esping-
Andersen 2001; Huber and Stephens 2001). Growing income inequality
in the United States over the past three decades provides perhaps the
most obvious manifestation of the failure of public policies to blunt the
force of class divisions (Page and Simmons 2001; Jacobs and Skocpol 2006;
Bartels 2008). The impact is most visible in recent changes in tax policy that
have disproportionately benefited capital and higher earners (Graetz and
Shapiro 2005), and also in the failure of the minimum wage to keep pace with
inflation (Bartels 2008, ch. 8).

One intriguing new line of work highlights how class divisions manifest
themselves in relation to the responsiveness of policy to citizens' preference.

For example, there is robust evidence that public policy responds to aggregate public opinion (Erikson, MacKuen, and Stimson 2002). While there are important sources of variation in the degree of responsiveness of policy to opinion (Manza and Cook 2002), the weight of the evidence suggests that politicians listen to the public at least some of the time. However, the question of *whose* opinions are listened to is a critical one. Martin Gilens (2005) and Larry Bartels (2008, ch. 9) argue that responsiveness in the United States is significantly higher for the rich than the poor. Analyzing the policy attitudes of rich and poor, Gilens (2005) finds that when attitudes between the two groups vary, it is the rich who are more likely to enjoy policies that are in accord with their preferences. Research on the average levels of responsiveness may thus mask class-linked variation in the degree to which politicians respond to public opinion.

How Much Does Class Matter in American Politics?

The previous section argues that class impacts can be found across the micro and institutional contexts of democratic capitalist political systems. At the same time, we noted that measuring and analyzing these impacts is challenging. We now turn to three applications: political participation, voting behavior, and campaign finance, focusing on evidence and debates concerning class politics in the contemporary United States.

Political Participation: Class Differences in Participation

Writing in 1949, V. O. Key (1949/1964, 527) asserted that "the blunt truth is that politicians are under no compulsion to pay much heed to classes and groups of citizens that do not vote." It is thus appropriate to start with the question of voter turnout. Some key facts are not in dispute. A hallmark of American elections is the comparatively low rate of participation.[7] And the aggregate matters in relation to class differences in participation. In elections where turnout is far from universal, resource-rich groups vote at higher rates than do more disadvantaged groups, but this is not the case in countries with much higher rates of turnout (Lijphart 1997, 1–2). The United States is thus not surprisingly marked by a substantial cleavage-based skew in political participation. For example, a turnout gap of some 25 percent or more between the highest and lowest turnout classes (such as professionals versus unskilled workers) has been found in many analyses (Hout, Brooks, and Manza 1995; Lijphart 1997).[8]

Both individual-level and institutional explanations have been proffered to account for class skews in participation. The sociodemographic attributes of individuals linked to class position, such as education, income, gender, and labor force status, all contribute to subsequent class differences in turnout rates. One long-standing staple of the turnout literature has been the importance of education (Wolfinger and Rosenstone 1980, 13–36; Teixeira 1992; Verba, Schlozman, and Brady 1995). To be sure, educational effects on turnout are often mediated by other, associated factors, such as knowledge of the candidates and issues, newspaper reading, perceptions of political efficacy, and concern with the outcome of the election (Teixeira 1992; Conway 2000, 25–28). But there can be little doubt that education is the dominant individual-level influence on American voter participation. Because education levels are unevenly distributed across the class structure, the powerful effects of education on turnout contribute to class differences in participation.

As alluded to earlier, social networks have long been thought to have significant impacts on individual political participation. Networks provide a key source of both information and motivation. The basic idea is straightforward: interactions about politics with others enhance the likelihood of one's political participation, and the greater the degree of interaction, the greater the effect (Huckfeldt 1986; Rosenstone and Hansen 1993; Mutz 2006). Networks also provide incentives to participate; as Sidney Verba and his colleagues (1995, 16) pithily put it, one reason people do not participate is "because nobody asked." This finding appears to hold across both aggregate contextual measures of social environment and measures of individual networks.[9] The impact of social networks on turnout reinforces class differences in participation, in part because of the similarity in turnout propensity between individuals and members of their surrounding networks.

Turning to political and institutional sources of class differences in turnout, we should begin by noting one of the least recognized sources of participation, namely, eligibility. Official turnout statistics are based on a denominator that includes the entire voting-age population. But barriers to participation for legal immigrants, convicted felons and ex-felons, and several other small groups are an increasingly important source of nonvoting (McDonald and Popkin 2001). Eligibility has an impact on some classes more than others. The share of immigrants and disenfranchised felons at the bottom of the class structure has grown steadily over time, following the 1965 immigration reforms and with rising incarceration and criminal conviction rates since the 1970s (Manza and Uggen 2006; McCarty, Poole, and Rosenthal 2006). Nolan McCarty and his colleagues (2006, ch. 3) have further shown that over time the share of immigrants in the population is associated with trends in income inequality.

Other analysts have suggested the importance of the mobilizing activities of parties and political organizations as a powerful source of class inputs into participation (Rosenstone and Hansen 1993). Mobilizing elections, in which the parties seek to expand the electorate, produce higher turnout rates. Declining mobilization efforts from the 1960s onward, however, have been associated with declining (or stagnating) turnout, even in the face of increases in education levels within the electorate as a whole (see esp. Rosenstone and Hansen 1993; see also Burnham 1982; Piven and Cloward 2000). These scholars have argued that the Democratic Party and the social movements and organizations affiliated with it have generally lost the capacity to reach out to disadvantaged voters as part of a broader trend toward a more elite-oriented, money-driven party. Steven Rosenstone and John Hansen's (1993) widely cited analysis produced statistical evidence from individual-level survey data suggesting that declining mobilization accounted for one-half of the turnout decline between 1960 and 1988. The importance of mobilization in relation to skewed class turnout rates is based on the simple dynamic in which well-endowed groups with high turnout rates are largely unaffected by mobilization efforts. But mobilization can be quite important with lower turnout rates (Leighley 2001), such as minorities and the working class.[10]

In specifying institutional factors, analysts have pointed to several class-related mechanisms: the difficulty of voter registration in the United States compared to countries that use an automatic system of voter registration (Piven and Cloward 2000; Powell 1986); the higher costs of voting when national elections are held on a workday, in contrast to (most) democratic polities that schedule elections on weekends or national holidays (Crewe 1981; for discussion of the extraordinary differences in turnout between Puerto Ricans voting in Puerto Rico, where elections are held on either Sunday or a national holiday, versus Puerto Ricans living on the U.S. mainland, see Freeman 2004); and the limited range of ideological choices available to voters in the American two-party system, and in particular the absence of a labor or social democratic party to mobilize working class voters (see, for example, Burnham 1982; see also Jackman 1987).

Trends in Class Bias in Political Participation

From the standpoint of the impact of class divisions on turnout, a key question has been how much group-based inequalities in participation have grown, if at all. In other words, is the turnout decline (whatever its precise magnitude) concentrated disproportionately among certain groups, most notably the working class or the poor? An extensive body of research has produced agreement on a key point: there is no evidence of any narrowing in turnout inequality. But on the question of whether there has been any *increase* in participation inequalities, contradictory results abound. Evidence of an increased skew in participation has been found using income and education to measure socioeconomic status (Bennett 1991; Rosenstone and Hansen 1993; Freeman 2004) and occupation (Burnham 1982). Most studies measuring educational differences in turnout have found greater decline among less-well-educated groups (Leighley and Nagler 1992; Teixeira 1992; Abramson, Aldrich, and Rohde 2002), even among analysts who are skeptical of any overall increase in social cleavage-related bias (esp. Leighley and Nagler 1992).

However, a number of other analysts have found little to no evidence of an increasing skew and emphasize instead that turnout decline reflects electorate-wide trends. Jan Leighley and Jonathan Nagler (1992) argue that income is the best single measure of the class skewness of the electorate and that there has been no change in the relative participation rates of different income groups (on midterm elections, see also Shields and Goidel 1997). Utilizing a new data set—the Roper Social and Political Trends Data—with over-time measures of participation across a range of political and charitable activities, Henry Brady and his colleagues (2002) find largely trendless patterns in the turnout ratio of upper to lower socioeconomic groups; these authors conclude that while substantial participation inequalities remain, "the voters remain the same." Using an occupational measure of class, we find limited evidence that turnout has fallen among working class voters, principally among skilled workers (see Hout, Brooks, and Manza 1995; see also Manza and Brooks 1999, ch. 7).

Overall, the trend debate has proven difficult to resolve, in part because estimates based on self-reported turnout are subject to nonrandom reporting biases, and different model specifications yield different results. These sources of uncertainty hold across the major data sets (the National Election Study and the Voter Supplement Module of the Current Population Survey [CPS]) and across different specifications of class. We conclude that there is at best only modest evidence for an *increase* in class divide on turnout. But this should in no way obscure the fact that by any measure the *persisting* class-based skew in participation rates in elections in the United States is substantial and consequential.

Class Divisions in U.S. Voting Behavior

The most widely analyzed question of class politics in the electoral arena concerns the choices that voters actually make at the ballot box. As with participation, there are questions about both the magnitude of the class divide and the existence of possible trends in the alignment of classes and parties.

Turning to the question of trends, a wide range of scholars have argued that traditional group-based political alignments have eroded, often directly paralleling the decline of left-right political cleavages (Franklin 1992; Franklin, Mackie, and Valen 1992a, 1992b; Van der Eijk et al. 1992; Dalton and Wattenberg 1993; Carmines and Huckfeldt 1996; Dalton 1996;). Ronald Inglehart and his collaborators' arguments about the emergence of a "new politics" rooted in a clash between materialist and postmaterialist values start from the assumption that there has been a decline in social cleavages such as class and religion (see, for example, Inglehart 1990, 1997).

Much of this debate is cross-national, with the comparatively higher rates of class voting in Europe making them potentially more susceptible to decline. The debate is complex: there is evidence of declining class voting in some countries, but not in all (Brooks, Nieuwbeerta, and Manza 2006; Evans 1999). Much of the question depends on how one analyzes "class voting." In the traditional approach, introduced and popularized by Robert Alford (1963), class voting is the proportion of "manual workers" voting for left parties minus the proportion of nonmanual workers voting for the same parties. In the "Alford index," working class voters are expected to align with left parties, and vice versa for nonmanual workers. Later extensions tweaked the basic formula but left its underlying assumptions in place.

More recent scholarship on class voting challenges the assumptions of the Alford index. Critics point to the limitations of a simple, dichotomous model of classes, alongside problems with constraining "class voting" to a single dimension that imposes a strict ordinality on class and party alignments. In our earlier work (Hout, Brooks, and Manza 1995; Manza and Brooks 1999), we sought to develop an approach that does not require assumptions of any specific correspondence between particular classes and parties but rather measures class voting as the sum total of each class's divergence from the electorate-wide average.

In the debate over trends in class voting in the United States, recent work has suggested two striking findings. Income-based models have found persistence of the classical alignment, with lower-income voters remaining as Democratic as before (Bartels 2006; McCarty, Poole, and Rosenthal 2006). To be sure, growing affluence from the 1950s through the early 1970s pushed all voters to the right (Brooks and Brady 1999), but the relationship between *relative* income groups and vote choice has remained as strong as ever (McCarty, Poole, and Rosenthal 2006).

However, an occupational-based model of class voting produces a more nuanced picture. Classes have realigned politically. In our own six-class model distinguishing professional, managers, the self-employed, routine white collar workers, skilled manual workers and supervisors, and nonskilled workers, we find that considerable realignment has occurred (Manza and Brooks 1999, ch. 3; see also Hout and Moody 2006). Professionals moved from being the second-most Republican class to the most *Democratic* class by the 1990s. The self-employed moved from a centrist position to a strongly Republican bloc in recent elections. Skilled and nonskilled workers shifted toward the center, with nonskilled workers remaining in a weaker Democratic alignment. These trends suggest some important features of class-based political alignments that are not picked up by income measures.

The question of trends in class voting—and their impact on elections more generally—has been reignited by the debate over Thomas Frank's (2004) recent polemic. Frank argues that white working class voters have defected to the Republicans and into an alliance with affluent voters, creating a coalition "uniting business and blue collar" (Frank 2004, 8). His argument is that class-based voter alignments have declined because of successful Republican inroads into the working class electorate based on appeals to symbolic social issues and traditional family values. Our own investigation of these trends suggests a somewhat different picture (Manza and Brooks 1999, ch. 3). We do find evidence that social issues have become an important source of class realignment, but *not* because conservative views on such issues have pushed working class voters to the right. Rather, we find strong evidence that social issue liberalism has pushed professionals (and to a lesser extent other middle class voters) toward the Democratic Party.[11]

Putting It All Together: Political Class Coalitions

There is no single way of capturing the overall electoral impact of class divisions. But one approach that we believe is promising is to focus attention on the ways in which biases in turnout combine with changes in class-based political alignments and the size of social classes to shape major party coalitions. Focusing on the class bases of the parties—where the voters come from—enables a sharper understanding of some of these processes. In other words, by taking into account the relative *size* of social classes as well as their turnout and vote choice, we can obtain a better sense of the combined impact of class politics on the electoral strategies and policies that politicians and parties ultimately pursue. Indeed, because such processes as the declining size of the number of manual workers and their increasing unwillingness to support Democratic candidates are difficult to reverse over short periods of time, they set in place powerful constraints that party officials cannot readily ignore.

How have class voters' turnout levels, alignments with parties, and relative size influenced the major parties' coalitions? A few previous analysts have advanced different estimates addressing these questions (see, for example, Axelrod 1972; Erikson, Lancaster, and Romero 1989; Stanley and Niemi 1993; Bartels 1998). Our own earlier effort (Manza and Brooks 1999, ch. 7) considered trends through the early 1990s. We found that in the postwar era the Democratic Party experienced a major shift from a party with more working class voters than professional and managerial voters to one with far larger representations of the latter. As displayed in the estimates shown in figure 7.1, we estimate that the ratio of working class voters to professional or managerial voters fell from nearly three-to-one in 1960 to parity by 1992.[12] Decomposing this shift reveals several dynamics. Professionals have both grown in size and become significantly more Democratic (see Brooks and Manza 1997). Both skilled and nonskilled workers have moved toward the center—skilled workers in the 1960s and nonskilled workers in the 1980s and 1990s, although the latter remain a reliably Democratic bloc. Because both classes have declined in size, however, their relative contributions

Figure 7.1   The Ratio of Working Class Voters to Professionals and Managers in the Democratic Party Electoral Coalition, 1960 to 1992

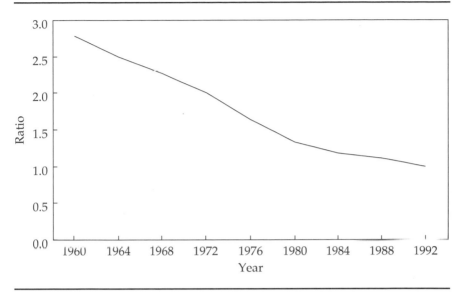

Source: National Election Study; for further details, see Manza and Brooks (1999, chapter 7).

to the Democratic coalition have decreased. These trends have only deepened in recent elections, with professionals and managers now providing slightly *more* votes than skilled and nonskilled voters for Democratic candidates. A smaller increase in the share of votes has come from routine white collar workers since the 1960s.

With such a significant shift in the source of the votes, it can hardly be surprising that Democratic strategists and elected officials have found fewer electoral rewards in maintaining the economic and social policies of the New Deal. Indeed, it is precisely the growing prominence of middle class voters within the Democratic coalition that provides officials with incentive to give greater emphasis to market-related and meritocratic policy ideas.

These results suggest, then, a pair of thematic impressions. Clearly, the growing prominence of the new middle classes in the contemporary Democratic Party, when coupled with the relative decline of the traditional working class, exerts pressure away from the modestly egalitarian agenda the party pursued between the 1930s and 1960s. Further, viewed in conjunction with the relatively high level of representation of these groups within the Republican column, we find evidence of contraction in the occupational polarization of working class forces versus middle class voters as a source of party competition.

Financing American Elections: Class Capacities and American Exceptionalism

When it comes to the politics of class in the United States, nothing is more unusual compared to other democratic countries than the American system of financing elections. In other countries, public financing of elections, mandatory free media access, or strict limits on the amounts that can be spent set limits on the importance of money in the political system. But in the United States, extraordinary, and rapidly increasing, amounts of money are spent on political campaigns.[13] This system's potential for class-based influence on politics is thus considerable.

To be certain, the availability of large amounts of money to finance American political campaigns is hardly a recent phenomenon. Affluent individuals and groups have long taken advantage of opportunities for political influence (see, for example, Corrado 1997).[14] But recent increases suggest the possibility of a widening class divide in influences on elections. Concerns about the political role of money have received widespread media and popular attention, both in relation to the potential for corruption and with respect to domination by monied interests. At the same time, however, a number of analysts have argued that these impacts are frequently overstated (Ansolabehere, de Figueiredo, and Snyder 2003; Burstein 2008).

Where does political money come from, and how can we characterize it in class terms? Broadly speaking, contributions come from either individual donors or political action committees (PACs). PAC contributions can be divided into three categories: business-related PACs, labor PACs, and "ideological" PACs, the last category including all types of groups organized around specific issues, such as the National Rifle Association (NRA) and the National Organization of Women (NOW). Business PACs include both those associated with individuals and groups. Labor PACs are generally associated with single unions, although the most prominent labor PAC is the AFL-CIO's Committee on Political Education (COPE). While PAC money receives a great deal of public attention, it is individual donations that account for the largest share of total donations. The vast majority of the largest of these contributions are made by affluent individuals.

The overall trends in campaign finance can be seen in table 7.1, which presents our estimates of total PAC and individual contributions to congressional campaigns through the 1978 to 2006 election cycles in real (2006) dollars, collapsing "hard" and "soft" money donations (as well as "527" donations after 2002).[15] The table shows that total contributions from business sources ratcheted up by some 950 percent in midterm elections, and by 823 percent in presidential election years. While the amounts contributed by organized labor and ideological PACs also increased (quite considerably for ideological PACs), the totals are dwarfed by those from business

Table 7.1 Trends in National Election Campaign Finance, 1992 to 2006 (in Millions of Dollars, Inflation-Adjusted)

Election Year	Total Business PAC Contributions	Total Labor PAC Contributions	Total Ideological PAC Contributions	Total Individual Contributions
1978	$66.5	$31.8	$8.3	n.a.
1980	93.4	35.3	13.1	n.a.
1982	106.7	43.2	22.9	n.a.
1984	122.4	48.4	28.3	n.a.
1986	111.4	54.2	34.0	n.a.
1988	152.3	58.0	32.9	n.a.
1990	139.4	52.7	22.4	n.a.
1992	263.1	62.4	26.7	$459.8
1994	262.7	63.6	30.4	353.6
1996	407.7	71.8	33.5	536.5
1998	357.3	65.5	37.8	407.2
2000	669.7	104.7	54.0	817.6
2002	615.5	96.1	68.6	719.3
2004	769.4	101.6	77.1	1,014.2
2006	631.7	88.9	67.1	703.0
Change from 1978 to 2006 (midterm elections)	950%	280%	810%	
Change from 1980 to 2004 (presidential)	823%	288%	589%	
Change from 1992 to 2004 (individual)				154%

Source: 1978 to 1984: Corrado (1987); 1986 to 2000: Federal Election Commission reports (http://www.fec.gov) and Center for Responsive Politics (http://www.opensecrets.org).

Note: All estimates shown in 2006 dollars. "Total" includes hard and soft (unregulated) contributions from 1992 to 2002 to all candidates for national office (U.S. House, Senate, and the presidency). After 2002, totals include hard and estimated 527 (ideological advocacy) contributions. Note that 1992, 1996, 2000, and 2004 are presidential years and thus reflect higher overall contributions than in midterm congressional elections without a presidential ballot.

sources. The ratio of business to labor contributions rose from a little over two-to-one at the beginning of this period to approximately seven-to-one at the end.

Focusing on corporate donations, however, understates the full impact of political money from upper class sources. Millions of Americans make campaign donations in their own names (or those of family members), often alongside donations to their corporate PAC. While most of these donations are in modest amounts, when we consider larger individual contributions—which in the aggregate provide the vast bulk of the total amount donated—the class disparity in individual donations is substantial. For example, in 2002 the Center for Responsive Politics was able to categorize about 70 percent of donations over $200 for the 2000 election cycle. It reports that individuals associated with business interests contributed a total of $533.7 million to election campaigns, compared with less than $1 million contributed by individuals associated with organized labor.

Survey data on individual-level giving to political campaigns are consistent with this finding: patterns of significant giving are heavily skewed toward individuals from affluent households. For example, Verba and his colleagues (1995, 191–96) found that 56 percent of households with incomes over $125,000 donated to a political campaign in 1989, with the average amount of such donations being $1,183, compared with just 6 percent of households with incomes below $15,000 (who gave an average of $86). Surveying large ($200 or more) contributors to the 1996 congressional campaign, Robert Biersack and his colleagues (1999) report that 79.5 percent of large donors had incomes over $100,000, and 42.4 percent had incomes over $250,000. These authors find that large donors are far more conservative politically than NES respondents (with only 29 percent identifying as Democrats, compared with 52.4 percent of the NES sample for that year), though they are more liberal on social issues than the NES sample. While many affluent individuals and households give to the Democrats or pro-Democratic advocacy groups, the economic interests of these donors mark them as distinctly different than the Democratic Party of the New Deal era.

Skewing Outcomes? Assessing the Political Impact of Money in American Politics

In the vast social science literature on campaign finance, the ultimate question is whether political money skews election outcomes and public policy. There are, as Bartels and his colleagues (2005, 113) put it, two ways in which money might matter: "It can influence elections and it can affect the behavior of elected representatives." We can, however, break down the question further by distinguishing the role of money in influencing who runs for political office; the role of money in influencing election outcomes; the role of money in shaping the voting patterns of those who are elected; and the impact of money on other significant types of legislative behavior. At every stage of the political process, there are arguments in favor of the power of money to skew outcomes, but at the same time, in none of these areas has the existing body of research established firmly that money is the decisive factor.[16]

Who Runs   Political recruitment—who runs for office—is clearly influenced by the need to be able to raise large amounts of money to finance competitive campaigns for national or important state offices. The bloated war chests of incumbents (or the large amounts raised by one candidate for an open-seat election) have been shown to deter potential challengers. Only those with the networks and resources to raise the funds needed to be competitive will seek political office (see, for example, Box-Steffensmeier 1996). The money system works as a kind of signaling process in which early fundraising plays a much greater strategic role than late fundraising. Because early fundraising is much easier for candidates who already have access to elite money networks, some have argued that the early fundraising process constitutes a "money primary" (Magleby and Nelson 1990, 58–61; Clawson, Neustadtl, and Weller 1998, ch. 1; Domhoff 2006, ch. 6). Another increasingly important recent development has been the growing number of affluent candidates who can give or loan start-up funds to their campaign out of their own pocket and signal, right off the bat, the viability of their campaign.

In the "money primary"—not unlike the actual election—momentum and visible evidence of a high probability of ultimate success are key factors in being able to raise money. Political reporting is increasingly paying attention. The money primary is important because it serves to eliminate potential challengers who do not have access to the same types of resources as incumbents or front-runners. In a more speculative vein, it may force challengers to tailor their message in ways that will appeal to potential donors. Although an incumbent's large war chest may not deter challengers who expect to have access to significant resources themselves, it makes grassroots efforts significantly more difficult than in the past.

Who Wins   Aside from the impact of money on candidate selection, there are extensive controversies over the question of whether the amount of money spent during an election significantly influences the outcome. Some research suggests that money plays a much bigger role in determining the success of challengers, while greater amounts are of more marginal benefit for incumbents (see, for example, Jacobson 1990; Abramowitz 1991). However, the endogenous role of money in elections makes such conclusions problematic. Rational incumbents will raise and spend more money in close elections—that is, in elections that they are more likely to lose—than in races that weigh heavily in their favor from the outset (Green and Krasno 1988; Gerber 1998). Because many incumbents spend little and win easily, while those who spend more often face tougher challenges (and thus have a greater likelihood of losing), the spending effect can appear spurious.

Nonetheless, it is impossible to avoid the conclusion that to beat an incumbent or to win an open seat a challenger needs to be able to raise large amounts of money and that those funds must come primarily, though not exclusively, from business interests or affluent individuals. (The national parties are also providing increasing support to their candidates, but generally only after those candidates have already shown themselves adept at raising money on their own.) In terms of who wins, then, the impact of money may show up either at the stage of political recruitment, when the universe of potential candidates winnows, or in the election outcome, which is harder to measure and document.

Legislative Voting Patterns   Does money influence legislative votes on policy, either for individual legislators or in the aggregate? Periodic vote-selling scandals excite journalistic outrage. But what is the larger picture? With little, if any, direct evidence of systematic vote selling, much hinges on the assumptions of measures and statistical models. Key to the question is whether money matters after controlling for party and ideology. Early examinations split inconclusively between those who find that contributions influence voting patterns (Ginsberg and Green 1986) and those who find no effect (Welch 1982). Such different results have often been attributed to the variance of issues on which votes are cast and to competing approaches to measurement issues.

A related but more sophisticated version of the influence argument suggests the existence of a "spot market" in which votes are exchanged for contributions. Proponents of this approach (Austen-Smith 1995; Baron 1989; Stern 1992; Stratmann 1992) claim that contributions are short-term investments through which the donor secures political favors (such as votes on relevant issues or the framing of legislation in ways that are beneficial to the donor) or ensures that legislators honor past agreements. Short of legislators admitting that their voting behavior was influenced by PAC donations, however, direct evidence of money buying votes is almost impossible to find. Members of Congress can always claim that their voting behavior leads to contributions from like-minded PACs rather than vice versa. In lieu of direct evidence, scholars have attempted to support the spot market hypothesis by showing that PAC behavior closely corresponds to behavior that one would expect if votes were being exchanged for contributions. Thomas Stratmann's (1992) analysis of the behavior of PACs associated with the farming industry is illustrative: he shows that these PACs tend to contribute more money to legislators whose voting decisions are uncertain than to those who are expected to vote in the PAC's interest. This suggests that a relationship between PAC contributions and voting patterns cannot be solely attributed to shared political interests (that is, PACs give money to certain candidates *because* they vote in accordance with the PAC's interest) but instead indicates attempts by PACs to sway undecided legislators.

Critics of the spot market thesis abound. A second generation of research on the influence of money on votes has introduced techniques for distinguishing how voting behavior influences PAC contributions as well as how PAC contributions influence voting behavior (see, for example, Levitt 1998; Wawro 2001). This line of work suggests that contributions do not dictate voting patterns in a unidirectional fashion from money to subsequent votes. Other recent critics of the view that money changes votes have pointed out that the scholarly attention given to the influence of PAC contributions on voting patterns is exaggerated because PACs do not contribute enough money to be very influential. Legislators are, in this view, not capable of being bought off with contributions from a single PAC (even if the PAC gives the maximum $5,000). House incumbents are likely to spend $1 million on reelection (and Senate incumbents far more), and this amount rises even higher in competitive races. Those who hold a "safe" seat should be even less subject to influence (see, for example, Milyo, Primo, and Groseclose 2000).

The theoretical case for the impact of money on voting thus requires a more nuanced interpretation than a simple vote-buying thesis would suggest. Indeed, one model argues that the relationship between contributors and legislators is best understood as a long-term commitment between those parties. Alan Neustadtl (1990, 559), for example, reports that "PAC directors indicate that there is a long-term give-and-take established between interest groups and members and that, as a political player, one cannot be concerned only with legislative outcomes." In explicitly theorizing this relationship, Dan Clawson, Neustadtl, and Mark Weller (1998) draw on Mauss's famous analysis of the gift to argue that donations create a "gift" relationship in which periodic small favors are exchanged, but not any specific or immediate responses on the part of the recipient legislator (such as voting a particular way on a particular issue) (see also Schram 1995). Like a gift, the donation implies unnamed obligations and acts of reciprocity—that is, that legislators will attend, where possible, to the interests of contributors with whom they have a relationship (see Clawson, Neustadtl, and Weller 1998, 84–87).

Conclusion

Class matters in American politics. There are multiple dimensions through which class-based inequalities are felt, and one of the challenges for a class analysis of politics is to pay attention to the layering of these impacts. To conclude that class is a minor factor in American politics, as Paul Kingston (2000, ch. 6) has asserted, requires an unduly restrictive focus on those arenas—for example, public opinion and vote choice—where class has its most limited impact. Viewed more broadly, and taking into account the full range of ways in which class divisions become manifest, we arrive at a rather different set of conclusions.

The starting point of our analysis was to note that American political institutions are internationally distinctive in ways that encourage some kinds of class politics while discouraging others. Class remains a source of electoral division—especially in relation to political participation, but less so in terms of vote choice. The existence of institutional barriers to participation (such as holding elections on workdays and placing the onus for registration in most states on voters) is one key example. The system of campaign finance provides yet another pathway for the affluent to exert influence.

Turning to the question of *how* class matters, we posited three mechanisms: economic interests, group identities, and social networks. Individuals may think about politics or behave politically in ways that relate to their own economic circumstances or their views of the economic well being of the country as a whole. Subjective identification with a class or class-based social group can reinforce, or in some cases produce, a certain kind of class-linked behavior. Finally, exposure to, or involvement with, class-based social networks reinforces class influences on politics.

In our review of the evidence of class impacts on American politics, we noted large differences in participation and political money but more modest differences in class voting. However, even though in most models class has only a modest impact on voting behavior, it is still useful to think about how changes in the class structure are influencing political outcomes. A class analysis of electoral politics reveals sharp changes in the class character of the electoral coalitions of the major parties, with the weight of working class voters diminishing significantly in the Democratic Party's electoral coalition. We know that policy outputs over the past few decades have favored a widening of class inequality in the United States. If we are to understand the reasons why policy is more responsive to the wishes of the affluent, a class analysis of politics remains of vital import.

Research assistance was provided by Sarah Lowe. We thank Annette Lareau and Dalton Conley for their generous and helpful comments on this chapter.

Notes

1. Analysts of class politics use the term "class" in a number of different ways. We discuss these, and our own preferred approach, in the next section.

2. Such a rendering assumes that (class) voters evaluate the expected utility of the political choices offered by candidates and parties. In this view, "groups" are ultimately aggregates of self-interested actors (albeit with similar calculations of utility), and group-based voting is explained in terms of calculations regarding which party is more likely to bring about the desired economic outcomes (see, for example, Lipset et al. 1954, 1136).

3. Morris Fiorina's (1981) pioneering work developed an economic model of vote choice that distinguished between the retrospective versus prospective orientations of economic expectations and behavior. Whereas retrospective voting involves comparisons between present and past economic evaluations, prospective voting requires comparisons between future and current economic expectations. Fiorina argues that because voters tend to be more concerned with the outcomes of government policies than the details of policy implementation, retrospective voting is the more common orientation found in the American electorate. Roderick Kiewiet's (1983) research illustrates the importance of conceptualizing and measuring the variable target of economic evaluations: voters' evaluations are egocentric when they involve perceptions of economic conditions experienced by an individual; voters' evaluations are sociotropic when they involve considerations of national economic prosperity (Kinder and Kiewiet 1981). Either may provide the basis for economic voting.

4. We discuss in more detail the dynamics of the "ethno-religious" cleavage in American society in relation to other kinds of political identities in Manza and Brooks (1999, esp. ch. 4).

5. We discuss this point in further detail in Brooks, Manza, and Bolzendahl (2003).

6. In American political history, the two-party system (and the institutional rules that enforce it) has long been seen as an important source for blunting the political expression of working class interests (see, for example, Burnham 1982; Piven and Cloward 1997).

7. Richard Freeman (2004) cites one recent international survey showing that turnout in national elections in the United States ranks an extraordinary 138th among the 170 countries that hold elections—far lower than all similar capitalist democracies except Switzerland (which ranked 137th).

8. Such sharp socioeconomic-based cleavages are not generally found to the same degree in other countries, although cross-national research frequently finds that in those countries without compulsory voting there are small to moderate effects of education on turnout (Powell 1986, 26–27; Font and Viros 1995; Dalton 1996; Lijphart 1997, 2–3; but see Topf 1995).

9. Diana Mutz (2006) has recently produced new survey-based evidence suggesting that individuals with substantively cross-cutting and conflictual networks are less likely to participate. This finding suggests that the content of network interactions matters, although not the basic fact of their importance.

10. It is worth noting that since the late 1980s both the Democratic and Republican Parties and their allies have significantly increased their efforts to mobilize voters; National Election Study (NES) data show that while 22 percent of voters were contacted by one of the parties in 1960 (the year with the highest postwar turnout), in 1996, 29 percent of voters were contacted, and in 2000 fully 36 percent of voters were contacted (the highest total ever recorded), without stimulating an increase in aggregate (or working class) turnout rates (on party mobilization, see Abramson, Aldrich, and Rohde 2002, 90). The field experiments undertaken by Alan Gerber and Donald Green (2000, 2004) suggest that certain kinds of contacts—especially those based on person-to-person contact— are much more likely to raise turnout. One explanation for the decline in

turnout rates in spite of increased party contact with potential voters is the inefficient mode through which such contacts are made, which in turn may be linked to the organizational decline of the labor movement and other grassroots organizational capacities that use in-person contacts.

11.   Bartels (2006) challenges Frank's (2004) evidence of shifting class voting, in relation to both income groups and educational level. Bartels shows that neither voters with low education nor voters with low income have moved toward the Republicans, as Frank claims.

12.   For full details of this analysis, see Manza and Brooks (1999, ch. 7). In a striking replication for Britain, Anthony Heath and his colleagues (2001, ch. 7) find an equally dramatic shift in the ratio of workers to professionals and managers in the Labour Party, from 5.2-to-1 in 1974 to 1.7-to-1 in 1997.

13.   The financing of political campaigns in the United States is governed by a complex set of regulations and laws. Fears that wealthy corporate and individual campaign donors were buying government influence early in the twentieth century led to an initial attempt at campaign finance reform, the Tillman Act of 1907, which sought to ban corporate contributions to federal campaigns. The effectiveness of this legislation was limited, however, by lack of enforcement and its susceptibility to loopholes. Similar limitations have characterized the numerous attempts at campaign finance reform up to the present (Corrado 1997; Goidel, Gross, and Shields 1999; Mutch 2001).

    The Federal Election Campaign Act (FECA) of 1971, along with key modifying amendments in 1974, 1976, and 1979, defines the landscape of money and politics today. The act put into place new requirements for the disclosure of money received by candidates while placing new limitations on contributions to candidates and political parties. Under the 1974 amendments to the act, in each election individuals may contribute up to $1,000 to a candidate, $5,000 to a political action committee (PAC), and $20,000 to national parties, but no more than $25,000 total; PACs are allowed to contribute up to $5,000 each election to a candidate, $5,000 to other PACs, and $15,000 to national parties. "Soft-money" contributions were made legal in the 1979 amendment to the FECA; these contributions have no ceiling but are limited to non-candidate-specific, party-building activities, such as get-out-the-vote drives and issue advertisements (see Potter 1997; Magleby 2002).

    In a recent attempt to eliminate the influence of very large soft-money contributions coming overwhelmingly from business sources, the Bipartisan Campaign Reform Act of 2002 prohibited (after the 2002 election) national party committees (that is, the Democratic and Republican Parties) from accepting and spending soft-money contributions. But it also allowed for increased individual contributions and, perhaps more importantly, continued to allow unrestricted soft-money expenditures. The latter—which can be used for voter registration, get-out-the-vote efforts, voter "education" efforts, and other activities so long as these are not formally coordinated with the parties—exploded in 2004 and showed no signs of diminishing during the 2008 election season.

14.   For example, in the first of her pioneering studies of campaign contributions, Louise Overlacker (1932) found that nearly 70 percent of all money contributed to the 1928 federal election campaigns came from donations of over $1,000.

15.   Unlike soft-money contributions, which are not regulated or limited by federal
law and may be used for party-building activities, such as voter registration
drives and general campaigning for the party (see note 13), direct, "hard-
money" election expenses are regulated by the FECA. Before 1990, soft-money
contributions were not required by law to be reported, so systematic data on
soft-money contributions are only available beginning with the 1992 election
cycle, and they were ended by federal legislation in 2002. During this ten-year
span, however, there was a dramatic increase in business soft-money contributions: from $92 million to $351 million in 2002 (in real 2004 dollars). Soft-
money contributions were barred after the 2002 election by the campaign
finance reform legislation known as the McCain-Feingold Act. This measure
raised the amount of allowable hard-money donations for individuals and
PACs, but eliminated soft-money expenditures on behalf of a candidate. The
upshot was that in 2004 hard-money expenditures increased. And because
McCain-Feingold permits election-related "issue advocacy" that does not
explicitly mention a candidate, a new type of campaign organization known
as a "527 group" (named after a section of the act) has sprung up. In 2004, even
though they got off to a late start, 527s spent over $500 million on activities
such as partisan get-out-the-vote drives and issue advertising.
16.   Many of the recent debates turn on complex methodological issues—what
two leading analysts once described as "the statistical morass that surrounds
the study of campaign finance" (Ansolabehere and Gerber 1994, 1115). We do
not have the space here to discuss all of the debates over competing statistical
approaches, but there are a couple of common issues that appear repeatedly.
Most notably, there are linked questions about simultaneity bias and assumptions about the exogeneity of money in the political process. For instance, models that treat campaign contributions as an exogenous variable tend to ignore
the possibility that PACs give legislators money *because* these legislators vote
in a particular way. Such models are unable to distinguish between these two
scenarios. The most sophisticated models for the role of money at any of the
four stages attempt to build in parameters for capturing processes that may
shape *both* the amounts of money received and their impact.

References

Abramowitz, Alan. 1991. "Incumbency, Campaign Spending, and the Decline of
Competition in the U.S. House." *Journal of Politics* 53(1): 34–57.
Abramson, Paul R., John H. Aldrich, and David W. Rohde. 2002. *Change and
Continuity in the 2000 Elections.* Washington: Congressional Quarterly Press.
Alesina, Alberto, John Londregan, and Howard Rosenthal. 1989. "Partisan Cycles
in Congressional Elections and the Macroeconomy." *American Political Science
Review* 83(2): 373–98.
———. 1993. "A Model of the Political Economy in the United States." *American
Political Science Review* 87(1): 12–33.
Alford, Robert. 1963. *Party and Society.* Chicago, Ill.: Rand-McNally.
Ansolabehere, Stephen, and Alan Gerber. 1994. "The Mismeasure of Campaign
Spending: Evidence from the 1990 U.S. House Elections." *Journal of Politics*
56(4): 1106–18.

Ansolabehere, Stephen, John M. de Figueiredo, and James M. Snyder. 2003. "Why Is There So Little Money in U.S. Politics?" *Journal of Economic Perspectives* 17(1): 105–30.

Austen-Smith, David. 1995. "Campaign Contributions and Access." *American Political Science Review* 89(3): 566–81.

Axelrod, Robert. 1972. "Where the Votes Come From: An Analysis of Electoral Coalitions." *American Political Science Review* 66(1): 11–20.

Baron, David. 1989. "Service-Induced Campaign Contributions and the Electoral Equilibrium." *Quarterly Journal of Economics* 104(1): 45–72.

Bartels, Larry. 1998. "Where the Ducks Are: Voting Power in a Party System." In *Politicians and Party Politics,* edited by John Geer. Baltimore: Johns Hopkins University Press.

———. 2004. "Partisan Politics and U.S. Income Distribution." Unpublished paper, Princeton University, Department of Politics.

———. 2006. "What's the Matter with *What's the Matter with Kansas?*" *Quarterly Journal of Political Science* 1(2): 201–26.

———. 2008. *Unequal Democracy: The Political Economy of a New Gilded Age.* New York: Russell Sage Foundation.

Bartels, Larry, Hugh Heclo, Rodney E. Hero, and Lawrence R. Jacobs. 2005. "Inequality and American Governance." In *Inequality and American Democracy: What We Know and What We Need to Learn,* edited by Lawrence Jacobs and Theda Skocpol. New York: Russell Sage Foundation.

Bennett, Stephen E. 1991. "Left Behind: Exploring Declining Turnout Among Noncollege Whites, 1964–1988." *Social Science Quarterly* 72(4): 314–33.

Biersack, Robert, John C. Green, Paul E. Herrnson, Lynda W. Powell, and Clyde Wilcox. 1999. "Individual Congressional Campaign Contributors: A Preliminary Report." Paper prepared for the annual meeting of the Midwest Political Science Association. Chicago, Ill., April 15–17, 1999.

Box-Steffensmeier, Janet. 1996. "A Dynamic Analysis of the Role of War Chests in Campaign Strategy." *American Journal of Political Science* 40(2): 352–71.

Brady, Henry E., Kay Lehman Schlozman, Sidney Verba, and Laurel Elms. 2002. "Who Bowls? The (Un)changing Stratification of Participation." In *Understanding Public Opinion,* edited by Barbara Norrander and Clyde Wilcox. Washington: Congressional Quarterly Press.

Brooks, Clem, and David Brady. 1999. "Income, Economic Voting, and Long-Term Political Change in the U.S., 1952–1996." *Social Forces* 77(4): 1339–74.

Brooks, Clem, and Jeff Manza. 1997. "The Social and Ideological Bases of Middle Class Political Realignment, 1972–1992." *American Sociological Review* 62(2): 191–208.

———. 2007. *Why Welfare States Persist: The Importance of Mass Opinion in Democracies.* Chicago, Ill.: University of Chicago Press.

Brooks, Clem, Jeff Manza, and Catherine Bolzendahl. 2003. "Voting Behavior and Political Sociology: Theories, Debates, and Future Directions." *Research in Political Sociology* 12: 137–73.

Brooks, Clem, Paul Nieuwbeerta, and Jeff Manza. 2006. "Cleavage-Based Voting Behavior in Cross-National Perspective: Evidence from Six Postwar Democracies." *Social Science Research* 35(1): 88–128.

Burnham, Walter Dean. 1982. *The Crisis in American Politics.* New York: Oxford University Press.

Burstein, Paul. 2008. "Is Congress Really for Sale?" In *The Contexts Reader,* edited by Jeff Goodwyn and James Jasper. New York: Norton.

Campbell, Angus, et al. 1960. *The American Voter.* New York: Wiley & Sons.

Carmines, Edward G., and Robert Huckfeldt. 1996. "Political Behavior: An Overview." In *The New Handbook of Political Science,* edited by Robert E. Goodin and Hans-Dieter Klingemann. New York: Oxford University Press.

Centers, Richard. 1949. *The Psychology of Social Class.* Berkeley, Calif.: University of California Press.

Clawson, Dan, Alan Neustadtl, and Mark Weller. 1998. *Dollars and Votes.* Philadelphia, Pa.: Temple University Press.

Conway, M. Margaret. 2000. *Political Participation in the United States.* Washington: Congressional Quarterly Press.

Corrado, Anthony. 1997. "A History of Campaign Finance Law." In *Campaign Finance Reform: A Sourcebook,* edited by Anthony Corrado, Thomas E. Mann, Daniel R. Ortiz, Trevor Potter, and Frank J. Sorauf. Washington: Brookings Institution Press.

Crewe, Ivor. 1981. "Electoral Participation." In *Democracy at the Polls,* edited by David Butler, Howard R. Penniman, and Austin Ranney. Washington: American Enterprise Institute.

Dalton, Russell. 1996. "Comparative Politics: Micro-Behavioral Perspectives." In *A New Handbook of Political Science,* edited by Robert E. Goodin and Hans-Dieter Klingemann. New York: Oxford University Press.

Dalton, Russell, and Martin Wattenberg. 1993. "The Not So Simple Act of Voting." In *Political Science: The State of the Discipline,* edited by Ada W. Finifter. Washington: American Political Science Association.

Dawson, Michael C. 1994. *Behind the Mule.* Princeton, N.J.: Princeton University Press.

De Graaf, Nan D., Paul Nieuwbeerta, and Anthony Heath. 1995. "Class Mobility and Political Preferences: Individual and Contextual Effects." *American Journal of Sociology* 100(4): 997–1027.

Domhoff, G. William. 2006. *Who Rules America? Power and Politics in the Year 2000.* 5th ed. Boston, Mass.: McGraw-Hill.

Erikson, Robert S., Thomas D. Lancaster, and David W. Romero. 1989. "Group Components of the Presidential Vote, 1952–1984." *Journal of Politics* 51(2): 337–47.

Erikson, Robert S., Michael MacKuen, and James A. Stimson. 2002. *The Macro Polity.* New York: Cambridge University Press.

Esping-Andersen, Gøsta. 2001. *Social Foundations of Postindustrial Economies.* New York: Oxford University Press.

Evans, Geoffrey, editor. 1999. *The End of Class Politics? Class Voting in Comparative Context.* New York: Oxford University Press.

Fiorina, Morris. 1981. *Retrospective Voting in American National Elections.* New Haven, Conn.: Yale University Press.

Font, Joan, and Rosa Viros, editors. 1995. *Electoral Abstention in Europe.* Barcelona: ICPS.

Form, William. 1995. *Divided We Stand: Working-Class Stratification in America.* Urbana, Ill.: University of Illinois Press.

Frank, Thomas. 2004. *What's the Matter with Kansas?* New York: Metropolitan Books.

Franklin, Mark N. 1992. "The Decline of Cleavage Politics." In *Electoral Change: Responses to Evolving Social and Attitudinal Structures in Western Countries,* edited by Mark N. Franklin, Thomas T. Mackie, and Henry Valen. New York: Cambridge University Press.

Franklin, Mark N., Thomas T. Mackie, and Henry Valen. 1992a. *Electoral Change: Responses to Evolving Social and Attitudinal Structures in Western Countries.* New York: Cambridge University Press.

———. 1992b. "Introduction." In *Electoral Change: Responses to Evolving Social and Attitudinal Structures in Western Countries,* edited by Mark N. Franklin, Thomas T. Mackie, and Henry Valen. New York: Cambridge University Press.

Freeman, Richard B. 2004. "What, Me Vote?" In *Social Inequality,* edited by Kathryn Neckerman. New York: Russell Sage Foundation.

Gerber, Alan. 1998. "Estimating the Effect of Campaign Spending on Senate Election Outcomes Using Instrumental Variables." *American Political Science Review* 92(2): 401–11.

Gerber, Alan, and Donald P. Green. 2000. "The Effects of Canvassing, Telephone Calls, and Direct Mail on Voter Turnout: A Field Experiment." *American Political Science Review* 94(3): 653–63.

———. 2004. *Get Out the Vote: How to Increase Voter Turnout.* Washington: Brookings Institution Press.

Gilens, Martin. 1999. *Why Americans Hate Welfare.* Chicago, Ill.: University of Chicago Press.

———. 2005. "Inequality and Democratic Responsiveness." *Public Opinion Quarterly* 69(5): 778–96.

Ginsberg, Benjamin, and John Green. 1986. "The Best Congress Money Can Buy: Campaign Contributions and Congressional Behavior." In *Do Elections Matter?* edited by Benjamin Ginsberg and Alan Stone. Armonk, N.Y.: Sharpe.

Goidel, Robert K., Donald A. Gross, and Todd G. Shields. 1999. *Money Matters: Consequences of Campaign Finance Reform in U.S. House Elections.* New York: Rowman & Littlefield.

Graetz, Michael, and Ian Shapiro. 2005. *Death by a Thousand Tax Cuts: The Fight over Taxing Inherited Wealth.* Princeton, N.J.: Princeton University Press.

Green, Donald P., and Jonathon Krasno. 1988. "Salvation for the Spendthrift Incumbent: Reestimating the Effects of Campaign Spending in House Elections." *American Journal of Political Science* 32(4): 884–907.

Grusky, David, and Jesper B. Sorensen. 1998. "Can Class Analysis Be Saved?" *American Journal of Sociology* 103(5): 1187–234.

Hacker, Jacob. 2002. *The Divided Welfare State.* New York: Cambridge University Press.

Haynes, Stephen, and David Jacobs. 1994. "Macroeconomics, Economic Stratification, and Partisanship: A Longitudinal Analysis of Contingent Shifts in Political Identification." *American Journal of Sociology* 100(1): 70–103.

Heath, Anthony, Roger Jowell, and John Curtice. 2001. *The Rise of New Labor: Party Policies and Voter Choices.* New York: Oxford University Press.

Hibbs, Douglas. 1987. *The American Political Economy.* Cambridge, Mass.: Harvard University Press.

Hibbs, Douglas, R. Douglas Rivers, and Nicholas Vasilatos. 1982. "The Dynamics of Political Support for American Presidents Among Occupational and Partisan Groups." *American Journal of Political Science* 26(2): 313–32.

Hicks, Alex. 1999. *Social Democracy and Welfare Capitalism: A Century of Income Security Politics.* Ithaca, N.Y.: Cornell University Press.

Hout, Michael, and Benjamin Moody. 2006. "The Realignment of U.S. Presidential Voting, 1948–2004." Working paper. Berkeley: University of California, Survey Research Center.

Hout, Michael, Clem Brooks, and Jeff Manza. 1993. "The Persistence of Classes in Postindustrial Society." *International Sociology* 8(3): 259–77.

———. 1995. "The Democratic Class Struggle in the United States, 1948–1992." *American Sociological Review* 60(6): 805–28.

Huber, Evelyne, and John Stephens. 2001. *Development and Crisis of the Welfare State: Parties and Policies in Global Markets.* Chicago, Ill.: University of Chicago Press.

Huckfeldt, Robert. 1986. *Politics in Context: Assimilation and Conflict in Urban Neighborhoods.* New York: Agathon Press.

Huckfeldt, Robert, and John Sprague. 1995. *Citizens, Politics, and Social Communication: Information and Influence in an Election Campaign.* New York: Cambridge University Press.

Inglehart, Ronald. 1990. *Culture Shift in Advanced Industrial Societies.* Princeton, N.J.: Princeton University Press.

———. 1997. *Modernization and Postmodernization.* Princeton, N.J.: Princeton University Press.

Jackman, Robert W. 1987. "The Politics of Economic Growth in the Industrial Democracies, 1974–1980: Leftist Strength or North Sea Oil?" *Journal of Politics* 49(1): 242–57.

Jacobs, Lawrence, and Theda Skocpol, editors. 2005. *Inequality and American Democracy.* New York: Russell Sage Foundation.

Jacobson, Gary. 1990. "The Effects of Campaign Spending in House Elections: New Evidence for Old Arguments." *American Journal of Political Science* 34(2): 334–62.

Key, V. O. 1949/1964. *Southern Politics in State and Nation.* Cambridge, Mass.: Harvard University Press.

Kiewiet, D. Roderick. 1983. *Macroeconomics and Micropolitics.* Chicago, Ill.: University of Chicago Press.

Kinder, Donald, and D. Roderick Kiewiet. 1981. "Sociotropic Politics: The American Case." *British Journal of Political Science* 11(2): 129–61.

Kinder, Donald, and Lynn Sanders. 1996. *Divided by Color.* Chicago, Ill.: University of Chicago Press.

Kingston, Paul. 2000. *The Classless Society.* Stanford, Calif.: Stanford University Press.

Korpi, Walter. 1984. *The Democratic Class Struggle.* London: Routledge.

———. 2003. "Welfare-State Regresses in Western Europe: Politics, Institutions, Globalization, and Europeanization." *Annual Review of Sociology* 29: 589–609.

Leighley, Jan E. 2001. *Strength in Numbers: The Political Mobilization of Racial and Ethnic Minorities.* Princeton, N.J.: Princeton University Press.

Leighley, Jan E., and Jonathan Nagler. 1992. "Socioeconomic Class Bias in Turnout: The Voters Remain the Same." *American Political Science Review* 86(3): 725–36.

Levitt, Steven. 1998. "Are PACs Trying to Influence Politics or Voters?" *Economics and Politics* 10(1): 19–35.

Lijphart, Arend. 1997. "Unequal Participation: Democracy's Unresolved Dilemma." *American Political Science Review* 91(1): 1–14.

Lipset, Seymour M. 1960/1981. *Political Man: The Social Bases of Politics.* Expanded edition. Baltimore, Md.: Johns Hopkins University Press.

Lipset, Seymour M., Paul Lazarsfeld, Allan Barton, and Juan Linz. 1954. "The Psychology of Voting: An Analysis of Political Behavior." In *Handbook of Social Psychology,* edited by Gardiner Lindzey. Cambridge, Mass.: Addison-Wesley.

Magleby, David B. 2002. "A High-Stakes Election." In *Financing the 2002 Election,* edited by David B. Magleby. Washington: Brookings Institution Press.

Magleby, David B., and Candice J. Nelson. 1990. *The Money Chase: Congressional Campaign Finance Reform.* Washington: Brookings Institution Press.

Mair, Peter. 1997. *Party System Change.* New York: Oxford University Press.

Manza, Jeff, and Clem Brooks. 1999. *Social Cleavages and Political Change: Voter Alignments and U.S. Party Coalitions.* New York: Oxford University Press.

Manza, Jeff, and Fay Lomax Cook. 2002. "A Democratic Polity? Three Views of Policy Responsiveness to Public Opinion in the United States." *American Political Research* 30(5): 630–67.

Manza, Jeff, and Christopher Uggen. 2006. *Locked Out: Felon Disenfranchisement and American Democracy.* New York: Oxford University Press.

McCarty, Nolan, Keith Poole, and Howard Rosenthal. 2006. *Polarized America: The Dance of Ideology and Unequal Riches.* Cambridge, Mass.: MIT Press.

McDonald, Michael P., and Samuel L. Popkin. 2001. "The Myth of the Vanishing Voter." *American Political Science Review* 95(4): 963–74.

Milyo, Jeffrey, David Primo, and Timothy Groseclose. 2000. "Corporate PAC Campaign Contributions in Perspective." *Business and Politics* 2(1): 75–88.

Mutch, Robert E. 2001. "Three Centuries of Campaign Finance Law." In *A User's Guide to Campaign Finance Reform,* edited by Gerald C. Lubenow. New York: Rowman & Littlefield.

Mutz, Diana. 2006. *Hearing the Other Side: Deliberative Versus Participatory Democracy.* New York: Cambridge University Press.

Neustadtl, Alan. 1990. "Interest-Group PACsmanship: An Analysis of Campaign Contributions, Issue Visibility, and Legislative Impact." *Social Forces* 69(2): 549–64.

Overlacker, Louise. 1932. *Money in Elections.* New York: Macmillan.

Page, Benjamin I., and James Simmons. 2001. *What Governments Can Do.* Chicago, Ill.: University of Chicago Press.

Pakulski, Jan, and Malcolm Waters. 1996. *The Death of Class.* Thousand Oaks, Calif.: Sage Publications.

Piven, Frances Fox, and Richard A. Cloward. 1997. *The Breaking of the American Social Compact.* New York: New Press.

———. 2000. *Why Americans Still Don't Vote.* New York: New Press.

Potter, Trevor. 1997. "Issue Advocacy and Express Advocacy." In *Campaign Finance Reform: A Sourcebook,* edited by Anthony Corrado, Thomas E. Mann, Daniel Ortiz, Trevor Potter, and Frank Sorauf. Washington: Brookings Institution Press.

Powell, G. Bingham. 1986. "American Voter Turnout in Comparative Perspective." *American Political Science Review* 80(1): 17–44.

———. 2000. *Elections as Instruments of Democracy.* New Haven, Conn.: Yale University Press.

Przeworski, Adam, and John Sprague. 1986. *Paper Stones: A History of Electoral Socialism.* Chicago, Ill.: University of Chicago Press.

Roemer, John. 1998. "Why the Poor Do Not Expropriate the Rich: A New Argument in Old Garb." *Journal of Public Economics* 70(3): 399–424.

Rosenstone, Steven J., and John M. Hansen. 1993. *Mobilization, Participation, and Democracy in America.* New York: Macmillan.

Schram, Martin. 1995. *Speaking Freely.* Washington: Center for Responsive Politics.

Shields, Todd G., and Robert Goidel. 1997. "Participation Rates, Socioeconomic Class Biases, and Congressional Elections: A Cross-Validation." *American Journal of Political Science* 41(2): 683–91.

Stanley, Harold, and Richard Niemi. 1993. "Partisanship and Group Support over Time." In *Controversies in Voting Behavior*, edited by Richard Niemi. Washington: Congressional Quarterly Press.

Stern, Phillip M. 1992. *Still the Best Congress Money Can Buy*. Washington: Regnery Gateway.

Stratmann, Thomas. 1992. "Are Campaign Contributions Rational? Untangling Strategies of Political Action Committees." *Journal of Political Economy* 100(3): 647–64.

Svallfors, Stefan. 2006. *The Moral Economy of Class: Class and Attitudes in Comparative Perspective*. Stanford, Calif.: Stanford University Press.

Teixeira, Ruy. 1992. *The Disappearing American Voter*. Washington: Brookings Institution Press.

Topf, Richard. 1995. "Electoral Participation." In *Citizens and the State*, edited by Hans-Dieter Klingemann and Dieter Fuchs. New York: Oxford University Press.

Van der Eijk, Cees, et al. 1992. "Cleavages, Conflict Resolution, and Democracy." In *Electoral Change*, edited by Mark N. Franklin, Thomas T. Mackie, and Henry Valen. New York: Cambridge University Press.

Vanneman, Reeve, and Lynn Cannon. 1987. *The American Perception of Class*. Philadelphia, Pa.: Temple University Press.

Verba, Sidney, Kay Lehman Schlozman, and Henry E. Brady. 1995. *Voice and Equality*. Cambridge, Mass.: Harvard University Press.

Wawro, Gregory. 2001. "A Panel Probit Analysis of Campaign Contributions and Roll-Call Votes." *American Journal of Political Science* 45(3): 563–79.

Weakliem, David L., and Anthony Heath. 1994. "Rational Choice and Class Voting." *Rationality and Society* 6(2): 243–70.

Weir, Margaret, editor. 1998. *The Social Divide: Political Parties and the Future of Activist Government*. Washington: Brookings Institution Press.

Welch, William P. 1982. "Campaign Contributions and Legislative Voting: Milk Money and Dairy Price Supports." *Western Political Quarterly* 35(4): 478–95.

Wilson, William Julius. 2001. *The Bridge Over the Racial Divide*. Berkeley, Calif.: University of California Press.

Wolfinger, Raymond E., and Steven J. Rosenstone. 1980. *Who Votes?* New Haven, Conn.: Yale University Press.

Wright, Erik Olin. 1985. *Classes*. London: Verso

Wuthnow, Robert. 1988. *The Restructuring of American Religion: Society and Faith Since World War II*. Princeton, N.J.: Princeton University Press.

Chapter 8

Social Inequality and Health: Future Directions for the Fundamental Cause Explanation

RICHARD M. CARPIANO, BRUCE G. LINK, AND JO C. PHELAN

W HILE VOLUMES of social science research have implicated social class as a critical element in many social and economic outcomes, a substantial body of evidence has also documented its pervasive association with what is arguably one of the most important elements of anyone's life: health. Collectively, this evidence, which spans several centuries, has consistently shown that, across geopolitical place and disease "regime" (infectious, chronic), higher social position (whether conceptualized as social class or socioeconomic status) is associated with lower morbidity and longer life expectancy (Link et al. 1998), and some evidence suggests that this association has even increased in magnitude over time (for the United States, see Pappas et al. 1993; for France, see Leclerc et al. 2006).

Although this social position–based health gradient has been monitored for years in a number of countries and has been critically considered since the beginnings of its surveillance, the attention paid to it by academics and policymakers has substantially increased since the early 1900s—and most markedly since the 1970s. Through such examinations, several explanations have been proposed for the direction of this social inequality–health association, including the argument that socioeconomic factors are a true cause of health outcomes and not merely confounding factors or markers for other unspecified characteristics or risk factors. Within this "social causation" explanation has emerged the "fundamental social causes" theory of health disparities, which contends that social gradients in health persist, despite changing mechanisms (including risk factors and medical innovations), because higher social and economic position embodies greater resources, such as money, knowledge, prestige, power, and beneficial social connections, that protect health no matter what mechanisms are relevant at any given time (Link and Phelan 1995).

This chapter discusses how social class "works" in producing health and illness. We begin by presenting a brief historical background for documented associations between social inequalities and health disparities. After discussing this historical context, we review several explanations for the association that have been offered: confounding, selection, and causation. Next, we focus on explanations for why social inequality is a cause of health inequalities, reviewing evidence concerning the fundamental cause theory of health inequalities, which suggests that such inequalities are not simply the product of relative or perceived social status but involve material conditions as well. Finally, we discuss current and future research directions that have important implications for further illumination of how social class affects health outcomes.

The Use of Social Class in This Chapter

The research reviewed here examines health disparities using both social class and socioeconomic status (SES) perspectives as well as measures appropriate for either perspective. In conceptualizing social inequality, social epidemiologists—whose field, in the past twenty years, has dominated the study of social determinants of health—have commonly used the terms "social class" and "SES" interchangeably (see Bolam, Murphy, and Gleeson 2004; Braveman et al. 2005), and they have frequently used measures such as personal or family income and educational level to capture such inequality. In doing so, they have allowed a gradational perspective (see Wright 2005) to dominate discussions of inequality in this literature, such that social position is predominantly viewed in hierarchical terms (that is, person A who has sixteen years of schooling is more likely to have better health than person B who has twelve years of schooling). Tied to this gradational perspective are some considerations of how people from various social positions are linked to unequally allocated resources—the amount and quality of which vary by social position—that may be used to pursue or maintain health, well being, and longevity. However, as we discuss in further detail later, there has been debate within this literature as to whether one's health is related to the *quantity* of resources one possesses (and the ability to use them) or merely one's *perceptions* of the quantity of resources one possesses relative to someone else.

Consequently, for parsimony, we intentionally use the term "social position–based health disparities" to describe the association between social inequality and health disparities, regardless of whether a class or SES approach was used. While social class and SES are conceptualized quite differently, measures used in prior studies capture aspects that are important to both. Additionally, because our focus is on discussing the fundamental cause theory of health inequalities, we do not provide here an extensive review of research findings pertaining to social class, SES, and the myriad health risks and outcomes for which linkages have been established (for such reviews, see Williams and Collins 1995; House and Williams 2000). Overall, we contend that the increasing attention to the many issues or characteristics of social inequality for which the concept of social class has been applied in other (nonhealth) literatures offers tremendous utility for better understanding how social class works for health inequalities. The issues or characteristics that are most relevant in this chapter include (but are not limited to) considerations of distributional location in systems of inequality, life chances, historical variation in the social organization of inequality, and emancipation from oppression and exploitation (see Wright 2005).

Social Inequalities in Health: A Brief Historical Context

The historical roots of linking social conditions to health and mortality can be traced to several influential figures within sociology, the sanitarian movement within public health, and social medicine. Beginning in the first half of the 1800s, the French physician Louis René Villerme focused considerable attention on the study of associations between social class and mortality (Coleman 1982). In Great Britain, the political appointee Edwin Chadwick (1842/1965) reported class-based death statistics in his influential—yet controversial (Hanley 2002)—*Report on the Sanitary Condition of the Laboring Population of Great Britain.* Soon thereafter, Friedrich Engels (1845/1999) published *Conditions of the Working Class in England,* which further documented the impact of class conditions on health and well being.

Overall, the social class–health association has long been monitored throughout Europe as well as Canada and elsewhere, particularly with regard to mortality rates. For example, in 1851 Great Britain began compiling mortality statistics by occupation (and later "social class" based largely on occupational categories) (MacIntyre 1997; Rose 1995). Although social inequalities in life expectancy in the United States in the 1800s and early 1900s have been reported (see Antonovsky 1967; Chapin 1924; Coombs 1941), the focus has historically been predominantly limited to racial-ethnic differences in mortality (Williams and Collins 1995). Hence, data on class or SES have not been consistently collected in the United States, as they have been in Great Britain and elsewhere. Consequently, American researchers have been forced to rely on limited data sets for studying socioeconomic inequality and health, particularly national samples collected within the past three decades. Examples of these include the National Longitudinal Mortality Study (NLMS) (Phelan et al. 2004; Sorlie, Backlund, and Keller 1995), the National Health Interview Survey (NHIS) (Pappas et al. 1993), and the Behavioral Risk Factor Surveillance Survey (BRFSS) (Link et al. 1998).

Consideration of the association between social class and health has not been limited to academic discussions. Throughout the nineteenth and twentieth centuries, social determinants of health and efforts to address them have received political attention and been part of reform movements throughout Europe, Canada, and South America. There was significant concern in nineteenth-century Europe—given voice, for example, by Villerme in France, Chadwick in Great Britain, and Rudolph Virchow in Germany—about the important role of poverty, squalor, and social class in shaping health and the overall health of the public. In South America, the recognition of social conditions, particularly work conditions, as causes of health disparities was part of twentieth-century socialist reform movement agendas (Waitzkin et al. 2001). More recently, commissioned policy reports such as the Lalonde Report in Canada (Lalonde 1974) and the Black Report in the United Kingdom (Department of Health and Social Security 1980) have helped generate today's renewed and intensified interest in the scientific study of social class–based health disparities not only within those countries but elsewhere as national and global health issues (WHO 2005).

Social Class and Health: Causation, Confounding, or Selection?

Although the association between social class and health has been documented for over two hundred years across places and disease periods, there has long been debate about the reasons for the existence of such a health gradient (for a detailed historical discussion of these issues in Great Britain, see MacIntyre 1997). A number of explanations have been proposed, which can be grouped into three categories (see figure 8.1):

1. The social position–health association is a spurious or noncausal relationship—the observed relationship is merely an artifact of their respective associations with other factors (such as genes and other biological factors) that, once accounted for, would make the association disappear.

2. Health has an impact on, or causes, social position.

These first two explanations have been termed "selection," or "drift," explanations.

Figure 8.1   Hypotheses for the Social Position and Health Association

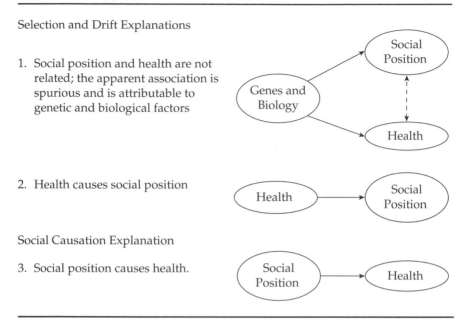

Selection and Drift Explanations

1. Social position and health are not related; the apparent association is spurious and is attributable to genetic and biological factors

2. Health causes social position

Social Causation Explanation

3. Social position causes health.

Source: Authors' compilation.

3. Social position has an impact on, or causes, health outcomes (the "causation" explanation) (Adler et al. 1994; Link and Phelan 1995; MacIntyre 1997).

Supporting the first selection and drift explanation requires evidence that genetic and biological factors are causing both social position and health, thereby making it only appear that social position and health are associated when in fact the association is an artifact of their respective associations with genetic and biological factors. Proponents of this hypothesis argue that once genetic and biological factors are controlled, the social position–health association should disappear. Related to this argument is the assertion by the epidemiologist Kenneth Rothman (1986, 90) that social class is "causally related to few if any diseases but is a correlate of many causes of disease."

The argument that genes serve as a major determinant of social class finds roots in hereditarian and eugenicist explanations for social class–based health inequalities dating back, respectively, to the latter half of the 1800s and the early 1900s (MacIntyre 1997). However, inherited genetic factors cannot explain social organization. Drawing on principles of genetics and gene function, Neil Holtzman (2002, 535) demonstrates that the contribution of genes to any phenomenon is so complex (involving interactions among themselves and with environmental factors) that it is "virtually impossible that the same genetic variants will be concentrated in any social class and transmitted more to children of that class than to children of another class." Additionally, Nancy Adler and her colleagues (1994) argue that if genetic predispositions for which we have yet to account are implicated in the SES-health association, it is quite likely that they become important as environmental and behavioral factors influence them.

The Whitehall I cohort study of British male civil servants—one of the most influential studies of social class and health—provides evidence to refute the genetic and biological confounding argument as a full explanation for class differences in health. Michael Marmot, Martin Shipley, and Geoffrey Rose (1984) found that a higher proportion of men in higher employment grades reported first-degree relatives with heart disease but had the lowest risk for cardiovascular disease-related deaths. If genetic predisposition is the major driver of health inequalities, then the cardiovascular disease mortality rates for men in these grades should have been more congruent with the disease rates of their relatives than was found.

In addition to genes, a more recent argument is that intelligence predicts both social class and health and thus explains the social class and health association (Gottfredson 2004). However, studies comparing the relative influences of IQ and social position on health have failed to corroborate this hypothesis. Using longitudinal data from two separate cohorts in the United States, Bruce Link and his colleagues (2008) found that SES (measured through income and education) was a stronger predictor of several health outcomes (general perceived health, chronic health conditions, and mortality) than IQ, which was not a confounder in the observed SES-health associations. Similarly, David Batty and his colleagues (2006), analyzing a Scottish sample, found that controlling for IQ led to some reduction in the association between several indicators of social position (such as childhood and current social class, income, area deprivation index, and education) and several measures of health status and mortality. However, among the twenty-five separate analyses in which a statistically significant gradient was initially observed, only five of these associations disappeared after adjusting for IQ.

Compared to this first selection and drift explanation or hypothesis, medical sociologists and social epidemiologists have devoted much more energy to testing the second selection and drift explanation and the social causation explanation. In fact, this selection versus causation "debate" is rather prominent across a number of specialty areas of sociomedical research, particularly the study of psychiatric disorders (see Dohrenwend et al. 1992). Evidence for not only the social position–health gradient but the association between social conditions and health overall has been gathered through three methodological strategies: quasi-experimental designs; identification of social risk factors that cannot be considered as having been caused by an individual's illness (for example, identifying ecologic conditions that cannot be explained by an individual's illness); and the use of longitudinal or prospective cohort study designs, a core methodological approach of epidemiology (Link and Phelan 1995).

It is clear that health status does affect social position in some circumstances (Kitagawa and Hauser 1973), and for some health conditions, such as schizophrenia, evidence supports selection as a stronger explanation than causation (Dohrenwend et al. 1992). However, the majority of evidence lends support to the causation hypothesis as the major explanation behind the social position–health association (Hahn, Kaplan, and Syme 1989; Wilkinson 1986). One type of evidence for the primacy of social causation is that education is often as strongly related to mortality as income, and education is typically achieved before serious illness emerges (Hahn, Kaplan, and Syme 1989). Moreover, population-based prospective studies that ascertain years of education and income several years before mortality (presumably, in most cases, before the emergence of serious illness that could lead to downward mobility and death) nevertheless find strong associations with mortality in the follow-up period (Fox, Goldblatt, and Jones 1985; Sorlie et al. 1995). Finally, there are strong associations between the health of children and wives and the social positions of their fathers or husbands, between the social position and mortality of retirees, and between social position and death by injury. These associations argue against a strong role for reverse causation, because social position is unlikely to be strongly affected by a family member's illness, by one's health status after retirement, or by meeting an untimely accidental death (Hahn, Kaplan, and Syme 1989). Although it is important to recognize that each of these study designs is limited in terms of causal inference, when considered collectively, the preponderance of empirical evidence suggests that social causation is more likely to account for the social position–health association relative to selection.

Explanations for Social Causation

If the social position–health association is more plausible as social position causing health than the reverse, what are the proposed pathways through which such an association exists? The majority of existing research has focused on three areas: individual social class or socioeconomic status, income inequality, and neighborhood effects. For the purposes of this review, we focus only on the first area, where the majority of the research has been focused. For in-depth reviews of the other areas, see Kawachi (2000) and Wilkinson and Pickett (2006) on income inequality and Diez-Roux (2001) and Pickett and Pearl (2001) on neighborhood effects.

Causation explanations have focused on one of two interpretations: psychosocial and material. In this section, we first review theories relating to the psychosocial and materialist interpretations and then discuss the empirical evidence used to test these explanations.

The Psychosocial Interpretation

According to the psychosocial interpretation, certain psychosocial factors mediate and therefore explain the social position–health association (Adler et al. 1994; MacIntyre 1997). One of the major proponents of this explanation, the social epidemiologist Richard Wilkinson (2005, 26), contends that social position has "a huge impact on whether people feel valued, appreciated and needed or, on the other hand, looked down on, ignored, treated as insignificant, disrespected, stigmatized, and humiliated." Wilkinson (2005) and Marmot (2004) contend that being in a lower position means being put down, left out, and having little control over one's life. The consequence is exposure to chronic stress that wears on the body and increases vulnerability to disease.

Interestingly, at least for Marmot and Wilkinson, the source of this stress is where one stands in relation to others, not one's "absolute" material resources, and this is what matters for health. "Relative deprivation" is argued to be the key social process that starts the cascade of social and psychological circumstances that produce social position–based gradients in disease and death (Marmot 2004; Wilkinson 2005). Thus, two people with the same income would differ in their health if one was surrounded by people with more money and the other with people with much less. Moreover, according to this view, the experience of relative deprivation can affect people either directly, by inducing stressful states such as feeling marginalized, hostile, angry, or depressed, or indirectly, as when these feelings cause them to smoke, binge-drink, forgo exercise, sleep erratically, or eat badly.

Of course, psychosocial explanations can be broader and need not rely on relative deprivation as the central factor generating health gradients. A broader view—that of the "hierarchy stress" explanation—posits that social position shapes differential exposure to stress, such that persons higher in the social hierarchy are less exposed to stressful circumstances and have more social and psychological resources to cope with the stress they experience than persons below them in the hierarchy (Adler et al. 1994; Link et al. 1998).

The Materialist Interpretation

Contrasting with the psychosocial interpretation is the materialist interpretation, which, historically, has been viewed among researchers and policy advocates as the major explanation for the social position–health association (MacIntyre 1997). This interpretation, which emphasizes the role of socioeconomic and social structural factors in the distribution of health, contends that social class and position produce health inequalities by shaping individuals' exposures to nearly all psychosocial and environmental risk factors for health (House and Williams 2000; MacIntyre 1997).

The critical difference between so-called materialist interpretations and psychosocial ones hinges on the importance of real differences in resources for health. The psychosocial interpretation attends to real differences but sees their impact as deriving from the social meaning of the differences rather than the differences themselves. Thus, Wilkinson (2005, 71) asserts that

> the reason why having an older car, a smaller freezer, or a less smart cell phone is related to health is not because they have direct effects on health; it is because of the social stigma attached to lower material standards. Second rate goods seem to tell people you are a second-rate person. To believe otherwise is to fundamentally misunderstand the pain of relative poverty.

A materialist interpretation, on the other hand, insists that health inequalities are shaped by real resource differences that are the products of social and economic conditions. These differences influence one's likelihood of encountering various life problems, experiencing psychosocial stress, and adopting different health-promoting or health-damaging behaviors (Raphael 2004). While income and educational attainment are two indicators of one's position in the social hierarchy, from a materialist perspective, they shape the real conditions of life that have an impact on one's health and well being. For example, income level influences one's ability to buy a quality home in a neighborhood where crime, noise, pollution, and vermin are kept to a minimum and safe parks, excellent medical facilities, and markets well stocked with fresh fruits and vegetables are conveniently located. Likewise, people use education to situate themselves in occupations that are safe and that include health insurance as a benefit. Therefore, the unequal distribution of actual resources creates social class gradients in health.

Next, we turn to the "fundamental cause" interpretation, an approach that is keenly attendant to real resource differences between people but also recognizes that some of the social mechanisms linking resources to health may work through psychosocial pathways.

The Fundamental Cause Interpretation

Set forth by Link and Phelan (1995), the fundamental cause interpretation seeks to understand the pervasive SES-health association by considering how social factors shape inequality in health and illness. Fundamental causes are defined as "involving access to resources . . . that help individuals avoid diseases and their negative consequences through a variety of mechanisms" (Link and Phelan 1995, 81). Although a common epidemiologic approach is to identify proximate "risk factors" for disease in an effort to understand and ultimately intervene, Link and Phelan note that risk factors change over time but the SES-health association persists.

For example, in the "infectious disease" era of the 1800s and early 1900s, an unsanitary living environment was a major risk factor for prevalent diseases such as cholera, typhus, and tuberculosis. Exposure to such an environment and other related risk factors for these diseases was stratified by social position, such that more affluent people were better able to avoid disease and death than were the less affluent. Eventually, efforts such as the sanitation movement and the discovery of the "germ" theory helped to reduce the mortality rates of infectious diseases. These efforts, combined with technological change in society overall, helped to promote an "epidemiologic transition" into a chronic disease era, when people had now become less likely to die of infectious disease and were living long enough to increase their risk of developing chronic diseases such as cancer and heart disease. These chronic diseases would replace many infectious diseases as the leading causes of death. Again, research has identified the major risk factors for these diseases (for example, smoking, lack of exercise, and a high-cholesterol diet), and technological developments have led to techniques and equipment that allow for early detection and treatment of such diseases, thereby contributing to reductions in mortality. Nevertheless, the morbidity and mortality rates for these and many other chronic diseases, as with the infectious diseases of nearly one hundred years ago, remain highly associated with social position: compared to the more affluent, poorer individuals are at greater risk for developing and dying from these conditions (see, for example, Phelan et al. 2004). Essentially, the diseases and risk factors have changed, but the social position–health gradient persists. This phenomenon is akin to Stanley Lieberson's (1985) discussion of "basic causes," which he argues have enduring effects on a dependent variable because, when the effect of one mechanism declines, the effects of others emerge or become more prominent. Drawing from Lieberson, James House and his colleagues (House, Kessler, et al. 1990; House, Lepkowski, et al. 1994) are credited with being the first to suggest that such a process might produce the pervasive association between socioeconomic status and mortality. Nevertheless, Lieberson's notion of basic causes does not offer clues as to which features of any particular basic cause allow it to reproduce its effects after the elimination of intervening mechanisms.

Link and Phelan (1995) use this predicament as the underlying basis for their fundamental cause argument: regardless of the disease, people use their available resources (money, education, networks and connections) to avoid or overcome risk factors for any disease, be it by obtaining access to quality health care, living in a clean, safe neighborhood, or even buying a gym membership. Because resources are differentially distributed across the socioeconomic hierarchy, people of higher social position have more resources at their disposal than those below them and are therefore better able to maintain good health and avoid disability and death. Essentially, this theory incorporates notions of the materialist and hierarchy stress hypotheses by recognizing that structural conditions systematically shape the exposure, course, and prognosis of disease, as well as the social resources to cope with all stages of the disease process (including susceptibility, vulnerability, and recovery).

A key feature of this theory is that it predicts that disparities will arise when humans develop the capacity to control specific health conditions. When this happens, the benefits of the newly developed ability are not evenly distributed throughout the population but are instead garnered more successfully by those segments of the population with more knowledge, money, power, prestige, and beneficial social connections. Disparities are "created" over time. Thus, for example, heart disease mortality was at one time more common in resource-rich groups (white collar workers, whites), but as the capacity to reduce death from heart disease increased and age-adjusted death rates plummeted, the association reversed, and death rates are now more prevalent among resource-poor groups (blue collar workers, blacks). Similarly, in the 1950s, before epidemiological studies showed that smoking caused lung cancer, rates of lung cancer mortality were higher in wealthier areas of the United States, but now the reverse is true. These reversals are challenging to any explanation that posits that the reason for current disparities resides in a factor that has *not* changed over time. Examples would be genetic differences or relative deprivation processes.

From a public health policy standpoint, the fundamental cause theory says that if disparities are to be reduced, efforts should not just be focused on proximate (or "downstream") risk factors, such as health risk behaviors, but on distal ("upstream") determinants as well, such as the economic processes that shape income distribution. A further implication of the idea is that policies that benefit everyone in a population regardless of their resources, such as fluoridation, air bags, meat inspection, and lead paint cleanup, are much less likely to create disparities than are policies that exhort people to floss, use seat belts, wash cutting boards, or monitor their children's potential ingestion of paint chips.

The Relative Deprivation and Hierarchy Stress Argument

Whereas the fundamental cause explanation posits that class-related resources shape exposure to both material and psychosocial risk and protective factors, the relative deprivation and hierarchy stress argument for the origins of the social position gradient in health strongly downplays material factors such as environmental exposures, health behaviors, and medical care. Because of this major difference in emphasis, we review the evidence concerning the plausibility of the relative deprivation and hierarchy stress explanation.

Relative deprivation constitutes the most complex of the psychosocial explanations for health inequalities. Support for this explanation is derived from three interrelated strands of empirical research.

First, when we restrict attention to societies with advanced economies, differences between countries in per capita income have little, if any, impact on life expectancy (Wilkinson 1997). With respect to longevity, countries with substantially more material wealth (measured, for example, in terms of gross domestic product) have no reliable advantage over countries with substantially less material wealth (for an interesting counterargument, however, see Lynch et al. 2000). At the same time, within each of these advanced economies we see the same expected gradient between measures of SES (education, occupation, or income) and mortality. This pattern of findings is consistent with the relative deprivation hypothesis. If absolute levels of material resources were important, we would expect a person directly in the middle of the income distribution in a relatively wealthy country (for example, median income $50,000 per year) to be better off than a person located in the middle of the income distribution of a country that was less wealthy (for example, median income of $25,000 per year). However, evidence from countries with advanced economies and from U.S. states suggests that this is not true (Wilkinson 2005). Instead, it is better to be more highly placed in a poorer country than to be equally wealthy but more modestly placed in a richer country. The conclusion is that the absolute level of material resources is less important than a person's relative position within a society.

Second, findings from the Whitehall study (Marmot 2004) reveal a strong social class (occupational grade) gradient for most major causes of death. This gradient was evident even at the top of the civil service hierarchy, with the highest rank (administrators) showing a consistent advantage over the next-highest rank (professionals and executives). However, none of the men in the study were extremely deprived in a material sense, the work was rarely dangerous or dirty, job security was very strong, and all the men received medical coverage from the British National Health Service. Moreover, only a portion (no more than one-third) of the differences in coronary heart disease mortality by employment grade could be explained by obesity, smoking, leisure time activity, baseline illness, blood pressure, or height. Because so many competing factors are held constant in the study design and so many other biological and behavioral risk factors were held constant in the analysis, the claim is that being lower down in the social hierarchy—that is, being relatively deprived—is inherently stressful.

Third, experimental studies of nonhuman primates conducted in the wild or in controlled circumstances show that having a lower position in the social hierarchy is associated with detrimental biological consequences (Adler et al. 1994; Marmot 2004). Experiments with rhesus macaques are particularly persuasive in assigning the direction of cause from status to health (social causation) rather than the other way around (social selection). Moreover, material conditions, including food and shelter, are held constant in these settings, so that the key factor associated with rank is status—the animal's position in the pecking order. In these experiments, the monkeys are raised in troops and hierarchies form within these troops. The experiment, then, is to take the two most dominant animals from different troops to create a new troop of monkeys. Similarly, the two least dominant animals are taken to create a different troop. As expected, the monkeys form new dominance hierarchies, and it is the animal's place in the new hierarchy that determines its health. The experimental manipulation of status and its separation from material factors are taken by Wilkinson and Marmot to be strong evidence for the health salience of relative position in a hierarchy. Wilkinson (2005, 75) puts it this way: "For monkeys and humans low social status is a stressor in itself . . . we are highly sensitive to feeling looked down on, being devalued and being treated as second rate."

An interesting feature of this theory is that it forcefully downplays the role of material resources (such as money), health behaviors (such as smoking, diet, and exercise), environmental exposures (such as air pollution and occupational exposures to toxins), and medical care as explanations for a social class gradient in health. Although status-based theorists acknowledge that these factors matter for health, they argue that they have relatively little bearing on the social gradient in health. For example, income is a means of "keeping score" in status competitions rather than an actual material resource that can be deployed to procure circumstances beneficial to health. Health behaviors are also deemed to have only a modest impact on the social position gradient because controlling for such behaviors reduces—but does not eliminate—the gradient in Whitehall or other studies. Furthermore, environmental exposures and access to medical care are held relatively constant in the Whitehall study, and yet the gradient remains. Overall, the dismissal of material resources, health behaviors, environmental exposures, and medical care as important explanations leads to a privileging of the psychosocial factors associated with relative position.

Testing relative deprivation is difficult because social status or prestige is often entangled with material circumstances. Therefore, it is difficult to test empirically whether social status is indeed the underlying driver of social class–based health inequalities. However, three strands of evidence lead us to strongly question this explanation as the main determinant of social gradients in health. First is the previously mentioned evidence concerning a reversal over time in the association between class position and two major killers—lung cancer and heart disease. Relative deprivation processes should have been operative in the 1950s as well as the 1990s and should have created—but, in fact, did not—a relatively consistent association between social position and death from these two diseases across time.

Second, relative deprivation processes should affect death from most diseases, since there is nothing in the theory that would lead us to expect that the social position–health gradient would be stronger for some diseases than for others. In a test of the fundamental cause hypothesis, Phelan and her colleagues (2004) used prospective data from the U.S. National Longitudinal Mortality Study to compare SES differences in survival rates between high- and low-preventability deaths. The reasoning from a fundamental cause approach says that gradients should be stronger for diseases that we can do more about because there are known and modifiable risk and protective factors. Consistent with this reasoning, the social position–mortality association was significantly stronger for high-preventability deaths. Why would relative deprivation, which supposedly operates through feelings of anger, hostility, humiliation, and shame, happen to affect diseases for which death is highly preventable more strongly than diseases for which death is not so highly preventable?

Third, while relative status and material resources often go hand in hand, it is possible to identify specific social situations where status is manipulated while income or social class remain relatively constant. Situations like awards ceremonies provide unique opportunities to test the relative deprivation hypothesis.

Donald Redelmeier and Sheldon Singh (2001a, 2001b) examined a high-status ceremony—the Academy Awards (the "Oscars")—to test relative deprivation among actors, actresses, and screenwriters. They found that Oscar-winning actors and actresses lived significantly longer than both Oscar nominees and other, less-recognized performers (respectively, 3.6 and 3.9 years). However, life expectancy for Oscar-winning screenwriters was a statistically significant 3.6 years shorter for winners than for losing nominees.

Link, Carpiano, and Weden (2006) expanded on this prior work by reconsidering these findings by Redelmeier and Singh (2001a, 2001b) with analyses of additional data from three high-status award groups: Major League Baseball players who were inducted, nominated but never inducted, or never nominated for the Baseball Hall of Fame; presidential and vice presidential election winners and losers; and actors and actresses who either were nominated for or received an Emmy Award.

Given that for each of these groups the "contestants" are all relatively equal in terms of social class standing (including education and income), if relative deprivation is the expected cause of health disparities, then, for each of these high-status award contest situations, we should expect to see a significant mortality advantage for winners. The results of the additional analyses showed that Emmy winners lived significantly longer than nominated losers; there were no differences between Hall of Fame inductees and both nominees who were never elected and players never nominated;

and elected presidents and vice presidents tended to die younger than the candidates they beat. Each one of these competitions induces enormous status differences between winners and losers, thereby powerfully manipulating the factor that Marmot and Wilkinson privilege in their explanation of SES gradients in mortality. The results of our empirical analysis and those of Redelmeier and Singh could have strongly supported the Marmot-Wilkinson explanation if winners consistently outlived losers. But this did not occur. Instead, some winners lived substantially longer than losers; others experienced no survival advantage at all; still others lived substantially less long than those they beat. As such, the evidence does not support the idea that relative status dominates over other factors in producing the SES-gradient in health.

Social Class as a Fundamental Cause of Health: Emerging Directions in Health Research

Research to date strongly suggests that social class is a true health determinant and that the effects of social position are mostly attributable to material conditions. However, many questions remain unanswered. As we mentioned at the start of this chapter, the explicit application of social class in the study of health is still a work in progress and has only recently begun to receive increased attention. In this section, we review some critical next steps for elucidating the mechanisms underlying how social class works in shaping both desirable and undesirable health outcomes and discuss some interesting emerging research directions aimed at improving this understanding.

Although evidence supports the idea of social class as a fundamental cause of health inequalities, essentially social class remains largely a "black box" of causal factors and mechanisms. In understanding how social class works, the questions that need to be answered for health are: how is social class embodied by individuals, and how does society ultimately get "under the skin"? Future work sorely needs to dissect the components of class membership that translate into health outcomes. To date, few authors have undertaken this challenging task. Research on social determinants of health has overwhelmingly utilized a variable-based approach, which, even when theoretically driven, still only assesses associations between measures and thus is limited in telling us about the processes or mechanisms underlying such associations.

Understanding Fundamental Cause Processes: Social Position as Metamechanism

In an effort to address criticisms that a variable-based approach to testing SES empirically as a health determinant does not sufficiently capture the processes through which SES shapes health outcomes, Karen Lutfey and Jeremy Freese (2005) identify and elaborate on the multiple mechanisms by which "fundamental causality" operates; they conceptualize SES as a "metamechanism" whereby it is associated with health through a constellation of pathways. These authors use ethnographic data obtained from two diabetes clinics (one treating predominantly disadvantaged patients, the other more affluent patients) to articulate some of the ways in which social resources are "translated into health advantages and may thus be implicated in the reproduction of a pervasive, well-documented quantitative association" (Lutfey and Freese 2005, 1329). Their analyses further three aspects of the fundamental causality argument.

The first aspect concerns various "compensatory elements" that are differentially provided to individuals as a result of their social class membership. Compensatory elements may provide greater benefits to those from disadvantaged groups, who have more to gain from them; however, in fundamental cause relationships, these elements are instead possessed in greater quantity by advantaged groups. One example provided by the authors is the pairing of lower-SES patients (who may be the least skilled at articulating their problems and may benefit the most from experienced medical interviewers) with inexperienced medical residents. The authors propose that disadvantaged patients might ultimately benefit more from experienced physicians, to whom affluent patients are more often paired, because the potential for improvement is greater.

A second aspect involves knowledge for pursuing or maintaining health. This issue was central to prior tests of fundamental causality by Link and his colleagues (1998; Phelan et al. 2004), who contend that knowledge about a disease and how to manage or treat it constitutes a major resource that contributes to the emergence and persistence of social inequalities in specific disease outcomes. Lutfey and Freese's (2005) analyses expand on this idea by illustrating that resources affect not only patients' access to people with knowledge regarding a disease and its treatment but also their ability to marshal this knowledge in a superior way to achieve further benefit (for example, by using resources to improve the communication of pertinent personal information to clinicians to maximize treatment efficacy).

The third issue is countervailing mechanisms. In conceptualizing SES as a metamechanism that reproduces health inequalities over time, Lutfey and Freese (2005) make the important point that for fundamental causality to work, not all pathways need to support the relationship. As their analyses demonstrate, not all social position improvement activities are health-promoting (and may be health-damaging for some persons). Nevertheless, when considered in terms of cumulative effects, the activities that produce the fundamental relationship need to be larger than the effects that countervail these relationships. Consequently, they recommend that we consider through this metamechanistic lens how countervailing mechanisms may be systematically plausible, since such contradictory behaviors can lead to a better contextualization of the issue of how greater social resources translate into better health in the midst of seemingly health-damaging behaviors (for example, examining how "hard-living" celebrities like Rolling Stones guitarist Keith Richards maintain health). Carpiano and Kelly (2007) consider this issue in examining the higher incidence and lower mortality of breast cancer experienced by whites versus blacks.

Class as Forms of Capital: Bourdieu-Based Approaches to Class and Health

As noted earlier in this chapter, research on the social determinants of health has often conflated social class and SES—the former being heavily rooted in a Marxist approach, wherein social class is a social group defined by its relation to the mode of production, and the latter being influenced by a Weberian conceptualization that includes a variety of social and economic characteristics capturing class, status, and party positions.

However, a third approach has recently emerged that emphasizes the theoretical project of Pierre Bourdieu and a relational approach to social class: a social class is defined in terms of social space by its possession and use of various forms of capital (that is, economic, cultural, social, and symbolic capital) relative to other social classes. To date, only a few authors have incorporated such a perspective (see Gatrell, Popay, and Thomas 2004; Veenstra 2007). A recent study by Gerry Veenstra (2007) best illustrates Bourdieu's approach for studying health inequalities.

Observing that existing research has yet to optimally consider the existence of different classes as well as between-class dynamics that influence health, Veenstra (2007), informed by Bourdieu's (1984) study of French class preferences and tastes, *Distinction,* applies the same methodology (correspondence analysis) to identify patterns of consumption and lifestyles among a sample of Canadians and observe how specific practices and activities associated with health and well being are clustered with the presence of different forms of capital (economic, cultural, and social), social background, and occupational categories. These analyses are used to identify groupings of variables that may be representative of particular social classes. Interestingly, Veenstra's interpretations of class groupings (for example, professional, middle class, and working class) were consistent with respondents' perceptions of their own social class and were fairly congruent with Bourdieu's findings for 1960s France. As we would expect, excellent self-rated health was statistically clustered close to a variety of physical activities (such as running, kayaking, yoga, aerobics, and weight training) as well as high educational and economic capital and "highbrow" cultural tastes (for example, reading *The New Yorker*). However, as argued by Veenstra (2007, 16), the novelty of this analysis lies in the "speculations that arise from adopting a structuralist vision of social space and the activities, tastes, and perceptions that inhere within it." In essence, this approach helps in generating hypotheses about the mechanisms through which class works for health. Furthermore—and perhaps most importantly—it contributes to applying a *relational perspective* to the conceptualization of social class in health research, where the class positions and resource possession of individuals are considered in relation to others.

Considering the Interplay of Structure and Agency: Health Lifestyles

Closely related to the Bourdieu-based approach to class and health is an emerging literature on "health lifestyles" aimed at integrating structural considerations into conceptualizations of individual health (see, for example, Cockerham 2005; Williams 2003). This theoretical enterprise draws heavily on the long-standing structure and agency debate in an effort to contextualize individual health practices and overcome the primacy typically given to personal agency as the sole or predominant determinant of a person's health.

In reacting to social epidemiological and public health conceptualizations of lifestyle as decontextualized collections of individualistic behavioral "risk factors," Katherine Frohlich, Ellen Corin, and Louise Potvin (2001) propose a "collective lifestyles" approach to reinserting social context into the study of health behaviors. Drawing on Weber's conceptualization of lifestyles, these authors develop a framework in which behaviors are conceived as patterns and ways of living that interact with social structures—or as generated *social practices* that emerge from, reinforce, and transform context. In this framework, lifestyle represents more than simply individualized behaviors (as usually viewed in public health). Here it is a collective attribute defined as the relationship between social conditions and the social practices in which people engage. Hence, the authors use the term "collective lifestyles."

Frohlich and her colleagues contend that this recontextualizing (or de-individualizing) of behaviors provides an improved opportunity for using social theories to better explain how social context shapes health outcomes, and they draw inspiration from several practice theories—namely, Amatyra Sen's capability theory, Bourdieu's theory of habitus, and Anthony Giddens's structuration theory. In terms of methodology, such theoretic considerations necessitate analyzing the dynamics between structure and agency—how each feeds into the other. Frohlich and her colleagues (2002) test this collective lifestyles framework in a mixed-method study of youth smoking initiation across neighborhoods. Examining both indicator data of local area resources and focus groups of smoking practices, they find that social practices are not always directly reflective of social structure, thereby suggesting the importance of considering how people interact with and interpret social structural conditions—essentially, how agency and structure interact in shaping health.

William Cockerham (2005) expands on the ideas of Frohlich and her colleagues (2001) by formulating a "preliminary paradigm" of health lifestyles—thereby providing important theoretic specificity to those ideas, particularly for understanding the role of social class in producing health lifestyles. Defining health lifestyles as "collective patterns of health-related behavior based on choices from options available to people according to their life chances," this paradigm draws heavily on Weber and Bourdieu in proposing that health lifestyles "are personal routines that merge into an aggregate form representative of specific groups and classes" and that class itself is the most critical influence on lifestyles (Cockerham 2005, 55, 56). Cockerham has applied this framework to the study of class-related patterns of health risk behaviors in an attempt to contextualize seemingly individualistic health lifestyles that have been theorized to be responsible for decreased life expectancy in the post-Soviet countries (see, for example, Cockerham, Snead, and Dewaal 2002; Cockerham et al. 2004).

When considered in total, theory and empirical research focused on health lifestyles provides a promising new direction in elaborating the importance of social class for health by considering the tastes and preferences associated with particular classes as well as the interplay between the actions of individual actors and the structural conditions that can constrain or liberate. This framework has potential for informing our understanding of not only health behaviors but other practices often viewed in terms of individualized behaviors labeled "risky" or "protective" (such as dropping out of school or making certain career choices).

Social Connections as Intra- and Inter-Class-Based Resources: Social Capital and Health

Another promising area of research concerns social capital and how the class positions of social network ties matter for achieving both desirable and undesirable health outcomes. While social capital is defined differently by a variety of authors, here we refer to it as the resources that inhere within social networks or relations. Although the intellectual roots of social capital can be traced back to Marx's idea of "a class for itself" (Portes 1998), to date, health research has almost exclusively considered the political scientist Robert Putnam's (2000) conceptualization of social capital (Moore et al. 2005), which conceptualizes social capital as a feature of geographic communities and emphasizes social cohesion factors such as interpersonal trust, norms of reciprocity, and shared values. This recent conflation of social capital with geographic community and communitarian perspectives is regrettable, since it eclipses recognition of the importance of other types of social network ties for social capital (for example, the parental and "key adult" ties of adolescents discussed by Lareau and Weininger, this volume) and their utility for understanding the social determinants of health (see, for example, Berkman et al. 2000; Erickson 2003).

Conceptualizing social class as a metamechanism for producing health necessitates a consideration (from a fundamental cause perspective) of the resources that inhere in social ties (that is, cultural, economic, political, and symbolic capital as well as the social capital possessed by others) and can be accessed for health (Carpiano 2006; Carpiano and Kelly 2005; Robert and Carpiano 2005). These considerations warrant applications of social capital theoretical perspectives other than Putnam's, including those of Pierre Bourdieu (1986), James Coleman (1988), and Alejandro Portes (1998), among others. However, to date, few have empirically applied any of these perspectives to studies of health (for a review, see Moore et al. 2005; for exceptions, see Carpiano 2004, 2007; Cattell 2001), although they have been considered for other issues of social well being (see, for example, Dominguez and Watkins 2003). Although the association between social position and social support has been explored in research on social stress and health, the social support literature has yet to explicate adequately the health implications of social class differences in social network composition, in the forms of capital that inhere within such networks and that translate into the relative value or quality of social ties, in access to and marshaling of such capital, and, ultimately, in the quality of the social support received for achieving positive and (although far less often considered) negative health outcomes (Carpiano 2004, 2007). Here is where a social capital perspective could offer much in furthering research on social support and health—an issue of long-standing interest within medical sociology and social epidemiology. In particular, social capital (whether within or between social classes) offers much for understanding the health consequences of status attainment and inter- and intra-generational social class changes. In terms of fundamental causality, such research provides necessary insights into how beneficial or advantageous social connections can be used in maintaining health and prolonging life. Although beneficial social connections are implicated in the underlying mechanisms of fundamental causes, this critical facet of social position has been relatively understudied compared to income and education—the two most commonly used indicators of social position—in which the level of social capital is implicitly assumed.

Class-Based Contexts: Neighborhood and Local Community Conditions

As noted by Pattillo (this volume), place is a crucial factor to consider in discussions about how class works, whether for health or other outcomes. People from various social class memberships are not randomly distributed across geographical localities but are differentially selected into—and consequently affected by—the communities in which they reside. While the interplay between place and social class has a long, rich history within sociology (see, for example, Logan 2003; Wacquant and Wilson 1989; Wirth 1969), consideration of neighborhoods and local area social effects is comparatively new to health research. Indeed, there has been an explosion in the past fifteen years of the "neighborhood effects" literature focused on health, which considers the social and economic conditions of neighborhoods on individuals' health above and beyond their social class or socioeconomic characteristics (Robert 1999; Sampson, Morenoff, and Gannon-Rowley 2002).

Why should considerations of social class and health include neighborhoods? Neighborhoods contain a variety of health-promoting and health-damaging characteristics (MacIntyre, Ellaway, and Cummins 2002). As numerous studies have shown, these health-promoting or -damaging characteristics are integrally tied to social conditions, be it at the end of the nineteenth century when New York City neighborhoods with crowded, unsanitary housing conditions were linked to epidemics of infectious disease (Markel 1997) or the present "chronic disease" period when socioeconomically deprived neighborhood conditions are found to be associated with individual health risk (see Diez-Roux 2001; Robert 1999). In short, the persistent association between social inequality and health also manifests at the neighborhood level: residents in more affluent neighborhoods enjoy better health outcomes than do residents in less affluent neighborhoods.

Reviewing health research on neighborhoods and local areas that use multilevel modeling analyses, Kate Pickett and Michelle Pearl (2001) find that twenty-three of twenty-five studies report at least one statistically significant association between a measure of the social environment and a health outcome after controlling for individual-level SES. These neighborhood measures included single and composite indicators of socioeconomic deprivation or disadvantage, proportion of working class residents, low income, and education (for a more extensive review of the measures used, see Pickett and Pearl 2001). Additionally, findings from the Moving to Opportunity study, a randomized, controlled trial that relocated families from high-poverty neighborhoods to more economically improved neighborhoods, further strengthen the argument that neighborhoods do matter for individual adult and child health and well being (Leventhal and Brooks-Gunn 2003). Despite this rapidly accumulating evidence, Jeffrey Morenoff (2003) argues that the existing findings are limited because many studies tend to focus only on whether neighborhood socioeconomic characteristics are associated with the health outcome of interest, yet fail to consider more proximate mechanisms that may offer insights into why the environment is associated with health.

While we know that neighborhood social conditions are associated with health, the question that needs to be answered is how they are associated.

Compositional factors, such as average age, income, education, or percentage of minority status certainly contribute to place-based health inequalities. However, as noted by Sally MacIntyre and her colleagues (1993), place-based health differences cannot be explained solely by the *composition* of the residents who live there—two other factors must also be considered: context and collectivity (see also MacIntyre, Ellaway, and Cummins 2002). *Contextual* factors are the opportunity structures in the social and physical environment, such as local area services and amenities, including, for example, health services, recreation facilities, affordable and safe housing, and decent-paying jobs—the lack of which has been implicated in creating an inner-city "underclass" (Wilson 1987). *Collective* factors concern sociocultural and historical features of places and emphasize the role of shared norms, values, and interests (MacIntyre, Ellaway, and Cummins 2002). Although these three factors may not always be distinct, they are integrally tied in shaping health outcomes (MacIntyre, Ellaway, and Cummins 2002). For example, neighborhood quality of life may be a function of composition (the social class composition of residents), context (local job opportunities), and collectivity (a shared commitment among residents to provide for one another and invest time in their community).

Overall, studying neighborhood conditions offers one way to understand some of the social and physical environmental conditions linked to social class that shape individual health (and the interplay of these conditions with demographic characteristics such as race-ethnic background, gender, and age). Nevertheless, much theoretical and methodological work remains to be done in elucidating the pathways through which neighborhood conditions affect the health of residents. The prior discussion on social capital figures prominently here, since social capital has been one of the most commonly considered intermediate mechanisms in this research (for further discussion of these issues, see Carpiano 2006; Robert and Carpiano 2005).

Power(lessness): Structural Violence

The structural violence framework, popularized by the medical anthropologist and physician Paul Farmer, provides great utility for conceptualizing structural determinants of health, particularly with respect to issues of power. In his explanation of structural violence, Farmer (1999, 79) notes that "historically given (and often economically driven) processes and forces conspire to constrain individual agency. Structural violence is visited upon all those whose social status denies them access to the fruits of scientific and social progress." This framework uses a critical theory approach to move beyond a focus on how positions within social and economic structures (class, race-ethnicity, gender) are linked to health to consider how the structures themselves create situations that make people occupying particular positions more vulnerable to disease and death than others—in essence, how structural conditions (for example, economic conditions and policies of discrimination and exclusion) enact a form of violence on individuals that is analogous to physical violence.

Although Farmer (1999) has applied this structural violence framework to the study of the political economy of health in developing countries (particularly with regard to infectious diseases like tuberculosis and HIV/AIDS), he has also shown its relevance for the American context in terms of inner-city poverty and tuberculosis. As his work demonstrates, structural violence is a particularly useful framework for conceptualizing power and policies of discrimination and exclusion. This perspective offers utility to our understanding of how social class–based health disparities may be either reduced or exacerbated by particular social and economic policies. For example, Carpiano's (2005) ethnographic research in Milwaukee, Wisconsin, neighborhoods has identified how recent substantial property tax increases and housing code policies may place fixed-income homeowning residents, who are already vulnerable to health threats, at an increased risk for poor health. Some residents may be forced to choose between spending money on medications and necessary services or paying significantly reassessed property taxes and making expensive (and sometimes unnecessary) home repairs—facing expensive fines and potential repossession by the city if they do not. Incidentally, this example highlights the role of social capital in acquiring health-enhancing resources: in Milwaukee, community-based organizations have become critical for providing this vulnerable and politically marginalized population with economic and political resources to help cope with—and ultimately lobby against—such policies.

A structural violence framework makes several contributions to a fundamental cause approach, particularly in terms of better incorporating social class. First are the issues of power (or powerlessness) and exploitation that are central to notions of class relations (Wright 2005). Certainly, aspects of power and exploitation are captured (at least implicitly) via education, income, occupational category, and the other conceptualizations and measures of social position used in most research on social determinants of health. However, a structural violence framework forces more explicit recognition of power and exploitation in the production of health inequalities and of how power differentials leave vulnerable those individuals with limited access to social, economic, and political resources. Such recognition helps foster improved theoretical specificity regarding how class matters for lifestyle and health, particularly in terms of the acquisition of health-beneficial compensatory elements and the marshaling of knowledge, both identified by Lutfey and Freese (2005) as central to fundamental causality. Second, it draws attention beyond individuals' education, income, and other resources to the "upstream" or macro-level economic, political, and cultural conditions and policies that differentially allocate those resources and shape their relative values (see, for example, the chapters by Manza and Brooks, Goldthorpe and Jackson, and McCall, this volume). Consequently, this helps to better contextualize fundamental causes in terms of historical variation issues of class (Wright 2005)—allowing for the identification of not only those social groups that can best maintain health regardless of the diseases prevalent at a particular time but also the social system processes that allow health inequalities to be socially reproduced. Third, by focusing attention on the policies and conditions of a particular context, the critical approach of the structural violence framework facilitates the formulation of policy solutions for addressing fundamental causes of health inequalities (for example, identifying the impact of policies on human rights or the reproduction of class-based differences in educational attainment and employment level, as discussed by Goldthorpe and Jackson, this volume)—in essence the emancipation issue raised within other applications of social class (Wright 2005).

Summarizing Emerging Directions

Revisiting our definition of fundamental causes as consisting of access to resources such as money, knowledge, power, prestige, and beneficial social connections, we can see that each of these emergent directions helps bring theoretical and empirical clarity to the health implications of class. Conceptualizing social class as a metamechanism provides an important step for considering the various pathways through which social class can have an impact on health. Likewise, the other emergent directions discussed here force us to broaden our consideration (and contextualization) of class-based resources—particularly with respect to their sources, allocation, access, and uses.

Conclusion

In light of our discussion on how social class works for health, we conclude this chapter with two key recommendations for social class researchers. First, because social scientists—particularly sociologists of class and stratification—have much to contribute to debates regarding social determinants of health, they need to increase their attention not only to health issues but to literature focused on social class and health published outside traditional sociology or social science journals. Social epidemiology has come to dominate this area of study, but calls are continually being made for the inclusion of more precise theoretical formulations for social class and other social determinants of population health (see, for example, Carpiano and Daley 2006a, 2006b). These are the debates to which sociologists of class, stratification, and population have much to offer but in which, to date, they have been substantially underrepresented compared to social epidemiologists, who publish extensively in international public health, epidemiology, and medical forums such as the *Journal of Epidemiology and Community Health, British Medical Journal, American Journal of Public Health, International Journal of Health Services,* and the *International Journal of Epidemiology.*

Second, although not directly addressed in this chapter, exploration of social class as a fundamental cause necessitates a consideration of how factors such as race-ethnicity, gender, and age matter for the metamechanisms contained within social class itself. Although federal initiatives like Healthy People 2010 aim to reduce health disparities, attention in the American research community has been heavily focused on racial-ethnic disparities (Raphael and Bryant 2006). Giving sole attention to disparities by racial-ethnic group implicitly assumes a social, cultural, and economic homogeneity within each group. Even in the midst of racism and discrimination, social mobility and integration have occurred for racial-ethnic minority groups throughout our nation's history, creating social class differences within and between members of various racial-ethnic groups. These differences are not limited to resources such as education and income but include cultural values as well (see, for example, Pattillo-McCoy's [1999] research on the black middle class). As Paula Braveman (2005) rightly notes, "The question is not: Is race or class more important?" Certainly, race-ethnicity complicates our understanding of the importance of social class, but it does not dismiss the importance of social class. Further complicating class mechanisms are other demographic factors such as gender and age, among others. As with race-ethnicity, focusing solely on disparities among categories of these demographic variables without considering their interactions with social class misses the mark of understanding how social, economic, cultural, and political structures differentially shape lifestyles.

In closing, research on social class determinants of health is presently in a very exciting period of intensified interest by researchers from a variety of disciplines and fields, including the social sciences, social epidemiology, public and population health, and social medicine. Although great strides have been made in furthering our understanding of social conditions as fundamental causes of health disparities, many questions remain regarding how such conditions translate to differential health outcomes. Although factors such as education, income, and beneficial social connections are implicated within social class as determinants of health outcomes, progress in discovering the mechanisms of fundamental causality hinges on carefully specified theoretical considerations, a variety of qualitative and quantitative methodological approaches, and avoidance of a risk-factor approach that merely seeks to test statistical associations between social class indicators and health outcomes. Such efforts will not only inform research regarding how individuals' health is inextricably linked to the social conditions in which they are immersed but contribute to the broader agenda of understanding how social class operates as a social fact that is a critical determinant of life chances and lifestyle.

Appendix: Key Terms

Fundamental causes explanation: A social causation explanation that contends that social gradients in health persist, despite changing mechanisms, because higher social class position embodies greater resources, such as money, knowledge, prestige, power, and beneficial social connections, that protect health no matter what mechanisms are relevant at any given time (Link and Phelan 1995).

Hierarchy stress: A psychosocial explanation that conjectures that social position shapes differential exposure to stress, such that persons higher in the social hierarchy have less exposure to stressful circumstances and more social and psychological resources to cope with the stress they do experience than persons below them in the hierarchy (see Adler et al. 1994).

Materialist explanation: A social causation explanation that emphasizes the role of socioeconomic and social structural factors in the distribution of health and contends that social class and position produce health inequalities by shaping individuals' exposures to nearly all psychosocial and environmental risk factors for health (House and Williams 2000; MacIntyre 1997).

Psychosocial explanation: A social causation explanation that emphasizes the role of social-psychological factors related to class position, such as relative deprivation, for why social class causes health.

Relative deprivation: A psychosocial explanation that conjectures that health inequalities are mostly attributable to people's perceptions of their placement in the social hierarchy or of their social status relative to others.

Social causation: An explanation for the persistent association between higher social class position and better health that contends that social class position is causal of health status.

Selection (drift): An explanation for the persistent association between higher social class position and better health that proposes two hypothesized mechanisms: that the apparent association between social class and health is spurious, or only due to their respective associations with unmeasured biological and genetic factors; and that health status causes social class position.

Richard Carpiano wrote this chapter while receiving support from the Robert Wood Johnson Foundation Health and Society Scholars Program and the Michael Smith Foundation for Health Research. The authors wish to thank Brian C. Kelly for providing helpful comments.

References

Adler, Nancy E., Thomas Boyce, Margaret A. Chesney, Sheldon Cohen, Susan Folkman, Robert L. Kahn, and S. Leonard Syme. 1994. "Socioeconomic Status and Health: The Challenge of the Gradient." *American Psychologist* 49(1): 15–24.

Antonovsky, Aaron. 1967. "Social Class, Life Expectancy and Overall Mortality." *Milbank Memorial Fund Quarterly* 45(2, Part I): 31–73.

Batty, G. David, Geoff Der, Sally MacIntyre, and Ian J. Deary. 2006. "Does IQ Explain Socioeconomic Inequalities in Health? Evidence from a Population-Based Cohort Study in the West of Scotland." *British Medical Journal* 332(February 1): 580–4.

Berkman, Lisa F., Thomas Glass, Ian Brissette, and Teresa E. Seeman. 2000. "From Social Integration to Health: Durkheim in the New Millennium." *Social Science and Medicine* 51(6): 843–57.

Bolam, Bruce, Simon Murphy, and Kate Gleeson. 2004. "Individualization and Inequalities in Health: A Qualitative Study of Class Identity and Health." *Social Science and Medicine* 59(7): 1355–65.

Bourdieu, Pierre. 1984. *Distinction: A Social Critique of the Judgment of Taste*, translated by Richard Nice. Cambridge, Mass.: Harvard University Press.

———. 1986. "The Forms of Capital." In *Handbook of Theory and Research for the Sociology of Education*, edited by John G. Richardson. New York: Greenwood.

Braveman, Paula. 2005. "The Question Is Not: Is Race or Class More Important?" *Journal of Epidemiology and Community Health* 59(12): 1029.

Braveman, Paula, Catherine Cubbin, Susan Egerter, Sekai Chideya, Kristen Marchi, Marilyn Metzler, and Samuel Posner. 2005. "Socioeconomic Status in Health Research: One Size Does Not Fit All." *Journal of the American Medical Association* 294(22): 2879–88.

Carpiano, Richard M. 2004. "The Forms of Social Capital: A Sociomedical Science Investigation of Neighborhood Social Capital as a Health Determinant Using a Bourdieu Framework." Ph.D. dissertation, Columbia University.

———. 2005. "Come Take a Walk with Me: Using Action Research to Build Theory and Inform Practice on Community Social Capital, Health, and Well-being." Paper presented to the University of Wisconsin Medical School at the University of Wisconsin Department of Population Health Sciences Seminar Series. Madison, Wisc., November 21, 2005.

———. 2006. "Towards a Neighborhood Resource-Based Theory of Social Capital for Health: Can Bourdieu and Sociology Help?" *Social Science and Medicine* 62(1): 165–75.

———. 2007. "Neighborhood Social Capital as a Health Determinant: An Empirical Test of a Bourdieu-Based Model." *Health and Place* 13(3): 639–55.

Carpiano, Richard M., and Dorothy M. Daley. 2006a. "A Guide and Glossary on Post-Positivist Theory-Building for Population Health." *Journal of Epidemiology and Community Health* 60(7): 564–70.

———. 2006b. "Theory-Building on the High Seas of Population Health: Love Boat, Mutiny on the Bounty, or Poseidon Adventure?" *Journal of Epidemiology and Community Health*, 60(7): 571–77.

Carpiano, Richard M., and Brian C. Kelly. 2005. "What Would Durkheim Do? A Comment on Kushner and Sterk's 'The Limits of Social Capital: Durkheim, Suicide, and Social Cohesion.' " *American Journal of Public Health* 95(12): 2120–1.

————. 2007. "Scientific Knowledge as Resource and Risk: What Does Hormone Replacement Therapy Tell Us About Health Disparities?" Paper presented to the annual meeting of the American Sociological Association. New York, August 2007.

Cattell, Vicky. 2001. "Poor People, Poor Places, and Poor Health: The Mediating Role of Social Networks and Social Capital." *Social Science and Medicine* 52(10): 1501–16.

Chadwick, Edwin. 1842/1965. *Report on the Sanitary Condition of the Laboring Population of Great Britain,* edited by Michael W. Flinn. Edinburgh: Edinburgh University Press.

Chapin, Charles V. 1924. "Death Among Taxpayers and Non-Taxpayers' Income Tax, Providence 1865." *American Journal of Public Health* 14(8): 647–51.

Cockerham, William C. 2005. "Health Lifestyle Theory and the Convergence of Structure and Agency." *Journal of Health and Social Behavior* 46(1): 51–67.

Cockerham, William C., Brian P. Hinote, Pamela Abbott, and Christian Haerpfer. 2004. "Health Lifestyles in Central Asia: The Case of Kazakhstan and Kyrgyzstan." *Social Science and Medicine* 59(7): 1409–21.

Cockerham, William C., M. Christine Snead, and Derek F. Dewaal. 2002. "Health Lifestyles in Russia and the Socialist Heritage." *Journal of Health and Social Behavior* 43(1): 42–55.

Coleman, James S. 1988. "Social Capital in the Creation of Human Capital." *American Journal of Sociology* 94(Supplement): S95–121.

Coleman, William. 1982. *Death Is a Social Disease: Public Health and Political Economy in Early Industrial France.* Madison, Wisc.: University of Wisconsin Press.

Coombs, Lolagene C. 1941. "Economic Differentials in Causes of Death." *Medical Care* 1: 246–55.

Department of Health and Social Security (DHSS). 1980. *Inequalities in Health: Report of a Working Group Chaired by Sir Douglas Black.* London: DHSS.

Diez-Roux, Ana V. 2001. "Investigating Neighborhood and Area Effects on Health." *American Journal of Public Health* 91(11): 1783–9.

Dohrenwend, Bruce P., Itzhak Levav, Patrick Shrout, Sharon Schwartz, Guedalia Naveh, Bruce Link, Andrew Skodol, and Ann Stueve. 1992. "Socioeconomic Status and Psychiatric Disorders: The Causation-Selection Issue." *Science* 255(5047): 946–51.

Dominguez, Sylvia, and Celeste Watkins. 2003. "Creating Networks for Survival and Mobility: Social Capital Among African-American and Latin-American Low-Income Mothers." *Social Problems* 50(1): 111–35.

Engels, Friedrich. 1845/1999. *The Conditions of the Working Class in England.* New York: Oxford University Press.

Erickson, Bonnie. 2003. "Social Networks: The Value of Variety." *Contexts* 2(1): 25–31.

Farmer, Paul. 1999. *Infections and Inequalities: The Modern Plagues.* Berkeley, Calif.: University of California Press.

Fox, A. J., P. O. Goldblatt, and D. R. Jones. 1985. "Social Class Mortality Differentials: Artifact, Selection, or Life Circumstances?" *Journal of Epidemiology and Community Health* 39(1): 1–8.

Frohlich, Katherine L., Ellen Corin, and Louise Potvin. 2001. "A Theoretical Proposal for the Relationship Between Context and Disease." *Sociology of Health and Illness* 23(6): 776–97.

Frohlich, Katherine L., Louise Potvin, Patrick Chabot, and Ellen Corin. 2002. "A Theoretical and Empirical Analysis of Context: Neighborhoods, Smoking, and Youth." *Social Science and Medicine* 54(9): 1401–17.

Gatrell, Anthony, Jennie Popay, and Carol Thomas. 2004. "Mapping the Determinants of Health Inequalities in Social Space: Can Bourdieu Help Us?" *Health and Place* 10(3): 245–57.

Gottfredson, Linda S. 2004. "Intelligence: Is It the Epidemiologists' Elusive 'Fundamental Cause' of Social Class Inequalities in Health?" *Journal of Personality and Social Psychology* 86(1): 174–99.

Hahn, Mary N., George A. Kaplan, and S. Leonard Syme. 1989. "Socioeconomic Status and Health: Old Observations and New Thoughts." In *Pathways to Health: The Role of Social Factors,* edited by John Bunker, Deanna S. Gomby, and Barbara H. Kehrer. Menlo Park, Calif.: Henry S. Kaiser Family Foundation.

Hanley, James. 2002. "Edwin Chadwick and the Poverty of Statistics." *Medical History* 46(1): 21–40.

Holtzman, Neil A. 2002. "Genetics and Social Class." *Journal of Epidemiology and Community Health* 56(7): 529–35.

House, James S., and David R. Williams. 2000. "Understanding and Reducing Socioeconomic and Racial-Ethnic Disparities in Health." Paper presented to the conference "Capitalizing on Social Science and Behavioral Research to Improve the Public Health," sponsored by the Institute of Medicine of the National Academy of Sciences and the Commission on Behavioral and Social Sciences and Education of the National Research Council. Atlanta, Ga., February 2–3, 2000.

House, James S., Ronald C. Kessler, A. Regula Herzog, Richard P. Mero, Ann M. Kinney, and Martha J. Breslow. 1990. "Age, Socioeconomic Status, and Health." *Milbank Quarterly* 68(3): 383–411.

House, James S., James M. Lepkowski, Ann M. Kinney, Richard P. Mero, Ronald C. Kessler and A. Regula Herzog. 1994. "The Social Stratification of Aging and Health." *Journal of Health and Social Behavior* 35(3): 213–34.

Kawachi, Ichiro. 2000. "Income Inequality and Health." In *Social Epidemiology,* edited by Lisa F. Berkman and Ichiro Kawachi. New York: Oxford University Press.

Kitagawa, Evelyn M., and Phillip M. Hauser. 1973. *Differential Mortality in the United States: A Study in Socioeconomic Epidemiology.* Cambridge, Mass.: Harvard University Press.

Lalonde, Marc. 1974. *A New Perspective on the Health of Canadians.* Ottawa: Ministry of Health and Welfare.

Leclerc, Annette, Jean-François Chastang, Gwen Menvielle, and Danie le Luce. 2006. "Socioeconomic Inequalities in Premature Mortality in France: Have They Widened in Recent Decades?" *Social Science and Medicine* 62(8): 2035–45.

Leventhal, Tama, and Jeanne Brooks-Gunn. 2003. "Moving to Opportunity: An Experimental Study of Neighborhood Effects on Mental Health." *American Journal of Public Health* 93(9): 1576–82.

Lieberson, Stanley. 1985. *Making It Count: The Improvement of Social Research and Theory.* Berkeley, Calif.: University of California Press.

Link, Bruce G., and Jo C. Phelan. 1995. "Social Conditions as Fundamental Causes of Disease." *Journal of Health and Social Behavior* (special issue): 80–94.

Link, Bruce G., Richard M. Carpiano, and Margaret Weden. 2006. "Red States and Blue States, Batter Up, and 'The Winner Is': Can Honorific Awards Give Us Clues

About the Connection Between Socioeconomic Status and Mortality?" Paper presented to the annual meeting of the American Sociological Association, Montréal, August 2006.

Link, Bruce G., Mary E. Northridge, Jo C. Phelan, and Michael L. Ganz. 1998. "Social Epidemiology and the Fundamental Cause Concept: On the Structuring of Effective Cancer Screens by Socioeconomic Status." *Milbank Quarterly* 76(3): 375–402.

Link, Bruce G., Jo C. Phelan, Richard Miech, and Emily Leckman Westin. 2008. "The Resources that Matter: Fundamental Social Causes of Health Disparities and the Challenge of Intelligence." *Journal of Health and Social Behavior* 49(1): 72–91.

Logan, John R. 2003. "Life and Death in the City: Neighborhoods in Context." *Contexts* 2(2): 33–40.

Lutfey, Karen, and Jeremy Freese. 2005. "Towards Some Fundamentals of Fundamental Causality: Socioeconomic Status and Health in the Routine Clinic Visit for Diabetes." *American Journal of Sociology* 110(5): 1326–72.

Lynch, John W., George Davey Smith, George A. Kaplan, and James S. House. 2000. "Income Inequality and Mortality: Importance to Health of Individual Income, Psychosocial Environment, or Material Conditions." *British Medical Journal* 320(7243): 1200–4.

MacIntyre, Sally. 1997. "The Black Report and Beyond: What Are the Issues?" *Social Science and Medicine* 44(6): 723–45.

MacIntyre, Sally, Ann Ellaway, and Steve Cummins. 2002. "Place Effects on Health: How Can We Conceptualize, Operationalize, and Measure Them?" *Social Science and Medicine* 55(1): 125–39.

MacIntyre, Sally, Sheila MacIver, and Ann Sooman. 1993. "Area, Class, and Health: Should We Be Focusing on Places or People?" *Journal of Social Policy* 22(2): 235–42.

Markel, Howard. 1997. *Quarantine: East European Jewish Immigrants and the New York City Epidemics of 1892.* Baltimore, Md.: Johns Hopkins University Press.

Marmot, Michael. 2004. *The Status Syndrome.* New York: Owl Books.

Marmot, Michael, Martin J. Shipley, and Geoffrey Rose. 1984. "Inequalities in Death—Specific Explanations of a General Pattern?" *Lancet* 1(8384): 1003–6.

Moore, Spencer, Alan Shiell, Penelope Hawe, and Valerie A. Haines. 2005. "The Privileging of Communitarian Ideas: Citation Practices and the Translation of Social Capital into Public Health Research." *American Journal of Public Health* 95(8): 1330–7.

Morenoff, Jeffrey D. 2003. "Neighborhood Mechanisms and the Spatial Dynamics of Birth Weight." *American Journal of Sociology* 108(5): 976–1017.

Pappas, Gregory, Susan Queen, Wilbur Hadden, and Gail Fisher. 1993. "The Increasing Disparity in Mortality between Socioeconomic Groups in the United States, 1960 and 1986." *New England Journal of Medicine* 329(2): 103–9.

Pattillo-McCoy, Mary. 1999. *Black Picket Fences.* Chicago, Ill.: University of Chicago Press.

Phelan, Jo C., Bruce G. Link, Ana V. Diez-Roux, Ichiro Kawachi, and Bruce Levin. 2004. " 'Fundamental Causes' of Social Inequalities in Mortality: A Test of the Theory." *Journal of Health and Social Behavior* 45(3): 265–85.

Pickett, Kate E., and Michelle Pearl. 2001. "Multilevel Analyses of Neighborhood Socioeconomic Context and Health Outcomes: A Critical Review." *Journal of Epidemiology and Community Health* 55(2): 111–22.

Portes, Alejandro. 1998. "Social Capital: Its Origins and Applications in Modern Sociology." *Annual Review of Sociology* 24: 1–24.

Putnam, Robert D. 2000. *Bowling Alone: The Collapse and Revival of American Community.* New York: Simon & Schuster.

Raphael, Dennis. 2004. "Introduction to the Social Determinants of Health." In *Social Determinants of Health: Canadian Perspectives,* edited by Dennis Raphael. Toronto: Canadian Scholars Press.

Raphael, Dennis, and Toba Bryant. 2006. "The State's Role in Promoting Population Health: Public Health Concerns in Canada, U.S.A., U.K., and Sweden." *Health Policy* 78(1): 39–55.

Redelmeier, Donald A., and Sheldon M. Singh. 2001a. "Survival in Academy Award–Winning Actors and Actresses." *Annals of Internal Medicine* 134: 955–62.

———. 2001b. "Longevity of Screenwriters Who Win an Academy Award: Longitudinal Study." *British Medical Journal* 323(7327): 1491–6.

Robert, Stephanie A. 1999. "Socioeconomic Position and Health: The Independent Contribution of Community Context." *Annual Review of Sociology* 25: 489–516.

Robert, Stephanie A., and Richard M. Carpiano. 2005. "Our Four Cents: Future Priority Directions of Research on Neighborhoods, Social Capital, Health, and Aging." Invited position paper for National Institute of Aging. Bethesda, Md., October 2005.

Rose, David. 1995. "Official Social Classifications in the U.K." *Social Research Update* (University of Surrey), July 9, 1995. Accessed at http://sru.soc.surrey.ac.uk/SRU9.html.

Rothman, Kenneth. 1986. *Modern Epidemiology.* Boston, Mass.: Little, Brown.

Sampson, Robert J., Jeffrey D. Morenoff, and Thomas Gannon-Rowley. 2002. " 'Assessing Neighborhood Effects': Social Processes and New Directions in Research." *Annual Review of Sociology* 28: 443–78.

Sorlie, Paul D., Eric Backlund, and Jacob B. Keller. 1995. "U.S. Mortality by Economic, Demographic, and Social Characteristics: The National Longitudinal Mortality Study." *American Journal of Public Health* 85(7): 949–56.

Veenstra, Gerry. 2007. "Social Space, Social Class, and Bourdieu: Health Inequalities in British Columbia, Canada." *Health and Place* 13(1): 14–31.

Wacquant, Loïc J. D., and William J. Wilson. 1989. "The Cost of Racial and Class Exclusion in the Inner City." *Annals of the American Academy of Political and Social Science* 501: 8–25.

Waitzkin, Howard, Celia Iriart, Alfredo Estrada, and Syria Lamadrid. 2001. "Social Medicine Then and Now: Lessons from Latin America." *American Journal of Public Health* 91(10): 1592–601.

Wilkinson, Richard G. 1986. "Socioeconomic Differences in Mortality: Interpreting the Data on Their Size and Trends." In *Class and Health: Research and Longitudinal Data,* edited by Richard G. Wilkinson. London: Tavistock.

———. 1997. "Health Inequalities: Relative or Absolute Material Standards?" *British Medical Journal* 314(7080): 591–5.

———. 2005. *The Impact of Inequality: How to Make Sick Societies Healthier.* New York: New Press.

Wilkinson, Richard G., and Kate E. Pickett. 2006. "Income Inequality and Population Health: A Review and Explanation of the Evidence." *Social Science and Medicine* 62(7): 1768–84.

Williams, David R., and Chiquita Collins. 1995. "U.S. Socioeconomic and Racial Differences in Health: Patterns and Explanations." *Annual Review of Sociology* 21: 349–86.

Williams, Gareth H. 2003. "The Determinants of Health: Structure, Context, and Agency." *Sociology of Health and Illness* 25(3): 131–54.

Wilson, William J. 1987. *The Truly Disadvantaged.* Chicago: University of Chicago Press.

Wirth, Louis. 1969. *The Ghetto.* Chicago, Ill.: University of Chicago Press.

World Health Organization (WHO). 2005. *Action on the Social Determinants of Health: Learning from Previous Experiences.* Geneva, Switz.: WHO. Accessed at http://www.who.int/social_determinants/home_coverpage/en/index1.html.

Wright, Erik Olin. 2005. *Approaches to Class Analysis.* New York: Cambridge University Press.

Chapter 9

Race, Class, and Neighborhoods

MARY PATTILLO

THIS CHAPTER takes a historical and ethnographic case study approach to illustrate how class works to stratify urban space and in particular how class elites use strategies of exclusion for the purposes of what Charles Tilly calls "opportunity hoarding." Tilly (1998, 8) argues that "people who control access to value-producing resources solve pressing organizational problems by means of categorical distinctions." "Class" is a primary category of distinction-making and thus the basis upon which resources are shared or hoarded, while a neighborhood is an example of an organization made up of residents, elected representatives, and other stakeholders who have class-based interests and act on them. Opportunity hoarding, or the exclusive securing of resources or access to resources, is one mechanism by which inequality is established. The hoarding of resources by one group or neighborhood necessarily leads to resource deficits for another group or neighborhood; these different levels of resources create a stratified metropolis made up of places that support and amplify efforts at mobility (or reproduce privilege) and places that challenge and frustrate mobility (or reproduce disadvantage).

In previous chapters, we have seen other examples of opportunity-hoarding, perhaps most acutely in the chapter by Carpiano, Link, and Phelan. In their analysis, segregated networks and neighborhoods are differentially endowed with health-promoting information and resources, yielding health benefits for the privileged and failing health for the disadvantaged. In many ways, this chapter is the antecedent to the fundamental cause theory elaborated in that chapter, since this chapter focuses on the process by which neighborhood actors create spatial segregation.

Yet considering class is not enough. I show how, in typical American fashion, class is entwined with *and inflects* race to erect complex systems of hierarchy, domination, and disadvantage. In the study of urban stratification in the United States, racial segregation often takes precedence over class owing to the visible color line that exists in most cities and the intensity with which it has been maintained (Massey and Denton 1993; Wacquant 1994, 1997). While understandable, this emphasis on racial segregation obscures two important processes elucidated in this chapter: the ways in which whites have utilized class distinctions alongside—and sometimes in lieu of—antiblack sentiments to secure and protect desirable urban locations, and how class works as the basis of exclusion *within* the black community.

When class is the primary subject of inquiry, especially in urban demography, it is often employed in gradational terms: urban residents are identified in terms of discrete income or occupational categories and then their levels of class isolation or integration are determined (Massey 1996; Massey and Fischer 2003). This method is very useful for describing the extent and nature of place-based class stratification, but not for understanding the actual class-based agency that explains how such scenarios came to be. Urban historians such as Robert Halpern and Gail Radford and scholars in the political economy tradition like Harvey Molotch, John Logan, Herbert Gans, and Peter Dreier have paid more attention to these relational aspects of class, emphasizing how elite class actors write legislation and execute plans that benefit members of their own class and exploit, disadvantage, or exclude poor and working class urban residents, thereby reproducing place-based economic inequalities (Dreier, Mollenkopf, and Swanstrom 2004; Gans 1991; Halpern 1995; Logan and Molotch 1987; Radford 1996). These scholars have illustrated how class relationships are inscribed onto the urban landscape through such exclusionary practices as segregation, suburbanization, gentrification, disinvestment, and eminent domain. I expand on this list of practices to analyze the role of neighborhood conservation in improving places by excluding certain faces.

Defining Class

Class is often construed as an individual attribute that includes some combination of how much money a person earns or has, what kind of work he or she does, and how far he or she went in school (Blau and Duncan 1967). Unlike other chapters in this volume, this chapter does not weigh in on the debates over what particular combination of these and many other attributes yields the best measurement of "class." Instead, I focus on the meaning of class in the neighborhood context. Neighborhoods are collections of individuals who vary to a greater or lesser degree on individual-level social and economic attributes, and neighborhoods both foster and take on identities based on the preponderance of residents' attributes. Neighborhoods that house the low-level workers of a manufacturing plant are deemed "working class," whereas neighborhoods where the managers of such plants live are considered middle or upper middle class. More homogeneous neighborhoods have stronger class identities and are more unified on issues of concern and in their activism. For example, because middle class and affluent families can for the most part meet their basic needs on their own, activism in middle class and affluent neighborhoods is likely to be more focused on issues of order, compliance, aesthetics, the abundance and diversity of goods and services, and public investments that are of high quality and enriching. On the other hand, residents of working class and poor neighborhoods are more likely to be concerned with affordability, access, and availability of social and economic services and supports. Because many important resources are spatially bound (for example, schools, clean air, open space, banks), affluent coresidents have considerable incentive to try to maintain certain entry restrictions so as not to diminish the supply and quality of neighborhood amenities. Drawing from Weber, Tilly (1998, 6) describes this as "social closure." As this chapter shows, such boundary maintenance is a mainstay of middle class community organizing.

Furthermore, neighborhoods are more than the sum of individuals with money, jobs, and educations. Individual-level traits are visibly manifest in neighborhoods in other ways as well, such as in home square footage, the makes and models of cars on the street, the presence of swimming pools or vacant lots, and the density and type of retailers. That is, neighborhoods are sites of consumption. Also, residents express class standing in how they tend their gardens, how they run homeowner association meetings, how they make vacation plans and decide on destinations, and how they socialize with their neighbors. The habits and manners people bring to how they use the things they buy, how they use their free time, and how they deploy their bodies constitute, in a Weberian framework, "styles of life," or lifestyles (Weber 1946, 193, 181; see also Bourdieu 1984; DiMaggio 1982; Lamont 1992; Lareau 1987, 2003). Investigating class at the neighborhood level requires paying attention to these three interrelated facets: individual economic attributes, physical markers of consumptive power, and negotiated modes of behavior and action. Using this approach, we can identify an upper class neighborhood as one that houses people similarly situated in the managerial and professional sector of the labor market, who have translated their wages and wealth into high-end consumption, and who partake in leisure activities or implement aesthetic standards that are economically prohibitive. Consequently, defending such a neighborhood might include keeping out unskilled workers by disallowing apartment complexes or public transportation, policing public basketball courts and street corners, or mandating specific home improvements through the use of municipal housing codes. Urban residents maintain and reproduce their class standing by excluding those who do not or cannot comply with such consumption and lifestyle standards, thereby hoarding high-quality, mobility-inducing neighborhood resources.

The Setting

The history of the North Kenwood–Oakland neighborhood on Chicago's South Side dates to the midnineteenth century, when wealthy industrialists established the area as a bucolic, aristocratic commuter suburb—"the embodiment of an elegant rural preserve" (Commission on Chicago Landmarks 1992, 2).[1] This chapter focuses on two periods in the neighborhood's development: its transition from middle class white to working and lower class black occupancy from the 1930s through the 1960s; and the replacement of poor blacks by middle and upper-income blacks beginning in the 1980s. I analyze the similarities and differences across those eras in strategies to exclude poor residents from the neighborhood.

Located along Chicago's south lakefront, a mile from the campus of the University of Chicago and a ten-minute drive from downtown (see figure 9.1), the North Kenwood–Oakland neighborhood has been rediscovered as ripe for new investment, as have many inner-city neighborhoods across the United States (Abu-Lughod 1994; Boyd 2000; Brown-Saracino 2004; Clark 2004; Dávila 2004; Hyra 2008; Jackson 2001; Lloyd 2005; Mele 2000; Pattillo 2007; Perez 2002; Prince 2004; Smith 1996; Spain 1993; Taylor 2002; Zukin 1982). A flurry of newspaper headlines like "South Side Lakeshore Ready to Catch Its Wave" (J. Linn Allen, *Chicago Tribune*, April 17, 1988, 1.), "Reverse Commute: North Kenwood/Oakland Enjoying an Influx of the Middle Class" (Jeanette Almada, *Chicago Tribune*, April 26, 1998, 1), "N. Kenwood–Oakland Back on Its Feet" (Leon Pitt, *Chicago Sun Times*, August 31, 1998, 8), and "The Unmaking of a Ghetto: How the North Kenwood–Oakland Neighborhood Came Back from the Grave" (Grossman and Leroux 2006) illustrates the attention being heaped on this neighborhood as it experiences a middle class renaissance.[2] The city of Chicago has actively facilitated this process, designating the neighborhood as a "conservation area" in 1990, a status that is legally supported in both state and federal law.

Prior to the current revitalization, or gentrification, of North Kenwood–Oakland, it had been a very poor, homogeneously African American neighborhood that exhibited all of the familiar characteristics of urban decline and concentrated poverty found in so many central-city black neighborhoods across the country. Kenwood lost over half of its population, and Oakland lost two-thirds, between 1960 and 1990. In 1990 Oakland was the poorest community in the entire city of Chicago, in terms of both median family income and the proportion of families who were poor; 70 percent of

Figure 9.1   North Kenwood–Oakland and Surrounding Areas

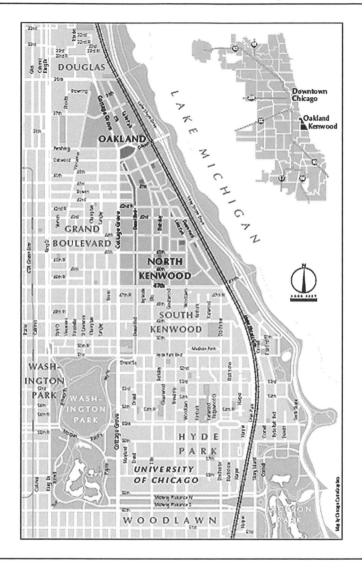

Source: Produced for the author by Dennis McClendon, Chicago CartoGraphics, used with permission.

its families had incomes below the federal poverty line. North Kenwood was only slightly better off, with 51 percent of its families living in poverty.

Between 1990, when the city recognized the neighborhood as a conservation area, and 2000, however, the overall demographic story shows considerable upward socioeconomic change (see table 9.1). By 2000, 20 percent of the families in the neighborhood earned more than $50,000 per year, a

Table 9.1   Demographic Changes in North Kenwood–Oakland, 1990 to 2000

	1990	2000
Total population	10,938	9,987
Percentage black	98.7	97.5
Median income (in 1999 dollars)	$9,391	$21,949
Percentage with income over $50,000	6	20
Percentage homeowners	9.5	17
Median home value (in 1999 dollars)	$44,160	$219,153
Family poverty rate	63%	39%

Source: Author's calculations from 1990 U.S. census, 2000 U.S. census, accessed at http://www.census.gov.

more than threefold increase from 1990. During the same time, the poverty rate declined precipitously, median family income more than doubled, the homeownership rate doubled, and the cost of housing skyrocketed. However, amid significant income flux, North Kenwood–Oakland remains predominantly black. Hence, North Kenwood–Oakland has been black since the 1950s, and it is for the most part experiencing "black gentrification," fueled by the growing affluence of some African Americans (Freeman 2006; Hyra 2008; Pattillo 2007; Street 2005).[3]

As a student of Chicago, of cities, and of black politics, class relations, and social life, I was drawn to the transformation of North Kenwood–Oakland. In 1998 I moved in and began my research. The neighborhood offers a case study of the utilization of race by whites as the primary vehicle for promoting both race *and class* stratification in the first historical period. And in the contemporary period the neighborhood exhibits the increasing salience of class *among* African Americans for similar spatial opportunity-hoarding ends.

Classic Conservation, 1940 to 1960: Race then Class

Between 1940 and 1960, North Kenwood–Oakland was "invaded" by African Americans (see figure 9.2). The war metaphor was pervasive in the rhetoric of community groups and scholars alike. The University of Chicago sociologist Robert Park (1936) borrowed the concept of "invasion and succession" from plant biology to describe the transition from one type of urban land use or resident population to another. Following this theoretical tradition, sociologists Otis Dudley Duncan and Beverly Duncan

Figure 9.2   Racial Composition of North Kenwood and Oakland,
            1920 to 1980

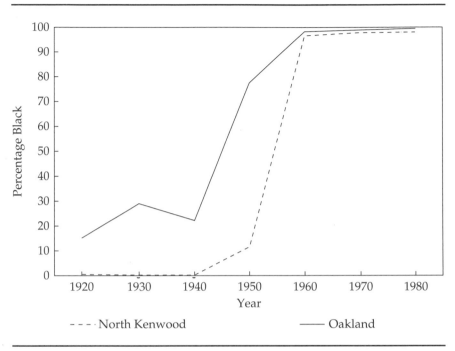

Source: Author's calculations.

(1957) analyzed 175 census tracts in Chicago and classified them in terms
of stages of racial transition in 1950. Because Oakland's minority-black
population in the 1920s and 1930s of roughly 25 to 30 percent was concentrated in a small section in the northwest of the neighborhood, the authors
classified most of Oakland and the western part of North Kenwood as
"invasion" areas from 1940 to 1950. A more detailed study of the "Negro
invasion" of Oakland identifies the precise moment of invasion of the
southern part of Oakland. "The public record shows that a parcel of land
in sub-area 'A,' which is adjacent to the Cottage Grove Avenue barrier, was
sold to a Negro in 1942" (Schietinger 1948, 22). Even though the African
American buyer did not move into the house he bought, this first purchase
signaled a crack in the armor, and like dominoes, "Negro acquisition of one
structure seemed to precipitate Negro occupancy of adjacent structures" (25).

"Conservation" was promoted as a strategy to stem this tide of black
in-migration. The idea of conservation was first introduced as a planning
category in the 1943 Master Residential Plan of Chicago (Chicago Plan
Commission 1943) and then legally codified in the Illinois Urban

Figure 9.3   Conservation Areas from 1943 Master Plan of Chicago

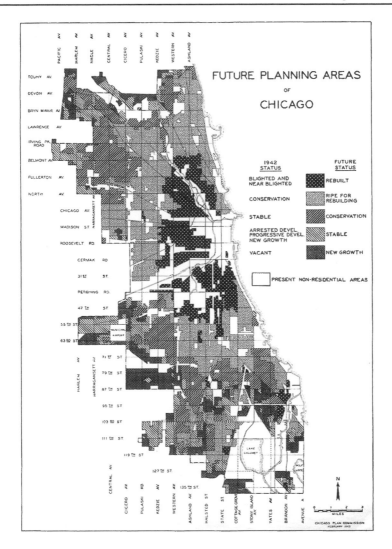

Source: Chicago Plan Commission (1943).

Community Conservation Act of 1953 and the U.S. Housing Act of 1954 (Flanagan 1997; Hirsch 2000; von Hoffman 2000).[4] The original conservation areas in the city (see figure 9.3), which covered 56 square miles and included 1.65 million residents, formed a "C" around the "blighted" and "near-blighted" areas of the central city, which were targeted for demolition and reconstruction. While these planning classifications were based objectively on the age, condition, and rents of an area's housing stock, there was a clear racial and class patterning to the designations of blighted areas, on the one hand, and conservation areas, on the other. Blacks of all classes and poor recent white immigrants were most likely to live in the oldest and least expensive parts of the city and thus were most likely to reside in blighted areas. Although a few of the areas where blacks predominated were included as part of the conservation "C," most of the conservation areas were white neighborhoods that sat precariously (from their perspective) adjacent to the swelling black and immigrant communities and were threatened with "the influx of families of lower economic status." The problem faced by conservation areas was that of "gradual deterioration and its arrest must be the objective of any immediate planning program for these areas" (Chicago Plan Commission 1943, 93–95).

The master plan made plain that conservation was a tool to be used by nonpoor neighborhoods against poor newcomers—which closely coincided with nonblack neighborhoods organizing against black newcomers—as a way to protect neighborhood assets. In more normative terms, the master plan proffered the assumption that conservation was about celebrating what already existed: "Planning is as much concerned with *what is good* and should be maintained as it is with that which is in need of reconstruction" (Chicago Plan Commission 1943, 91, emphasis added).

Debates about and establishment of "what is good" transforms *policies* into *politics* (Gans 1991). While we learned in the chapter by Jeff Manza and Clem Brooks that class matters for electoral politics, here the focus is on the local politics of community organizing and the manifestations of public policies and laws on the ground level. The relevant policies are those that guide state investments in neighborhoods. The logic of the largely conceptual master plan that there are community assets and liabilities was legally affirmed in the Illinois 1953 Urban Community Conservation Act, which emphasized that what is good should be "protected" in order to "prevent" decline. "In order to promote and protect the health, safety, morals and welfare of the public," the legislation reads, "it is necessary to provide for the protection of such conservation areas and prevent their deterioration into slum and blighted areas." What and whom should be protected or prevented are decisions based on the definitions of what is good. This is how normative class-based evaluations get translated into exclusionary actions.[5]

Given the rapidity of neighborhood change, many of the white conservation neighborhoods interpreted the master plan's mandate to prevent the bad and protect the good in brazenly antiblack terms. Organizing against a racial threat resonated with white residents and still had legal teeth through racial restrictive covenants—agreements between homeowners not to sell or lease their properties to blacks and sometimes not to other racial, ethnic, and religious groups as well. For example, in 1943 the

Oakland Kenwood Property Owners Association (OKPOA) listed the following as their accomplishments for the year (Long and Johnson 1947, 48):

1. The eviction of undesirables—Negroes—from dwellings at 4608 Drexel Boulevard, 44th and University, Northwest corner of 47th Street and Woodlawn Avenue; 2. Successful opposition, through appearances before the State Legislature, to a bill to nullify race restrictive agreements; 3. The initiation of suits to restrain sale to Negroes of four pieces of property between 39th and 40th Streets on Ellis and Oak [sic] Park Avenues and on Oakwood Boulevard; 4. The initiation of suits to restrain sale to Negroes of seven pieces of property between 36th and 42nd Streets on Ellis and Lake Park Avenues; 5. The renewal of interest in restrictive agreements through organization of block-by-block anti-Negro contracts.

In 1944 OKPOA spent over $3,000 in legal fees to enforce restrictive covenants barring black purchase of property in the neighborhood. These were defensive actions. But the organization also went on the offensive that year, gathering the signatures of more than 25 percent of the property owners for new restrictive covenants (Weaver 1945, 250).[6] There was also a militant fringe wing of the OKPOA. To visibly signal their contempt for the possibility of black newcomers, angry white homeowners hung signs in their windows that read THIS PROPERTY IS NOT FOR SALE. The more extreme residents were determined in their commitment to hold the racial line and ready to "do things the [Oakland-Kenwood] Property Association can't afford to do officially" (Ernest Lilienstein, "Mayor Kelly Threatened by Kenwood Ass'n.," *Chicago Defender*, February 9, 1946, 1).

In the 1930s the University of Chicago was a key player in organizing property owners' associations in Hyde Park and the neighborhoods that surrounded it like North Kenwood and Oakland. In a moment of poetic reflection, University of Chicago chancellor Robert Hutchins penned the following ditty about "Willie," the university administrator responsible for buying up nearby property and renting the apartments to whites only in an effort to forestall black settlement in and around Hyde Park (quoted in Hirsch 1983, 147):

The Chancellor and the President gazed out across the park,
They laughed like anything to see that things were looking dark.
"Our neighborhood," the Chancellor said, "once blossomed like the lily."
"Just seven coons with seven kids could knock our program silly."
"Forget it," said the President, "and thank the Lord for Willie."

Fortifying neighborhood boundaries is necessary for social and spatial closure. Chancellor Hutchins gave the university's perspective from the highest levels, making it clear that such racial boundary maintenance was key to keeping its residential surroundings lily-white and prosperously blossoming, despite the immiseration that such hoarding might cause adjacent overcrowded neighborhoods. In financing and encouraging white property owners' opposition to black neighbors, the university promoted the racist activities of these groups.

The role of the university in establishing these organizations ranged from planting the idea, as in the case of the Oakland Kenwood Property Owners Association, to financing their ongoing operations, as in the case of the Woodlawn Property Owners' League. The university made monthly payments to the Woodlawn group for "protective work," which probably meant protection against the settlement of blacks in the neighborhood (Hirsch 1983, 145; Oakland-Kenwood Planning Association 1952, 3). The historian Wendy Plotkin (1999) has documented the university's financial support of legal suits brought by white property owners against families who violated restrictive covenants. Of particular note, the university financed the court case *Hansberry vs. Lee,* one of the most well-known cases of white residents defending racial restrictive covenants to fend off African Americans. That whites so abhorred the arrival into Woodlawn of the Hansberrys—a family of substantial means and education—is proof that in the 1940s racial antipathies trumped class considerations when utilizing the conservation strategy.

Despite its early advocacy of racial exclusion, the role of the University of Chicago on the issue of conservation was *pivotal.* In 1948, the Supreme Court ruled that racial restrictive covenants were unenforceable. As a result, organizations like OKPOA lost the institutional and financial support and political sway of the University of Chicago in holding the racial line. On its own, OKPOA had insufficient organizational resources to realize its goals of either race- or class-based social closure. Although there are myriad reasons why racial turnover then happened so quickly in North Kenwood–Oakland while stalling elsewhere (Gamm 1999; Hirsch 1983), one necessary explanation is that the population pressures were just so powerful. The black population in Chicago was estimated to be growing by thirty thousand people every year from 1950 to 1955 (Duncan and Duncan 1957, 29). At the same time, whites in North Kenwood–Oakland left to follow the federal dollars and infrastructure to the rapidly growing suburbs (Hanchett 2000; Jackson 1985), which became the new frontier to protect and from which to prevent the in-migration of blacks and poor residents. The landscape of stratification was in flux, but the mechanisms of exclusion remained.

The University of Chicago—less able to pick up and follow the suburban drive—turned inward, shrinking the territory it committed to protect to include only Hyde Park and South Kenwood (see figure 9.1) and reevaluating its tactics. At this point, it transformed the conservation approach from a tool used primarily against blacks to a tool used against the poor, with the solace that the latter category would include many blacks.

The progression of the University of Chicago away from race to class as the explicit basis of exclusion was facilitated by an organization of civic and business leaders called the Metropolitan Housing and Planning Council (MHPC). In 1953, the university commissioned the MHPC to study the possibilities of conservation as a legal and practical development tool. The tangled language of the MHPC report (1953, 22) illustrates the inability to fully separate race from class and declares without reservation that targeting a race for removal or "prevention" is no longer tenable. "Conservation based on any policy of racial exclusion," states the MHPC, "is not only morally reprehensible, but practically impossible." Instead, conservation areas can be examples of "interracial communities maintained at a middle or upper middle class level." In the preceding sentences, the substitution of class for race is straightforward, but in the following passage it is less clear. "In a sense the criteria to be evolved are economic rather than racial. Because of the structure of the non-white community, such criteria will in a sense promote exclusion. This exclusion, however, will be at a different level in different conservation areas, and will not be based on race."[7] The MHPC's guide to conservation clearly conveyed that exclusion would not be based on race *by itself,* but that community groups could achieve significant racial exclusion through a focus on class.

The MHPC report represents the moment when elite actors became aware that race-based exclusion was both less acceptable and less effective in keeping out undesirable neighbors and that class-based exclusion was the most important factor in controlling access to high-quality amenities and services. Because "the structure of the non-white community" at that time was such that a majority of blacks had low incomes—and a greater proportion of blacks than whites had low incomes—then exclusion would more often be exercised against blacks than against whites. Despite ostensibly nonracial planning criteria, the effect would clearly be that blacks—*as a classed race*—would be disproportionately harmed. Because the university's answer to the master plan's implicit question, "What is good?" was ultimately "Middle-income residents," Hyde Park's conservation efforts tolerated, for the most part, "good" black residents—that is, those who were middle- and upper-income—but stubbornly resisted poor residents of any race, especially through the limits placed on public housing.[8] The university's evolution on the means and ends of conservation is the precursor to the conservation rhetoric used by middle- and upper-income African American North Kenwood–Oakland residents in the 1980s.

Contemporary Conservation: Class Within Race

There is obvious irony in the fact that North Kenwood–Oakland's middle class African American residents in the 1980s and 1990s chose the conservation area strategy, which in its first incarnations had been blatantly utilized to keep black people out of conservation areas. This mystery is better understood, however, by recognizing that the conservation area idea could also be wielded to construct a common foe in poor people. This is how the University of Chicago implemented its conservation area when it realized by the 1950s that barring blacks outright was indefensible. Newcomer black activists in North Kenwood–Oakland gazed at Hyde Park—their attractive, well-functioning, stable, integrated, and majority-*middle class* southern neighbor—as a worthy model to emulate. Indeed, emulation is one of the strategies outlined by Tilly for "transplanting" and making "durable" various forms of inequality. As Tilly (1998, 10) argues, opportunity hoarding is not restricted to the most elite actors in a particular hierarchy but can likewise be replicated and pursued by "people who lack great power . . . if encouraged, tolerated, or ignored by the powerful."

The reasons for gentrification in North Kenwood–Oakland are quite clear: proximity to downtown, the lake, and the university; large swaths of vacant land; and a stately vintage housing stock available at low cost (Pattillo 2007). The details of its implementation, however, are more convoluted. The establishment of the conservation area, plan, and council in North Kenwood–Oakland in the 1980s and 1990s was complicated, multilayered, and contested by the people who were involved. A roster of the key players serves to introduce the classed and raced actors who coalesced to envision and implement various strategies of closure. Robert Lucas was the executive director of the Kenwood Oakland Community Organization, which was a key early player in calling for a conservation area and in organizing block clubs and tenant organizations that gave human force to the revitalization efforts. Lucas was a veteran of Chicago's civil rights movement and one of a handful of black leaders who had worked closely with Dr. Martin Luther King Jr. during his time in Chicago. Shirley Newsome, a professional black woman who moved to Oakland in 1979, soon became committed to "getting this place straightened up." She also worked to organize block clubs and made key contacts with representatives of the economic, civic, and political elite outside of the neighborhood. One of those elites was the white real estate mogul Ferdinand "Ferd" Kramer, whose redevelopment designs for the neighborhood sparked as much controversy as the Conservation Plan itself. Kramer was a 1922 alumnus of the University of Chicago. Kramer took his vision to Jonathan Kleinbard, vice president for community affairs at the university, enlisting Kleinbard and the university in promoting plans for North Kenwood–Oakland's revitalization.

Poor residents of North Kenwood–Oakland—especially the residents of six high-rise public housing projects that overlooked Lake Michigan and were thus called the Lakefront Properties—also wanted a cleaner and safer neighborhood. Community improvement began, however, with their dislodgment: all nine hundred units in the high-rises were vacated in 1986 by the Chicago Housing Authority (CHA) due to the buildings' disrepair. The residents were scattered across the city of Chicago through various CHA-sponsored relocation methods, but there was minimal effort to track their exact whereabouts. The plan was to renovate the buildings and bring the residents back, but in 1998 four of the six high-rises were demolished instead. It is the relationship between the slate of mostly middle class actors and their allies and the few low-income public housing residents who remained or attempted to move back that illuminates both the figurative and literal processes of exclusion during neighborhood revitalization.

Searching for strategies to "straighten up" the neighborhood in the late 1970s, Shirley Newsome made a move that might have been unthinkable for someone steeped in the local history: she contacted the University of Chicago. Distrust of the university ran deep for more than a few community residents, and given the details already recited, such mistrust had its grounds. By the 1980s, however, the accusations levied at the university were not that it was trying to *insulate* itself from the surrounding black community, as it did in the 1950s and 1960s, but rather that it had designs to *impose* itself on its neighbors. Residents frequently rehearsed rumors that the university had certain intentions to colonize North Kenwood–Oakland. "I had heard that the University of Chicago was supposed to buy [the land] all the way north to Michael Reese [Hospital at Twenty-ninth Street]," asserted one resident (see figure 9.1). Newsome was aware of these fears, but she was even more convinced that the influence of the university was unavoidable and needed to be marshaled. At the University of Chicago, she contacted Jonathan Kleinbard, who suggested that she visit the Conservation Community Council in Hyde Park and meet with its president. Making this connection constituted the first step toward the emulation of the conservation strategy in North Kenwood–Oakland.

Yet another train departed with a conservation destination in 1987, when the developer Ferd Kramer declared his interest in developing a plan for North Kenwood–Oakland. Kramer put forth his plan in response to the emptying and planned renovation of the Lakefront Properties public housing complex. Instead of renovating the six hulking high-rises, Kramer proposed their demolition and reconstruction as low-rise, low-density buildings scattered across the larger North Kenwood–Oakland community (Illinois Housing Development Authority 1990). The *Chicago Tribune* reported on the unveiling of the plan in 1987 as follows:

> An ambitious plan to raze four 16-story public housing high-rises located on prime South Side lakefront land and replace them with low-rise housing for people of all income levels will be presented Tuesday to federal housing officials in Washington. If implemented, the proposal, conceived by Ferd Kramer, a prominent Chicago real estate developer, and backed by the Illinois Housing Development Authority, would revitalize one of the most deteriorated neighborhoods in the city and fill in one of the last underdeveloped gaps along the lakefront between the University of Chicago on the south and the

middle-income Lake Meadows and Prairie Shores apartment complexes on the north (Stanley Ziemba, "CHA Urged to Raze 4 High-Rises." *Chicago Tribune,* November 24, 1987, 1).

The first line of the article contains a word that would become a standard descriptor in the discussion of the Lakefront Properties site: "prime." The phrase "prime real estate" is a common reference to land that is attractive for a variety of reasons, in this case its proximity to both the lakefront and downtown. But "prime real estate," a social construct like any other, is historically and politically contingent. After an esteemed beginning, North Kenwood–Oakland experienced a precipitous decline in desirability, or "prime-ness." In the 1950s and 1960s, when the high-rises were built, downtown was a deteriorating center of congestion and disorder; from whites' perspective, the city was being overrun by African Americans. Whites turned their eyes toward the hinterland, where, thanks to the federal government, modern, air conditioned houses were relatively cheap and could be easily accessed by smooth new roads. At that time, "prime real estate" was the land adjacent to such highways or commuter rail lines in the suburbs. Neighborhoods like North Kenwood–Oakland—far away from the new suburban shopping malls and entertainment centers, still accommodating new black migrants from the South, and full of high-maintenance, attached old graystones with little yard space and no room for a garage—held none of the charm for which buyers are willing to pay a half-million dollars today. The power to define prime-ness is established partly through a group's ability to pay for land and partly through state subsidization; once again, class relationships are inscribed onto space as elites reclaim and secure particular places through their outbidding of poor residents. The return of North Kenwood–Oakland to "prime" status was not lost on public housing and other poor residents, but they interpreted North Kenwood–Oakland's second dawn as signaling a dusky future for them.

A long list of supporters of the Kramer plan began to materialize, from local representatives like Shirley Newsome and Robert Lucas to institutional players like the University of Chicago, Michael Reese and Mercy Hospitals, citywide banks, and other private developers. The group's vision—for which Kramer was the "catalyst" and financier—was put to paper by a design team from the nationally renowned architectural firm Skidmore, Owings, and Merrill (Hedlund 1989; Stanley Ziemba, "CHA Urged to Raze 4 High-Rises." *Chicago Tribune,* November 24, 1987, 1). The final product was an elaborate urban design initiative for the neighborhood that included new parkways, community squares, and a commercial "town center." The plan was soon called a "conservation plan"—lowercased since it was not developed under the Conservation Act, which requires such a plan. But it was the definite precursor to being recognized under that legal designation. The Kramer plan won a citation for excellence in urban design from the American Institute of Architects. The citation commended the plan for the way in which it "form[ed] cohesive areas that reaffirm[ed] the importance of the community fabric."

Not all residents, however, were well woven into that fabric, and the Kramer plan was not without its staunch critics. As might be expected given the plan's call to demolish the high-rise public housing, the displaced poor residents of the buildings were the most passionately critical. The former residents, who had organized into the Lakefront Community Organization, had with no small effort brokered an agreement with the Chicago Housing Authority that promised the renovation and repopulation of the high-rises, and they were not keen on any plan that would endanger those assurances. A handful of the residents stayed in the high-rises even after the Chicago Housing Authority ceased maintenance and management of the buildings. It was their way of resisting invisibility. Carlos Roberts, a leader of the Lakefront Community Organization, conveyed the residents' resolve: "Just because we're poor and living in public housing doesn't mean we'll allow ourselves to be taken advantage of. We'll do whatever is necessary to ensure that we remain where we're at" (Stanley Ziemba, "CHA Urged to Raze 4 High-Rises." *Chicago Tribune,* November 24, 1987, 1).

If nothing else, the public hoopla created by the Kramer plan debates got everyone looking at North Kenwood–Oakland. Local residents and organizations, city agencies and leadership on up to the mayors, state and federal departments, business leaders, and the federal courts were all taking sides to decide the fate of local public housing, which symbolized (and some argued determined) the fate of the whole neighborhood. Public housing also frustrated the attempts of gentrifiers toward residential class closure. Urban elites agree that the way to improve a neighborhood is to encourage the settlement of higher-income families, thereby maximizing land uses, increasing tax revenues, and creating an economic base to attract businesses and services (Logan and Molotch 1987). Poor people are a drag on such efforts, and poor people housed in conspicuous high-rises are an even greater hindrance. These were also the same principles espoused in the conservation of Hyde Park, where "the question of public housing aroused some of the bitterest debate and soul-searching" (Abrahamson 1959, 256). The resolution in Hyde Park was to make minimal allotments for poor families and affordable housing and demolish much of the area where working class and black families resided to redevelop them for parkland or institutional uses. Would North Kenwood–Oakland emulate such activities?

Between 1988 and 1989, hundreds of neighborhood residents participated in a series of community meetings to discuss community development (Neighborhood Planning Committee 1989). It was in these forums that the conservation area idea became more tangible and efforts began with various city agencies to gain the official conservation area designation.

The North Kenwood–Oakland Conservation Area was legally established in 1990, yet this culminating act only ushered in more controversy. One of the reasons the conservation notion was so appealing to residents was that it required the creation of a Conservation Community Council (CCC), which would be the community voice in the creation of a conservation plan that would govern future development in the area. These two processes would, again, turn policy into politics, since choosing people and ideas required translating interests into actions. The initial brainstorming activities had been relatively inclusive and democratic, with representation from more affluent newcomers as well as poor and working class old-timers. As the game changed to require more official leadership to interface with public officials, planning professionals, private developers, and potential commercial investors, the importance of elite social and cultural capital increased. With its ability to instantiate its vision in a plan that would be made binding by the certification of the entire Chicago City Council, the CCC became a coveted appointment. "It makes a difference, the educational levels of the black people living here," commented one middle class newcomer who relished the professional credentials of the new activists.

There were forty-three nominations for the CCC's fifteen positions, and residents scrutinized every step of the nomination and selection process. The first bone of contention was the fact that CCC members were ultimately appointed by the mayor, not elected by the community. The community's power was further attenuated by the legal fact that the CCC was an *advisory*, not a decisionmaking, body. Under these legal guidelines, the power of residents was secondary to that of the bureaucrats in the city administration. Residents could nominate their neighbors, or themselves, but the final roster to be presented to the mayor for his action would be filtered through a string of officials and city agencies. This process prompted the criticism that such oversight essentially undercut community control.

Still, community members coordinated letter-writing campaigns and petition drives to offer CCC nominees. The debates over the Kramer plan had clearly established camps of residents on the issues of public housing and community autonomy. These camps were reflected in the nomination and selection of council members. Residents who were wary of the imperial designs of Ferd Kramer and the University of Chicago and instead favored more community-driven development put forth a slate of candidates. The most conspicuously omitted name from that petition was Shirley Newsome.

Residents were only one part of the organizational brew in the neighborhood. Of particular note, the University of Chicago was hardly a neutral party, having invested time and energy and lent its name to parts of the process. Jonathan Kleinbard was a strong advocate of a conservation area and a Conservation Community Council because it would "ensure over time that the people who live there and are invested in it have advised what happens. [And] that they have a real voice and they can hold things up that they don't like." While his respect for local control was obviously genuine, Kleinbard seemed less conscious of how instrumental the university was in promoting a *particular kind* of leadership, one that had been willing all along to work collaboratively with the university rather than one that might have been antagonistic to university interests. Although he celebrated the fact that the community had a "real voice," subsequent events, as he narrated them, called into question the independence of that voice:

> We submitted names and they [the Department of Housing] came up with this awful list. I mean, I don't know where it came from. And so we had sort of an internal discussion [and a] fight with the administration over that. . . . So I said to [the mayor's chief of policy Frank] Kruesi, I want you to meet with this woman [Shirley Newsome]. She ought to be chairman of the CCC, and she ought to help you figure out who ought to be on it. She knows everybody. Not everybody's going to vote the way I wanted, but at least she'll get a sense of the community. So they met . . . I arranged for all three of us to meet . . . and I just introduced them and left. And he was very impressed. He had her in to see the mayor.

Since Kleinbard had recurrent reservations that the university would be perceived as the heavy, this is an example of a lighter touch. As a representative of the University of Chicago, Kleinbard championed community participation, but primarily the participation of those who seemed most appropriate by dint of education, experiences, self-presentation, agendas, and connections—in other words, by their class qualifications. Shirley Newsome had the necessary class-inflected cultural and social capital to impress the university and its officers. Always professionally dressed, flawlessly well spoken, confidently assertive, skillfully diplomatic, and very smart, Shirley Newsome has since been profiled on national and local public radio, in television documentaries and on public interest shows, and in countless newspaper articles—including a *Chicago Tribune* metro section front-page feature naming her the "South Side's Renaissance Woman" (Noreen Ahmed, "South Side's Renaissance Woman Shirley Newsome Has Devoted 20 Years to Reviving Community." *Chicago Tribune*, February 24, 2000, 1). Her day job as a judicial assistant also did not hurt; her officiating style was imbued with the decorum and precision of the courtroom.

Newsome's intelligence and charisma made a strong case for her to be the CCC chair on her own merits, but the university had the social capital (and economic and political capital) to ensure that outcome. The university was well within its bounds to make recommendations for the council. The enabling legislation directs the Department of Urban Renewal to "cooperate and consult with public and private agencies and individuals interested in the area" when evaluating council nominees (Illinois Revised Statutes, par. 91.121). As long as its nominees lived within the conservation area, the university was an acceptable nominator. The imbalance occurred, however, when weighing the handwritten letters and unnotarized petitions that North Kenwood–Oakland residents sent to support their candidates against the phone calls and introductory lunches that Kleinbard arranged.

The scale of history shows that the university's candidate, Shirley Newsome, won the position of chairman of the Conservation Community Council.[9] Newsome was without question a highly qualified choice and had earned the respect of many community residents. Moreover, the frequent deference to her judgment displayed by university officials and others suggests that perhaps *she* was steering the university (and the neighborhood's future) rather than the other way around. Having reenergized the block clubs and co-chaired the Neighborhood Planning Committee, she seemed to know the history of every parcel of land in the conservation area and, just as importantly, was comfortable referring to people's homes and yards as "parcels." At this point, the counterfactuals are unknowable: Who would have emerged as CCC chairman had a community-wide election been held? Would the mayor have appointed Shirley Newsome chairman without the bug that the University of Chicago planted in his ear? Could other candidates have been as adept at shepherding the conservation planning and implementation process? Would other leaders have spearheaded a plan that was more, or less, friendly to public housing residents? To homeowners? To the city? To developers? To the university? While these questions have no sure answers, the details of the front- and backstage efforts to secure a conservation area and appoint the Conservation Community Council, and the array of interests so involved, highlight several important points: the important role that social networks play in steering urban change; the middle class bias of those networks; the differential power that inheres in the networks of elite institutions versus working class and poor residents; and the production of interlocutors who are likely to support the opportunity-hoarding missions of elites.

Even more directly illustrative of exclusionary processes, a final controversy brewed over the first and most basic requirement for appointment to the CCC—that the member reside within the conservation area. Because of this stipulation, the public housing residents who had been moved out of the Lakefront Properties but who still hoped to be returned to rehabilitated apartments were not eligible to serve on the CCC. Representing the public housing residents, John Williams delivered the following impassioned statement at the public hearing to gather nominations for the CCC:

> Mr. Chairman and all those interested at this meeting, this is not actually a question. It is also a statement similar to the one that was just read. But I have been on the Board of Directors of the Lakefront Community Organization. Since 1985, we have been involved in negotiations with the Chicago Housing Authority, HUD and contractors, and anyone that has an interest in seeing the rehabbing of the six buildings known as [L]akefront [P]roperties. We are

here as representatives of the 700 plus families. Notice I said "families" not "people" that were forced to leave these six buildings.

I now refer you to your letter dated May 23, 1990. This is a notice you sent to inform everyone of this meeting. In Paragraph 3, you stated that all members of this Council must reside within the North Kenwood–Oakland Conservation Area. You say that this is in compliance with the City of Chicago, Department of Urban Renewal Procedures and the Urban Renewal Consolidation Act of 1961 as amended.

We, the Lakefront Community organization, strongly protest these procedures in this Consolidation Act. We feel that those that passed this Act 29 years ago could not have foreseen the unique situation we have before us now. It is unique because we have the 700 families who are residents in absentia who have been guaranteed in writing the right to return to these rehab buildings if they choose to do so. Therefore, it follows that a resident of any of these six buildings that left the lakefront because of rehabbing of these buildings, must be afforded the same right to decide what happens to the area as those residents who remain in the area. The area to mean the same area as described in your notice.

Mr. Vincent Lane, Chairman of the Housing Authority, when he appeared before you, he made you aware of this very situation that I speak of now. The memorandum before us sets forth in writing these guarantees. And we, the Lakefront Community Organization, as representatives of these residents in absentia, must insist that they be fully allowed to participate in any and all decisions affecting this conservation area.[10]

Applause followed Williams's speech. But the reply from the presiding public officials was not as sympathetic. The law was clear on the residency requirement and allowed no flexibility. Former residents of the Lakefront Properties were just that—former residents—and thus were not eligible for positions of community leadership.

The prohibition against displaced public housing residents serving on the CCC returns the discussion to the master plan that originally put forth the notion of conservation areas and the legislation that followed ten years later. The goals were to "preserve" and "protect" the community assets— or "what is good"—and to prevent the infiltration or preponderance of those people or factors thought to lead inevitably to community decline. This exchange suggests that public housing in North Kenwood–Oakland was on the list of things to prevent, not to protect—in other words, public housing was something to exclude, not to hoard. This was similarly the case in the Hyde Park Conservation Plan, and it had its precedent in the master plan, which named the object of exclusion as "families of lower economic status" (Chicago Plan Commission 1943, 95). Public housing and, by extension, its residents had for so long been placed in the "bad" category that they had very few protectors.

Indeed, the officials who summarily dismissed North Kenwood–Oakland's poor, displaced families were not alone in undercutting the entitlement of public housing residents to the buildings and neighborhoods they had long called home. During this same time, the U.S. Congress was hacking away at the funding and authority of the Department of Housing and Urban Development (Dreier, Mollenkopf, and Swanstrom 2004, 138–46). The Quality Housing and Work Responsibility Act of 1998 rescinded one-for-one replacement rules, allowing public housing authorities to demolish public housing without building commensurate replacement apartments and thereby lowering the supply of housing for poor families in cities across the country.[11] The land ceded by the removal of public housing, which is often located near city centers that elites are redefining as "prime" real estate, is thus open for reclamation (Wyly and Hammel 1999). The *relational* nature of class is once again apparent in urban space: one group loses ground (in a literal sense) just as it becomes more valuable, while another group appropriates the land and profits from it.

After public housing residents in North Kenwood–Oakland were denied the right to participate in planning for the future of the neighborhood in which they had once lived, and as the neighborhood became more and more gentrified, it was soon decided that the buildings themselves should be demolished. By the mid-1990s, there were heated debates over how much, if any, of the public housing demolished in the Lakefront Properties should be replaced. A group of black middle and upper class North Kenwood–Oakland residents waged a case against replacement public housing apartments by arguing that concentrations of public housing in black neighborhoods levied a negative economic toll on black neighborhoods and their black residents and thus constituted racial discrimination (Pattillo 2007). This gloomy reality would persist, they maintained, if new public housing was rebuilt in the neighborhood. It would stymie their struggle to *reverse* years of disinvestment, depopulation, and decay.

While such arguments are clearly reminiscent of the exclusionary practices apparent in white resistance to black settlement and middle class resistance to lower class settlement, I return to the topic of race to argue that it is not so simple. With nearly one-half of its housing stock publicly subsidized and a poverty rate of over 60 percent when the planning process began, North Kenwood–Oakland was bearing more than its fair share of low-income housing and poor people. Even with this concentration, when there was a chance to demolish the high-rises and be rid of the projects forever, local leaders like Shirley Newsome and the local alderman Toni Preckwinkle worked hard to broker an agreement that would allow at least some of the displaced families to come back. Urban renewal and conservation in Hyde Park allowed for a paltry 120 units of public housing in the whole neighborhood, sixty of which were reserved for senior citizens (Hirsch 1983, 163; see also Abrahamson 1959, ch. 16). Other Chicago neighborhoods virulently protested plans for a mere three public housing units (Fran Spielman, "Scattered-Site Could Spark Flight from City, Daley Says."

Chicago Sun-Times, April 29, 1996, 6). North Kenwood–Oakland, on the other hand, approved 240 replacement apartments for public housing residents on top of the hundreds of apartments set aside for low-income families that already existed. Given the comparisons, conservation in North Kenwood–Oakland was wildly progressive and *inclusive.*

The point is this: when we look at the importance and interaction of class *and race,* the North Kenwood–Oakland case illustrates the differential abilities of neighborhoods, as organizations, to succeed in their efforts at social closure. African American North Kenwood–Oakland residents were not simply battling, or trying to prevent, public housing and the poor people it sheltered; they were trying to prevent the possibility that the neighborhood would become invisible again because of both its blackness and its poorness. The neighborhood was embroiled in two systems of categorical inequality— race and class. Like the black middle class youth in the chapter by Lacy and Harris, North Kenwood–Oakland's black elite placed a high value on their black identity and thus could not as easily allow for the wholesale exclusion of poor African Americans because doing so would constitute a challenge to that racial collectivity. Moreover, black residents were cognizant of the fact that they remained tied to poor blacks as the out-group in processes of racial social closure by whites. Yet having fully learned the lessons of a history in which black neighborhoods are disadvantaged but poor black neighborhoods are left for dead, North Kenwood–Oakland residents saw putting a check on, but not completely excluding, public housing as part of their strategy to prevent this race- and class-based doom.

Conclusion

The study of social class has, as the chapters in this volume suggest, been one that focuses on the impact of social class position on individual outcomes. While useful, this approach pays too little attention to the crucial institutional patterns through which elite groups maintain boundaries and hoard opportunities. As I have shown in this chapter, the use of class position to exclude individuals who are poor is a crucial pattern in neighborhoods. Indeed, this chapter provides clear evidence of exclusion. From the first utilization of the conservation area idea through its legislative manifestations and practical applications, the point has been to hoard and guard resources in one place—in white North Kenwood–Oakland, in interracial but middle class Hyde Park—and concomitantly to withhold resources from other places, thereby writing class onto neighborhoods and perpetuating class (and race) inequalities. The history of conservation in North Kenwood–Oakland exists within a series of policy decisions and actions by elites to shape the city in ways that maintain class (and race) privilege. The national policy context—in which the federal government has been deeply implicated in the class and racial stratification of urban space (Bauman

1987; Biondi 2003; Dahl 1961; Gillette 1995; Gotham 2002; Hartman 2002; Jackson 1985; O'Connor 1999; Seligman 2005; Sugrue 1996)—grounds the micro-level actions and arrangements in areas like North Kenwood–Oakland where middle class and aspiring middle class organizations, like neighborhoods and universities, have wanted to create and then protect residential spaces that reflect and reproduce their class position. Activists achieve these ends through efforts at social closure, or exclusion, and through opportunity hoarding, or the securing of mobility-enhancing social goods for the sole use of those within the organization. The result is the shuffling around and dispossession of poor households to fit the tastes of urban elites for what is "good" and "prime" and what should be "protected" and conserved. In sum, this chapter highlights the processes of exclusion. The study of social class would benefit by increasing attention to the crucial processes of marshaling resources to exclude others and thus hoard opportunities.

This chapter also points out the inadequacy of studying either class or race and illustrates the entanglement of race and class. As I have shown, during the post–World War II period, race was an easy and generally effective shorthand for class. Separating the poor from the middle class was often achieved by separating blacks from whites. Gradually, however, race-based exclusion became less legally available. The terms then shifted more squarely onto class as the basis of exclusion. At this point, even African Americans could take advantage of such tools to enact their own version of opportunity hoarding. I have demonstrated how African Americans in North Kenwood–Oakland worked vigorously to prevent groups they saw as undesirable from moving into their neighborhood. This chapter, then, suggests the growing importance of class, particularly among African Americans, although the latter story must always be set in the context of collective racial disadvantage and exclusion. In general, considering class is not enough, and an exclusive emphasis on racial segregation also is flawed. Instead, as part of the American experience, class is entwined with *and inflects* race to erect complex systems of hierarchy, domination, and disadvantage.

Notes

1. North Kenwood–Oakland is the neighborhood's real name, as are the names of the individuals quoted.

2. There have been a few attempts to identify the community areas in Chicago that are undergoing gentrification using comparable demographic indicators. D. Garth Taylor and Sylvia Puente (2004) list both Kenwood and Oakland among the "most gentrifying areas" from 1990 to 2000. Nancy Hudspeth and Janet Smith (2004) include only Kenwood on their list of gentrifying community areas. In personal communications, however, one of the authors wrote,

"Keep in mind this is all based on census data—2000 is the most current and a lot has changed since then. We are seeing gentrification in many near south areas now, including Grand Blvd (Bronzeville), Douglas, Oakland and Bridgeport." Elvin Wyly and Daniel Hammel (1999) list neither Oakland nor North Kenwood as core or fringe gentrifying areas based on data from 1960 to 1990, although they do list South Kenwood as one of Chicago's gentrifying neighborhoods.

3. Mortgage lending data for 2003 show that of the 127 loans made in the Oakland neighborhood, 32 percent went to families with incomes between $56,000 and $82,000, and 39 percent went to families with incomes above $82,000. I report only the data from Oakland because the Kenwood data are complicated by the mixing of North and South Kenwood (see Woodstock Institute 2003).

4. Together these acts granted powers of eminent domain for the "removal of dilapidated buildings and other obstructions"; zoning powers for the "discontinuance of property uses that downgrade the neighborhood"; aggressive code enforcement with the ability to place liens on private property; and state and federal loans for rehabilitation and new construction (Community Conservation Board of Chicago 1957, 10–11, 16; see also Hirsch 1983, 136.)

5. The complete introduction to the act reads: "It is hereby found and declared that there exist in many urban communities within this State conservation areas, as defined herein; that these conservation areas are rapidly deteriorating and declining in desirability as residential communities and may soon become slum and blighted areas if their decline is not checked; that the stable economic and physical development of these areas is endangered by the presence of blighting factors as manifested by progressive and advanced deterioration of structures, by the over-use of housing and other facilities, by a lack of physical maintenance of existing structures, by obsolete and inadequate community facilities and a lack of sound community planning; that as a result and concomitant of the decline of conservation areas, there is a growth of delinquency, crime, and of housing and zoning law violations in such areas, together with an abnormal exodus of families; that the decline of these areas threatens to impair the tax base of such communities and produce the conditions characteristic of slum and blighted areas which threaten the health, safety, morals, and welfare of the public; that in order to promote and protect the health, safety, morals and welfare of the public it is necessary to provide for the protection of such conservation areas and prevent their deterioration into slum and blighted areas. The granting to the municipalities of this State of the powers herein provided is directed to that end, and the use of such rights and powers for the prevention of slums is hereby declared to be a public use essential to the public interest" (Illinois Revised Statues 1961).

6. Zorita Mikva (1951, 66) reported even greater expenditures on enforcing restrictive covenants: "During 1944 [OKPOA's] budget was $13,243, over one-fourth of this spent on legal fees."

7. Another example of this convoluted language is the following: "As developed in this study, conservation—in many areas, at least—must really mean maintenance of such communities at roughly a middle class economic level. This, of course, means de facto exclusion of certain groups on economic grounds."

The suggestion here seems to be that de facto exclusion is acceptable, or at least necessary. As long as it is not legally inscribed, then, exclusion is a reasonable strategy.

8. Many other players were involved in the establishment of Hyde Park–South Kenwood as a conservation area. The Hyde Park–Kenwood Community Conference (1952) was a much more liberal organization than the University of Chicago and worked hard to keep the issues of racial and class integration on the table, but it was often overpowered by the university and its community development arm, the South East Chicago Commission; on this history, see Abrahamson (1959) and Rossi and Dentler (1961). On various neighborhoods' reaction to potential public housing in Chicago, see Meyerson and Banfield (1955).

9. A similar process occurred with the choosing of the Hyde Park–South Kenwood Conservation Community Council. Community representatives from the Hyde Park–Kenwood Community Conference secured three seats on the CCC, but Julian Levi, executive director of the university-financed South East Chicago Commission, "attended Council meetings and acted in a quasi-*ex-officio* capacity" (Rossi and Dentler 1961, 147). Given Levi's "aggressive" visible presence (75), the university's meddling in the North Kenwood–Oakland CCC was comparatively minimal.

10. From the transcript of the public meeting regarding CCC nominations, June 6, 1990, Department of Planning and Development (DPD) files, pp. 38–40.

11. Quality Housing and Work Responsibility Act of 1998, Title V, "Public Housing and Tenant-Based Assistance Reform" of PL 105-276, accessed at http://frwebgate.access.gpo.gov/cgi-bin/getdoc.cgi?dbname=105_cong_public_laws&docid=f:publ276.105.pdf (accessed July 1, 2005). Other provisions of the law also decrease the number of hard units for very low-income families. Section 513 on income targeting establishes that no fewer than 40 percent of new public housing residents must have incomes below 30 percent of the area median income—that is, they must be very poor families—but it also requires an "income-mixing by bringing higher income tenants into lower income projects." It further prohibits the concentration of poor families. Section 514 repeals federal preferences for very low-income or housing-challenged families in favor of a preference system created by each local public housing authority. Section 531 eliminates the requirement that demolished public housing be replaced on a one-for-one basis. See also Popkin (2000).

References

Abrahamson, Julia. 1959. *A Neighborhood Finds Itself.* New York: Harper & Row.

Abu-Lughod, Janet L. 1994. *From Urban Village to East Village: The Battle for New York's Lower East Side.* Cambridge, Mass.: Blackwell.

Bauman, John F. 1987. *Public Housing, Race, and Renewal: Urban Planning in Philadelphia.* Philadelphia, Pa.: Temple University Press.

Biondi, Martha. 2003. *To Stand and Fight: The Struggle for Civil Rights in Postwar New York City.* Cambridge, Mass.: Harvard University Press.

Blau, Peter and Otis Dudley Duncan. 1967. *The American Occupational Structure.* New York: Wiley.

Bourdieu, Pierre. 1984. Distinction: *A Social Critique of the Judgement of Taste.* Cambridge, Mass.: Harvard University Press.

Boyd, Michelle. 2000. "Reconstructing Bronzeville: Racial Nostalgia and Neighborhood Redevelopment." *Journal of Urban Affairs* 22(2): 107–22.

Brown-Saracino, Japonica. 2004. "Social Preservationists and the Quest for Authentic Community." *City and Community* 3(2): 135–56.

Chicago Plan Commission. 1943. *Master Plan of Residential Land Use of Chicago.* Chicago, Ill.: Chicago Plan Commission.

Clark, Terry Nichols, editor. 2004. *The City as an Entertainment Machine.* London: JAI.

Commission on Chicago Landmarks. 1992. *Revised North Kenwood Multiple Resource District.* Chicago, Ill.: City of Chicago, Landmarks Commission.

Community Conservation Board of Chicago. 1957. *Save Your Neighborhood: The Chicago Conservation Program.* Chicago, Ill.: Community Conservation Board.

Dahl, Robert Alan. 1961. *Who Governs? Democracy and Power in an American City.* New Haven, Ct.: Yale University Press.

Dávila, Arlene M. 2004. *Barrio Dreams: Puerto Ricans, Latinos, and the Neoliberal City.* Berkeley, Calif.: University of California Press.

DiMaggio, Paul. 1982. "Cultural Capital and School Success: The Impact of Status Culture Participation on the Grades of U.S. High School Students." *American Sociological Review* 47(2): 189–201.

Dreier, Peter, John Mollenkopf, and Todd Swanstrom. 2004. *Place Matters: Metropolitics for the Twenty-First Century.* Lawrence, Kan.: University Press of Kansas.

Duncan, Otis Dudley, and Beverly Duncan. 1957. *The Negro Population of Chicago: A Study of Residential Succession.* Chicago, Ill.: University of Chicago Press.

Flanagan, R. M. 1997. "The Housing Act of 1954: The Sea Change in National Urban Policy." *Urban Affairs Review* 33(November): 265–86.

Freeman, Lance. 2006. *There Goes the Hood: Views of Gentrification from the Ground Up.* Philadelphia, Pa.: Temple University Press.

Gamm, Gerald. 1999. *Urban Exodus: Why the Jews Left Boston and the Catholics Stayed.* Cambridge, Mass.: Harvard University Press.

Gans, Herbert J. 1991. *People, Plans, and Policies: Essays on Poverty, Racism, and Other National Urban Problems.* New York: Columbia University Press.

Gillette, Howard. 1995. *Between Justice and Beauty: Race, Planning and the Failure of Urban Policy in Washington, D.C.* Baltimore, Md.: Johns Hopkins University Press.

Gotham, Kevin Fox. 2002. *Race, Real Estate and Uneven Development: The Kansas City Experience, 1900–2000.* Albany, N.Y.: State University of New York Press.

Grossman, Ron, and Charles Leroux. 2006. "The Unmaking of a Ghetto: How the North Kenwood–Oakland Neighborhood Came Back from the Grave." *Chicago Tribune Magazine*, January 29, 2006: 10.

Halpern, Robert. 1995. *Rebuilding the Inner City: A History of Neighborhood Initiatives to Address Poverty in the United States.* New York: Columbia University Press.

Hanchett, Thomas W. 2000. "The Other 'Subsidized Housing': Federal Aid to Suburbanization, 1940s–1960s." In *From Tenements to the Taylor Homes*, edited by John F. Bauman, Roger Biles, and Kristin M. Szylvian. University Park, Pa.: Pennsylvania State University Press.

Hartman, Chester. 2002. *City for Sale: The Transformation of San Francisco*, rev. ed. Berkeley, Calif.: University of California Press.

Hedlund, Nevin. 1989. "Too Good to Be True?" *Inland Architect* 33(1): 27–30.
Hirsch, Arnold. 1983. *Making the Second Ghetto: Race and Housing in Chicago, 1940–1960.* Cambridge: Cambridge University Press.
———. 2000. "Searching for a 'Sound Negro Policy': A Racial Agenda for the Housing Acts of 1949 and 1954." *Housing Policy Debate* 11(2): 393–441.
Hudspeth, Nancy, and Janet Smith. 2004. "The Effects of Gentrification in Chicago: Displacement and Disparity." Paper presented to the annual conference of the Urban Affairs Association. Washington, March 31–April 3, 2004.
Hyde Park–Kenwood Community Conference. 1952. *Community Appraisal Study: Report on Housing and Social Survey.* Chicago, Ill.: Hyde Park–Kenwood Community Conference and South Side Planning Board.
Hyra, Derek. 2008. *The New Urban Renewal: The Economic Transformation of Harlem and Bronzeville.* Chicago, Ill.: University of Chicago Press.
Illinois Housing Development Authority. 1990. *Kenwood–Oakland Neighborhood Conservation Plan.* Springfield, Ill.: Illinois Housing Development Authority.
Illinois Revised Statutes. 1961. *Urban Renewal and Consolidation Act of 1961,* ch. 67-1/2, sects. 91, 101–91, 136. (Revised 1989).
Jackson, John L. 2001. *Harlemworld: Doing Race and Class in Contemporary Black America.* Chicago, Ill.: University of Chicago Press.
Jackson, Kenneth T. 1985. *Crabgrass Frontier: The Suburbanization of the United States.* New York: Oxford University Press.
Lamont, Michèle. 1992. *Money, Morals and Manners.* Chicago, Ill.: University of Chicago Press.
Lareau, Annette. 1987. "Social Class Differences in Family-School Relationships: The Importance of Cultural Capital." *Sociology of Education* 60(2): 73–85.
———. 2003. *Unequal Childhoods: Class, Race, and Family Life.* Berkeley, Calif.: University of California Press.
Lloyd, Richard. 2005. *Neo-Bohemia: Art and Commerce in the Postindustrial City.* New York: Routledge.
Logan, John R., and Harvey L. Molotch. 1987. *Urban Fortunes: The Political Economy of Place.* Berkeley, Calif.: University of California Press.
Long, Herman, and Charles Johnson. 1947. *People vs. Property: Race Restrictive Covenants in Housing.* Nashville, Tenn.: Fisk University Press.
Massey, Douglas S. 1996. "The Age of Extremes: Concentrated Affluence and Poverty in the Twenty-First Century." *Demography* 33(4): 395–412.
Massey, Douglas, and Nancy Denton. 1993. *American Apartheid: Segregation and the Making of the Underclass.* Cambridge, Mass.: Harvard University Press.
Massey, Douglas, and Mary Fischer. 2003. "The Geography of Inequality in the United States, 1950–1990." *Brookings-Wharton Papers on Urban Affairs* (2003): 1–40.
Mele, Christopher. 2000. *Selling the Lower East Side: Culture, Real Estate, and Resistance in New York City.* Minneapolis, Minn.: University of Minnesota Press.
Metropolitan Housing and Planning Council (MHPC). 1953. *Conservation: A Report to the Conservation Committee of the Metropolitan Housing and Planning Council.* Chicago, Ill.: MHPC.
Meyerson, Martin, and Edward C. Banfield. 1955. *Politics, Planning, and the Public Interest: The Case of Public Housing in Chicago.* Glencoe, Ill.: Free Press.
Mikva, Zorita. 1951. "The Neighborhood Improvement Association: A Counter-force to the Expansion of Chicago's Negro Population." Master's thesis, University of Chicago.

Neighborhood Planning Committee. 1989. *North Kenwood–Oakland Neighborhood Planning Process*. Chicago, Ill.: City of Chicago, Department of Planning.

Oakland–Kenwood Planning Association. 1952. "A Report to the Oakland–Kenwood Community." Mimeography in Collections of the Chicago History Museum.

O'Connor, Alice. 1999. "Swimming Against the Tide: A Brief History of Federal Housing Policy in Poor Communities." In *Urban Problems and Community Development*, edited by Ronald Ferguson and William Dickens. Washington: Brookings Institution Press.

Park, Robert E. 1936. "Human Ecology." *American Journal of Sociology* 42(1): 1–15.

Pattillo, Mary. 2007. *Black on the Block: The Politics of Race and Class in the City*. Chicago, Ill.: University of Chicago Press.

Perez, Gina. 2002. "The Other 'Real World': Gentrification and the Social Construction of Place in Chicago." *Urban Anthropology* 31(1): 37–68.

Plotkin, Wendy. 1999. "Deeds of Mistrust: Race, Housing, and Restrictive Covenants in Chicago, 1900–1953." Ph.D. dissertation, University of Illinois at Chicago.

Popkin, Susan. 2000. *The Hidden War: Crime and the Tragedy of Public Housing in Chicago*. New Brunswick, N.J.: Rutgers University Press.

Prince, Sabiyha. 2004. *Constructing Belonging: Class, Race, and Harlem's Professional Workers*. New York: Routledge.

Radford, Gail. 1996. *Modern Housing for America: Policy Struggles in the New Deal Era*. Chicago, Ill.: University of Chicago Press.

Rossi, Peter Henry, and Robert A. Dentler. 1961. *The Politics of Urban Renewal: The Chicago Findings*. New York: Free Press of Glencoe.

Schietinger, Egbert Frederick. 1948. "Real Estate Transfers During Negro Invasion: A Case Study." Master's thesis, University of Chicago.

Seligman, Amanda. 2005. *Block by Black: Neighborhoods and Public Policy on Chicago's West Side*. Chicago, Ill.: University of Chicago Press.

Smith, Neil. 1996. *The New Urban Frontier: Gentrification and the Revanchist City*. New York: Routledge.

Spain, Daphne. 1993. "Been-Heres Versus Come-Heres: Negotiating Conflicting Community Identities." *Journal of the American Planning Association* 59(Spring): 156–71.

Street, Paul. 2005. *Still Separate, Unequal: Race, Place, Policy, and the State of Black Chicago*. Chicago, Ill.: Chicago Urban League.

Sugrue, Thomas J. 1996. *The Origins of the Urban Crisis: Race and Inequality in Postwar Detroit*. Princeton, N.J.: Princeton University Press.

Taylor, D. Garth, and Sylvia Puente. 2004. "Immigration, Gentrification and Chicago Race/Ethnic Relations in the New Global Era." Paper presented at The Changing Face of Metropolitan Chicago, May 12–13, 2004. Accessed at http://www.about.chapinhall.org/uuc/presentations/TaylorPuentePaper.pdf.

Taylor, Monique M. 2002. *Harlem Between Heaven and Hell*. Minneapolis, Minn.: University of Minnesota Press.

Tilly, Charles. 1998. *Durable Inequality*. Berkeley, Calif.: University of California Press.

Von Hoffman, Alexander. 2000. "A Study in Contradictions: The Origins and Legacy of the Housing Act of 1949." *Housing Policy Debate* 11(2): 299–326.

Wacquant, Loïc. 1994. "The New Urban Color Line: The State and Fate of the Ghetto in Postfordist America." In *Social Theory and the Politics of Identity,* edited by Craig J. Calhoun. Cambridge, Mass.: Blackwell.

———. 1997. "Three Pernicious Premises in the Study of the American Ghetto." *International Journal of Urban and Regional Research* 21(2): 341–53.

Weaver, Robert Clifton. 1945. *Hemmed In: ABCs of Race Restrictive Housing Covenants.* Chicago, Ill.: American Council on Race Relations.

Weber, Max. 1946. *From Max Weber: Essays in Sociology.* H. H. Gerth and C. Wright Mills, editors. New York: Oxford University Press.

Woodstock Institute. 2003. "Community Area 36—Oakland." *Community Lending Fact Book—City of Chicago.* Accessed July 1, 2005 at http://woodstockinst.org/document/2003-36.pdf.

Wyly, Elvin, and Daniel Hammel. 1999. "Islands of Decay in Seas of Renewal: Housing Policy and the Resurgence of Gentrification." *Housing Policy Debate* 10(4): 711–81.

Zukin, Sharon. 1982. *Loft Living: Culture and Capital in Urban Change.* Baltimore, Md.: Johns Hopkins University Press.

Chapter 10

What Does Class Inequality Among Women Look Like? A Comparison with Men and Families, 1970 to 2000

LESLIE MCCALL

A T LEAST some of the impetus for a new book about class is driven by the steep rise in market earnings inequality in the United States and other advanced industrial nations during the 1980s and 1990s. In the United States, this rise in earnings inequality occurred for women as well as for men. Although estimates vary somewhat depending on data sources and definitions, the level of earnings inequality is roughly the same for men and women, and the rate of increase in earnings inequality is also comparable. This is particularly true for measures of inequality that tap into the top half of the earnings distribution: the ratio of earnings for college-educated versus high school-educated workers and the ratio of earnings between the top 10 percent and middle ten percent of the earnings distribution (for the latter, see figures 10.1 through 10.4).[1] Despite this similarity between men and women in the level and growth of inequality, there has been little discussion of inequality among women, especially relative to the attention devoted to inequality among men, inequality among families, and inequality between men and women. Why is this?

I focus on two factors that I believe underlie the neglect of "class" analysis among women (more on definitions in a moment). The first is a perspective that might be held especially among scholars of gender inequality: that the same level and trend in earnings inequality may mean something very

Figure 10.1   Weekly Earnings Ratio for Female Workers, 1970 to 2000

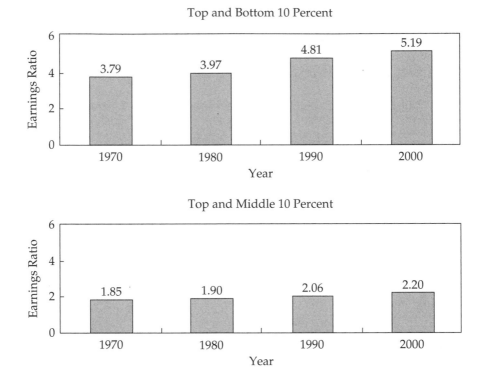

Top and Bottom 10 Percent

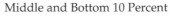

Top and Middle 10 Percent

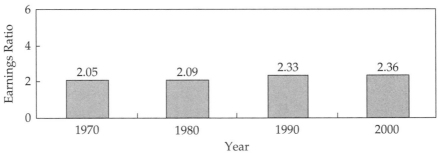

Middle and Bottom 10 Percent

Source: Author's compilation from the Annual March Current Population Surveys; see Data Appendix for further details.

Figure 10.2   Weekly Earnings Ratio for Male Workers, 1970 to 2000

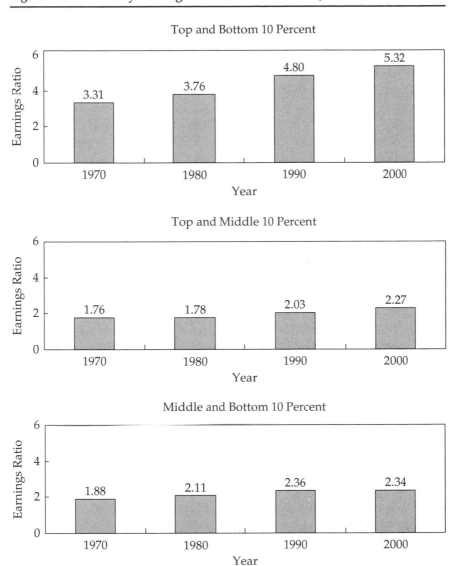

Source: Author's compilation from the Annual March Current Population Surveys; see Data Appendix for further details.

Figure 10.3   Weekly Earnings Ratio for Full-Time Female Workers, 1970 to 2000

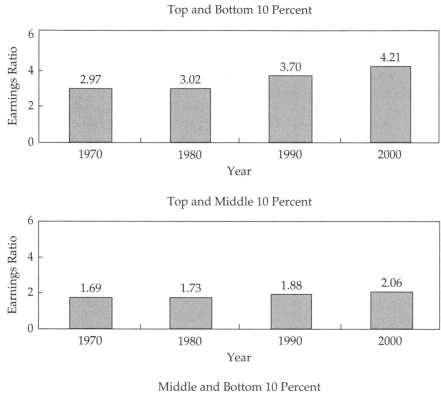

Top and Bottom 10 Percent

Top and Middle 10 Percent

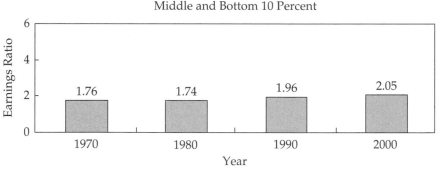

Middle and Bottom 10 Percent

Source: Author's compilation from the Annual March Current Population Surveys; see Data Appendix for further details.

Figure 10.4   Weekly Earnings Ratio for Full-Time Male Workers, 1970 to 2000

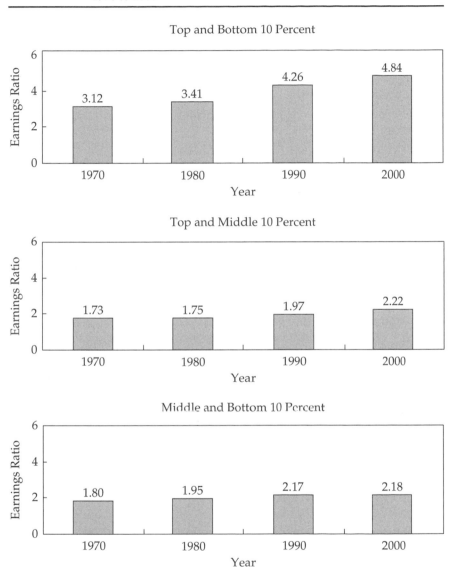

Source: Author's compilation from the Annual March Current Population Surveys; see Data Appendix for further details.

different for men and women. That is, inequalities related to social class may "work" differently for women than for men. Among women, for example, rising class inequality may be considered a reflection of growing gender equality as opportunities for women expand across the occupational hierarchy. I lay out this position in greater detail in the first part of this chapter and then provide a multidimensional portrait of what class inequality among women looks like in terms of the occupational and family characteristics of women in the top, middle, and bottom tenths of the female earnings distribution.[2] I provide a similar portrait of men and examine changes for both men and women over the decades between 1970 and 2000. In describing these changes, I find evidence to support the claim that inequalities among men and women are qualitatively different if quantitatively similar, suggesting that we do need to examine gender and class inequalities simultaneously. I also find, however, that this applies much more to the earlier time period than to the later time period.

The second factor that may limit the amount of attention devoted to class inequalities among women is another indication of how class works differently for men and women: the assumption that a woman's class position is determined less by her own earnings—and therefore by earnings inequality among women—than by her family income, which, if she is married, is composed primarily of her husband's earnings. This assumption stems from the breadwinner-homemaker model of class analysis in which men are the primary earners and women are the primary caretakers (Goldthorpe 1983, 2000; Western and Baxter 2001). Although much has been written on this subject, and more generally on the changes in families and employment structures wrought by married women's increasing employment, it is difficult to assess this claim because it has not been examined in a direct way.

In the second part of the chapter, I try to provide a precise measure of the degree to which women's and men's position in the earnings distribution differs from their position in the family income distribution. I focus on measuring the relative roles of family factors and an individual's own employment and earnings in determining his or her economic location, with one's own individual earnings presumably playing a greater role for men and family factors a greater role for women. This pattern should change over time, however, as family factors become less important for women and more important for men. As in the first part of the chapter, I find that the association between one's own earnings and family income is more similar among men and women than it once was, but that the association among women is still just six-tenths the size of the association among men—highlighting once again the need to understand how class continues to work differently for women than for men.

As should be clear by now, in assessing these two challenges to a class analysis of women, I focus less on conceptual definitions of class than on empirical definitions that are consistent with the voluminous literature on rising earnings and income inequality in the United States (see, for example, Katz and Autor 1999). My approach involves a "gradational account of class in which class is itself directly identified within inequalities in income" (Wright 2001, 23; Grusky and Weeden, this volume; Wright, this volume). This differs from a more conceptually oriented approach that begins "with the social relations that determine the access of people to economic resources"—and, one might add, to other kinds of outcomes in the arenas of politics and culture (see, for example, Hout, this volume; Weeden and Grusky 2005).

Although the social relations that I emphasize in this chapter—the social relations of gender and the family—may not be the ones that some have foremost in mind, they most definitely determine access to economic resources, though in ways that have changed significantly over time. My objective is to focus on the empirical evidence of those historic changes using the kind of multidimensional approach advocated by Grusky and Weeden in this volume in a descriptive way to understand how changes in the United States in occupational status and family formation practices are coinciding with increasing earnings and income inequality as well as declining gender earnings inequality. Thus, I go beyond the focus on earnings and income alone. Given the paucity of research on inequality among women, I hope the findings in this chapter will spark both greater theoretical work and more extensive empirical tests and elaborations.

Earnings Inequality: Does it Mean the Same Thing for Men and Women?

The first reason why there may have been little exploration of class differences among women, especially relative to class differences among men, stems from the idea that women are crowded into a small number of female-dominated jobs in which differences among them in earnings and status are minimal.[3] Since this might especially have been the case historically, some accommodation must be made for changes over time. Such an accommodation can be made easily: if earnings inequality has risen among women over time, it should be taken less as an indicator of growing class inequality among women and more as an indicator of expanding occupational opportunities for women. In this view, earnings inequalities were not large to begin with and have grown over time as a natural result of greater gender equity. Part of this account—that earnings inequality could be a natural result of expanding opportunities for women—is certainly plausible.

However, the other part of this account does not accord well with the actual trends in earnings inequality among women, since levels of earnings inequality have been comparable among women and men since at least the late 1960s. As shown in figures 10.1 and 10.2, earnings ratios between the top and middle, middle and bottom, and top and bottom are generally higher among women in the earlier period and comparable or slightly lower in the later period, if all part-time and full-time workers are included (for details on the data, see the data appendix). Since part of the disparity among women is due to disparities in hours worked—the weekly hours of women at the top are typically greater than the weekly hours of women at the bottom—the ratios are larger among men once hours are controlled; see figures 10.3 and 10.4, which include full-time, full-year workers only. Levels of inequality increased substantially over time for both men and women, though somewhat more for men than for women (by 55 percent for full-time men, overall, and 42 percent for full-time women). Therefore, it cannot be said that inequality among women was negligible historically because of the crowding of women into a few low-wage jobs.

There is a second possible view that is closely related to the first one. In this view, it is not necessarily disputed that earnings inequalities are as large among women as they are among men, both in the past and in the present. In this sense, this view accords better with actual trends. Rather, the argument is that the two types of inequality are not strictly comparable because the underlying distributions are so different. Specifically, although the *relative* distance between the top and middle and bottom may be the same for men and women, the *absolute* distance is not. Absolute differences are in fact considerably smaller among women as a result of lower mean earnings and a smaller range of earnings, especially in the earlier period. For example, in 1970 the ratio of average earnings among the top and bottom 10 percent was greater for women than for men (3.79 versus 3.31; see figures 10.1 and 10.2), but the absolute difference was little more than half as large for women as it was for men ($463.53 versus $805.86; see tables 10.1 and 10.2). As in the first view, then, widening inequality could be considered a natural result of widening opportunities for women. At the point of equality in distributions, in which *both* relative and absolute disparities are comparable for men and women, earnings differences can take on the same meaning among women as they do among men—that is, they can be interpreted unequivocally as class differences.

These are, of course, highly stylized views, and when pressed, almost no one would argue that class differences among women never existed or do not exist today. Nor would proponents of these views argue that class differences among women consisted primarily of differences outside of paid work, such as differences in family background, marital status, husbands' income, and educational level. Important qualitative and quantitative differences among women have always existed in the realm of paid work as well: for example, between the work that household servants performed and the work that office administrators performed. Still, there is something valid in the objections raised earlier to treating measures of

Table 10.1   Weekly Earnings and Occupations of Women in the Top, Middle, and Bottom 10 Percent (2000 Dollars)

	1970	1980	1990	2000
Top 10 percent earnings range	$558.33 to $739.26	$622.53 to $817.51	$764.47 to $1049.33	$920.75 to $1346.15
Top 10 percent earnings (average)	$629.83	$705.51	$885.29	$1,088.79
Managers	7.21%	11.88%	24.43%	32.32%
Professionals	40.77	44.90	46.45	44.13
Noncollege teachers	20.62	16.25	12.91	12.59
Nurses	8.16	8.80	11.44	8.16
Professors and scientists	1.50	2.26	2.50	2.99
Doctors, lawyers, and judges	0.35	0.74	1.48	1.77
Sales	1.67	3.12	6.98	8.14
Clerical	29.31	26.01	14.17	8.97
Secretaries	10.74	6.38	3.32	1.55
Services	3.28	3.00	1.68	1.99
Crafts	1.36	2.46	2.30	1.88
Operators and laborers	9.54	8.60	3.83	2.45
Middle 10 percent earnings range	$319.05 to $364.17	$347.15 to $400.04	$393.19 to $465.85	$460.67 to $532.14
Middle 10 percent earnings (average)	$340.81	$371.21	$429.05	$493.82
Managers	2.77%	6.71%	12.00%	15.24%
Professionals	7.53	13.82	17.56	21.44
Noncollege teachers	3.29	4.10	4.54	5.75
Nurses	2.14	3.06	2.15	2.99
Sales	3.57	3.19	7.81	9.11
Clerical	38.02	45.90	41.05	35.15
Secretaries	10.66	14.11	12.01	7.12
Services	10.74	10.94	8.35	8.46
Crafts	1.65	2.22	2.88	2.73
Operators and laborers	30.49	16.72	9.99	7.34

(continued)

Table 10.1   *Continued*

	1970	1980	1990	2000
Bottom 10 percent earnings range	$140.23 to $190.85	$147.71 to $206.07	$149.90 to $216.53	$168.54 to $243.11
Bottom 10 percent earnings (average)	$166.30	$177.85	$183.98	$209.60
Managers	1.64%	3.29%	3.42%	5.02%
Professionals	6.57	9.62	10.02	10.93
Noncollege teachers	3.69	3.47	3.76	4.33
Nurses	2.35	2.07	0.67	0.63
Sales	8.59	8.34	16.08	14.97
Clerical	18.65	31.56	23.00	22.03
Secretaries	5.41	6.54	5.14	3.93
Services	21.23	27.98	27.99	26.94
Crafts	0.87	1.35	1.81	2.23
Operators and laborers	26.01	16.61	16.49	16.19

Source: Author's compilation from the Annual March Current Population Surveys; see Data Appendix for further details.
Note: Percentages for the seven major categories sum to 100 within each year and earnings group (top, middle, and bottom 10 percent). Percentages of subcategories are percentage of total, not of subcategory. Part-time workers are included.

earnings inequality among women in exactly the same way as measures of inequality among men. In this section, I take these objections seriously and ask, quite literally, what does class inequality among women look like, and how has it changed over the past three decades? I answer this question by examining the earnings, occupations, and family characteristics of three groups of women—the top, middle, and bottom tenths of the female earnings distribution—and then comparing these patterns to those for men.

Some of the objections raised earlier are clearly borne out in the occupational distributions provided in tables 10.1 and 10.2. In 1970 women at the top were concentrated in clerical work (29.3 percent), with one-third of these employed as secretaries. Another one-fifth were primary and secondary school teachers, and 10.9 percent worked in manual occupations, larger than the share of nurses (8.2 percent). The rest were distributed among assorted professions (roughly 10 percent) and management (7.2 percent). Overall, then, over two-thirds of women in the top tenth were clerical workers, teachers, manual workers, or nurses, while only an additional one-fifth were employed in the more elite male-dominated occupations (management, law, medicine, and other professions). Although most of these women were

Table 10.2   Weekly Earnings and Occupations of Men in the Top, Middle, and Bottom 10 Percent (2000 Dollars)

	1970	1980	1990	2000
Top 10 percent earnings range	$1011.25 to $1381.19	$1107.81 to $1546.31	$1174.25 to $720.06	$1353.19 to $2049.71
Top 10 percent earnings (average)	$1,154.25	$1,259.35	$1,372.10	$1,630.10
Managers	25.91%	28.28%	31.21%	33.85%
Professionals	34.13	29.64	30.51	34.40
Professors and scientists	3.83	3.48	3.45	2.37
Doctors, lawyers, and judges	0.89	2.62	3.52	4.14
Sales	7.54	7.25	11.82	12.91
Clerical	3.06	2.70	2.57	1.80
Services	1.35	0.52	0.52	0.25
Crafts	19.00	21.05	15.73	11.50
Operators and laborers	9.36	10.40	7.11	4.88
Middle 10 percent earnings range	$622.14 to $687.12	$666.99 to $743.75	$624.60 to $730.07	$670.10 to $769.23
Middle 10 percent earnings (average)	$654.82	$707.41	$675.56	$717.15
Managers	11.09%	13.75%	12.54%	14.21%
Professionals	15.46	20.59	18.09	20.50
Sales	4.80	5.00	10.74	10.90
Clerical	10.57	8.80	6.89	6.99
Services	2.61	2.05	2.69	3.07
Crafts	25.68	25.01	23.99	22.09
Operators and laborers	30.40	24.49	23.70	20.83
Bottom 10 percent earnings range	$276.77 to $400.59	$262.18 to $400.04	$224.34 to $338.96	$240.44 to $365.38
Bottom 10 percent earnings (average)	$348.39	$334.88	$285.66	$306.38
Managers	5.54%	5.14%	3.79%	4.11%
Professionals	6.90	10.49	6.84	6.79

(continued)

Table 10.2   *Continued*

	1970	1980	1990	2000
Sales	3.70	5.30	7.48	7.20
Clerical	5.96	6.17	5.79	6.29
Services	9.85	13.17	14.49	15.50
Crafts	18.69	20.05	18.88	18.78
Operators and laborers	48.08	36.06	35.39	34.11

Source: Author's compilation from the Annual March Current Population Surveys; see Data Appendix for further details.
Note: Percentages for the seven major categories sum to 100 within each year and earnings group (top, middle, and bottom 10 percent). Percentages of subcategories are percentage of total, not of subcategory. Part-time workers are included.

more highly educated than most, this is not a portrait of an especially elite group, at least not by today's standards or by male standards. The weekly average earnings for these women were comparable only to those of men in the middle tenth of the men's earnings distribution ($629.83 for women at the top versus $654.82 for men in the middle).

A quite different portrait emerges three decades later. By 2000 about one-third of women in the top tenth were clerical workers, teachers, nurses, or manual workers (as opposed to over two-thirds in 1970). Nurses were the only group to hold steady in their share of top employment; teachers' share declined from 20.6 to 12.6 percent, clerical workers' from 29.3 to 9.0 percent, and manual laborers' from 10.9 to 4.3 percent. Over half of all women in the top tenth worked in management and other professions. In contrast to popular perceptions, however, only 1.8 percent of high-earning women were employed as doctors, lawyers, or judges. This was five times the share in 1970, but it was still smaller than one would think given the vast increase in female enrollments in law and medical schools, now at near parity (Goldin 2006). Despite the high visibility of these occupations, then, they are actually a relatively small share of overall employment, with only 4.1 percent of men in the top tenth holding such jobs in 2000 (see table 10.2). In addition to these improvements in women's occupational standing, women at the top can no longer be compared to midlevel men in terms of their earnings, which are now well above those of men in the middle tenth ($1,088.79 on average for women in the top tenth versus $717.15 for men in the middle tenth).

We know that inequality among women increased—so women in the middle and bottom tenths could not have done as well as women at the top—but did their occupations and earnings improve as well? At the same time that clerical work decreased markedly among women at the top, it either increased or held relatively steady among women in the middle and bottom.

Women in the middle and bottom tenths also increased their presence in managerial and professional occupations, which accounted for over one-third of all occupations among women in the middle (up from one-tenth in 1970) and 15.9 percent of women in the bottom (up from 8.2 percent in 1970). While some of these are no doubt low-level supervisory positions, and the increase is consistent with an overall increase in "postindustrial" occupations in the economy more broadly, it is noteworthy that men in the middle and bottom tenths did not see as much of an increase in managerial and professional occupations. Employment levels in managerial and professional occupations were virtually the same in 2000 as they were in 1970 for men at the bottom, and they increased from 26.6 percent to 34.7 percent for men in the middle tenth—about the same level of employment for women in the middle tenth in 2000.

While there was a discernible shift to upper-level white collar occupations for women in the middle tenth as employment in service occupations and especially manual occupations declined substantially, there was less evidence of upgrading for women at the bottom as well as for men in the bottom half. For example, there was an increase in the share of low-level service jobs to a little more than one-quarter of all jobs held by women in the bottom tenth. This is three times the share held by women in the middle tenth in 2000. Overall, four out of five jobs for women in the bottom tenth were in manual, clerical, service, and sales occupations. Among men, there was relative stability among the male-dominated occupations in the middle and bottom tenths despite waves of industrial restructuring throughout this period. Male employment in the manual labor occupations ranged from 56 to 66 percent in 1970 and from 43 to 53 percent in 2000.

In sum, among the six groups of women and men in the top, middle, and bottom of the earnings distribution, the most noticeable positive changes in occupational standing occurred for women in the top tenth and, to a somewhat lesser extent, for women in the middle tenth. Although there is gender-based segregation *within* the broad categories of management and the professions, more detailed studies of occupational sex segregation bear these general trends out. Jerry Jacobs (1999) finds, for example, that the largest declines in occupational sex segregation occurred among men and women with a college or postgraduate degree (20- and 17.5-percentage-point declines, respectively, from 1971 to 1997). The next largest declines were for those with less than a high school degree (11.8 points) and some college (10.9 points), while those with a high school degree witnessed only a 4.9-percentage-point decline (see also Cotter, Hermsen, and Vanneman 2004). To explain these differences, Maria Charles and David Grusky (2005) argue that gender inequalities embedded in assumptions of male authority in managerial and professional jobs are easier to challenge than those embedded in hegemonic notions of femininity and masculinity in working class jobs. In addition, or alternatively, job growth was much greater in white collar than in blue collar jobs, facilitating integration more in the former than in the latter (MacLean 2006). The impressive degree of occupational integration and upgrading of women at the top documented here is therefore consistent with a number of different trends and explanations.

At the same time that women at the top made gains in the labor market, family dynamics shifted decisively to the advantage of men and women in the top tenth as well, provided we consider marriage—and other forms of cohabitation, which I do not consider here—to be a net plus economically because of the benefits of pooling earnings and risk and sharing household labor. In 1970 women at the top were *less* likely to be married than women in the middle and especially at the bottom, conforming (some might say) to the Mary Tyler Moore stereotype of an educated woman who sacrifices marriage and family for a career (though almost two-thirds of such women were married as shown in table 10.3) (Havens 1973). By 2000, however, women at the top had completely closed this "marriage gap." Results from a separate analysis of black women show that there was little difference in marriage rates among black women in 1970, but that by 2000 black women at the top were the most likely to be married (47.9 percent versus 39.1 and 31.5 percent in the middle and bottom, respectively).

Because marriage rates fell for all groups—owing, for example, to an increase in divorce and the age of first marriage—these shifts mean that marriage rates fell less for women at the top; in fact, they fell much less than for any other group of men or women.[4] As shown in table 10.3, 64.4 percent of women in the top tenth were married in 1970, as compared to 73.6 and 79.4 percent of women in the middle and bottom tenths, respectively. Between 1970 and 2000, the marriage rate declined by only 2.2 percentage points for women at the top, whereas it declined by 14 to 20 percentage points for the other groups of women. Among men, the declines were even greater, especially for the middle and bottom tenths: in those groups, marriage rates fell by 30 percentage points. Men at the top were more likely than other men to be married in 1970, but now they are even more so, by quite a large margin (74.4 percent versus 56.6 and 43.0 percent for the middle and bottom tenths, respectively). Overall, these patterns hold for both black and white men. For any given year, then, individuals with high earnings are now at least as likely to be married as others (white women), if not more likely than others to be married (black women and men, white men).

In addition to class differences in the likelihood of being married, it is important to know more about who is marrying whom, or what is called "assortative mating" or "marital homogamy." Here we are interested in whether women at the top are reinforcing their gains by marrying men at the top (double-income "yuppies") or whether they are spreading the wealth around by partnering with men of lesser means. We are also interested in men at the top, for traditionally they married women who worked less

Table 10.3   Family Characteristics of Women and Men in the Top, Middle, and Bottom 10 Percent

	1970	1980	1990	2000
Women, top 10 percent				
Married, spouse present	64.43%	58.20%	59.12%	62.16%
Single, never married	17.36	18.81	19.86	18.18
Other	18.21	22.99	21.02	19.66
Spouse earnings rank (average)	41.62	49.18	56.07	56.38
	(34.49)	(33.38)	(34.18)	(34.44)
Women, middle 10 percent				
Married, spouse present	73.62%	64.74%	62.80%	59.66%
Single, never married	8.46	13.11	15.53	18.49
Other	17.92	22.15	21.66	21.85
Spouse earnings rank (average)	35.34	42.30	44.76	46.12
	(30.58)	(30.92)	(31.15)	(31.35)
Women, bottom 10 percent				
Married, spouse present	79.42%	76.22%	67.26%	59.66%
Single, never married	5.22	6.95	12.63	17.68
Other	15.36	16.83	20.11	22.66
Spouse earnings rank (average)	35.98	43.09	41.10	40.58
	(32.05)	(32.50)	(32.17)	(31.51)
Men, top 10 percent				
Married, spouse present	91.04%	78.91%	76.31%	74.38%
Single, never married	4.83	11.27	13.42	13.52
Other	4.12	9.83	10.26	12.10
Spouse earnings rank (average)	22.79	40.00	45.44	47.28
	(35.07)	(35.31)	(34.45)	(34.61)
Men, middle 10 percent				
Married, spouse present	88.11%	63.23%	57.45%	56.58%
Single, never married	7.41	22.24	27.69	28.32
Other	4.48	14.52	14.86	15.10
Spouse earnings rank (average)	27.25	33.86	38.89	38.88
	(36.55)	(33.02)	(30.42)	(30.52)
Men, bottom 10 percent				
Married, spouse present	73.89%	44.34%	37.79%	43.03%
Single, never married	15.56	36.52	42.68	37.75
Other	10.55	19.15	19.53	19.22
Spouse earnings rank (average)	27.01	31.88	27.73	28.54
	(34.54)	(32.08)	(28.27)	(28.70)

Source: Author's compilation from the Annual March Current Population Surveys; see Data Appendix for further details.
Note: Standard deviations of average spouse earnings rank are in parentheses.

than other married women, thereby reducing the concentration of earnings (see, for example, Becker 1973; Juhn and Murphy 1997). We begin with men at the top because it was for them and their wives that the most remarkable shifts occurred. In 1970 the traditional pattern held sway, with the wives of men at the top falling pretty low on the totem pole of earnings (including zero earners). Not only was their average rank in the female earnings distribution low, but it was lower than that of women who were married to men in the bottom half. But by 2000 the ranking of women married to men at the top had doubled from 22.8 (out of 100) to 47.3, which catapulted them above the rankings of other wives. Thus, the average earnings of women married to men at the top are now greater than for women married to men in the bottom half, serving to reinforce the earnings advantages of the highest-paid men.

The trend over time is largely the same for married women at the top, whose husbands' ranking rose from 41.6 in 1970 to 56.4 in 2000. The average ranking of husbands' earnings for these women has always been greater compared to other women, and now their advantage is even greater. Among married women in the middle tenth, the average ranking of husbands' earnings grew by almost as much as it did among married women at the top, but there was little change in the rankings of spouses for both men and women in the bottom tenth, rising from 36.0 to 40.6 for women and from 27.0 to 28.5 for men. Thus, both the process of getting (and staying) married and the process of choosing one's spouse has changed over the past three decades in ways that reinforce the concentration of earnings among families at the top.

With this fuller picture of the occupational and family characteristics of men and women from different class positions in mind, we can return to the views expressed at the beginning of this section about the peculiarity of class inequality among women. Specifically, the question was whether class inequality based solely on labor market earnings means something different when we are talking about women rather than men, even though the actual levels of earnings inequality are quite comparable. In particular, earnings differences between the top and bottom could be comparable in relative terms but much smaller in absolute terms for women, reflecting the smaller range of earnings for women. Moreover, growing class inequality among women could reflect growing opportunities for women as gender inequality declines. This in turn could explain why there has been little attention to the issue of earnings inequality among women, especially compared to earnings inequality among men, among families, and between men and women.

In fact, in 1970 the portrait of women at the top very much resembled a portrait of *women* at the top: over two-thirds were employed in clerical, teaching, nursing, and manual occupations, and fewer were likely to be married than women in the middle and bottom tenths. This portrait confirms the skepticism about treating earnings differentials among men and women as similar indicators of class inequality. However, since 1970, absolute progress in the occupational standing, family position, and earnings growth of women at the top has generally been much greater than for other groups of men and women, including men at the top. The portrait of women at the top looks much less gender-typed in 2000 than it did in 1970, and less gender-typed than in the middle and bottom tenths of the distribution as well, since occupational sex segregation has declined more rapidly for those with higher education. In an apparent historic reversal that demands further attention, women at the top are also now slightly more likely to be married than women in the middle and bottom tenths. While inequalities among women were not especially comparable to inequalities among men in the beginning of our period, they are today.

Of course, this does not mean that gender inequality has been eliminated, or eliminated more for top earners than for everybody else. Once again, a distinction between absolute and relative progress is required to understand the joint dynamics of class and gender inequality. Although women at the top made greater *absolute* progress than other women, *relative* gender earnings inequality declined somewhat less for women at the top.[5] Figure 10.5 provides the female-male earnings ratios for the top, middle, and bottom tenths, using the weekly average earnings for each group shown in tables 10.1 and 10.2 (ratios for full-time workers only are shown in figure 10.6). Among all part-time and full-time workers, the gender earnings ratio increased from 0.55 to 0.67 for the top tenth, from 0.52 to 0.69 for the middle tenth, and from 0.48 to 0.68 for the bottom tenth. Because gender disparities in hours worked are greater for those in lower earnings groups, the ratios are much higher for those groups once hours are controlled, as shown in the ratios for full-time, full-year workers in figure 10.6.

It is still unclear exactly why women at the top made such strong absolute progress without closing the gender gap in earnings to a greater degree than occurred for other groups of women. A likely explanation is that declining discrimination in higher education and increasing demand in the professions and management were major causes of the strong earnings growth of women at the top, but it is likely that men benefited from these top-heavy demand shifts as well (Black and Juhn 2000; Blau and Kahn 1997). Men at the top saw a 41.2 percent increase in their weekly earnings from 1970 to 2000, whereas men in the middle saw only a 9.5 percent increase, and men in the bottom group lost ground. Thus, the path to achieving greater gender equality has not been the same for all groups. We can grant that increasing inequality among women is indeed a reflection of expanding opportunities for women; at the same time we must acknowledge that it is also a reflection of how those opportunities have been unequally distributed across class lines.

Figure 10.5   Weekly Earnings Ratio Between Female and Male Workers, 1970 to 2000

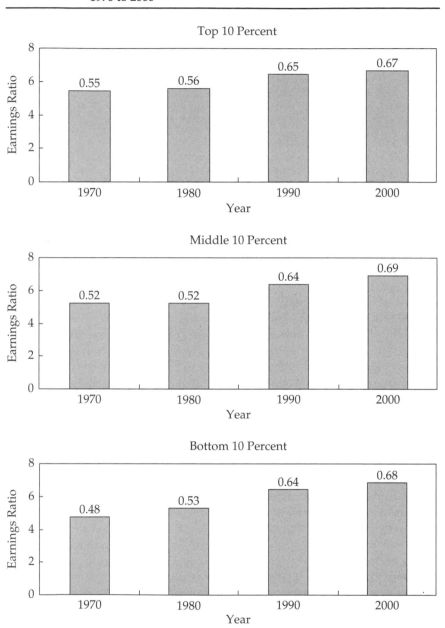

Source: Author's compilation from the Annual March Current Population Surveys; see Data Appendix for further details.

Figure 10.6   Weekly Earnings Ratio Between Full-Time Female and
               Male Workers, 1970 to 2000

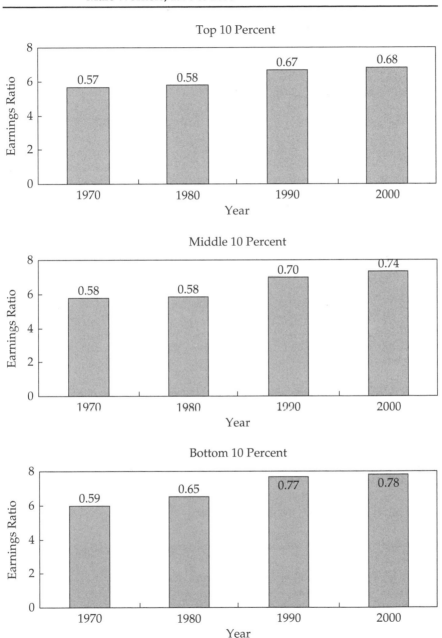

Source: Author's compilation from the Annual March Current Population Surveys; see Data
Appendix for further details.

Income Attainment: How Much More Important Is the Family for Women Than for Men?

The second reason class differences among women, especially in labor market earnings, might have received relatively little attention is the assumption that women's economic well being is determined more by their total family income, which is provided in large part by their husbands, than by their own earnings. This assumption is undoubtedly true in many contexts and for many groups, but it is not universal in degree—differences by race are substantial, for example—and researchers have generally devoted little effort to measuring whether this assumption is valid, focusing instead on the related, but still distinct, question of women's dependency on men *within* marriage (see, for example, Sorensen and McLanahan 1987).

Determining the extent to which women are still dependent on men for achieving their position *in the family income distribution* should be an equally important objective given the transformations in women's occupations, family position, and earnings. How much of an effect have these transformations had on where women end up in the income distribution? Is the family becoming less important to women for achieving their position in the income distribution? Is the family becoming more important for men? Perhaps most importantly, is the relative importance of their own earnings and other family income becoming more similar for men and women, regardless of the level of dependency? I suggest that gender inequality can be defined as asymmetry in the role of the family in the income attainment process rather than as dependency within marriage per se. In this way, gender equality could be achieved through an equal level of dependency on the family rather than an equal level of independence from the family.

In this section, I propose a simple measure of the relative importance of family income sources in assessing women's and men's economic position: the correlation between one's own annual earnings and family income. I chart substantial changes in this measure for women over the last three decades and surprisingly small changes for men. I also discuss the ratio of women's and men's correlation as a measure of gender inequality. Finally, I reanalyze the data for blacks only and show that these changes have been relatively mild in comparison to the changes among the population as a whole, which is dominated by white individuals and families.

As implied earlier, the association between one's own earnings and the income of one's family as a whole is defined separately for men and women, allowing for a comparison of the degree of dependency on sources other than one's own earnings for where one ends up in the income distribution. Taking women as an example, the association is a measure of where women fall in the earnings distribution of all women relative to where they fall in the family income distribution of all women.[6] If the association is high—that is, if one's position in the distribution of earnings is relatively similar to one's position in the distribution of family income—then we can conclude that family-specific factors are relatively unimportant and that the variances of earnings and family income distributions are similar. This describes the prototypical situation of men: to the extent that family income is composed primarily of income from husbands, there should be a high correlation between a man's position in the men's earnings distribution and his position in the family income distribution. The variances of those distributions should be similar as well. In the extreme, women do not work, men are fully "independent," and there is a perfect positive correlation between men's own earnings and their family income (ignoring the role of family size). For these reasons, I occasionally refer to the correlation as the "independence" correlation for short.

In contrast, conventionally we would expect the opposite for women, whose position in the earnings distribution is weakly associated with their position in the family income distribution, which is heavily influenced by the income of their husbands. In this scenario, there is less of a correspondence between the structure of variance of women's earnings and the structure of variance of family income. This is particularly the case if a large number of wives do not work and thus have zero earnings or work only part-time. As the mix of work and earnings shifts and converges among wives and husbands, and among women and men, so should the prototypical associations for men (high) and women (low). Since black wives have historically been more likely to work than white wives, both the initial associations (in 1970) and the changes over time will differ from these prototypical patterns, which for the sample overall will be dominated by white families.

These changes over time in the independence correlation depend not only on changes in the structure of labor market opportunities for women and men, however, but also on changes in how families are formed; these changes were discussed earlier in terms of "who gets married" and "who's marrying whom." For example, we saw a convergence over time in the marriage rates of women in the top, middle, and bottom tenths, indicating a broader representation of married women in the labor market. This in turn implies that the dissonance between one's own earnings and family income among all women will decline, all else being equal, since that dissonance is created in large part by the zero earnings of many wives. In addition, as marriage becomes less common for everyone (in the cross-section), other family income sources will become less important and the correlation between one's own earnings and family earnings will increase. And finally, as men and women at the top increasingly find spouses who also have relatively high earnings (that is, as positive assortative mating increases), the correlation between one's own earnings and the income of the family will also increase.

The primary way I identify the role of these confounding factors is by examining covariation within groups of individuals who are married and unmarried. My base sample consists of all households regardless of marital or earning status (both zero and positive earners are included); I subsequently distinguish between married (spouse present), married with wife working, and unmarried households.[7] Average earnings for each group are provided in order to assess whether married individuals are becoming a more or less select group, though these differences reflect changes in earnings as well as labor force participation rates, since annual earnings and family income are used.[8] I also examine the correlation between spouses' earnings, which is an indicator of the degree to which men and women of like earnings marry one another (marital income homogamy).

The correlations between one's own annual earnings and annual family income from 1970 to 2000 for all households (of all races) and for households broken down by marital status are presented in table 10.4. The prototypical differences between men and women are precisely what we observe, with high associations between one's own earnings and family income for men and low associations for women. The correlation between women's own earnings and their family income was 0.27 in 1970—starkly different from the correlation of 0.83 for men in the same period. Over time the correlation nearly doubled for women, climbing to 0.51 in 2000, whereas it held steady for men at 0.82. The relatively low correlations among women in 1970 were driven by the presence of nonworking married women, as can be seen by comparing the correlations among all married women with the correlations among only those married women who worked. For all married women, the correlations rose from 0.36 to 0.57 over the three decades, whereas the correlation among only those who worked was already significantly higher in 1970 (0.55) and then rose less dramatically over time to 0.63 in 2000. The highest correlations were among unmarried women, rising from 0.72 in 1970 to 0.88 in 2000, at which point the correlation was very similar to that of unmarried men (0.91).

Table 10.4 sheds light on a number of reasons for the large increase in the correlation for women over time. First, compositional shifts have been an important factor, as shown by the decrease in married women from 83.2 to 65.5 percent of all women. In addition, the share of married couples with a working wife has also increased, especially wives who work full-time (results not shown). Second, the relative mean earnings of married women are lower than those of unmarried women, but they have grown substantially. The mean earnings of married women were 49 percent of those of unmarried women in 1970 and 82 percent in 2000. This increase is driven not only by the growing share of married women who work but by the fact that the earnings of married women who work are very close to those of unmarried women. For the first time in fact, in 2000, married women who work enjoyed an earnings premium over unmarried women who work, a

Table 10.4   Marital Sorting, the Independence Correlation, and Marital Homogamy by Marital Status: All Households

	1970	1980	1990	2000
Women				
Full sample mean annual earnings (2000 dollars)	$7,823.72	$11,647.18	$16,798.65	$21,466.53
Married mean	$6,665.87	$9,897.47	$14,998.53	$19,938.27
Married mean, self works	$13,129.64	$15,565.76	$20,664.28	$26,695.77
Nonmarried mean	$13,544.41	$16,656.57	$20,685.03	$24,370.72
Ratio married-nonmarried means	0.49	0.59	0.73	0.82
Men				
Full sample mean annual earnings (2000 dollars)	$35,427.94	$37,538.38	$37,864.11	$41,249.60
Married mean	$36,319.01	$39,515.48	$40,742.90	$45,011.58
Married mean, wife works	$33,256.23	$37,401.75	$39,566.78	$44,058.40
Nonmarried mean	$27,436.76	$29,349.34	$30,104.44	$32,897.72
Ratio married-nonmarried means	1.32	1.35	1.35	1.37
Marital status				
Women, percentage married, spouse present	83.17%	74.11%	68.34%	65.52%
Women, percentage married, spouse present, self works	42.20	47.12	49.61	48.94
Men, percentage married, spouse present	89.97	80.55	72.94	68.94
Men, percentage married, spouse present, wife works	45.65	51.21	52.94	51.49
Correlation of own earnings and family income				
Married and nonmarried combined				
Women	0.27	0.28	0.43	0.51
Men	0.83	0.84	0.84	0.82

(continued)

Table 10.4   *Continued*

	1970	1980	1990	2000
Married				
Women	0.36	0.38	0.51	0.57
Men	0.82	0.83	0.82	0.80
Married, self/				
wife works				
Women	0.55	0.49	0.59	0.63
Men	0.80	0.81	0.83	0.81
Nonmarried				
Women	0.72	0.76	0.85	0.88
Men	0.90	0.93	0.92	0.91
Correlation of spouses' earnings, married couples				
All (men, their spouses)	−0.0645	−0.0267	0.0838	0.1098
All, wife works	0.0843	0.0743	0.1865	0.2021

Source: Author's compilation from the Annual March Current Population Surveys; see Data Appendix for further details.

pattern more typical of men. This could be an indication that the marriage pendulum is swinging now in the direction of enhancing women's labor market productivity rather than detracting from it. Perhaps a clearer case can be made for men, as the earnings advantage of married men over unmarried men increased further by five percentage points from 1970 to 2000.[9]

Third, the increase in women's correlation is also due to an increase in marital income homogamy. The correlation between husbands' and wives' earnings in married-couple families has increased from a very low negative value of −0.06 in 1970 to a positive 0.11 in 2000. The lower and even negative correlations in the earlier period reflect the coupling of high-earning husbands with zero-earning wives (Cancian, Danziger, and Gottschalk 1993). The correlation between spouses' earnings is higher if we examine only those couples in which both spouses work; it rose from 0.08 to 0.20 between 1970 and 2000. Although income marital homogamy has clearly increased over the past several decades, it has tapered off somewhat in recent years and at present remains quite small in absolute terms. To the extent that the much higher (and possibly increasing) degree of educational homogamy sets the stage for greater income homogamy in an era of high female labor force participation among wives, income homogamy could begin to track educational homogamy more closely than in the past (Schwartz and Mare 2005).

Thus, the overall rise in the correlation of one's own earnings and family income for women is attributable to increasing shares of single-adult and dual-earning households, increasing similarities in the employment and earnings of married and unmarried women, increasing marital income homogamy, and increasing earnings among women across the board. Since the structure of earnings for men and women is now much more similar than it once was, the *ratio* of women's and men's correlations nearly doubled as well, from 32 percent to 62 percent between 1970 and 2000. Although this increase is impressive, the dependency on family factors is still much greater for women than for men in determining where they fall in the income distribution. If we think of the correlation as a measure of independence from family factors—the independence correlation—the female-male ratio in the degree of independence is 62 percent for the population as a whole, 71 percent for those who are married (between 65 and 69 percent of the population), and 78 percent for those married couples with a working wife (about half of the population).

Among black women, however, both the degree of independence and the relative degree of independence compared to men are much higher. Table 10.5 replicates the analysis in table 10.4 for blacks only and shows quite different patterns than for the population as a whole, which is dominated by white families and individuals. The most striking differences are for women. First, the earnings of married and unmarried women have been comparable throughout the entire period, although they too are now moving in the direction of favoring married women. Second, marriage rates are much lower, though here too they are trending in the same downward direction as in the population as a whole. Third, and most notably for our purposes, the independence correlation for married women has held steady and even declined somewhat over time. This appears to be due to trends in marital income homogamy, which historically is much higher among blacks but has been declining precipitously, particularly among married couples with a working wife over the 1990s. In 2000 it reached a level that was not much different than in the population as a whole (0.24 for blacks versus 0.20 for the general population).

As we can see, some of the most important forces that have been strengthening the independence correlation for white women (as represented by the population as a whole)—namely, the relative increases in the employment and earnings of married women and marital income homogamy—have been either less dramatic or declining for black women. In contrast, it is mainly the increase in the independence correlation for *unmarried* women that is driving up the correlation for all black women over time.

I do not have the space here to discuss these patterns fully, but they are important for signaling the very different ways in which "independence" from family factors can be achieved, both in an absolute sense for women and in a relative sense compared to men. For example, the increase in

Table 10.5   **Marital Sorting, the Independence Correlation, and Marital Homogamy by Marital Status: Black Households**

	1970	1980	1990	2000
Women				
Full sample mean annual earnings (2000 dollars)	$8,313.91	$12,222.86	$15,917.74	$20,142.71
Married mean	$8,140.54	$12,496.06	$16,730.60	$21,354.00
Married mean, self works	$12,190.34	$17,312.06	$20,960.37	$26,418.76
Nonmarried mean	$8,586.42	$11,972.97	$15,325.14	$19,317.35
Ratio married-nonmarried means	0.95	1.04	1.09	1.11
Men				
Full sample mean annual earnings (2000 dollars)	$22,545.49	$25,598.42	$25,765.21	$29,838.72
Married mean	$23,775.67	$27,942.89	$29,182.73	$33,708.86
Married mean, wife works	$23,822.60	$28,229.77	$30,212.98	$34,755.66
Nonmarried mean	$17,907.54	$21,013.25	$20,982.45	$25,103.56
Ratio married-nonmarried means	1.33	1.33	1.39	1.34
Marital status				
Women, percentage married, spouse present	61.12%	47.77%	42.16%	40.53%
Women, percentage married, spouse present, self works	40.81	34.48	33.66	32.76
Men, percentage married, spouse present	79.04	66.17	58.32	55.03
Men, percentage married, spouse present, wife works	52.77	47.75	53.45	44.48

(*continued*)

Table 10.5   *Continued*

	1970	1980	1990	2000
Correlation of own earnings and family income				
Married and nonmarried combined				
Women	0.55	0.58	0.65	0.65
Men	0.78	0.81	0.82	0.78
Married				
Women	0.67	0.65	0.69	0.67
Men	0.76	0.77	0.81	0.77
Married, self/ wife works				
Women	0.73	0.70	0.70	0.67
Men	0.78	0.79	0.84	0.79
Nonmarried				
Women	0.68	0.80	0.85	0.88
Men	0.86	0.92	0.92	0.89
Correlation of spouses' earnings, married couples				
All (men, their spouses)	0.2133	0.2077	0.2868	0.2244
All, wife works	0.3314	0.3059	0.3141	0.2405

Source: Author's compilation from the Annual March Current Population Surveys; see Data Appendix for further details.

unmarried black women's independence correlation is most likely due to a decline in other, nonspousal income (for example, income from the government), creating a closer relationship between actual earnings and family income for low-income black women with children. To some degree the increase in the independence correlation among single white women is also most likely a result of the increase in single women with children who rely almost exclusively on their own earnings. Thus, an increase in the independence correlation itself—and the components that reinforce it, such as marital income homogamy—is not necessarily a desired outcome from an equity perspective, whereas a declining disparity with men, regardless of the level of dependency, might be. These trade-offs between independence from marriage, on the one hand, and financial well-being, on the other, especially for poor women with children, have been noted by others and reinforce the need to understand the context of women's growing independence from marriage as well as its relation to men's independence (Edin and Reed 2005; Ellwood and Jencks 2004; England 2000; Oppenheimer 1997).

Conclusion

Although it is tempting to draw sweeping conclusions about gender giving way to class—such as "class is becoming degendered" and "gender is becoming classed"—the reality, as is usually the case, is more complicated. On the one hand, it is clear that gender inequality has not simply withered away so that it can be replaced by an encompassing analysis of class. As shown in the first part of the chapter, occupational distributions between men and women remain different in several respects, most especially in the bottom and middle tenths, but also in the top tenth if a more disaggregated occupational and earnings distribution could be provided (see, for example, Crompton 2001; McCall 2007a). And as was shown in the second part, men's overall economic position is still much more strongly determined by their own earnings than is the case for women. Although women's independence from sources of income other than their own has more than doubled, men's independence has barely declined, highlighting the asymmetrical nature of recent transformations in the family.

On the other hand, it is equally clear that challenges to the class analysis of women hold less water today than they did a generation ago. Although earnings ratios between the top and bottom have been comparable for men and women throughout the three decades of this study, it was only in the later period that the earnings levels and occupational attainment of women at the top began to resemble those of men at the top. Most women in the top tenth were employed in female-dominated professions and clerical work in the earlier period, and that is no longer true today. Moreover, women at the top were once less likely to marry than women in the middle and bottom tenths, but now they are slightly more likely to do so. The earnings of married women who work also exceeded the earnings of unmarried women for the first time in 2000, suggesting that a marriage premium for women— long associated only with men—may be on the horizon, though this needs to be studied more closely. Although still small in absolute terms, income homogamy among married couples has grown swiftly from a negative (or essentially zero) correlation between spouses' earnings—a reflection of zero-earning wives being married to high-earning husbands—to 0.11 for all married couples, and from 0.08 to 0.20 for married couples in which the wife works. All of this suggests that expanding opportunities and changes in the formation of families have both been unequally distributed across class lines, favoring better-off women in multiple ways and in many of the same ways that they have favored better-off men all along.

Taking these disparities among women seriously opens up possibilities for addressing the multiple ways in which class works *among* women differently than it does among men. Such an analysis would need a stronger emphasis than now exists on the relationships of inequality among women that have developed as a result of increasing stratification among the employed and among families. More controversially, it might also involve a weaker emphasis than now exists on the similarities among women resulting from common sources of gender inequality in the labor market (discrimination and segregation) and in the family (dependency on husbands' income). This does not mean that universal solutions to inequities that affect all women are impossible. It means only that a well-developed understanding of growing class inequalities among women could provide a unique lens into how these problems operate and thus, perhaps, better insights into how to solve them. Regardless of one's position on such matters, however, further investigations of the issues raised in this chapter are needed, as the scholarly record on disparities among women is slim (though growing), and many of the findings presented here should be understood as only an initial foray into the field.

Data Appendix

All results presented in this chapter are calculated from the annual March Current Population Survey (CPS) uniform files provided by Unicon for 1962 to 2005. All samples exclude the self-employed and individuals under age twenty-five and over fifty-five (in order to limit biases associated with school attendance and retirement). The four time periods are referred to as 1970, 1980, 1990, and 2000 as a shorthand but include three years of pooled data for each time period (1968 to 1970, 1978 to 1980, 1988 to 1990, and 1998 to 2000). CPS weights are used in all calculations.

Earnings Groups

The top, middle, and bottom earnings groups were calculated using weekly earnings (as measured by annual earnings divided by weeks worked in the year previous to the survey) for earners in the eighty-fifth to ninety-fifth percentiles, forty-fifth to fifty-fifth percentiles, and fifth to fifteenth percentiles, respectively, after individuals with less than half the minimum wage in 1982 are excluded (as is common in studies of wage inequality). Full-time workers are defined as those who work thirty-five or more hours per week (if hours data are available) and forty or more weeks per year. All other workers are defined as part-time. Earnings are presented in inflation-adjusted 2000 dollars using the Personal Consumption Expenditures deflator. All analyses are weighted using CPS person and family weights.

Occupational Groups

The occupational classification I use is based on U.S. Census Bureau categories and is similar in broad outline to the categorization defined by Weeden and Grusky (2005) as the Featherman and Hauser classification (see also Grusky and Weeden, this volume). Several differences should be noted, however: I exclude the self-employed, farmers, and farm workers; I group laborers, operatives, and most material-moving occupations into a single category; aircraft pilots, engineers, and controllers, transportation supervisors, protective service workers, and technicians are all included in the professions category; I separate out nurses, teachers, and secretaries because of their status as elite female occupations; and similarly, I separate out doctors and lawyers because of their status as elite male occupations. This breakdown mixes the "big class" approach with the more detailed occupational approach advocated by Weeden and Grusky.

Annual Earnings and Family Income

The sample of individuals with annual earnings and family income includes all men and women in what the Census Bureau refers to as "primary" families and individuals, which excludes subfamilies. I also include secondary unrelated individuals as separate observations. Both family income and annual earnings are unadjusted for family size. Both annual earnings and family income are top-coded by taking the minimum top-code value across all years and assigning it as the top code for all years (after adjusting each year by one and a half times the original top-coded value) (see Martin 2006). All negative values are set to zero for annual earnings and family income. Other family income includes income from all other sources, including from tax and transfer programs and earnings from other family members.

I am very grateful for comments from Annette Lareau, Molly Martin, Lincoln Quillian, Pamela Smock, Megan Sweeney, and two anonymous reviewers on an earlier version of this chapter and for research assistance from Yingying Deng.

Notes

1. Measures of earnings inequality at the bottom of the distribution (for example, the median relative to the bottom tenth percentile) are sensitive to low values at the very bottom, particularly among women, who are the lowest earners. As a result, some measures show higher levels of inequality at the bottom among women, while others with higher cutoff points for selection into the sample show lower levels of inequality at the bottom among women. I have a relatively strict

cutoff: half the value of the minimum wage in 1982, as used in many other studies of earnings inequality (see, for example, Katz and Autor 1999). For all other details on the data used in this chapter, see the data appendix.

2. On the need to examine relationships among multiple dimensions of inequality, see Grusky and Weeden (this volume).

3. Since earnings disparities or class relationships among women are rarely analyzed among sociologists, except in the special case of employers of domestic service workers (a subject of much research, in fact), it is not possible to attribute this position to any particular author. A somewhat related and thoughtful discussion is provided by Rosemary Crompton (2001). The empirical documentation of rising earnings inequality among women has been provided primarily by economists (for example, Dinardo, Fortin, and Lemieux 1996).

4. This is consistent with growing evidence of an "educational crossover" in lifetime marriage rates (the percentage ever married) that now favors college-educated women (Goldstein and Kenney 2001). These data are also consistent with the argument that "high-quality" women are becoming more attractive as marriage partners in the same way that high-quality men have always been considered more attractive marriage partners (Oppenheimer 1997; Sweeney and Cancian 2004). However, I do not know of any research that examines marriage rates by earnings levels of employed women. Note also that marriage rates are much lower at any one point in time (for example, in a cross-sectional analysis such as this one) than over the lifetime; lifetime marriage rates remain relatively high by historical standards.

5. This conclusion depends to a certain degree on the categories being compared (for example, percentiles of the distribution versus education groups), and there are more differences than first meets the eye. For a more thorough discussion of earnings trends by gender and class, see McCall (2007a). For a more general discussion of long-term changes in gender inequality, see Goldin (2006) and Blau and Kahn (1997).

6. Translated into covariances, which I examine in detail elsewhere (McCall 2007b), the covariance of the women's distribution and the covariance of the men's distribution make up the within-group components of the overall covariance when women and men are grouped together.

7. An analysis of only three marital status groups is an oversimplification of the data. In particular, unmarried individuals include the never-married as well as those who are divorced, widowed, separated, or cohabiting, while married women who work include part-time and full-time workers (see, for example, Martin 2006; Smock 2000). In addition, the distinction between those with and without children is not addressed. These distinctions are made in a more detailed analysis provided in a separate paper (McCall 2007b), whose findings I report where relevant.

8. Differences between married and unmarried individuals can be attributed to differences prior to marriage (an exogenous effect of selection into marriage) or differences resulting from marriage (an endogenous effect of specialization within marriage). I do not differentiate between these two causal models (see, for example, Cohen 2002).

9. Since age distributions may affect the relative means of married and unmarried individuals, I examined mean annual and weekly earnings for men and women in two other age groups, thirty-five- to forty-four-year-olds and forty-five- to fifty-four-year-olds, and found the same patterns of mean differences between the married and unmarried as in the larger sample.

References

Becker, Gary. 1973. "A Theory of Marriage: Part I." *Journal of Political Economy* 81(4): 813–46.

Black, Sandra, and Chinhui Juhn. 2000. "The Rise of Female Professionals: Are Women Responding to Skill Demand?" *American Economic Review* 90(2): 450–5.

Blau, Francine D., and Lawrence Kahn. 1997. "Swimming Upstream: Trends in the Gender Wage Differential in the 1980s." *Journal of Labor Economics* 15(1): 1–42.

Cancian, Maria, Sheldon Danziger, and Peter Gottschalk. 1993. "Working Wives and Family Income Inequality Among Married Couples." In *Uneven Tides: Rising Inequality in America,* edited by Sheldon Danziger and Peter Gottschalk. New York: Russell Sage Foundation.

Charles, Maria, and David Grusky. 2005. *Occupational Ghettos: The Worldwide Segregation of Women and Men.* Stanford, Calif.: Stanford University Press.

Cohen, Philip N. 2002. "Cohabitation and the Declining Marriage Premium for Men." *Work and Occupations* 29(3): 346–63.

Cotter, David A., Joan M. Hermsen, and Reeve Vanneman. 2004. *Gender Inequality at Work.* New York and Washington: Russell Sage Foundation and Population Reference Bureau.

Crompton, Rosemary. 2001. "The Gendered Restructuring of the Middle Classes." In *Reconfigurations of Class and Gender,* edited by Janeen Baxter and Mark Western. Stanford, Calif.: Stanford University Press.

Dinardo, John, Nicole Fortin, and Thomas Lemieux. 1996. "Labor Market Institutions and the Distribution of Wages, 1973–1992: A Semiparametric Approach." *Econometrica* 64(5): 1001–44.

Edin, Kathryn, and Joanna Reed. 2005. "Why Don't They Just Get Married? Barriers to Marriage Among the Disadvantaged." *The Future of Children* 15(2): 117–37.

Ellwood, David T., and Christopher Jencks. 2004. "The Uneven Spread of Single-Parent Families: What Do We Know? Where Do We Look for Answers?" In *Social Inequality,* edited by Kathryn M. Neckerman. New York: Russell Sage Foundation.

England, Paula. 2000. "Theory on Gender/Feminism on Theory." In *The Ties That Bind: Perspectives on Marriage and Cohabitation,* edited by Linda J. Waite. New York: Aldine de Gruyter.

Goldin, Claudia. 2006. "The Quiet Revolution That Transformed Women's Employment, Education, and Family." Working paper 11953. Cambridge, Mass.: National Bureau of Economic Research.

Goldstein, Joshua R., and Catherine T. Kenney. 2001. "Marriage Delayed or Marriage Forgone? New Cohort Forecasts of First Marriage for U.S. Women." *American Sociological Review* 66(4): 506–19.

Goldthorpe, John H. 1983. "Women and Class Analysis: In Defense of the Conventional View." *Sociology* 17(4): 465–88.

———. 2000. *On Sociology: Numbers, Narratives, and the Integration of Research and Theory.* New York: Oxford University Press.

Havens, Elizabeth. 1973. "Women, Work, and Wedlock: A Note of Female Marital Patterns in the United States." *American Journal of Sociology* 78(4): 975–81.

Jacobs, Jerry A. 1999. "The Sex Segregation of Occupations: Prospects for the Twenty-first Century." In *Handbook of Gender in Organizations,* edited by Gary N. Powell. Thousand Oaks, Calif.: Sage Publications.

Juhn, Chinhui, and Kevin M. Murphy. 1997. "Wage Inequality and Family Labor Supply." *Journal of Labor Economics* 15(1): 72–97.

Katz, Lawrence F., and David H. Autor. 1999. "Changes in the Wage Structure and Earnings Inequality." In *Handbook of Labor Economics,* vol. 3A, edited by Orley Ashenfelter and David Card. Amsterdam: North Holland Press.

MacLean, Nancy. 2006. *Freedom Is Not Enough: The Opening of the American Workplace.* Cambridge, Mass., and New York: Harvard University Press and Russell Sage Foundation.

Martin, Molly A. 2006. "Family Structure and Income Inequality in Families with Children: 1976 to 2000." *Demography* 43(3): 421–45.

McCall, Leslie. 2007a. "Increasing Economic Inequality Among Women and the Politics of Gender Equity." In *The Sex of Class: Women Transforming American Labor,* edited by Dorothy Sue Cobble. Ithaca, N.Y.: Cornell University Press.

———. 2007b. "Women's and Men's Position in the U.S. Income Distribution 1970–2000: New Linked Measures of Economic Dependency and Gender Inequality." Unpublished paper, Department of Sociology, Northwestern University.

Oppenheimer, Valerie. 1997. "Women's Employment and the Gain to Marriage: The Specialization and Trading Model." *Annual Review of Sociology* 23: 431–53.

Schwartz, Christine R., and Robert D. Mare. 2005. "Trends in Educational Assortative Marriage from 1940 to 2003." *Demography* 42(4): 621–46.

Smock, Pamela J. 2000. "Cohabitation in the United States: An Appraisal of Research Themes, Findings, and Implications." *Annual Review of Sociology* 26: 1–20.

Sorensen, Annemette, and Sara McLanahan. 1987. "Married Women's Economic Dependency, 1940–1980." *American Journal of Sociology* 93(3): 659–87.

Sweeney, Megan M., and Maria Cancian. 2004. "The Changing Importance of White Women's Economic Prospects for Assortative Mating." *Journal of Marriage and the Family* 66(4): 1015–28.

Weeden, Kim, and David Grusky. 2005. "The Case for a New Class Map." *American Journal of Sociology* 111(1): 141–212.

Western, Mark, and Janeen Baxter. 2001. "Introduction." In *Reconfigurations of Class and Gender,* edited by Janeen Baxter and Mark Western. Stanford, Calif.: Stanford University Press.

Wright, Erik Olin. 2001. "Foundations of Class Analysis: A Marxist Perspective." In *Reconfigurations of Class and Gender,* edited by Janeen Baxter and Mark Western. Stanford, Calif.: Stanford University Press.

PART III

REFLECTIONS ON CLASS

Chapter 11

Logics of Class Analysis

ERIK OLIN WRIGHT

EW CONCEPTS in sociology are more contested than the concept of class: different people mean quite different things when they use the word. The result is that in many discussions people talk past each other; they use the same word, but they are really talking about quite different concepts.

Two issues underlie much of this confusion. First, there are many different sorts of questions people ask for which class is thought to provide at least part of the answer. Different concepts of class are often rooted in different questions or clusters of questions. Second, even when people are addressing the same broad question and thus trying to explain the same sorts of things, the word "class" may be used to identify different kinds of causal mechanisms: sometimes it is used to identify attributes of persons, sometimes the nature of the positions they occupy, and other times the nature of the relations among positions.

In this chapter, I try to locate the various contributions of this volume within the diversity of ways of approaching the analysis of class. I do this by first examining an *inventory of questions* posed within class analysis and then elaborating a *typology of causal mechanisms* identified by different traditions of class analysis. My central conclusion is that nearly all of the contributions to this book embody a quite narrow version of class analysis in a double sense: first, they mainly revolve around a single question in class analysis (the analysis of life chances); and second, in addressing that question, they focus almost entirely on one type of causal mechanism (the effects of individual attributes and conditions). This narrowing of questions and mechanisms, I argue in the conclusion, reduces the critical content of class analysis and ultimately blunts its moral and political relevance.

The Questions of Class Analysis

There are six particularly important general questions for which the concept of class often figures centrally in the answers:[1]

1. *Distributional location:* How are people objectively located in distributions of material inequality?

2. *Subjectively salient groups:* How do people, individually and collectively, subjectively locate themselves and others within a structure of inequality?

3. *Life chances:* What explains inequalities in life chances and material standards of living?

4. *Antagonisms and conflicts:* What cleavages in society systematically generate overt antagonisms and conflicts?

5. *Historical variation:* How should we characterize and explain the variations across history in the social organization of inequalities?

6. *Emancipation:* What sorts of transformations are needed to eliminate oppression and exploitation within capitalist societies?

There are, of course, other questions that could be added. For example, class is sometimes offered as an answer to the question: what explains the political attitudes and voting behavior of individuals? This question, however, is very closely tied to several of the six questions in the list, since the arguments for why class is linked to attitudes and voting usually work through the way class shapes subjective identities (question 2), life chances (question 3), and conflicts (question 4). In any case, this inventory of six questions covers the main agenda of class analysis. Let us look at each of the questions in turn.

Distributional Location

Class is often central to the descriptive question: how are people *objectively located* in distributions of material inequality? In this case, class is defined in terms of material standards of living, usually indexed by income or, possibly, wealth. Class, in this agenda, is a *gradational* concept; the standard image is of rungs on a ladder, and thus locations have names such as upper class, upper middle class, middle class, lower middle class, lower class, underclass. This is the concept of class that figures most prominently in popular discourse, at least in countries like the United States that lack a strong working class political tradition. When American politicians call for "middle class tax cuts," what they characteristically mean is tax cuts for people in the middle of the income distribution. Class, in this context, is contrasted with other ways in which people are objectively located within social structures—for example, by their citizenship status, their power, or their subjection to institutionalized forms of ascriptive discrimination.

Subjectively Salient Groups

Class is one of the possible answers to the question: how do people, individually and collectively, *subjectively locate* themselves and others within a structure of inequality? In this case, the concept would be defined something like this: classes are social categories that generate subjectively salient experiences that shape the identities used by people to locate those categories within a system of economic stratification. With this definition of class, the actual content of these evaluative attributes varies considerably across time and place. In some contexts, class-as-subjective-classification revolves around lifestyles, in others around detailed occupations, and in still others around income levels. Sometimes the economic content of the subjective classification system is quite direct, as in income levels or occupational categories; in other contexts, it is more indirect, as in expressions such as "upper class." The number of classes also varies contextually depending on how the actors in a social situation themselves experience and define the relevant distinctions and the salient groups. Class in this sense of the word would be contrasted to other forms of subjectively salient evaluation (religion, ethnicity, gender, and so on) that may have economic dimensions but are not centrally defined in economic terms.

Life Chances

Perhaps the most prominent question in contemporary sociological research for which class is offered as part of the answer is this: what *explains* inequalities in life chances and material standards of living? This question plays a role, in one way or another, in virtually all approaches to class analysis. It is a more complex and demanding question than the first question about distributional location, for here the issue is not simply descriptively locating people within some kind of system of stratification, but identifying causal mechanisms that help determine salient features of that system. When class is used to explain inequality, typically the concept is not defined primarily by subjectively salient attributes of a social location but rather by *the relationship of people to income-generating resources* or assets of various sorts. Class thus becomes a *relational* rather than simply *gradational* concept. In this usage, class is contrasted to the many other determinants of a person's life chances—for example, geographical location, forms of discrimination anchored in ascriptive characteristics, or genetic endowments. Geographical location, discrimination, and genetic endowments may, of course, still figure in the analysis of class—they may, for example, play an important role in explaining why different sorts of people end up in different classes, or the effects of class location on life chances may vary across such ascriptive categories—but the definition of class as such centers on how people are linked to those income-generating assets.

The problem of life chances is closely linked to the normative issue of equality of opportunity. A very broadly held view in liberal societies is that inequalities in material rewards and status are not in and of themselves morally objectionable so long as individuals have equal opportunity for achieving these rewards. This issue is especially salient in terms of inter-generational mobility—to what extent do children born into families of different economic standing have equal opportunities to succeed in life?—but it also bears on issues of intra-generational opportunities. Equality of life chances, therefore, is a background normative idea in discussions of class as a determinant of life chances.

The basic insight of a class analysis of life chances is captured by this formula: what you have determines what you get. This leaves open, however, the range of resources or assets that are included under "what you have" and the kinds of outcomes that are included in "what you get." Of class theorists who focus on life chances, Pierre Bourdieu (1984) clearly has the most expansive notion of resources and the broadest conception of life chances. In Bourdieu's class analysis, the relevant resources for answering the life chances question include financial assets (capital in the ordinary sense), skills and knowledge (or what is often called human capital), and, most distinctively, what he calls cultural capital. Bourdieu also has a quite expansive notion of the scope of life chances relevant to class analysis, for he includes not simply material standard of living in the narrow economic sense but also chances for the symbolic rewards that are crucial for establishing inequalities in social status. For Bourdieu, then, life chances for both material goods and symbolic status are determined by the relationship to these three forms of capital. Marx, in contrast, adopts the narrowest inventory of resources relevant to the question. At least in his relatively systematic discussions of class, the only assets that really matter for defining class in capitalist society are capital and labor power. Weber's class analysis falls between these two, for he, like Bourdieu, explicitly includes skills as a distinctive kind of resource that shapes market capacities and thus life chances in a market society.

Antagonisms and Conflicts

The fourth question of class analysis adds further complexity to the underlying explanatory function of the concept of class: what cleavages in society systematically generate overt antagonisms and conflicts? Like the third question, this question suggests a concept of class closely linked to the causes of inequalities in economic opportunities, but here the concept attempts to identify those aspects of economic inequality that, by generating not only *differences* in interests but *antagonisms* of interest, tend to generate overt conflict. For this question, classes would not be defined simply by a commonalty of the conditions that generate economic opportunities, but by those specific clusters of common conditions that inherently tend to pit people against each other in the pursuit of those opportunities. Class here would be contrasted, on the one hand, with non-economic sources of social cleavage—such as religion or ethnicity—and, on the other hand, with nonclass forms of economic cleavage, such as economic sector or geographical region.

This question about the basis of conflict figures especially prominently in the Marxist tradition, although class also plays a role in explaining social conflict in non-Marxist theoretical traditions. Weber certainly sees class as a potential basis for conflicts, but he explicitly rejects any claims that there is an inherent tendency for class relations to generate overt conflicts. Marx, in contrast, saw conflict as an intrinsic consequence of class relations. This does not imply that Marx saw explosive class conflict as a constant feature of capitalist society, but he certainly did believe, first, that capitalist societies would be characterized by recurrent episodes of intense struggles generated by antagonistic class interests, and second, that there would be a systematic tendency for these episodes to intensify over time.

When one of the central questions of class analysis is explaining conflict, a concept like "exploitation" is likely to play a particularly important role. For Marx and most neo-Marxists, this concept is elaborated in terms of the process through which labor effort is appropriated from one class by another. In Aage Sorenson's (2005) approach to class, exploitation is elaborated in terms of the process through which economic rents are extracted. In both cases, conflicts of interests are not treated as contingent properties of class but rather are seen as built into the very structure of class relations.

Historical Variation

The fifth question of class analysis centers on a broad macro-level problem: how should we characterize and explain the variations across history in the social organization of economic inequalities? This question implies the need for a macro-level concept rather than simply a micro-level concept that captures the causal processes of individual lives, and it requires a concept that allows for macro-level variations across time and place. This question plays an especially central role in both the Marxist and Weberian traditions, but the two traditions treat the problem of historical variation in quite different ways.

Within the Marxist tradition, the most significant aspect of historical variation in inequality is how economic systems vary in the *manner in which an economic surplus is produced and appropriated.* Capitalism, in these terms, is contrasted to feudalism on the basis of the specific mechanisms through which exploitation takes place. In capitalism this occurs through the ways in which labor markets enable propertyless workers to be employed by capitalists and capitalists' control over the labor process enables them to appropriate labor effort from workers. In feudalism, in contrast, the surplus is extracted from serfs through the direct exercise of coercive power by lords. Both of these ways of organizing economic relations constitute class structures because both are built on the appropriation of the economic surplus by an exploiting class, but they are qualitatively different because of the process by which this is accomplished.

For Weberians, in contrast, the central problem of historical variation is the *relative salience of different forms of inequality,* especially class and status. In these terms, the critical contrast between capitalism and feudalism is not between two types of class structures, but between a society within which class is the fundamental basis of power and inequality and a society within which status is the fundamental basis. While classes did exist in feudalism—since feudalism did contain markets and thus people engaged in market exchanges with different resources and market capacities—the market system was subordinated to the status order, and it was the status order that most fundamentally determined the advantages and disadvantages of lords and serfs.

Emancipation

The most controversial question asked by social theorists for which class is an important part of the answer is this: what sorts of transformations are needed to eliminate economic oppression and exploitation within capitalist societies? This question implies not simply an explanatory agenda about the mechanisms that generate economic inequalities but a normative judgment about those inequalities—they are forms of oppression and exploitation—and a normative vision of the transformation of those inequalities as part of a political project of emancipatory social change.

This is the question that I believe most fundamentally anchors the Marxist approach to class analysis and infuses each of the other core questions with a particular set of meanings within the Marxist tradition. In the context of the Marxian emancipatory agenda, the problem of historical variation includes trying to understand possible future forms of social relations within which the exploitation and oppression of capitalist class relations have been eliminated. The historical variation relevant to class analysis thus revolves around the contrast not simply between capitalism and feudalism as empirically observable historical forms of class relations, but also between capitalism and a hypothetical communism (understood as an egalitarian, classless society). Similarly with respect to the problem of class conflict: characterizing the antagonistic interests embedded in class relations as "exploitation" and "oppression" suggests that the conflicts generated by those relations involve issues of social justice, not simply morally neutral material interests. Within the broad agenda of Marxist class analysis, therefore, the concept of class contributes to the critique of capitalist society rather than just to description and explanation.

While class analysts generally address more than one of these questions, different theoretical traditions of class analysis give different weight to each of the questions within this inventory. The Weberian tradition of class analysis is most tightly organized around the problem of life chances and historical variation. Bourdieu's class analysis is also centrally concerned with life chances, but it gives much less weight to historical variation and more to the problem of the subjective boundaries of class. Marxist class analysis is anchored in the problem of emancipation, historical variation, and class conflict; the problem of life chances enters the analysis mainly as it bears on these other questions. These different configurations of questions, in turn, place different theoretical demands on the concept of class. A concept that is called on to map broad historical variations in social structures as well as variations across persons in life chances is likely to be quite different from a concept that functions mainly on the terrain of subjective identity and life chances.

Because of the ideologically charged character of many of the debates over class, alternative frameworks of class analysis often appear to be hostile camps, each trying to recruit supporters and defeat opponents. Students interested in class analysis thus often feel that they have to make a choice and adopt one or another of these approaches to the exclusion of others. But if it is the case that these various approaches are organized around different mixes of anchoring questions, then, depending on the specific empirical agenda, different frameworks of class analysis may provide the best conceptual menu. One can be a Weberian in the morning for the study of class mobility, a Bourdieuian in the afternoon for the study of the class determinants of lifestyles, and a Marxian in the evening for the critique of capitalism.

A full survey of research on social class and how it works would include studies anchored in all of these questions. A central theme could then be how research around one set of questions might influence the ideas and agendas of other questions. Understanding the historical variations in class structures and the dynamics of class conflicts, for example, might change the way one studies the micro processes that shape individual life chances, for these macro questions would highlight the ways in which the opportunities available to individuals depend not just on their own attributes and circumstances but on the character of the structures within which they live. Equally, a full account of class conflict and its effects on transforming class structures should be informed by our understanding of the micro processes that shape individual life chances, since the inter- and intra-generational patterns of individual mobility are likely to be important determinants of the stability of systems of inequality and the prospects for collective action challenging those inequalities. If we want to really under-stand "how class works," class needs to be explored at the macro as well as micro levels of analysis, subjectively as well as objectively, statically as well as dynamically.

The contributions to this volume, however, nearly all revolve around only one of the six class analysis questions: how can we explain variations in life chances in contemporary American society? This is perhaps not sur-prising, since this question has been such a preoccupation of American sociology. There is, of course, nothing wrong in research focusing on a nar-row slice of the full inventory of class analysis questions, and the problem of inequalities in life chances linked to class is certainly a salient issue on both sociological and moral grounds. Nevertheless, with such a restricted agenda, the research assembled in this book presents only a partial under-standing of the overarching theme of how class works. I return to the ram-ifications of this limitation in the conclusion to this chapter.

Mechanisms

While the studies in this book are mainly concerned with aspects of the problem of class and life chances, they differ in the kind of life chances with which they are concerned (health, social inclusion, economic opportunity) and the specific causal mechanisms they see as central to determining those life chances. In the broader sociological literature on class and life chances, three clusters of causal mechanisms can be distinguished: mechanisms con-nected to the ways in which *unequal life conditions and individual attributes* generate salient effects in the lives of individuals; mechanisms connected to a variety of *forms of social closure* that give some individuals and groups advantages in access to resources and opportunities by virtue of the exclu-sion of others; and mechanisms linked to the ways in which individuals and groups benefit from their ability to *control the activities of others.* These three clusters of mechanisms can be referred to as class-based individual attri-butes and conditions, class-based opportunity hoarding, and class-based domination and exploitation. Stratification research in American sociology is most closely associated with the first of these mechanisms, Weber-inspired approaches to class and inequality with the second, and Marxist class analysis with the third. All of the chapters in this book include some discussion of the first of these clusters of causal mechanisms; a few of them include some analysis of the second; none of them includes the third.

In what follows I examine the logic of each of these causal mechanisms and locate the various contributions in this book with respect to these approaches. I then indicate how the three logics can be combined into a more comprehensive framework of class analysis.

Individual Attributes and Life Conditions

Among both sociologists and the lay public, the principal way most people understand the effects of class on life chances is in terms of individual attributes and life conditions. People have all sorts of individual attributes, such as sex, race, religion, intelligence, income, wealth, education, and geographical location. They have some of these attributes from birth; other attributes are acquired but once acquired are very stable, and still others are quite dependent upon a person's specific social location at any given point in time and may accordingly change. These attributes are consequential for various things we might want to explain, from health to voting behavior to child rearing practices. "Class," then, is a concept that covers one of these attributes or a cluster of them.

Within this style of class analysis, most research revolves around two kinds of mechanisms through which class is thought to have consequences for people's lives: *lived experiences* and *resources or capacities* of various sorts. In the first of these mechanisms, certain things happen to you, by virtue of your class, that shape your life in enduring ways. Class-based experiences include experiences like the frustrations and insecurities of looking for a job, the pressures within work from a boss, and the signs of respect and disrespect one receives from class markers in various contexts. The second mechanism concerns the different opportunities and choices people face by virtue of the resources they can deploy in social actions: housing and educational choices are affected by wealth constraints; saving and investing opportunities are affected by discretionary income; and caregiving choices are affected by work and time constraints. In a stripped-down form, the causal logic of these kinds of class processes is illustrated in figure 11.1.

When the study of class and inequality is anchored in these individual-level processes, the degree of economic inequality in a society is seen mainly as a function of the degree of inequality in the distribution of those individual attributes and conditions. All sorts of things determine how people acquire these economically relevant attributes, and many of these are social in character, such as the child rearing norms in different communities, the peer pressures in schools, and the quality of the schooling itself. But it is not the case in this approach to inequality that there are strong causal interconnections between the success and affluence of some and the failure and deprivations of others. I thus refer to this approach as the *individual* attributes and life conditions approach, not because it ignores all social determinants, but because the relevance of social determinants always works through the ways they shape the characteristics of individuals.

Figure 11.1   The Individual Attributes and Life Conditions Approach to Class and Inequality

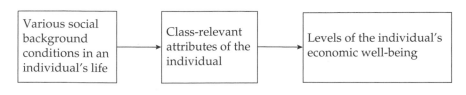

Source: Author's compilation.

This is, roughly, the dominant stance taken by quantitative sociological research on inequality in the United States, particularly before the 1970s, but even today still. The central idea of the research area that came to be known as "social stratification" is that we can understand the distribution of unequal economic statuses by understanding how individuals come to acquire their status. Given that economic status and rewards are mainly acquired through employment in paid jobs, the central thrust of most research has been on the determinants of individual access to occupations and earnings. The elaborate "status attainment models" of this research tradition thus have focused on the process by which people acquire the cultural, motivational, and educational resources they use to acquire their position in the system of stratification, mainly through the way these resources affect their entry into jobs through the labor market. Little has been said about the determinants of the *inequalities in the positions themselves* that people occupy.

Class analysis in both its Weberian and Marxian variants adopts a very different strategy for understanding systems of inequality. Rather than focusing mainly on the process by which individuals are sorted into positions, class analysis begins by analyzing the nature of and relations among the actual positions into which people are sorted. Both Weberian and Marxist class analysis see the resulting patterns of inequality as deeply structured by causal connections among these positions.

Opportunity Hoarding

The Weberian tradition emphasizes the process by which various mechanisms of exclusion and closure are built into occupational positions (a theme also stressed in the class analysis of Pierre Bourdieu). The central logic of this approach is schematically presented in figure 11.2.

Superficially, it might seem that there is scant difference between certain individual attributes that give people enhanced opportunities and mechanisms that enable people to monopolize opportunity. Consider higher education, for example: should this be understood as *human capital* that simply

Figure 11.2   The Opportunity Hoarding Approach to Class and Inequality

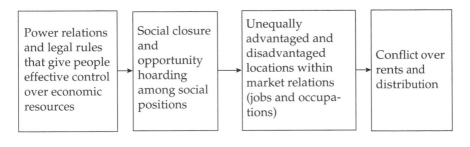

Source: Author's compilation.

makes a person's labor more productive and thus valuable, or is higher
education a *mechanism of social closure* through which people acquire credentials that effectively restrict access to certain kinds of jobs in the economy? The key difference here is that if the causal process is derived strictly
from individual attributes, then the well being and opportunities of individuals are independent of each other, so enhancing the education—
understood as human capital—of people with little human capital in no
way adversely affects people who already have higher levels of education.
It is like having two subsistence farmers on adjacent identical plots of land,
one of whom knows a lot about farming and the other little, with the result
that one has much to eat and the other little. Increasing the knowledge of
the poor farmer will improve that farmer's productivity, and thus life
chances, without in any way reducing the well being of the more prosperous farmer. In the strictly individual attributes approach to class, a person
who ends up poor has deficits in the relevant income-generating individual attributes such as education; a person who ends up rich has high levels of these same attributes. The social relation between the rich person and
the poor person does not enter into the explanation: the poor are not poor
because of what the rich do to become rich, but rather because of their
deficits in the relevant attributes that would enable them also to achieve
higher statuses. The degree of inequality is thus primarily a function of the
inequality in those attributes, and remediation in these deficits would
reduce poverty without in any way undermining the welfare of the currently advantaged.

In contrast, if one mechanism by which higher education generates high
economic standing is opportunity hoarding, then there is a real causal
interdependence between the advantages of one group and the disadvantages of another, and thus improvements in the latter are a threat to the former. High education generates high income in part because it enhances
productivity, but also because there are restrictions of the supply of highly

educated people. Credentialing, admissions procedures, tuition costs, risk aversion to large loans, and so on, all block access to higher education, and this benefits those with higher education. If a massive effort was made to improve the human capital of those with little human capital, this would itself render the human capital of those with high human capital less valuable, for its value depends to a significant extent on its scarcity.

Credentialing and licensing are particularly important mechanisms for opportunity hoarding, but many other institutional devices have been used to restrict access to given types of jobs: color bars, marriage bars, gender exclusions, cultural capital criteria for access, and so on. Private property rights in the means of production are also a form of exclusion and closure and are central to determining access to the "job" of capitalist. When workers attempt to take over a factory and run it themselves, they are violating this process of closure by challenging their exclusion from control over the means of production. The capacity of owners to appropriate profits depends on their defense of this exclusion, which we call "property rights." The core class division within Marxism between capitalists and workers can therefore be understood as reflecting a specific form of opportunity hoarding enforced by the legal rules of property rights.

These various forms of closure, as Aage Sorenson (2005) has emphasized in his analysis of class, systematically generate a flow of rents to incumbents of such jobs, and these rents contribute significantly to the overall levels of inequality in a society. In these terms, the advantages of people in such rent-appropriating jobs depend on the causal processes that exclude others from access to those jobs. It may also be the case, as outlined in individualistic approaches to inequality, that individual attributes help explain who actually gains access to such rent-appropriating positions, but inequalities in individual attributes alone do not adequately explain the resulting inequality. The inequality is crucially shaped by the effectiveness of the exclusionary mechanisms, and in this sense the prosperity of the advantaged causally depends on the exclusionary mechanisms that contribute to the deprivations of the disadvantaged.

The idea of opportunity hoarding is at the center of Max Weber's approach to the study of class and also informs the work of sociologists, like Frank Parkin (1971), Anthony Giddens (1973), and Charles Tilly (1998), whose work draws heavily on the Weberian tradition. Pierre Bourdieu's focus on cultural capital and the mechanisms of class distinction is fundamentally concerned with social closure and opportunity hoarding as well. This is also a central theme in class analyses that focus on social networks as channels for the dissemination of information and other kinds of resources. Social networks, and the closely connected idea of social capital, confer advantages to people in the network precisely because they give their members privileged access to resources and information. In all of these cases, class generates its effects not simply through the attributes of

Table 11.1   The Role of Social Relations in Different Logics of Class Analysis

Logics of Class Analysis	Conditions of Life	Economic Activities
Individual attributes	Nonrelational	Nonrelational
Opportunity hoarding	Relational	Nonrelational
Domination and exploitation	Relational	Relational

Source: Author's compilation.

individuals but also through the social relations within which those individuals live and interact.

Domination and Exploitation

Marxist class analysis takes the relational interdependency of Weberian class analysis one step further by identifying exploitation as an additional causal process that generates inequality. In a relation of exploitation, it is not simply the case that one group obtains rents by monopolizing certain resources or positions. In addition, the exploiting group is able to control the laboring effort of another for its own advantage. Consider the following classic contrasting cases. In the first case, a large landowner seizes control of common grazing lands, excludes peasants from gaining access to this land, and reaps economic rents from having exclusive control of this land for his own use. In the second case, the same landlord seizes control of the grazing lands, excludes the peasants, but then brings some of those peasants back onto the land as agricultural laborers. In this second case, in addition to gaining rents from the monopoly of the land, the landowner dominates and exploits the labor of the farm workers. This is a stronger form of relational interdependency than in a relation of simple exclusion, for here there is an ongoing relationship between the *activities* of the advantaged and disadvantaged persons, not just a relationship between their *conditions*. Exploitation and domination are forms of structured inequality that simultaneously require the continual active cooperation between exploiters and exploited, dominators and dominated, and generates systematic antagonisms of their interests. This contrast in the role of social relations within the logics of class analysis is summarized in table 11.1.

The domination and exploitation approach to class is represented in figure 11.3. Like the opportunity hoarding approach, power and legal rules that enforce social closure are important in defining the basic structure of social positions, particularly the potent form of social closure and exclusion we call "private ownership of the means of production." But here the

Figure 11.3   The Domination and Exploitation Approach

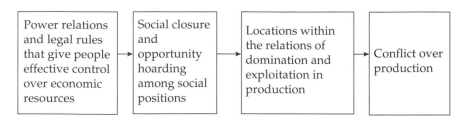

Source: Author's compilation.

critical effect of opportunity hoarding is domination and exploitation, not simply market advantage.

In both Marxist- and Weberian-inspired class analysis, power plays an important role. The inequalities generated by closure and rent appropriation require the use of power to enforce exclusions, and exploitation requires supervision, monitoring of labor effort, and sanctions to enforce labor discipline. Accordingly, the level of inequality depends in significant ways on the effectiveness of political struggle against the social structural bases of power and privilege. This is not simply because there is a zero-sum quality to distributional struggles, but because a sustainable reduction of inequality requires transformations of the underlying mechanisms of exclusion, domination, and exploitation. In this way, class analysis suggests not simply an analysis of the structural mechanisms that generate and sustain inequality but a critique of the social institutions that embody those mechanisms.

The Contributions of this Book and the Logics of Class Analysis

Most of the contributions to this book anchor their analysis in some version of the individual attributes and life conditions approach to class and inequality, with occasional discussions of opportunity hoarding.

Michael Hout's chapter is mainly concerned with the relationship between various aspects of the objective economic conditions of individuals' lives and their subjective identification with social classes. There is no explicit discussion about the social structural relations that bind these conditions together.

David Grusky and Kim Weeden ground their analysis in a comprehensive list of life conditions that, taken together, "adequately characterize the multidimensional space of inequality." While there are places where they allow processes of social closure to play a role in the analysis—social closure, for example, is one possible mechanism that could explain the existence and reproduction of micro classes—opportunity hoarding figures in neither their conceptualization of class nor directly in their analysis of classes.

John Goldthorpe and Michelle Jackson's chapter is devoted to a critique of a line of research that is resolutely individualist in its approach and argues for an increasingly "meritocratic" system of stratification in which the acquisition of educational credentials is strictly determined by ability and effort and the acquisition of economic opportunities is strictly determined by education. In such a world, there would be no role for power and exclusion as mechanisms. Goldthorpe and Jackson are mainly concerned with empirically evaluating the predictions of the increasingly popular meritocracy theory and show these to be unsatisfactory. One of their central points is that there are a variety of "soft skills"—similar to Bourdieu's idea of cultural capital—that are transmitted through families and that severely undercut the possibilities of a talent-based, educationally constructed meritocracy. Soft skills, like hard skills, become embodied in a person as individual attributes that shape his or her opportunities and life chances.

Annette Lareau and Elliot Weininger's chapter on class and child rearing emphasizes the ways in which middle class families have a cultural orientation to child rearing that leads them systematically to help their children navigate the complex process of applying to college, whereas working class and poor families rely on school personnel to guide their children through this process. Given the admissions rules and standards of academic institutions, these cultural orientations, linked to class, significantly affect children's prospects. There is nothing explicit in the analysis, however, that suggests that the fate of children from one class is causally linked to the strategies of parents in another class.[2]

Dalton Conley's analysis of parental investments in siblings also centers on the problem of individual class attributes and their acquisition. His purpose is to demonstrate that the individual life conditions of people growing up should not be assumed to be the same for all the children in a family, since parents may not treat siblings equally. The specific social context of families, therefore, can result in differential attributes and resources of children, and thus their life chances.

Karyn Lacy and Angel Harris's chapter on the interactions of race and class in patterns of socialization of black adolescents sees a particularly salient aspect of individual attributes—the form of racial understanding and identity among black youth—as varying across class contexts. This has significant implications for their life chances insofar as it affects their ease of functioning in the broader society.

Leslie McCall explicitly identifies her approach to class with individuals' income (either in terms of individual earnings or family income) rather than with anything about the nature of the positions they occupy as such. She suggests that changes in patterns of inequality among women are deeply connected to changes in the opportunities women face in the labor market, and that such changes in opportunity probably involve changes in *gendered* patterns of exclusion and opportunity hoarding (through mechanisms of gender discrimination in various forms), but she does not treat class inequality itself as a problem of social closure.

A few of the chapters adopt in part or in whole the opportunity-hoarding approach to class. While Jeff Manza and Clem Brooks's chapter on class and politics is mainly concerned with the effects of individuals' class attributes on their political behavior (participation, voting, party preference), part of their analysis also focuses on the strategies used by businesses and wealthy individuals to secure privileges through the political process. The use of campaign financing to influence politicians and political parties is one aspect of the larger problem of opportunity hoarding in class analysis.

Richard Carpiano, Bruce Link, and Jo Phelan's analysis of class and health and Mary Pattillo's analysis of race, class, and neighborhoods are firmly located within the opportunity-hoarding approach to class. Carpiano, Link, and Phelan reject the notion that the health effects of class can be entirely linked to the habits or dispositions of people living in different class situations. Rather, they argue, class positions enable some people to hoard health opportunities and gain access to the best care and the best information. The strategies of people with these class advantages therefore adversely affect the health outcomes of the disadvantaged. Pattillo demonstrates that the class advantages of certain kinds of neighborhoods are the result of deliberate strategies of social closure enacted by elites rather than simply the home-buying choices of individuals. Opportunity hoarding—in this case of desirable neighborhoods—is an essential part of the explanation for the negative outcomes for those excluded.

None of the chapters in this book adopt a domination and exploitation approach to class.[3] I do not think that this was the result of any ideological screening or objection to concepts of domination and exploitation, but rather a reflection of the general preoccupation of Anglo-American sociologists studying class with the problem of the micro determinants of individual life chances rather than the macro determinants of systems of inequality, power, and privilege. On the basis of the studies in this book, one would not understand that classes systematically interact with each other in ways in which members of one class exercise control over aspects of the lives and activities of members of another class. The unequal life chances linked to class are not part of a system of interdependency and interaction; at most they are shaped by exclusions of various sorts, but not by forms of interdependency.

Elements of a More Comprehensive Macro-Micro Model of Class Processes

To summarize the analysis so far, three clusters of causal mechanisms are involved in the class analysis of life chances:

1. *Individual attributes and life conditions:* The micro-level mechanisms linked to the ways in which individuals acquire economically relevant resources and traits and the ways in which these individual attributes influence access to positions and other economic outcomes

2. *Opportunity hoarding:* The mechanisms by which boundaries and exclusions are linked to the positions filled by individuals, thus generating potential rents and shaping distributional conflicts

3. *Exploitation and domination:* The mechanisms linked to the power relations among positions that allow for the domination and exploitation of laboring activity, thus shaping conflicts within production

While research typically focuses on one or another of these three clusters, they are all pertinent to a full understanding of class and inequality. The particular patterns of inequality we observe empirically result from the complex forms of interaction among these mechanisms. The theoretical task is to think through the different ways in which these mechanisms are linked and combined; the empirical task is to figure out ways to study each mechanism and their interconnections. One possible nested micro-macro model is illustrated schematically in figure 11.4.

In this model, the power relations and legal rules that give people effective control over economic resources (means of production, financial capital, and human capital) generate structures of social closure and opportunity hoarding connected to social positions. Opportunity hoarding, then, generates three streams of causal effects: it shapes the micro-level processes through which individuals acquire class-relevant attributes; it shapes the structure of locations within market relations (occupations and jobs) and the associated distributional conflicts; and it shapes the structure of relations within production, especially relations of domination and exploitation, and the associated conflicts within production. The first of these causal streams, in turn, shapes the flows of people into the class locations within the market and production. Jointly, the class attributes of individuals and their class locations (defined within the market and production) affect their levels of individual economic well being.

This picture, even as a schematic simplification, is in one critical respect fundamentally flawed: it treats power relations and institutional rules as

Figure 11.4   Combined Class Analysis: Macro and Micro Processes

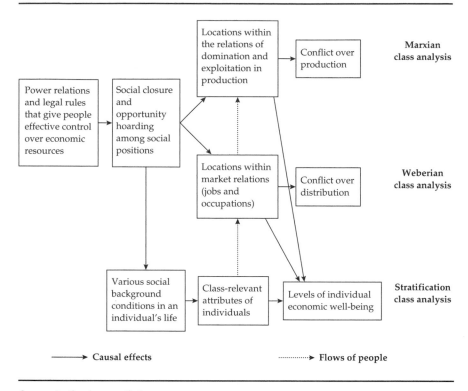

Source: Author's compilation.

exogenous structures, whereas in fact these basic power relations are themselves shaped by class processes and class conflicts. Why does this matter? It matters because structures of inequality are dynamic systems, and the fate of individuals within the system depends not just on the micro-level processes they encounter in their lives but on the trajectory of the system as a whole within which those micro processes occur. Treating the underlying power relations that support a given structure of class locations as fixed parameters is deeply misleading and contributes to the incorrect view that the fate of individuals is simply a function of their attributes and individual circumstances.[4] What we need, therefore, is a dynamic macro model, as pictured in a highly simplified form in figure 11.5.

The recursive quality of the linkages among power, locations, conflicts, and individual outcomes becomes obvious in periods in which dramatic collective challenges to the rules occur. Consider, for example, the radical transformation in the civil rights era of the power relations and legal rules that governed racial patterns of opportunity hoarding in the United States. The conflicts generated by these racialized forms of opportunity hoarding

Figure 11.5   The Dynamic Macro Model

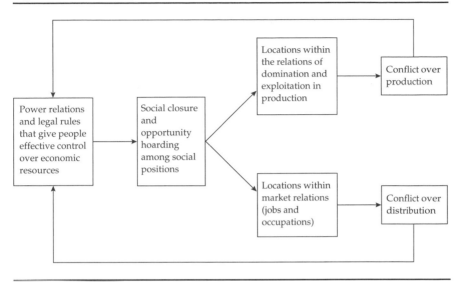

Source: Author's compilation.

ultimately transformed the power relations and legal rules that sustained such opportunity hoarding. The life chances of an African American born in 1950 depended not simply on the micro processes within a fixed structure but also on the trajectory of transformations of the structure generated, in part, by the conflicts produced by that structure.

A fully elaborated class analysis, then, combines this kind of dynamic macro model with the macro-micro multilevel model. These models link the class analysis questions about life chances with the questions about class conflict and historical variation. In such a model, the key insights of stratification approaches, Weberian approaches, and Marxist approaches are combined.

Conclusions

Class analysis, anchored in these three clusters of causal mechanisms and the dynamic model of macro processes, offers a wide-ranging agenda for research and theoretical development. In recent years, at least in the United States, there seems to have been some waning of interest in the macro-structural questions of class conflict and historical variation linked to problems of power, exclusion, and exploitation and a return to the more micro-level concern with individual life conditions, attributes, and life chances associated with the stratification tradition of research. Most of the chapters in this volume follow this basic logic of analysis.

This retreat within sociology from a full-bodied class analysis is, in part, a reflection of broader theoretical trends in social science linked to the ascendancy of neoclassical economics thinking. The neoclassical economic analysis of inequality typically has two central components. The first is the idea that in a capitalist market economy individuals are paid on the basis of their productivity; thus, if everyone's productivity goes up, everyone earns more, and if inequalities in productivity across people are reduced, inequality in economic conditions are reduced. The only important problem is improving the human capital of those at the bottom so that their productivity will increase. The assumption here is that raising the human capital of people at the bottom automatically induces the creation of jobs that will productively utilize that human capital. There is no recognition of the ways in which the structure of jobs is shaped by power relations and access to well-paying jobs is structured by strategies of social closure and not simply the human capital of individuals looking for jobs. To the extent that this is the case and opportunity hoarding remains a potent expression of power relations, simply increasing education at the bottom will be insufficient to dramatically reduce overall levels of inequality.

The second component of the neoclassical economics analysis of inequality is the idea that economic growth is the surest way of improving the lives of people who for whatever reasons are disadvantaged within markets. The attempt by the state to counteract the inequalities generated by the forces of the market creates such inefficiencies, the argument goes, that ultimately this hurts everyone, and thus redistribution is a self-defeating project. Poverty cannot be countered by politically challenging capitalists and wealthy elites, but rather by reducing the fetters on their freedom to invest and make money. Class conflicts are counterproductive; workers should embrace win-win cooperation with their employers and let the market do its magic. These claims ignore the ways in which poverty and inequality serve the interests of powerful elites because of the link between their advantages and the processes of exploitation and domination. So long as that power is unchallenged, then the fruits of economic growth are unlikely to be distributed in a way that would dramatically reduce inequalities.

Sociologists should sharply counter these arguments. While, of course, the micro-level processes by which people acquire class-relevant attributes, especially human capital, matters, the solution to poverty and inequality should not focus simply on remediation of these deficits. Poverty and inequality are anchored in macro relations of opportunity hoarding, domination, and exploitation, and thus a serious challenge to poverty requires a serious challenge to privilege and power. The narrow focus on micro processes obscures this necessity. It is the responsibility of sociological class analysis to clarify the nature of these fundamental structures and contribute to this challenge.

Notes

1. Parts of this section are drawn from Wright (2005).

2. The processes of family transmission of cultural capital explored in both the Goldthorpe and Jackson chapter and the Lareau and Weininger chapter can also be regarded as a special form of opportunity hoarding insofar as children from "disadvantaged" families are excluded from access to the socialization activities that instill these valuable subjective resources. However, both of these chapters are less concerned with the ways in which power is deployed to sustain these exclusions and more focused on the consequences of the resulting variations in individual attributes.

3. The original paper that Michael Hout presented at the NYU conference on which this volume is based contained an extended discussion of the causal relationship between the increasing wealth of the top of the American economic structure, the stagnation of earnings in the middle, and the enduring poverty at the bottom. He argued that since in this period there was also a sharp rise in productivity, the widening gap could most reasonably be interpreted as reflecting an increase in the transfer of the social product generated by the higher productivity of the labor of those in the middle and bottom of the distribution to those at the top. That analysis reflected an exploitation and domination approach to class but was dropped for the book.

4. For exemplary empirical research that in different ways embodies key elements of this dynamic macro-micro model of power, conflict, and life chances, see Kenworthy (2004, 2008), Esping-Andersen (1990), and Przeworski (1985).

References

Bourdieu, Pierre. 1984. *Distinction*. Cambridge, Mass.: Harvard University Press.

Esping-Andersen, Gøsta. 1990. *The Three Worlds of Welfare Capitalism*. Cambridge: Polity Press.

Giddens, Anthony. 1973. *The Class Structure of the Advanced Societies*. New York: Harper & Row.

Kenworthy, Lane. 2004. *Egalitarian Capitalism*. New York: Russell Sage Foundation.

———. 2008. *Jobs with Equality*. Oxford: Oxford University Press.

Parkin, Frank. 1971. *Class Inequality and Political Order*. New York: Praeger.

Przeworski, Adam. 1985. *Capitalism and Social Democracy*. Cambridge: Cambridge University Press.

Sorenson, Aage. 2005. "Foundations of a Rent-Based Class Analysis." In *Approaches to Class Analysis*, edited by Erik Olin Wright. Cambridge: Cambridge University Press.

Tilly, Charles. 1998. *Durable Inequality*. Cambridge: Cambridge University Press.

Wright, Erik Olin. 2005. "If Class Is the Answer, What Is the Question?" In *Approaches to Class Analysis*, edited by Erik Olin Wright. Cambridge: Cambridge University Press.

Chapter 12

Two Oppositions in Studies of Class: A Reflection

JOHN GOLDTHORPE

I AM GENERALLY called upon to do sessions with Erik Olin Wright so that we can argue with each other over Marxist versus non-Marxist forms of class analysis. But on this occasion, this is largely not going to be the case, since Erik has done that part of the wrap-up very well in his chapter. Instead, I will pick up two themes that I think have recurred throughout the whole range of chapters in this volume. I say two themes, but these are really two oppositions that have emerged and that we should think about.

On one side of the first opposition is thinking about class as some kind of *umbrella concept* that aims to capture all the various aspects of social inequality that we know exist in contemporary societies. It may exclude racial and ethnic inequalities or gender inequalities, but it still covers a pretty broad swath of other inequalities. This concept of class is not one for which I have very much sympathy: it just leads to muddled and confused thinking. What I would favor in place of that—and I think other contributors to this volume share this view, including Erik Olin Wright (2005a, chapter 11, this volume)— is a *fairly specific, narrowly defined concept of class* (Goldthorpe 2007a, 2007b) that one could then use along with other concepts that try to capture other aspects of structured social inequality.

Just to illustrate from my own experience, I have been working on class analysis for longer than I care to think (Goldthorpe et al. 1969; Goldthorpe et al. 1987; Goldthorpe and Jackson, this volume), but my current work is actually about social status. I take very seriously the Weberian distinction between class and status as two qualitatively different forms of social stratification, the relationship between which is historically quite contingent.

Recently, my colleague Tak Wing Chan and I have tried to look at different domains and different outcomes and to consider the relative importance of class and status (Chan and Goldthorpe 2007). Not surprisingly, when we look at things like risk of unemployment or the long-term, lifetime development of earnings, it is clear that class, not status, is important. If we shift, however, to another field, that of cultural consumption—the extent to which people participate in various forms of music, theater, dance, cinema, and the visual arts—then we get the reverse result. When we have both concepts in the analysis, and appropriately measured, we find that status is the dominant factor rather than class. In some other fields the situation is more complex and more mixed. When we look at politics in Britain, for example, we find results very much in line with those of Jeff Manza and Clem Brooks (this volume): in actual voting—especially left-right voting (Labour as opposed to Conservative)—class is important and status is not. Looking at a scale of right-left political orientations produces the same result: class is all-important and status is not. However, using another scale that is concerned with libertarian-authoritarian attitudes—attitudes on basic questions about the limits of freedom and the limits of authority—produces completely different results. Status accounts for the variation, not class. I should add that there is considerable status variation within the classes of the class schema that informs several chapters in this volume, although that variation is greater within some classes than others. So there is plenty of scope to get different effects of class and status from one domain of life chances and life choices to another.

What I found especially fascinating in the chapter on health by Carpiano, Link, and Phelan is the way in which the debates that are now going on among social epidemiologists—between those who favor social-psychological or socio-cultural explanations of inequalities in health and those who favor materialist or "political economy" explanations—could rather neatly be translated into debates about whether stratification by class or stratification by status is chiefly important in generating these inequalities. My view is that there is little point in falling out about this. It may well be—in fact I would be willing to bet that it is the case—that certain kinds of health differentials are more related to class and others are more related to status.

So that is one kind of opposition that I have seen coming through in the chapters in this volume: between those authors who use an umbrella concept of class and those, including myself, who draw on more specific concepts of class and who use class as just one concept among others to grapple with the structure of inequality.

The second opposition that I want to discuss is that between an emphasis on individual attributes and an emphasis on social relations in thinking about class. Here again, I am clearly on the same side of the fence as Erik Olin Wright.

Where we differ is in regard to Wright's famous "question 6" on how far we should build normative commitments into our class analysis and how much we should leave them out, so I will say just a word on that here (Wright 2005b, this volume). I suspect that my sociopolitical commitments and values are very close to Wright's, but I want to leave them out of my class analysis—to have them free-standing—because I am rather old-fashioned. I am still a Humean. I do not believe that we can in any way derive an "ought" from an "is." And as a sociologist, I am concerned about the "ises," not the "oughts" that concern me as a citizen.

But there is a more practical point. I want to be able to at least have the possibility of persuading people about the validity of my sociological analysis even when I know they disagree with me politically. I recently had a one-hour session with the new Conservative "shadow" secretary for education. I think that in this discussion I persuaded him about what is really going on as regards social mobility in Britain, especially the relationship between social mobility and education. He got the point, and I think he agreed with the analysis, although it was quite clear that our sociopolitical commitments were very far apart. If we had been discussing the question of what we were going to do about this situation, then we would certainly have disagreed. But at least to a large extent we could share a common analysis and understanding of the situation.

On the question of attributes versus relations in class analysis, my position is very close to Wright's. I would guess that Wright wants to start from a kind of counterfactual position of what things would be like if we really had a democratic-socialist regime—where workers are hiring capital rather than capital hiring workers—while I start more from the situation as it is: from the fact that we have a capitalist free market economy. But then, like Wright, I am interested in what follows from the implied social relationships in labor markets and production units. That is, I am interested in the effects on life chances and life choices of the fact that some people are employers (they deal with their customers, suppliers, and workers), other people are self-employed (they deal, again, with their suppliers and with bank managers and clients), and other people—most of us—are just employees, and we deal with our employers. But then, among employees, there are some of us who work on a very specific kind of labor contract: just so much money for so much work, measured by the time or piece, with special provision for working overtime perhaps and with very limited career prospects. Others of us work on a salaried basis with incremental salary structures and career prospects. These are quite different forms of labor contract, especially when we take into account the implicit as well as the explicit terms.

I think that people who have these different social relations in their economic lives are living in very different social worlds, and that it is the task of class analysis to see how far these differences translate into various outcomes. But, as I have said, I would expect class to be far more consequential for certain sets of life chances and life choices than for others, and—to return to the first opposition—that is why I want to make a clear distinction between class and status. Following Weber, I take status to be a quite different relational structure of inequality to class. Status has to do with which people you treat as your social equals, which you regard as your superiors, and which as your inferiors. And following Weber again, I think the best test of this is, as Weber said, "commensality and connubium"—who eats with whom, who sleeps with whom.

Our status scale (Chan and Goldthorpe 2004) is derived from work that Ed Laumann (1966) did in Chicago back in the 1960s and that, to my mind, has been incomprehensibly neglected in American sociology. Laumann developed a status scale through the analysis of patterns of close friendship—that is, he emphasized the *relational*, not the attributional, aspects of stratification, as in scales of "socioeconomic" status. When we bring status measured like this—through structures of intimate association—into the analysis, we find areas where this particular aspect of structural social inequality is far more consequential than class, and vice versa. That, for me, is the program of social stratification analysis: to understand these different relational structures of inequality and to determine their implications for different domains of social life.

This is an edited transcript of a portion of the concluding session of the April 2006 conference. The editors are grateful to John Goldthorpe for graciously permitting the transcript to be published as well as for his editorial suggestions.

References

Chan, Tak Wing, and John H. Goldthorpe. 2004. "Is There a Status Order in Contemporary British Society? Evidence from the Occupational Structure of Friendship." *European Sociological Review* 20(5): 383–401.

———. 2007. "Class and Status: The Conceptual Distinction and Its Empirical Relevance." *American Sociological Review* 72(4): 512–32.

Goldthorpe, John H. 2007a. *On Sociology*, vol. 1, *Critique and Program*, 2nd ed. Stanford, Calif.: Stanford University Press.

———. 2007b. *On Sociology*, vol. 2, *Illustration and Retrospect*, 2nd ed. Stanford, Calif.: Stanford University Press.

Goldthorpe, John H., Catriona Llewellyn, and Clive Payne. 1987. *Social Mobility and Class Structure in Modern Britain*. Oxford: Oxford University Press.

Goldthorpe, John H., David Lockwood, Frank Bechhofer, and Jennifer Platt. 1969. *The Affluent Worker in the Class Structure*. Cambridge: Cambridge University Press.

Laumann, Edward. 1966. *Prestige and Association in an Urban Community*. New York: Bobbs-Merrill.

Wright, Erik Olin, editor. 2005a. *Approaches to Class Analysis*. London: Cambridge University Press.

———. 2005b. "If Class Is the Answer, What Is the Question?" In *Approaches to Class Analysis*, edited by Erik Olin Wright. London: Cambridge University Press.

Chapter 13

Reflection on "Class Matters"

JANNY SCOTT

THIS IS like some sort of strange dream.

In the dream, you're a reporter who has spent a year calling up strangers and asking them to tell you everything they know about a subject you don't understand and they do. In fact, they've spent entire careers studying the thing that you're going to profess to know something about in, oh, six minutes. You go off and write something inevitably facile—this is journalism, after all—based on things they told you. Afterward, you're never quite sure they even saw what you wrote. Nor are you quite sure you would have wanted them to. Then, a year later, early one morning on too little sleep and not enough caffeine, you find yourself in a room on a college campus. You're at a table, and there are rows and rows of chairs facing you. And every one is filled with the very people you spent a year pestering.

If you're lucky, that's when you wake up. If you're lucky.

I figured I'd talk about the conception and pachyderm-style gestation period of the project that *The New York Times* did in 2005 on class, "Class Matters," because it seems to me to shed some light on some of the questions I was asked to consider: Why does the myth of the classless society persist? Is there an awareness of class as an issue? Why is there no language of class? What are the difficulties in framing class-based issues? And what does the reader—or, say, the editor—think class is?

It had occurred to me sometime before we ever embarked on the class series that maybe I could try to cover class as a beat at the *Times*. I'd been covering demographics and the release of the data from the 2000 census; after a while, it had begun to seem to me that all stories—crime stories, school stories, zoning stories, health stories, immigration stories, labor stories, transportation stories—were in some way about class. But we never wrote those stories as if they were about class. We wrote them as though they were about money, education, power, culture, gender, race.

I remember having breakfast with the then-metro editor of the *Times* back in 2003. He wanted to know what I wanted to do next. I said I had been thinking about whether there was a way to make a beat out of writing about class. It seemed to me that class difference was out in the open in New York City in a way that was maybe less so in other places. Once you got tuned into it for whatever reason, class assumptions and dynamics seemed to permeate nearly every encounter. Class was the subtext in our daily lives, I suggested. But we rarely looked at it squarely. Maybe I could write about that.

He looked at me across the table. He was really smart. He cocked his head. "I think you might be saying something really interesting," he said, "but I don't know what it is."

The problem was, neither did I.

Later that year, a high-ranking editor at the *Times* decided to see if there was a big project to be done on class. After editing a series we had done on race in 2000, she had come to think of class as the last unexplored country, a place where journalists rarely went. She asked me and David Leonhardt, who covered economics, to spend a few months looking into what there might be to say. It would have to be new, the *Times* being a *news*-paper. It would have to be tellable as a story. And it couldn't be predictable, feeding the assumptions of critics who liked to paint the *Times* as hand-wringing and reflexively liberal.

David tackled economists, who, of course, don't even use the word "class." I took the sociologists, who at least used the word, even if they had long ago stopped agreeing about what it meant. On the part of at least one of our editors, you will be amused to know, there was some suspicion of sociologists; to him, interviewing sociologists to get a handle on the existence of class was like relying on psychics to give you an objective opinion about the existence of the paranormal. I remember him asking one day, "Could we do this project without talking to any sociologists?"

Our editors scheduled lots and lots of meetings—a sure sign that we were wandering in a desert no one seemed sure how to cross. Lots of reporters and editors and outsiders were dragged in to test out the idea. Everyone's first question seemed to be: What is it you're talking about? What is class anyway? A man in the graphics department said it was something his mother had, raising him and his siblings in a parish in Louisiana with no husband and no money. What about P. Diddy? people kept asking, as though now they had really tripped us up; what class was he? One of the television critics made it clear she thought the idea was lame; the only issue in America anymore, she said, is money.

We needed a working definition. Some of the people we were interviewing told us class is defined by income. Some said it is more about education, or about wealth. Some said occupation is the key. We were ruthless, and we had a deadline. We decided, almost for the sake of argument, that class is the product of a combination of all four. Like a hand of cards? someone at the paper asked us. Maybe you don't have face cards in all four categories, but if you have them in three, you're safely upper-middle-class? Sure, why not? Once we had a definition, no matter how fallible, it became possible to talk.

After two or three months, we submitted a proposal for a series. Here was the general idea: Class has become in many ways less visible in the United States over the past thirty years, thanks to things like demographic change; racial, ethnic, and gender diversity; globalization; the rise of credit; and changes in consumption. But at the same time, in important areas, the impact of class has increased—in access to higher education, in health and longevity, and in where people live and who gets ahead, the power of class has been on the rise.

I took the quick approval of the series as a testament that people (editors) know on some level that class is a potent force but one that we most of the time choose not to examine. When we polled Americans about class for the series, we found little support for the truism that all Americans think they're middle-class. The people we polled seemed to have a surprisingly sophisticated understanding of where they fit in the scheme of things. They seemed to understand the impact of class well enough to support the idea of class-based affirmative action. Where they seemed confused was on the question of their chances of getting ahead.

Some months later, a group of reporters on the project had a conversation about what exactly we were telling our subjects we were up to. For many of us, our stories required insinuating ourselves into the daily lives of people and watching how the power of class played out in their experiences over many months. Should we tell them it's a series about class? one reporter wondered. Some were nervous about using the word, as though it would be off-putting, which it might have been. I had decided to use it up front, to avoid misunderstandings. Still, my subjects rarely, if ever, used the word, even talking to me.

Little was clear-cut in the reporting and writing of this series. The data on mobility were murky to a degree that made editors nervous. In our stories, were we seeing the impact of class differences or of something else? Did the upper middle class man in my story do better after his heart attack because he was an upper-middle class man—an educated patient with good health insurance, a flexible work schedule, and an attentive, non-working, younger wife to provide him with the kind of social support that made a difference? Was he the beneficiary of the kind of agency and entitlement that accrues to the privileged? Or did he do better because of his personality? Or blind luck? Did the working class woman do worse after her heart attack because she was uneducated and a smoker with a bad diet, a sedentary lifestyle, and a physically punishing job? Or did she do worse because she was female? Or unlucky?

Daily journalism often works best with black and white. What to do with gray?

We handed in our stories, and they were kicked back repeatedly for rewriting. We were told that it had to be clear immediately that each one was a story about class, not something else. Not simply a story about college dropouts or expensive suburbs or changes in the way people shop. I had briefly entertained the idea that I might write my entire six-thousand-word piece without using the word "class," that it could just be implicit. That was out; the editors worried that we could not count on readers to pick up the implication that the story was all about class.

I do not believe readers are tone-deaf to issues of inequality and opportunity. Well-done stories about inequality often elicit outpourings of impassioned responses from readers sending money, wanting to help, calling to offer whatever they can. I do think the media and readers—I don't know which came first—have a bias in favor of stories about sudden, serendipitous moments of opportunity seized rather than stories about opportunity withheld or taken away.

Are sources not speaking the right tongue? What can academics do to better educate the public about class as a powerful force that shapes American lives? It would be helpful if there was more agreement about what we mean when we use the word "class." In the series, we ended up for the most part dodging the inevitable question from readers and subjects alike: okay, so what class am I in? With some people telling us there were no longer big classes, just micro classes, maybe 150 or more, there was no way we could begin to answer that question. But I have a feeling that that's what people wanted to know.

Both the *Wall Street Journal* and the *Los Angeles Times* did series that might be said to have been about class at the same time that we did. But they defined theirs differently. The *Journal*'s series was about what had happened to mobility in America; the *L.A. Times* covered the loss of the safety net. In American journalism, we talk about class when we write vaguely snide, often humorous stories about the absurdities of the old-time upper crust. But when we write about the more profound implications of class position on the course of people's lives, we seem to think we're writing about something else.

After the series was over, a new metro editor took me out to lunch. It was before my favorite class story of recent months, the New York City transit strike, a story in which the word "class" or the idea of class barely surfaced directly in the coverage, even though everything about the event and the public reaction seemed to scream class. The new metro editor wanted to know what I wanted to do next. I said I wanted to cover inequality. Particularly in New York City, but throughout the country, it seemed to be everywhere, and yet we chose to live with it. Maybe I could write about that.

"I think you might be saying something really interesting," she said, "but how about writing about the rich?"

Chapter 14

Class Notes

ROGER D. HODGE

WHY DOES the myth of the classless society persist in America? Is the myth itself a myth? Is the public more aware of class as an issue than social scientists generally think? Are Americans afraid to talk about class? What can academics do to better educate the public about class as a powerful force that shapes American lives? These were some of the guiding questions that we were asked to address at the 2006 conference.

I think the myth is itself a myth. Americans are obsessed with class, and although they might not always use that word, they possess a highly refined and sophisticated vocabulary for discussing it. The concept is at work everywhere—in conversation, in street-level interactions, in our entertainment, and in the news media. (Just watch one episode of *Trading Spouses, Cops, The Simpsons, South Park, Married with Children, My Name Is Earl, The Beverly Hillbillies,* or *The Simple Life.* Class anxiety is the dramatic engine of all of them.) We express our class anxieties and allegiances by means of our clothing, the cars we choose to drive, the neighborhoods we live in, and the schools we attend. Body types and haircuts. Jewelry. How and where we vacation. The sports we play or follow. What newspapers we read. The same person who might deny that America has a "class system" when a pollster interrupts his dinner and convinces him to submit to a questionnaire will without a second glance precisely categorize a new acquaintance, someone he's just met at a cocktail party or in a business meeting, within the infinitely nuanced American micro-class economy.

Herewith, then, a short list of terms that signify class in America.

Rich, poor, white trash, ghetto, snob, WASP, JAP, striver, yuppy, artsy, hipster, professional, blue collar, white collar, redneck, hillbilly, hick, low-rent, high-rent, hoity-toity, chic, glamorous, fabulous, fashionable, trendy, celebrity, Wall Street, suit, local, covite, Eurotrash, homeboy, bum, home-less, country, gangsta, projects, suburban, inner city, uptown, downtown, wrong side of the tracks, elitist, Ivy League, state school, preppy, public, col-lege boy, frat boy, good ole boy, self-made, trust fund, nouveau riche, hoi polloi, exclusive, cultured, cultivated, wetback, illegal, immigrant, outer borough, bridge and tunnel, trustee, country club, service worker, loser, slacker, trailer park, trailer trash, skanky, upscale, classy.

It's not clear to me, however, that class is, properly speaking, an "issue." We speak of racism as an issue. The collapse of the health care system, our decaying schools, and the war in Iraq are all issues. Is class itself an issue, something that can be fixed or overcome? That strikes me as something akin to saying that desire is an issue. Is death an issue? The weather? Class is a fact, a whole world of facts.

Class, from my perspective as a magazine editor, is not particularly interesting in itself, but it does figure prominently in many of the stories we tell in *Harper's Magazine,* in our narrative and investigative journalism as well as in the fiction we publish. In other words, I don't see the point of running stories that attempt to demonstrate the obvious fact that class is a powerful force in American life. What's more interesting is the story of how the American ruling class, or at least its dominant faction, has engaged in the wholesale looting of our society. The point is not *that* we have a rul-ing class but *how* and *why* our ruling class has come to be so reckless. Historically, such inordinate civic corruption (and the collapse of political legitimacy that so often ensues) has led to political violence in one form or another—and that, it seems to me, is a very important issue.

Chapter 15

Holding Up a Mirror to a Classless Society

RAY SUAREZ

I WANT TO thank the conference organizers for thinking that a journalist has something to say that's fit to be heard at an ambitious conference. Reporters are sociologists on the fly. We traffic blithely and consistently in class-rooted images, especially on TV, but certainly in the printed press as well. We do this so habitually that it achieves a kind of transparency, a meta-wink at the audience. That wink is most powerful to that portion of the audience watching in metropolitan areas, in homes that cross every boundary of class and status. When I say we traffic in those images on television, I mean that we use them in place of language. The images themselves are a language thoroughly understood at every end of the transaction—by the interviewer, by the interviewee, and by the end user of the images, the audience. These images are a vocabulary so complete that they don't need to be pointed out, identified, or underscored in any way when we marry a narration track to a series of pictures to convey information in a nuts-and-bolts, "just the facts, ma'am" kind of way connotatively, and denotatively, in this other language. We don't need subtitles to decode this language because everybody watching is bilingual, or thinks they are.

You are unlikely to turn on the television and see a group of white young men face down on the streets with their hands behind their necks. Is it because white young men never do anything wrong? No, you know it's not that. It's just that when young white men get arrested, police are less likely to roust them out of a cell and parade them in front of cameras. Also, television stations have their resources concentrated in dense urban areas, and they are more likely to shoot events that happen closer to the station. These factors tend to reinforce unspoken assumptions about correlations between race and class, and between race and crime, that are not in fact true but that are sustained by the language and images streaming from the television day after day.

When there is a tragic death of a young person, do middle class people not lose their composure? Do middle class people not mourn in an emotional way? Of course they do. We just tend not to see their mourning in the same way, and because their private moments are less likely to happen in a public way, they are less likely to be seen and photographed, and any such photographs are thus less likely to be thrown in the hopper with other images. With money comes the ability to exert control over when and where and under what circumstances one is seen. With money comes the ability to put mediating layers between one's self and the unwanted gaze. There is a corollary in the economy of images presented by television: with less money comes less ability to control the gaze of others, less ability to control self-representation, less ability to block the unwanted gaze.

It is a very powerful thing to have the privilege of self-description, the ability to be an expert about the facts of your own life. Much of journalism is the practice of identifying and locating credible sources of opinion and striking a bargain. Give me your credentialed opinion, and I will give you my access to the public's eyes and ears. We will live symbiotically, you and I. Because I put you on TV, you will be made an expert; because you are an expert, you will give my product a kind of public heft.

If your life is one marked by lower educational attainment, lower income, and lower class, you are less likely to be considered an expert about anything, even your own life. While you may be able to explain what's hard about getting health care when you have no insurance, your plight will be used as an illustration and explained by an expert. A low-status person is raw material; a higher-status person is given the job of providing context, sketching the big picture, describing the systemic challenges of being a lower-status individual.

The public has a very finely tuned calibration about how it assigns class location. It's a funny, supple, mutable world, and communications media like the news business play with and manipulate these definitions with that knowing wink I spoke of earlier. When the guys at the loading dock buy one Powerball ticket and split an $80 million jackpot, reporters chronicle in loving detail the life choices the winners are about to make: whether or not they keep their job; whether or not they plan to move; what kind of boat they are going to buy. Without ever saying it, the grinning anchorwoman and the reporter live from the scene jocularly describe a rich low-class person. A winner's authenticity is praised—having money will not change him or her. I would love to see the face on one of these grinning, college-educated, six-figure-earning faux regular guys if the jackpot winner said, "Please, leave me alone, and if you come to my house, I will call the police." Or if the winner said, "I'm going to get my teeth fixed, and I'm going to pay off my mortgage and go to college. And I'm not taking any further questions."

Because mass-market news is a story told by high-status people about higher- and lower-status people to lower-status people, class is woven into the DNA of the news. It is an enterprise that proposes to operate in the public service interest of the greatest number of people while, in the profit-making end of the business, creating dividends for the wealthiest Americans. The class tensions inside national network news, and even the commercials that pay for that news, can sometimes be hilarious.

If you were a stranger to our country and had been assigned to learn about it by watching television and reading the papers, the America you would assemble in your head would be wildly different from the one that actually exists. You would come away from your week or month or year in front of the tube convinced that American households are richer than they are. You would be convinced that more people are knowledge workers, business travelers, and rich than actually are any of those things. You would think that the average American is not strung out on debt, carrying more than $9,000 in credit card debt from month to month. Turn on *The Today Show* in the wintertime and there's a grinning feature reporter doing a live shot from the Consumer Electronics Show in Vegas. The reporter in the field is happily walking the hosts back in New York through the high-priced gee-whiz that will soon be coming to the shelves. Tune in a month later, and another reporter might be doing the same from the Detroit Auto Show. In a country where families in the middle quintile are earning about $45,000 in annual household income, cars costing that much and more are featured. The effect of dollar weakness on the cost of overseas travel is detailed for a country where between 10 and 15 percent of citizens have a passport. In a country where an ever-shrinking portion of the population owns a greater and greater share of the wealth, gyrations in the stock market are detailed to the hundredths of points, without much of an effort made to connect the activities of market players to the small holdings of most American stock funds or to the jobs that make up the vast majority of the dollars that working Americans live on each year.

That most black and Latino households have no net worth at all, and that the inability to hold real estate in a family portfolio as a performing asset to make intergenerational transfer of wealth impossible, does not intrude on the class-riven but allergic-to-talking-about-class world presented in the popular press. Athletes, entertainers, and performer millionaires like Donald Trump all inhabit different class realms in the mass media world, but the kind of structural underpinnings of class that make TV what it is, and that make newspapers what they are, are realities of class in America that intrude only in elite media. It's as if the news is a kind of hazardous material that can only be handled by properly trained individuals.

The secret knowledge that a class straddler or climber learns on the way up from the barrio, the shape shifting, the self-composition that individual might undergo on the subway ride from Merrill Lynch downtown to Washington Heights uptown—these are simply not fit topics for conversation. It is a game the media have decided to cover only in the most tangential way—like reporting only the scores and giving no details on how the winners won.

The people who write and research and present in mass media do know plenty; however, their roles are heavily proscribed. The expectations are so well understood by all the players in the game that no one even needs to describe what they're doing. A reporter describes a person who is killed on his stoop as being at the wrong place at the wrong time, without ever unpacking that idea that the place where you live could be so deadly that living there could put you in the fatally wrong place to be.

When the tables are turned and a high-status or wealthy person is killed in some place where people don't normally get killed, the tone of the reporter is often one of shared outrage and surprise, channeling the fear of people who thought they had made enough and paid enough that they didn't have to worry about the mess of the real world barging into their orderly enclave.

The distaste for, and condescension toward, the poor in a lot of conventional news reporting can sometimes be jaw-droppingly obvious, as it was, for instance, when millionaire anchors described the violence in Los Angeles following the Rodney King verdicts in rising panic and outrage. Take a look at the easy, seamless acceptance of police-generated umbrella narratives of tension in poor and minority neighborhoods and of the need for acceptable leaders to go down and talk to "those people" and calm them down. It is at these moments that the calm and happy world of liberty and consumption for all is plunged into the messy intricacies of class.

Cases like the Amadou Diallo shooting immediately throw up a scaffolding of class interest in which certain people, almost as if they were sent the script in advance, side with the police. Others, in a similar way, side with the victim, and the news business worriedly tries to do both: granting deference to the mayor, who seemed to always side with the police when civilians were killed, and creating a lot of space for the shooting victim's West African mother, Katiatou Diallo, who came to New York for the trials of the police.

A lot of reporting results in morality plays. These plays are cast with archetypical players: the spoiled rich girl . . . her salt-of-the-earth slum sister . . . the honor student shooting victim . . . the hardworking guy who can't get a break . . . the smart and nervy nobody who suddenly gets ahead.

How much less attention would Dennis Kozlowski's trial for looting his company, Tyco, have gotten if there had been no video of his opulent birthday party complete with waitstaff in Greco-Roman garb and a reproduction of Leonardo's David with vodka pouring from the penis? The $6,000 shower curtains were but a maraschino cherry on L'Affair Kozlowski. We like these images because they distract us from the hardening boundaries of class in America, the increasing difficulty of class mobility, and the very real chance that you can work hard, and constantly, your whole life and still be poor. Confronting these realities would make the news, and the entertainment programming around it, a fairly exhausting place to live. We would rather be happy than smart it seems, and on most days American journalism would rather be complicit in class narratives than fearless about them.

Chapter 16

Reading Class Between the Lines (of This Volume): A Reflection on Why We Should Stick to Folk Concepts of Social Class

DALTON CONLEY

Mmuch academic ink (academic in both senses of the word) has been spilled in debates as to whether class is gradational—à la Max Weber's classic notion of life chances in the marketplace—or whether it is relational—more akin to Marx's definition of class as defined by the relations of production (or Wright's in this volume, for that matter). Is class best thought of as a fundamental social cleavage or as a continuum of sorts? Does it rest in the individual person or in the person's "role" in the economic system?

The constant changing of the nature of our economy keeps these debates lively. For example, writing about the Internet information economy in *No Collar*, Andrew Ross (2002) identifies what he calls a fundamental cleavage in the computerized workplace: classes, he argues, can be defined by whether the acceleration of computational speed makes your life easier (by making you more efficient) or harder (by increasing the pressure on your own human "processing time"). These debates are sometimes waged without the formal jargon of academe. In the online magazine *Slate*, Jason Furman and Barbara Ehrenreich (2006), for example, recently debated whether Wal-Mart is good or bad for America's "working class." Wal-Mart drives down wages but also depresses prices for low-income shoppers, so what is the company's net effect on the so-called working class? Hard to

366

tell. Who gains and who loses does not appear to fall within neat class lines or boxes, but the Wal-Mart model certainly does create oppositional (and perhaps even exploitative) relationships. The biggest sure losers, for instance, may be other capitalists up the supply chain, whose profits are driven down to nothing by the monopsonistic pressures that Wal-Mart exerts.

I leave theoretical controversies about the conceptualization of class and economic interests to Erik Olin Wright to address in his chapter, "Logics of Class Analysis." Here, instead, I want to focus on reconciling (or not) the colloquial sense of what class is and how it works with the ways in which we social scientists try to capture it. The bottom line of my position is that when sociologists and other academics debate the difference between class and status, between relational and gradational notions of class, and in how best to measure it, they are, in essence, trying to sweep dust or sand into neat little piles. They can make these epistemological molehills, but what good are they? Dust bunnies soon blow across the landscape, and piles of dirt have little power when we push on them to explain things. Put another way, I would say that sociologists are a lot like the character Lenny in Steinbeck's *Of Mice and Men:* Lenny adored his pet mouse so much that he squeezed it to death. We do the same when we try to grasp what I am going to argue is an inherently indescribable concept. Rather than spend more time and effort in trying to refine lofty conceptual apparatuses, I would argue for a "kitchen sink" (or what Goldthorpe calls an "umbrella") approach: even when we include every form of social hierarchy we can measure, our empirical models do rather poorly in explaining meaningful outcomes. (Theoretically elegant measures of class tend to do worse than simple measures of SES; see, for example, the exchange between Charles Halaby and David Weakliem [1993] and Erik Olin Wright [1993] in the *American Sociological Review;* also see Halaby [1993]). What's more, like Wittgenstein's theory of the relationship between words and meaning, when we measure any social hierarchy—class included—we tend to point to, but never name precisely, exactly what we mean. As a result, I argue that we should embrace a folk concept of class and include in our models all forms of social hierarchy that appear to hold empirical weight, ascriptive or achieved. These may range from social networks (what Goldthorpe is calling "relational status position") to income flows and wealth stocks to physical appearance. Especially in an age when cultural, social, human, bodily, and financial capital are fluid and exchangeable, this would appear to be the most robust strategy, lest we end up like the blind men and the elephant (if the reader will indulge yet another metaphor in this crowded paragraph).

Put another way, essays by a volume's editor typically stress what is in the book. This one, by contrast, is going to tell you what is missing—that is, what to reflect on when reading between the lines of the chapters in the collection. And to do this, I will start with a parable that may be familiar.

If we want to ask how this folk concept of class works, perhaps there is no better example than to turn to our current president, George W. Bush. The election and presidency of Bush put class right in our faces on a number of dimensions: how did a man who was a self-confessed alcoholic until age forty; a man who was a C student throughout his academic career; a businessman who ran Arbusto (the Spanish word for Bush and the name he gave his Midland, Texas–based oil company) into the ground—how did this man end up occupying what is arguably the most powerful position in the world? Yes, it is a story of political shifts in the United States. But it is primarily a case study in how class works.

The material aspects of class are evident here, of course. Like his father before him, Bush received an elite education, paid in full, first at Andover for high school, then at Yale for his bachelor's degree, and finally at Harvard for his MBA. He was given ample campaign funding to run (unsuccessfully) for the U.S. Congress in 1978. When that did not work out as hoped, he then received capital from "investors" to start Arbusto, his oil exploration firm. (George Bush Sr. had received his own $1 million bequest to "get started.") When Arbusto went belly up during the era of cheap oil in the 1980s, Bush fell softly (and kindly) onto the boards of several corporations. Then, in 1994, he again benefited from the "kindness of strangers" (or, in his case, family friends) when he was installed as managing director of the Texas Rangers baseball team, a deal that allowed him to "purchase" a share of the team for a mere $600,000, which he later sold for $15 million.

In addition to the material advantages that George Bush enjoyed directly from his family and from his family's connections to big business, there was, of course, the political pedigree that came with his name. This name had been a potent brand in politics for three generations, so after his stint in business Bush managed to land the governorship of Texas on his first try. And after reelection, he positioned himself (or rather had been positioned) so firmly as the presidential front-runner that he had raised a record amount of money before even the first primary. Furthermore, despite his admitted problem with alcoholism that lasted until age forty, Bush's elite status protected him to such a degree that he made it almost all the way through the 2000 presidential campaign without a drunk driving conviction coming to light.

While the importance of these financial and social capital endowments that Bush enjoyed cannot be understated, it would not be fair to say that they tell the whole story of how upper class (or in this case, elite) status works in America. It neglects the social-psychological aspects of class.

Many sociologists and anthropologists have written about how many working class youths are socialized into a reproduction of that status in their own coming of age. For example, Paul Willis (1977) has vividly described how working class teenagers in the United Kingdom (though he might as well have been writing about the United States) are taught to obey authority in school and to mitigate their aspirations for anything greater than a skilled manual occupation. In the American context, Jay MacLeod (1995) describes a similar process by which peer culture serves to blunt the aspirations and expectations of poor white and black teenagers.

More recently, the co-editor of this book, Annette Lareau, has described how class is not only inscribed through societal institutions, such as school and work, but also in the very ways in which families function. In her 2003 book *Unequal Childhoods*, Lareau argues that working class parents tend to instill a sharp division between the world of children and the world of adults among their offspring. Middle class children, she shows, are often shown how to navigate the adult world of social institutions through extensive involvement in organized activities with adult nonkin. Meanwhile, working class kids in her study were taught to shy away from entitlement claims at school; by contrast, middle class kids were taught to expect adult attention in a process she calls "concerted cultivation." In other words, more important than the content of music lessons, SAT tutorials, or soccer leagues is their very form—the organized relationships to nonkin adults.

There has been less scholarship, however, on how class works—that is, how it pays off—for the elite (as opposed to how it fails the working class). Bush is illustrative here as well. Just as the social reproduction of the working class involves a constraining of the horizons of the minds of its members, the construction of an upper class involves the expansion of the sense of possibility among its members. A key part of this construction, I would posit, is the "envisioning" process—the simple familiarity with and demystification of certain social roles that is afforded those in privileged positions. To explain what I mean, do the following thought experiment with me (at the risk of making myself sound like a get-rich-quick guru on a late-night infomercial): try to imagine yourself sitting at the president's desk in the White House.

Pretty hard to imagine, I am willing to bet. Thanks to a West Wing tour given by a friend of mine who worked in the Clinton administration, I have seen the Oval Office; I even got to shake Bill Clinton's hand on the South Lawn. Still, I cannot generate an image in my mind of myself sitting at the desk, doing whatever it is that presidents do. I would speculate, however, that George Bush had little trouble envisaging himself as president, given the fact that his father showed him how the job worked. This inheritance of "possibility" is, I would argue, just as important as all the social and economic resources that George Bush Sr. (and his connections) provided his son. The presidency, for George W. Bush, was not a totally abstract idea. It was a job that people (and even relatives) did.

For George Bush Sr., or Al Gore Jr., being the son of a senator might have been enough to make big-time politics seem "doable." Of course, occasionally someone who has not been born into such privilege can still rise to these heights—someone like Dwight Eisenhower, Jimmy Carter, or Bill Clinton, for instance. But in these cases, perhaps there is another moment in which the class possibilities are expanded—such as the time when young Bill shook the hand of President John Kennedy in the Rose Garden. Alternatively, perhaps it is a gradual process, as in the case of Eisenhower, whose military career provided a step-by-step steepage in the nature of power and politics.

While, of course, the thought experiment of "becoming president" may be a tad extreme, the basic theory applies to all rungs of the socioeconomic ladder. For instance, what is the best background predictor of getting a college degree? It's not race, not income, not even parental occupation. The single most important (measurable) factor is one's own parent's education. If a child has a parent who went to (and completed) college, the odds that she will also complete a bachelor's degree are much greater than those of her counterpart from a family of no college graduates. Of course, this statistic is picking up a number of aspects of class reproduction—everything from the inheritance of genes to the economic resources and social connections and actual learned knowledge (human capital) that a college-educated parent can more easily provide his or her child. All these aspects of a parent's education are no doubt important. Some of these dimensions of class can be measured—albeit with difficulty and lots of random and nonrandom measurement error. Others (genes, for example) remain a giant black box.

However important these factors are, I would argue that they do not represent the most powerful aspects of how the folk concept of class works. The most potent aspect of the college-educated parent is the very fact that she has shown the possibility of college to her child—perhaps not just the possibility but the probability too, or at least the expectation. Expectations, possibilities, probabilities, aspirations—these are notoriously difficult to measure quantitatively (or qualitatively, for that matter). The realistic vision of sitting in the college lecture hall taking notes (or at the president's desk, for that matter) is a matter of not just having a glimpse of what a college setting really looks like—from an immersion program or merely from TV, say—but also comprehending the instruction manual of what to do to get there. Each little step must be envisioned—taking the SATs, requesting applications, revising a personal essay, and so on. There are plenty of exceptions, of course—remarkable individuals who manage to "wing it" up the class hierarchy, improvising and seizing opportunities along the way. But as the proverb goes, these exceptions—let's call them "upward mobiles"—generally show the validity of the social class rule. That is, they illustrate how remarkable someone must be to pull off such a feat.

Elliot Liebow (1967), author of the classic ethnography *Tally's Corner*, makes a related point. While policymakers may want to target children—the deserving poor—and avoid rewarding adults (and adult men in particular)—the so-called undeserving poor—their efforts to break the intergenerational reproduction of poverty (read: class) will come to naught as long as older generations are left to struggle and flounder in the face of limited economic possibilities, thereby defining the "opportunity horizon" for those maturing children. In other words, perhaps we do not want to help the older men hanging out on the street corners of Washington's ghetto communities, but changing their fates is key to changing the fates of the kids, who, we may agree, deserve the class possibilities of occasional mentoring, the Fresh Air Fund, free SAT prep courses, summer immersion courses, and outreach, outreach, outreach. These programs are all well and good. But even together, they cannot do enough to completely counteract the message of limited prospects conveyed by dads and uncles hanging out on the corner.

I began this concluding essay by saying that it was going to tell you what is not in the book. The chapters in the volume describe class in one way or another: whether classes should best be thought of as large occupational groupings or smaller ones (Grusky and Weeden); how neighborhood boundaries are drawn and redrawn along class lines (Pattillo); the extent to which husbands' and wives' economic statuses are independent or correlated with each other (McCall); or how income is related to voting patterns (Manza and Brooks). These are but a few of the many important contributions contained herein. What they all have in common, however, is an attempt to proxy class, whether through occupation, income, education, or wealth.

But the very paradox of class is that the moment we are measuring some aspect of it adequately—say, income—and specifying a causal pathway of some sort, then we have taken our finger off what class really is. If it is income buying us advantage, then it is not social class exactly, but rather financial resources. If it is explicit skills or credentials that land us the killer job, then it isn't social class per se that gets us there. Rather, it is the silent force between the cracks of wealth, income, occupation, and education that constitutes the mortar of the class system. We researchers use these four pillars of SES to act as a proxy for something latent—something they are related to but are not themselves—when we try to "model" the effects of social class. Steven Lukes writes that power is most potent when it is least recognized or explicit. Class, of course, is one of the most important forms of power, and it too is most virile when it is least visible.

To elucidate what I mean, take the example of Roger Hodge, editor of *Harper's* magazine and a contributor to this volume. As one-half of a struggling young couple, he lived in a poor section of Brooklyn in a tenement building. He was working at an entry-level job in the magazine business, making more or less what his neighbors made. He was struggling economically, like they were, to raise his kids on his low pay. But, he confesses, there was never any doubt—among any of the parties—that he was of a different class than his neighbors. Nor was this difference ever made explicit. It merely sat there in the air, thickly, between the parents as the kids played with each other.

That unspoken—unspeakable even—thing that hangs in the air . . . that is the essence of social class. In Roger's case, it was certainly proxied to a certain extent by his education. It no doubt was related to his race (Roger is white). But plenty of white people do not have Roger's class privileges. Nor do most college graduates, especially many who—like Roger—come from modest economic backgrounds themselves. Conversely, some people with high class quotients, so to speak, have not gone to college or failed to finish. (Think Bill Gates, Woody Allen, or Matt Damon, just to name a few famous examples.) No, it was a certain je ne sais quoi that Roger possessed—which was related to his race and education but was not exactly captured by them—that served as the class factor that distinguished him from his tenement coresidents.[1]

Sure enough, Roger worked his way up the editorial ladder, and a mere ten years later was named *Harper's* youngest editor ever. He no longer lives in the same building. One might argue that in order to get a complete picture of his class status we needed to watch him for a decade or more to adequately measure it. In other words, Roger's income or place of residence back in 1996 did not adequately proxy his class only because it was a poor snapshot. Merely collecting more years of data to capture his "permanent income," in the language of economists, would have solved the problem of "misclassification." However, that is a cop-out, since it denies the power of that invisible force that divided Roger from his neighbors and that he felt on a daily basis. (He claimed that he thought his neighbors abhorred him.) It is also to take something (namely, his ultimate class position) as obvious *after the fact*. After all, what good is class (or its various stand-ins) if it is not predictive?

We are, of course, caught between the proverbial rock and a hard place: I want something that is ultimately silent and unnameable to be predictive. I am asking the impossible of my own dust bunny. But please keep this tension in mind as you reflect on the collection of wonderful essays herein. Think of social class as a ghost that haunts this volume, tapping you, dear reader, on the shoulder occasionally as you are about to turn the page. But each time you spin your head around to catch a glimpse, it has disappeared from view.

Notes

1. Susan Mayer (1997), in the first pages of *What Money Can't Buy: Family Income and Children's Life Chances,* tells a similar story of being a struggling single mother while also having a class status that did not match her income.

References

Furman, Jason, and Barbara Ehrenreich. 2006. "Is Wal-Mart Good for the American Working Class?" *Slate,* June 30, 2006. Accessed November 20, 2007 at http://www.slate.com/id/2144517/.

Halaby, Charles N. 1993. "Reply to Wright." *American Sociological Review* 58(1): 35–36.

Halaby, Charles N., and David L. Weakliem. 1993. "Ownership and Authority in the Earnings Function: Nonnested Tests of Alternative Specifications." *American Sociological Review* 58(1): 16–30.

Lareau, Annette. 2003. *Unequal Childhoods: Class, Race, and Family Life.* Berkeley, Calif.: University of California Press.

Liebow, Elliot. 1967. *Tally's Corner: A Study of Negro Streetcorner Men.* Boston, Mass.: Little, Brown.

MacLeod, Jay. 1995. *Ain't No Making It: Aspirations and Attainment in a Low-Income Neighborhood.* Boulder, Colo.: Westview Press.

Mayer, Susan E. 1997. *What Money Can't Buy: Family Income and Children's Life Chances.* Cambridge, Mass.: Harvard University Press.

Ross, Andrew. 2002. *No Collar: The Humane Workplace and Its Hidden Costs.* Philadelphia, Pa.: Temple University Press.

Willis, Paul. 1977. *Learning to Labor: How Working-Class Kids Get Working-Class Jobs.* New York: Columbia University Press.

Wright, Erik Olin. 1993. "Typologies, Scales, and Class Analysis: A Comment on Halaby and Weakliem's 'Ownership and Authority in the Earnings Function.' " *American Sociological Review* 58(1): 31–34.

Index

Boldface numbers refer to figures and tables.

equality of opportunity, 95, 109, 332, 333

equalizing model for parental investment in children, 185–86, 189

Erikson-Goldthorpe-Portocarero (EGP) class scheme, 32–33, 97

ethnographic vs. survey research, 17*n*8

eugenic explanations for class-health relationship, 236

exclusion, social. *See* neighborhoods

exploitation: and class analysis, 333, 334–36, 341–42, 344; and class definition, 26; Goldthorpe vs. Wright, 19*n*17; and social stratification, 14–15

extra-market rewards, 74

family life: child rearing, 123–24; economic models of family, 181; family income and gender, 298, 312–14, **315–16,** 316–17, **318–19,** 319, 320, 322; working family vs. working class concepts, 31. *See also* parents

Farmer, Paul, 253, 254

feudalism vs. capitalism in Marxist tradition, 334

financing of electoral politics, 216–21, 224*n*13, 225*n*15

fractal individualized inequality, **76,** 76–77

Frank, Thomas, 203, 213–14

Freese, Jeremy, 247, 254

Frohlich, Katherine, 249–50

fundamental causes interpretation of class and health, 232–33, 240–42, 245, 246–55, 257

Gans, Herbert, 265

Gender and Academic Research Program (GARP), 157

gender and class inequality: earnings and occupational inequalities, 293, **294–97,** 298, 299–300, **301–2,** 302, **303–4,** 304–6, **310–11,** 321, 322; education and women's social status, 305, 323*n*4; and family income, 298, 312–14, **315–16,** 316–17, **318–19,** 319, 320, 322; introduction, 293, **294–97,** 298–99; marriage factor in, 17*n*6, 306, **307,** 308–9, 317, **318–19,** 319–20,

324*n*9; methods and data, 314, 321–22, 322–23*n*1; and sibling social status correlation, **183;** as sociological focus, 7, 256

gender consciousness and working man concept, 31

General Household Survey (GHS), 101, 106

General Social Survey (GSS), 28, 29, 30

genes as cause of social position and health, 236–37

gentrification of neighborhoods, 267–69, 276–85, 286*n*2

geographic boundary maintenance by class. *See* neighborhoods

GHS (General Household Survey), 101, 106

Giddens, Anthony, 249, 340

gift relationship between political donors and legislators, 221

Gilens, Martin, 209

Goldthorpe, John, 11–12, 19*n*17–18, 79–80

government: attitudes toward and class identification, **48,** 49–50; need for analysis of role in class structure, 18*n*13; undermining of public housing by, 284

gradational approach: and distributional location of class, 330–31; gender factor in class inequality, 299; and health disparities by social position, 233; introduction, 13; and measurement of inequality, 67, 68, 74–76, **75;** vs. relational approach, 13–14, 366–72

group-based consciousness and political participation, 205–6

Grusky, David, 10, 26, 299, 305

GSS (General Social Survey), 28, 29, 30

habitus, 27, 249

Halle, David, 31

Halpern, Robert, 265

Hansberry vs. Lee, 274

Hansen, John, 211

hard vs. soft money in campaign financing, 225*n*15